One More for the Road

One More for the Road

A Director's Notes on Exile, Family, and Film

Rajko Grlić

berghahn
NEW YORK · OXFORD
www.berghahnbooks.com

Published in 2022 by
Berghahn Books
www.berghahnbooks.com

English-language edition © 2022 Rajko Grlić

Originally published in Croatian as *Neispričane price*
© 2018 Hena Com, Zagreb

Translated from Croatian by Vesna Radovanović
and Americanized by Ellen Elias-Bursać

All rights reserved. Except for the quotation of short passages for the purposes of criticism and review, no part of this book may be reproduced in any form or by any means, electronic or mechanical, including photocopying, recording, or any information storage and retrieval system now known or to be invented, without written permission of the publisher.

Library of Congress Cataloging-in-Publication Data

A C.I.P. cataloging record is available from the Library of Congress
Library of Congress Cataloging in Publication Control Number:
2021037206

British Library Cataloguing in Publication Data

A catalogue record for this book is available from the British Library

ISBN 978-1-80073-241-4 hardback
ISBN 978-1-80073-254-4 paperback
ISBN 978-1-80073-242-1 ebook

*For Rubi
and Lou*

Use a knife to cut through the foil just below the second notch on the neck of the bottle (*grlić* in Croatian) in order to keep the wine from dripping as it pours. A deft cut does take practice but rest assured that once you have mastered the skill, your guests will be impressed.

Be sure the corkscrew is always positioned perpendicular to the table or the surface on which the bottle stands, to prevent the point from entering the cork at an angle and any possible complications which may arise while extracting the cork, such as breaking, crumbling, or wedging. Place the point on the middle of the cork and twist it slowly and evenly until the spiral has penetrated the cork halfway.

After this, with your thumb press the metal lever over the rim of the bottle and start slowly drawing the handle upward in such a way that the cork begins to move up out of the neck. Once three-quarters of the cork has been drawn up, gently twist it to prevent the "pop" sound—but if this is done prematurely, it may cause the cork to snap while still in the bottleneck.

—From vinarija.com

CONTENTS

Introduction. Rajko Grlić and Cadences of Reality x
Aida Vidan

Preface xxiii

LEXICON OF UNTOLD TALES

A
Animal Movies 3
Anticlimax 7

B
The Beginning & The End 10
Biopic 12
Black Wave 14
Bollywood 16
Box Office 17

C
Cameo 19
Camera Angle 20
Character Arc 21
Chase Movies 22
Children's Movies 23
Cineaste 24
Cinema's Exiles 25
Cinema's Exiles II 26
Cinematography 27
Cliché 28

Close-Up 31
Cold Open 32
Completion Guarantee 32
Continuity 34
Courtroom Movies 34
Courtroom Movies II 36
Courtroom Movies III 36

D
Damnatio memoriae 39
Defining Premise 42
Deliverance 42
Dialogue 43
Director 43
Director's Cut 44
Director's Language 45
Documentary (Autobiographical) 47
Double Feature 52
Dream Sequence 53
Dream Sequence II 54
DVD 55

E
Editor 56
Entertainment Trade Magazine 58
Epic Movies 60
Epiphany 64
Escape Movies 65
Escape Movies II 66

Establishing Shot 68
Extras 69

F
Faces 70
Fade to Black 72
False Ending 73
Festival de Cannes 76
Festival Opening Speech 77
Festival Selector 78
Fiction & Nonfiction 85
Fifty-Fifty 88
Film Critics 89
Film Festival 92
Film History 96
Film Library 97
Film Manifesto 98
Film Stock 99
Film Style 101
Filming Permit 102
Filmmaking 112
Flashback 113
Flash Cutting 114
Foley 115
Food Movies 116
Food Movies II 118

G
Gentleman 121
Great Movie Quotes 124
Guarantee 125

H
Head & Final Shot 128
Hollywood Blacklist 129
Horror Movies 132
How to Film in Front of a Mirror 132
How to Make Your Movie 133

I
Imaginary Line 134
Independent Production 137

In Memoriam 138
In Memoriam II 143
In Memoriam III 145
Intermission 146
Internal Dialogue 147
Invisible Editing 148
Italian Neorealism 148

J
Jewish Film Festival 150
Jump Cut 150

L
Lady 153
La Paloma Blanca 156
Larger Than Life 163
The Last Picture Show 164
The Last Picture Show II 169
Legal Movies 170
Lifetime Achievement Award 171
Location 173
Lost in Translation 174
Lost Movies 175
Love Letters 177
Lunatic Asylum Movies 180

M
Magic Hour 183
Master Class 184
Maverick 190
Mediterranean Cinema 193
The Melody Haunts My Reverie 196
Military Movies 196
Monologue 199
MOS 200
Movie Star 200
Movie Theatre (Cinema) 204
Movie Violence 205
Movies with a Number in the Title 207
Multimedia 208

N
The New Hollywood   213
Newsreel   214
No & Yes Man   215
No & Yes Man II   217
No & Yes Man III   217

O
Opening Scene   219
Oscar   222
Oscar II   223

P
Paradox   225
Partisan Movies   226
Partisan Movies II   228
Partisan Movies III   229
Performer   229
Phobia   230
Photographer   231
Photographer II   232
Photographer III   233
Photographer IV (& Painter)   235
Plagiarism   236
Point of View—POV   237
Porno Movies   238
Porno Movies II   238
Porno Movies III   239
Preproduction   239
President Movies   240
Prison Movies   246
Producer   250
Product Placement   250

R
Reality Check   252
Research   253
Revenge Movies   254
Road Movies   255
Rock and Roll Documentaries   256
Romantic Comedy   256
Romantic Comedy II   257
Rome   258

Rules of the Game   258
Russian Cinema   259

S
Script   265
The Secret to Great Film
   Acting   270
Selfie   271
The Seventh Seal   272
Silent Movies   273
Silver Screen   274
Sound   275
Soundstage Isolation   277
Special Screenings   278
Sports Movies   280
Sports Movies II   281
Spy Movies
   "Based-on-a-True-Story"   282
Stage Fright   284
State Award   284
Subtitles   285
Superstar   286
Suspense   287
Sync Sound   292

T
Television   294
Third Act   295
Time   295
Timing   297
Travel Movies   298
Twist Ending   299

W
Walt Disney   300
Western   301
Wipe   302
Wrap   303
Wrap Party   304

Works by Rajko Grlić   306

Index   309

INTRODUCTION
Rajko Grlić and Cadences of Reality
Aida Vidan

Rajko Grlić's *One More for the Road* provokes in the reader both a sense of great joy and one of deep sadness. The joy arises from the narrative opulence, balancing on an existential and political brink and propelling us to ask some of the most pertinent questions a human being can pose. At the same time, Grlić's stories, presented in the form of lexicon entries, immerse us in a complex set of artistic, ethical, and political topics while traversing the globe and offering a taste of a life lived in diverse social and cultural circumstances. Much like in his films, overtones of humor, irony, mischief, and resilience pervade the scenes before us. The sadness, on the other hand, descends upon the reader as they reach the final pages and realize that these notes about slivers of lives both real and imagined from the director's notebook will never be made into movies. Disillusioned with both socialist censorship and capitalist profiteering that prevented the production of at least some of them, one is grateful for the eye-opening journeys they afford us while capturing the recent tumultuous decades in which individual fates and feats stood up against belligerent political projects.

Rajko Grlić was born in 1947 in Zagreb, Croatia (then Yugoslavia) to a family who, over the centuries, had been settling in Zagreb and then leaving it, carrying with them memories of images, ideas, stories, songs, and tastes, and losing anew with each generation what little material possessions the previous one managed to acquire. As Grlić adeptly puts it: "In all these centuries-long migrations, in the maze of places they lived, the only anchor for arrivals and departures has always been Zagreb, a small town on the edge of Europe. They all came to it bright with hope, lost nearly everything each time they were here, and then set off on a quest for new lands" (Preface, p. xxiii). His own life follows this same pattern of departures and arrivals, as well as accomplishments undercut by retributions and lost opportunity. His family—of mixed German, Slavic, and Jewish background, which in previous centuries migrated between Germany, Spain, Hungary, Austria, and England to Zagreb, and in more recent ones from Zagreb to Canada, Brazil, Congo, Switzerland, New Zealand, Pakistan, Italy, England, and the US—has been a repository of cultural memory that has colored his upbringing in the most profound way and which he selflessly shares with his readers. Unfortunately, one need not look far back to uncover horrors and suffering—despite fighting on the antifascist side, both of the director's parents spent time on Goli Otok (Bare Island), the most ruthless Yugoslav labor camp for political prisoners. Although his father, philosopher Danko Grlić, eventually became a university professor and was among the founding members of the Praxis group which brought together influential European Marxists, the shadow of uncertainty and suspicion continued to hover over the family even after Yugoslavia was no more. And yet, despite the hardships he depicts, his narrative reveals a defiant spirit, a seemingly inexhaustible persistence, and a subtle joy of living which measure up to relentless challenges.

A small Bell & Howell camera, the auspicious gift Rajko Grlić received from his uncle who had been living in the West, launched him on a path of cinematic exploration when he was only fourteen. His early engagement with the medium as a member of a local cine club resulted in the first amateur films made during his teenage years and acceptance at the renowned Academy of Performing Arts in Prague (FAMU) where he was deemed sufficiently advanced to skip his first year. His mentor, Elmar Klos, prominent Czech filmmaker and 1965-Oscar winner in the category of Best Foreign Language Film for his *The Shop on Main Street*, appears in multiple narratives. Klos had a major impact on Grlić's artistic vision, especially when Klos's creative output was obliterated by the Soviet invasion of 1968. Klos, however, was not silenced: he resisted by raising a new generation of directors who, in addition to learning the nuts and bolts of scriptwriting and directing, were also instilled with a strong sense of political responsibility and adherence to ethical values. Grlić's time at FAMU was a period of major stylistic development through the study of works by important auteurs, whose poetics left a lasting resonance with him. He was particularly drawn to Godard and the French New Wave as well as Italian directors Antonioni and Fellini with whom he felt he shared a kindred spirit and geographic connection.

Over the years, FAMU educated several South Slavic directors of the post–World War II generation, among them Goran Paskaljević, Srđan Karanović, Lordan Zafranović, Goran Marković, and Emir Kusturica, some of whom forged life-long friendships while others found themselves on opposing sides of political barricades. Rajko Grlić and Srđan Karanović's multiple collaborations as well as his friendship with the eminent Serbian director Dušan Makavejev, both portrayed here in several stories, provide further testimony of solidarity prevailing over political extremism. Through an account of Grlić's studies in Prague, the reader relives the frightening uncertainty of Soviet oppression and witnesses the collapse of cultural and social institutions in a sovereign country while at the same time learning about the efforts of the local population to preserve a semblance of normal life. Several chapters and decades later, we encounter Rajko Grlić and several other young Yugoslav filmmakers in Moscow at the invitation of *Mosfilm* and the Ministry of Culture of the USSR. The stern official protocol is challenged by the disheveled appearance and informal attitude of the invitees who scramble to improvise the expected laudatory speeches. The nonconforming toasts culminate in the Yugoslav delegation's public praise of Isaak Babel and Boris Pilnyak, Russian writers executed during the Stalinist period. Consequently, the delegation's effort to meet Andrei Tarkovsky remains unanswered, however, they are lucky to be escorted by Larisa Shepitko, a former student of Alexander Dovzhenko. Their last nocturnal walk through Red Square, during which they outline the Coca-Cola logo with their footsteps in pristine snow, would these days possibly be called an installation. Back then it was a mischievous provocation, a punch back for old unsettled accounts, which did not escalate only because of Yugoslavia's special status between the East and the West.

Never a part of the mainstream, Grlić was affiliated early in his career with the intellectually provocative underground scene which resented the official "Red Wave" film production meant to glorify Partisan conquests during World War II and achievements of the socialist period. Maturing in a family distrustful of the political establishment at a time when the new order was starting to exhibit serious cracks, he had the impulse to look behind the scenes and capture raw unfiltered reality. No wonder the GEFF (Zagreb's *Genre Film Festival*), a venue for experimental film which, among many others, showed the work of Jonas Mekas, had caught Grlić's attention even before his Prague years. His FAMU experience did not turn into a long-term engagement with the Czech film industry because of abysmal political circumstances so he returned to Zagreb upon graduation. In addition to the skills of the trade, he took with him the ability to envelop his films in both humor and tragedy (reflected also on the pages of this book), and to employ ambiguity and metanarrative devices as core elements of his scripts. He directed his first award-winning film *If It Kills Me* at twenty-seven and proceeded to make *Bravo Maestro* in 1978, which was nominated for the Palme d'Or at the *Cannes Film Festival*. A story about a wasted talent abandoned for social advancement, the film is as much about a young musician as it is about society depicted through its music microcosm.

Grlić's next film *You Love Only Once* (a.k.a. *The Melody Haunts My Reverie*) from 1981 was equally well received at Cannes where it was included in the category Un Certain Regard for its "original and different" vision. The film focuses on the period immediately after World War II and on a young Partisan hero rising rapidly through the socialist hierarchy; the narrative gradually shifts its upbeat momentum for a tragic downfall. The hero, who falls in love with a beautiful ballerina from a bourgeois family, becomes suspect by the sheer act of affiliating himself with the wrong class. The true reason for his punishment, however, turns out to be the envy of his comrades, rather than any political or revolutionary motivation. Although censorship relaxed after Tito's death in 1980, as the Yugoslav leadership turned to address a cohort of pressing economic and political issues, the film still caused major consternation. Anticipating harsh criticism, the director smuggled a copy out of the country and managed to enter it into the Cannes Film Festival competition. Once it was included in the official program, it became impossible for censors to remove the film from the public domain and consequently it was seen by a large audience. Many critics consider this film one of the best Yugoslav/Croatian productions. Its subtle interplay between the notion of personal freedom and oppressive authority was a slap in the face to the leadership who responded with particular wrath to insinuations of corruption as the true motivator behind political action (Vidan 2017: 36–38). Some scholars (Gilić 2011: 129–30; Pavičić 2017: 228) find connections between *You Love Only Once* and Fassbinder's and Szabo's films from this period through their focus on family matters refracted through specific historical circumstances.

Although loosely based on a diary by Ruža Jurković, a Croatian prima ballerina and choreographer, the film pursues its own narrative course, and through a calibrated juxtaposition of characters becomes a sharp social critique. The principal protagonists, Tomislav and Beba, are trapped in a postwar province experiencing the harsh reality of life with a shock-brigade and surrounded by political watchdogs. Owing to their dissimilar backgrounds, their relationship is complicated enough and becomes additionally saddled when her family, with whom they share close quarters, is constantly interfering. His comrades too do not hesitate to pry, under the guise of duty, and ultimately turn everyone against the couple. The lack of freedom is accentuated by the impossibility of having any personal space, and this forces the couple to withdraw from social interactions. Against this stark social canvas, the erotic scenes serve as an emotional shelter and the only psychological stronghold. However, even the most intimate sphere is not safe from political schemes and rivalry which eventually compromise their marriage, landing Tomislav in prison and leading to his demise. Along with the protagonists, the viewer quickly becomes aware that Marxist idealism has nothing to do with the life in the provincial outpost, where differences of any sort are considered antirevolutionary. What is more, the seemingly organized society aspiring to high ideals of equality, justice, and prosperity quickly turns into a bloodthirsty pack while the idyllic space of joined labor becomes a site of terror and lawlessness. Much could be said on account of gender relations in this and in Grlić's other films that bravely depict the rawness of patriarchal relations and machismo embedded in both the private and social aspects of life even in a system that nominally espoused gender equality. The male protagonist pays the price in part because of his failure to play along with the macho schemes. Prioritizing the ordinary things in life such as preferring a relationship over the revolutionary agenda and, moreover, signaling that the agenda has been tarnished by serious ethical concerns, was problematic even for this late-stage, more tolerant brand of Yugoslav socialism. The visual vocabulary of the film with its subdued color palette, spatial organization, and a gradual transition from long shots to mid-shots and closeups underscores the protagonists' psychological drama and their sense of captivity. Tomislav Pinter, who was the director of photography, is praised as the most influential Croatian cinematographer and is also known for his work with Orson Welles.

The nonconformism exhibited in his early films has persisted throughout Grlić's career. Irrespective of the system and the name of the country where he is residing, he finds himself walking the razor edge of criticism in many of his projects; this is never voiced overtly but wrapped in the palpable everyday reality of the protagonists whose psychology is carefully counterposed to their milieu. Even when they appear to be heroes carrying the weight of the narrative arc, their fate is typically anything but. Indeed, they come away stripped of any heroic aura and their activity ends up illustrating futile endeavors, the fruits of which are obliterated by systems, governments, wars, and corrupt ploys. Grlić's next film, *In the Jaws of Life*, completed in 1985 and based on Dubravka Ugrešić's novel *Steffi Cvek in the Jaws of Life* (*Štefica Cvek u raljama života*, 1981) is a case in point. The metanarrative intervention is brought to the fore by the interplay between the subplot of film production, which mimics the content of the film that is being produced. The lives of the characters and putative film crew entwine around soap opera plots serving as prime examples for a study in behavioral gender patterns. Ugrešić's novel is based on a parodic premise, which in its cinematic iteration acquires additional dimensions by exploiting political and gender stereotypes to the maximum: it plays off the profiles of a conformist, an anarchist, and an activist, while bringing into the mix regional ethnic nuances. Urban and rural mentalities clash in humorous encounters while each character is pitched against their metafictional doppelgänger. This East European version of *Bridget Jones's Diary*, appearing long before Hollywood's intellectually depleted version, provides a rich cultural script through its multilayered structure and witticism distributed along the axes of characterization, narrative pattern, cinematic devices, social analysis, and political activism. Although well-received by a wide audience, its noncommercial aspect places it in the niche category.

Needless to say, each of Grlić's films has had its own interesting journey reaching international audiences, festivals, and critics, which led him to enjoy a number of exciting encounters. One such example is his 1987 film *Three for Happiness*, which won the Grand Prix at the Salsomaggiore–Parma Film Festival with Sergio Leone presiding over the jury. Through the directors' informal exchange over a lunch, the reader is familiarized with the complicated editing saga of Leone's legendary *Once Upon a Time in America* and his unsuccessful quest to provide his own cut of the movie. After *Bravo, Maestro*, Grlić's path intersects with that of Erland Josephson, one of the most recognizable faces from Ingmar Bergman's films. An exceptionally gifted, modest, and open-minded actor, he accepted the invitation to act in Grlić's *You Love Only Once*. Grlić's trips to Paris included visits and walks with Milan Kundera, his former professor at the Prague Academy, during which they worked on a screenplay that, too, was sadly never realized. His stroll down the famous alley in Cannes ended in a funny episode of an enormous restaurant bill for an impoverished East European film crew with no credit cards, while his participation at Valencia Film Festival (the Mostra) afforded him a life-long friendship with Honorio Rancaño, an anti-Franco activist who was deported to the Soviet Union and worked for Fidel Castro. A dinner with Honorio turned into a movie-like scene with gunshots, robbery, and a political showcase for the ETA, the Basque separatist organization, which used Mostra as a stage for its proclamations. In Grlić's narratives, be it cinematic or literary, such ancillary episodes provide the ground for painting a complex historical picture in which regimes, outcasts, dictators, and movements shape everyday occurrences and catapult those who are caught in their orbits into unpredictable directions.

His film *Charuga* is the tale of one such individual, a legendary rebel-outcast figure from the northern part of Croatia living in the turbulent 1920s, a period of political instability similar to that of 1991, when the film was made. The film examines the topic of leadership in a humorous manner at the very moment when the region was at a historical and political crossroads, having just gotten rid of the communist government and facing the rise of nationalist leaders in all corners of southeastern Europe. He playfully explores the compelling need of the locals to embrace a fatherly hero-figure regardless of his ethical and political stance (which is subverted, needless to say, from the ostensible altruist mode to a self-serving agenda). Layering the film with the motifs of freedom, rebellion, and anarchy underscored by robbing escapades, sexual abandon, and Roma music, which in itself celebrates the notion of free living, Grlić, in this film, "in many ways pre-figures and comments on the events that were to unfold in the 1990s" (Vidan and Crnković 2012: 101). *Charuga* received funding under the old Yugoslav system but when the movie emerged, it was delivered to an entirely changed political landscape; in the meantime Croatia had become a newly established country. Owing to Grlić's engagement in Srđan Karanović's production, coincidentally taking place in the Dalmatian hinterland that was gradually being occupied by Serbian rebels, Grlić's own mixed family background was being questioned as was his long-time friendship with his Serbian colleague. Although he previously taught for the Academy of Dramatic Arts on multiple occasions, after his return to Zagreb from a Fulbright leave of absence, he found his contract annulled. He and his family were threatened, his films banned from movie theaters and TV programming. In such a cultural wasteland, exacerbated by war and a nationalist agenda, he decided to turn the page even if it meant that he would never again be able to make films. The paradox has it that while in the US he showed *Charuga* at New York University's Tisch School of the Arts to a curious audience of students and faculty whose excitement generated an offer from NYU to teach there along with Spike Lee and Arthur Penn. And so the journey continued.

This move opened a new educational chapter in Grlić's career which, like everything else, has spanned both continents. In three decades of teaching in the US, in addition to providing instruction to NYU film students, he was also a guest professor and artist in residence at Columbia University; the University of California, Los Angeles; Harvard University; and currently he has the post of Ohio Eminent Scholar in Film at Ohio University, Athens. His departure from Croatia, however, did not imply the severing of all ties. He returned there regularly and, at the time when the Croatian film industry faced its darkest period, he initiated the Motovun Film Festival with the intention of supporting independent productions from the region and abroad. Organizing such a venue with foreign financial support in 1999 amounted to a political statement as well, since the program of the national film festival held in the nearby Istrian city of Pula only considered Croatian productions that had been approved by the current government. Having inherited the Yugoslav—and, by extension, Russian—antiquated state-controlled production and distribution model, the new Croatian leadership had its fingers deep in film budgeting and programming, thereby preventing any ideological aberrations and effectively suffocating the next generation of filmmakers. Films produced to meet the ideological agenda quickly dispersed the war-impoverished audiences and brought the industry to its knees. The Motovun Film Festival served as a critical outlet not only by presenting itself as a cultural venue which brought together writers, journalists, filmmakers of all stripes and backgrounds, musicians, visual and media artists, but also by extending educational opportunities. For seven years Rajko Grlić and Nenad Puhovski ran the so-called Imaginary Academy and the latter went on to conceive the production house Factum and Zagreb Dox—one of the most respected documentary film festivals in Europe. This program launched a new generation of filmmakers among whom are some well-recognized names such as Jasmila Žbanić, Dalibor Matanić, Dana Budisavljević, and others. In the postwar decade, those reaching maturity were burdened with war experiences that they were unable to translate into films because of the scarcity of funding. The school offered both instructional mechanisms and a platform for engaging in more easily financed documentary projects. From these the new cohort of directors was gradually able to realize larger productions and introduce much-needed diversity in both Croatian and regional production. It has to be noted that the South Slavic statistics on female directors do not mirror the low numbers in the West; with Žbanić's generation and going forward we have witnessed the emergence of several gifted female filmmakers, a trend in part set by the Imaginary Academy.

In addition to bringing his students to the set and helping them realize their own projects as a part of coursework at the Ohio University School of Film, during the years when he was unable to make films, Grlić embraced an educational multimedia project. Rather than writing yet another manual on film production as requested by a publisher, he and a group of computer experts ventured to design a CD-ROM—a brand new technology at the time. The adventure, which was supposed to take only a few months, evolved into a complicated operation, both technologically and intellectually, as he found it necessary to dissect many processes over which an experienced filmmaker has an intuitive command. *How to Make Your Movie: An Interactive Film School Version* was pronounced the American film product of the year, reviewed in numerous IT publications and lauded at festivals as a supreme educational achievement. As in the case of his professor who had been silenced by political decree, Grlić was able to invest time in his students on both continents and affect the world of independent filmmaking for a long time to come. Luckily, unlike the older generation, he reentered the film scene again, initially through documentary projects, which he holds essential for a filmmaker of any orientation.

His *Croatia 2000—Who Wants To Be a President* (*Novo novo vrijeme*), which he codirected with Igor Mirković, introduces a pluralist perspective during the critical election period in Croatia when the monolithic coverage by national TV provided an anemic account of reality. By simply following the politicians on their daily tasks for three months, Grlić and Mirković captured a different, nonsterile political canvas that the audiences felt compelled to see in movie theaters even though they had been watching the same faces daily on their television sets. In many ways this documentary was for Grlić a testing-ground or probe into the reality of the Yugoslav disintegration, the subject of his *Border Post*, 2006, the first coproduction among the successor states of former Yugoslavia. Grlić cowrote the script with Ante Tomić, basing it on the latter's novel *Nothing May Surprise Us* (*Ništa nas ne smije iznenaditi*, 2003), the title of which evokes a country-wide military training program designed to prepare for an attack by a potential enemy. A war film in which two national agendas clash featuring "our good guys" against "their bad guys" was not something that interested him. Rather, he wanted to go back to the turning point in 1987 when tensions were still building, and the media incessantly added fire to the already collapsed socialist project (Vidan and Crnković 2012: 109). This disjointed moment—when Slobodan Milošević, the Serbian nationalist leader, first came into power—provided texture for crafting the memorable characters of soldiers stationed at a mountainous outpost on the border between Albania and North Macedonia. Their gossip and the street-smart attitudes of privileged urban youth listening to rock songs reveal their cynicism and disregard for any political platform, and especially for a socialist fairy tale and its slogans. Under the watchful eye of an abusive (and promiscuous) commander, this group of young men from various corners of Yugoslavia forge comraderies and rivalries, but they also support one another in amorous escapades. What unites them is their desire to outsmart their Bosnian commander, himself a frustrated casualty of political and military schemes who failed to be promoted and relocated. His rural Bosnian accent and gullible reckoning make him an easy target for pranks, but they also serve as the backdrop for cultural and political differentiation. In order to buy time he needs to treat a sexually transmitted disease; the commander announces a lockdown due to an alleged Albanian military threat. Deprived of the little entertainment and freedom the soldiers enjoyed, they start going stir-crazy. The two best friends, a Croat and a Serb, compete in mischief and disobedience: first, by eventually seducing the commander's wife on his trips to obtain the medications for the commander in a nearby town; and second, by misleading the officers about his trip on foot to Tito's memorial burial site in Belgrade. Each of them in his own way inadvertently causes an avalanche of uncontrollable events. As Levi points out "*Border Post*'s narrative asserts a connection between political turmoil and the assertion of phallic authority" (Levi 2007: 63). The tenor of the film changes over the course of events from humorous to tragic, turning it into an account of abrupt maturing and disillusionment. As Johnson correctly observes, "an ostensibly comic story, full of realistic details of life in a military outpost in the far reaches of Yugoslavia several years after Tito's death, becomes a metaphor for Yugoslavia's demise" (Johnson 2012: 162). The film brings into focus much of what held the country together (including the obligatory military service which forced young men of different ethnic and religious backgrounds to serve together), but also subtly reveals subcutaneous discords signaling the future collapse of the country.

Already early in his career Grlić was preoccupied with the notion of lost utopia and disillusionment or "utopia tripping over reality" as he once put it (Vidan and Crnković 2012: 108). Going into greater detail in this book, he connects his three films

> that examine three pivotal moments in the utopia where we see ourselves as having lived: *Charuga*, a story about the beginnings of the utopia; *You Love Only Once*, about the clash between that utopia and real life; and *The Border Post*, about the moment when the "Yugoslav" version of the utopia came to an end. In some way, all three movies tackle the same topic. I approached each of them in a completely different way because, told through three different characters, these were three distinct stories. (p. 102)

This trilogy thus tasks itself with the intention of understanding how things took a wrong turn and at which point the ideals became permanently severed from the realm of possibility and lost their ethical currency.

Taking a temporary break from politically charged topics in his next film, entitled *Just Between Us* from 2010, Grlić weaves an intimate humorous drama of infidelity and friendship in the spirit of the best Prague school tradition. A portrait of two middle-class families whose private affairs intersect at multiple levels, the film probes questions of relationships, attraction, and marriage by fleshing out convincing and well-acted characters. Despite the somewhat lighter nature of this film, a scandal erupted when the Catholic Church took a stance against sexual explicitness. During the previous era, Grlić may have been accused of subversive intentions, however nudity in his films had never prompted censors to act. A shift in social mores was visible already in these reactions. When asked about a hiatus in political topics and a choice to occupy himself with ahistorical characters and their foibles, he stated that in his view there are no more politics since "it is all about money. Politics have been reduced to money. The element of utopia has disappeared as well as the element of the social category in politics. Politics represents the process of arriving at a position of power that can be calculated through money. In particular, in transitional countries which have a portion of the new capital that was generated by crime, politics has become an empty category" (Vidan and Crnković 2012: 106).

Grlić's most recent film *The Constitution*, produced in 2016, reintroduces the political dimension and situates its characters in a typical four-story building in a Zagreb neighborhood. Sufficient time has elapsed since the last war for the protagonists to lead a normal life and for the most part ignore one another's ethnic backgrounds. The main character, Vjeko Kralj, rendered superbly by the late Nebojša Glogovac, is a high school teacher and a highly esteemed member of society owing to his family's right-wing political affiliations. At home he grudgingly cares for his bedridden father, an officer in the Croatian World War II Nazi-occupied puppet state and now a shadow of a man. Their love-hate relationship acquires a new dimension when Vjeko decides to come out and, after many years of abuse, admits he is gay. What is more, he himself becomes incapacitated after a herd of skinheads attacks him during one of his secretive outings, while dressed in drag. Although they live in the same entryway, Vjeko and his neighbors, a childless couple, avoid one another. Seeing him in this predicament, Maja (played beautifully by Ksenija Marinković), who is a nurse, comes to his aid. This hesitant and initially awkward relationship grows more intricate when her husband, who happens to be of Serbian descent, enters the picture. Serving in the Croatian police force, he has to pass an exam on the constitution and needs some coaching. Vjeko's father's demise eventually frees Vjeko but also forces him to face his own demons, and it is at this critical moment that the humane face of the neighborhood prevents a tragedy. *The Constitution* tackles difficult issues of nationalism, LGBT rights, oppression, revenge, solidarity, love, and hate and does so by providing a glimpse into a Croatian neighborhood while eerily reminding us of our own backyards. The topic of father–son relationships in recent Croatian film production is a layered one and deserves a separate examination but suffice it to say here that it raises the question of accountability and answerability for political outcomes that have a lasting negative impact on future generations. It just so happened that the main role was played by a Serbian actor, not as a statement, but because he was best able to portray the principal character. The anecdote shared in this book of Nebojša Glogovac's accent-coaching by a professional linguist is yet another example of the separations and connections so well captured in this film.

Grlić's sensibility for political issues is covert, woven into the textures of life, the inescapable traits and essences of an individual who stands in opposition to the system and who lives that system through his or her everyday actions. As the characters cannot escape the intricacies of their own temperament and habits, they are similarly entrapped in the circumstances dictated by a specific historical and political moment. These simple human stories uncover the absurdities that lie in plain view and invite us to reflect. The notion of solidarity looms large in Grlić's works as he puts to the test the values propagated against simple human truths. He shows how human life never fits into a binary universe and why dissidents are essential for the dispersal of dogma of any kind. Although ethical and political aspects are omnipresent in his films, they never obscure the aesthetic intention. By his own admission, he does not believe in unidimensional stories, rather he indulges his viewer (and, we can say, the reader here) to play with ambiguity and discover this multiplicity of levels as they see fit. Because ultimately, in Grlić's view, films are stories about specific people and specific places, not ideas, and this is what gives them their universal potential. To the complicated question of how to tell a film story, he answers as follows: "I usually start from the main protagonist. I ask myself: if he or she were to make a movie about themselves, how would they do it? In what kind of breath, what cadences, what images, color, sound? I search for a way to tell the story from within the mindset of the lead, in their life rhythm, in short—as their story" (p. 102).

The present volume is as multilayered as Grlić's movies in the sense that these are his stories inasmuch as they are his characters', friends', and family's stories. They are self-reflective and playful, hilarious and tragic, political and subversive, metanarrative and realistic, nuanced and colorful.

The one hundred and seventy-seven film terms provide sometimes a direct and at other times a metaphoric path to Grlić's stories and concurrently serve as a self-referential mechanism to comment on a series of film attributes. The entries can be read in any order, allowing for the reader's own "montage" of the book's universe. Through this palimpsest of fates, circumstances, encounters, and calamities emerges a subtle socioanthropological account which not only provides an insight into the ins and outs of the socialist film industries but also brings us face-to-face with important film figures and venues in the West. Grlić adroitly captures the absurdities and paradoxes in one's life resulting from the sort of tectonic shifts with which East European history abounds. His collection offers a taste of "the other" Europe's reality and yet demonstrates how much this liminal space, despite the political unrest, has also been an intrinsic part of Western culture. However, it also immerses us in scenes of living in many other places and times, while forcing us to ask the same essential questions.

As Jacob Mikanowski has put it in his reflections on this corner of the world, "the stories of Eastern Europe offer another way of looking at the world. They are a reminder that we are not always the masters of our own fate" (Mikanowski 2017). Given the state of the world's affairs, Grlić's stories could not have arrived at a more opportune moment.

Aida Vidan holds a PhD in Slavic Languages and Literatures from Harvard University, where she taught in the Department of Slavic Languages and Literatures for over a decade. Currently, she teaches in the Department of International Literary and Cultural Studies at Tufts University. Her areas of research include East European film as well as written and oral literature from the South Slavic region. She is the author/editor of four books, numerous articles, and several short and feature-length documentaries.

References

Gilić, Nikica. 2011. *Uvod u povijest hrvatskog igranog filma*. Zagreb: Leykam International.

Johnson, Vida. 2012. "Rajko Grlić: Border Post (*Karaula*, 2006)." In *Contrast: Croatian Film Today*, ed. Aida Vidan and Gordana P. Crnković. Zagreb, Oxford: Croatian Film Association and Berghahn Books.

Levi, Pavle. 2007. "Border Post by Rajko Grlic." *Cinéaste*. 32(3): 63.

Mikanowski, Jacob. 2017. "Goodbye, Eastern Europe!" *Los Angeles Review of Books*, January 27. Retrieved January 12, 2021 from https://lareviewofbooks.org/article/goodbye-eastern-europe/.

Pavičić, Jurica. 2017. *Klasici hrvatskog filma jugoslavenskog razdoblja*. Zagreb: Hrvatski filmski savez.

Vidan, Aida. 2017. "Perceptions of Authority and Freedom in Late Yugoslav and Post-Yugoslav Film." *Studies in Eastern European Cinema. Europeanization in East-Central European Fiction Film and Television (1980–2000)*. 9(1): 33–46.

Vidan, Aida, and Gordana P. Crnković. 2012. "A Conversation with Rajko Grlić: Films Are Stories About People, Not About Ideas." In *Contrast: Croatian Film Today*, ed. Aida Vidan and Gordana P. Crnković. Zagreb, Oxford: Croatian Film Association and Berghahn Books.

PREFACE

My studio at Ohio University is in a venerable red brick building. Here, where the local newspaper used to be printed, I sit at my computer and leaf through my director's notebook.

So far, I've made eleven feature films, but when I finished *Charuga* (*Čaruga*), my seventh, in 1991, I honestly believed it would be my last. Telling stories during those black-and-white times seemed so pointless. It was glaringly obvious that war was imminent, that it would break out whether we tried to stop it or not, and would serve as a smokescreen for grand and sweeping thievery.

As a Fulbright Artist in Residence at UCLA in Los Angeles, I started assembling something I've called *One Hundred of the Best Movies I'll Never Make*, so sure I was to be done for good with my romp with film. That was over twenty years ago, and I have since added remarks, stories and tales, photos and drawings to the notes about all the unborn films.

My folks, now that I think of it, are more like a moving company than a respectable middle-class family. "Professional, reliable, affordable movers! Choose us!" These words could be engraved on our family crest. Various people with the surnames Görlich, Grlić, Izrael, Klingerberger, Hun, Cekić, Kostinčer, Schwartz, Domany, Alačević, Brozović, Janeš, Hardy, Glavaš, Rušinović, and hundreds of others flowed onto and off of our family tree, as if moving was all they'd been doing for centuries. Moving across Europe, from Germany, Spain, Hungary, Austria, and England to Zagreb, and then from Zagreb to Canada, Brazil, Congo, Switzerland, New Zealand, Pakistan, Italy, England, the Americas.

In all these centuries-long migrations, in the maze of places they lived, the only anchor for arrivals and departures has always been Zagreb, a small town on the edge of Europe. They all came to it bright with hope, lost nearly everything each time they were here, and then set off on a quest for new lands.

There is a saying in Zagreb that moving three times is as bad as a moderate earthquake. In America, built mostly of wood, they say: "Moving three times is as bad as fire." If we embrace this logic, it's safe to say that my family has been through at least a dozen major earthquakes, to put it mildly, not to mention the fires.

Natural disasters like these usually demolish all material possessions and any trace of one's existence. And this is exactly what happened to us. Anything my ancestors, or the next generation coming after them, built or bought—they lost. Houses, apartments, estates, taverns, summer houses, pharmacies, and stores, they were all ravaged, sold, nationalized, expropriated, or signed over to mistresses, much faster than we'd made them ours.

A few generations ago, this trend drove one branch of the family to lose its faith in "material possessions" and to turn to "spiritual" values. As usually happens, the "nonmaterialists," the "black sheep" of the family, left behind them much more in the form of books, paintings, lithographs, photographs, and movies, more traces in general than did the "materialists."

With a hint of bourgeois irony, my grandfather used to call this branch the "circus performers." So, as a descendent of the "circus performers," I could hardly choose another profession than making movies—the only serious twentieth-century circus. Filmmaking, therefore, was not a choice of mine but my destiny that came down to me from my family.

This "family of movers" has yet another distinctive feature. No matter which of the two branches of the family they belonged to, all my ancestors—and I can remember three generations back—were filled to bursting with terrific stories. They were passionate storytellers who embellished, added to reality and subtracted from it, always with great joy. And they told the stories in full voice, in keeping with Grlić, our last name, which contains the adjective *grlen*, meaning full-throated. This was their struggle when faced with oblivion, their way of defying the nomadic life that has dogged us through the centuries. The last progeny of these branches of family storytellers were my mother and father. Perfect storytellers, exciting, witty, the best I have ever listened to.

And then it was my turn. Time was passing, the stories were happening, multiplying, being recounted; I have always loved the telling, just as I have enjoyed the listening. And slowly I came to realize that they, the stories, will keep following me, but most of them I will never have a chance to make into movies. The stories will be lost when I go, just as the hundreds and hundreds of the stories told by the rest of our family storytellers have gone. This is why I started feeding them into my computer memory. They were just clusters of sentences in my own defiance of oblivion. Nothing more. Nothing grandiose. More like the breadcrumbs Hansel and Gretel left behind to make a trail through the woods and mark their way home.

All my ancestors—my great-grandfather Julius who lived in Zagreb's Upper Town and was one of the city's first lithographers and photographers; my grandfather Alexander, an Upper Town pharmacist and one of the founders of the Grič literary group; my grandmother Olga, a painter, who studied under Vladimir Becić; my mother Eva, a journalist and writer; my father Danko, a philosopher from Zagreb's Lower Town; my sister Vesna who has been thoughtfully amassing the splinters of our family history—and myself as a narrator of Zagreb film stories have, each in our own way, been fueled by a like passion and have always loved Zagreb. Each of us has tried, as best as we could, to help our small town move a little, an invisible millimeter, an imperceptible micron, up the ladder of civilization. But the last four generations have been decimated by three major wars.

The most recent war, neatly signed, sealed, and delivered, proved once again, perhaps conclusively, that everything the past generations had accomplished was in vain. Everything we did, lived, and created, proved irrelevant and utterly redundant. All the women, the men, and children, the photos and books and movies, the shops and houses and paintings, the friends and acquaintances, the dinners and holidays, the births and the deaths. Everything. All efforts, progress, the finer touches, the cultural achievements, all of it—in vain. It was undone in a matter of days by the new wave of barbarians, in what has become a common practice for centuries now, every fifty years, in this part of the world. They razed to the ground all our efforts, erased them from the books, decided that anything they didn't need from the past did not exist, did not dare to exist.

Once again, the region is facing the old game of official oblivion, in which history is always reworked so as to commence anew with the arrival of newcomers. And now what? How to persuade myself, how to convince those who come after me, that having children, laughing again, working again are worthwhile? How to do this now when primitivism, in its latest triumphant rampage, intends to prove that all the efforts were pointless, that all the lives were lived for nothing? How quick and easy it is to destroy, how long and arduous to build, and how cruel are the lessons of this truism.

In spite of the monstrous experience each generation in this region must go through at least once in a lifetime, in spite of all the political name-calling and verbal lynching I have endured, despite the interrogations and anonymous threats, despite the ten-year ban on screening everything I had filmed . . . I am still trying to find a way back to my Zagreb, although there isn't a single rational reason out there for me to do so.

I've spent my life hiding behind my film characters. Living their lives and recounting their lives, I've hidden my own. The untold tales were stowed in my director's notebook as if in a well-sealed bottle. And then all of a sudden, probably in hopes of easing my return, I decided to uncork it.

And now that the bottle stands here before you, I am asking you to extract the cork from its neck gingerly. Everything you find inside—afloat on chronologically unlinked bits and pieces arranged in an imaginary lexicon, more or less as they were recorded—are the traces of a film life. Each piece is named after a term or phrase used in the world of film.

With a knock at my door, in peeks Ruth Bradley: "May I?"

I beckon her in.

Ruth is the best the 1960s had to give to America: a festival curator, a connoisseur and fan of experimental film and of the good underground, a Doctor of Literature, and the eternal hippie. Smart and cynical, completely uninhibited when it comes to behavior and, even more so, regarding appearance. Her studio is across from mine. Just like me, for the past few years she has been trying to quit smoking. As she sits, she opens a pack of cigarettes and softly says: "May I?"

I nod and she—her eyes filling with guilt—shrugs helplessly, exhales a puff of smoke, and says: "There are only two possible stories: a man goes on a journey, or a stranger comes to town!"

How true, I think, watching Ruth smile with glee at this nugget of wisdom. Indeed, Tolstoy said the same—all good stories, both in life and on film, come down to one of these two patterns: either a person sets out on a journey, or a stranger comes to town.

I'd say I'm both—the one who left, and the stranger who has arrived.

—Rajko Grlić
Athens, Ohio, 2011

Lexicon of Untold Tales

Animal Movies

Movies that feature animals as the lead: King Kong *(1933),* Lassie Come Home *(1943),* Jaws *(1975),* Babe *(1995),* 101 Dalmatians *(1996),* Lone Wolf *(1972), etc., as well as numerous cartoons, puppet-movies, and documentaries.*

Zagreb, Vienna, Wroclaw, 1966

I was a first-year student of philosophy and sociology at the Faculty of Humanities and Social Sciences in Zagreb. As an amateur, I acted in *Ars Longa, Vita Brevis,* a production put on by the student experimental theater.

We traveled to Poland for our first international performance. Vienna was the first stop on the journey and my first contact with the West. I had my picture taken in front of a giant billboard on which a voluptuous dark-haired girl is advertising *Paloma* bras. On the next billboard, a giraffe was inviting the citizens of Vienna to visit Schönbrunn Zoo.

In Wroclaw, we put the play on at the Grotowski Institute. That same evening, a few streets away, Ida Kamińska, the leading actress of the Oscar-winning *The Shop on Main Street* (*Obchod na korze*) by Klos and Kadár, was giving her farewell performance, closing the last Jewish theater in Europe.

Zagreb, 1982

With five-year-old Olga I watched a BBC documentary about the history of zoos. It said that the first European, animal zoo opened in Vienna, in Schönbrunn, and that its first denizen was a giraffe.

A few days later, I learned that in the mid-eighteenth century, the ruler of Egypt sent two giraffes to Europe as a gift to European rulers—one to Paris and the other to Vienna. The journey of the first giraffe, across the

Mediterranean to Marseilles and then to Paris, traveling along small channels, had been fully documented in several books. The journey of the second giraffe, however, had not been documented at all, or at least I didn't find anything. That is why I wrote this story. To be ready in case Olga had any questions about the giraffe.

Los Angeles, 1991

This is also the first story in my director's notebook.

Vienna, 1752

Emperor Francis I is given an unusual birthday present. Since he is a great lover of nature, the Empress has a vast glass palace built for him in Schönbrunn Park as a gift. The king takes his breakfast there every morning and spends hours and hours enjoying the view of the park. The birds chirp, the trees grow, the statues of Greek gods are aligned symmetrically, but the Empress notices the Emperor is still missing something. Despite his paradise, he is still very, very bored.

About that time, the palace receives a letter from far-off Africa, written by a Captain Koenigsmark. It contains a drawing of a strange animal, and a note: "These are drawings of the Camelopardalis, as observed close to the Cape of Good Hope. I believe this animal has not been seen in Europe since the times of Julius Caesar, who marched alongside one of them in his triumphant procession of 62 BC."

The strange drawing of the strange animal, which is thought to be a cross between a camel and a leopard, reaches the Empress. This is how the idea is born of bringing a camel-leopard to Vienna and building a zoo around the glass pavilion in the park, an idea which, or so hopes the Empress, will brighten the spirits of the Emperor.

But if the Emperor is to receive this wonderous gift for his next birthday, hundreds and hundreds of nearly insurmountable obstacles must first be overcome.

Those obstacles, the adventures, the long and arduous journey, the people, and the animal that every child today simply calls a giraffe are what this story is about.

Cape of Good Hope, 1752

Led by Captain Koenigsmark, hundreds of natives and a dozen experienced hunters track a great giraffe for days. Finally caught, it is taken to a ship built especially for it.

The Atlantic Ocean, the Mediterranean, the Adriatic Sea, 1752

The two-ton, six-meter-tall giraffe sails across the stormy ocean for two months before the ship comes to the Mediterranean and the calm Adriatic. Every day the giraffe devours ten kilos of alfalfa, five kilos of specially dried grasses, three kilos of oats, a barrel of sliced apples, and a barrel of grated carrots mixed with clover and dried bread. Captain Koenigsmark hardly sleeps a wink. He looks after the giraffe, feeds it, pampers it. For him, transporting it to Vienna is a matter of life or death, of honor and glory, an opportunity to accomplish the impossible.

Rijeka, 1752

The ship finally enters the port of Rijeka at the northern tip of the Adriatic Sea. At that point there is a mere seven hundred more kilometers yet to traverse between the bewildered giraffe and exhausted captain at one end and imperial Vienna at the other. Only then, however, when the greatest obstacles seem to have been overcome and glory within reach, do Captain Koenigsmark's real troubles begin.

The courageous Captain Koenigsmark is unfamiliar with a fact any child nowadays can easily discover: "The biggest problem zoos face when it comes to giraffes is the terrain underfoot. Most animals can walk on more or less anything, but giraffes are different. If the soil is too hard, they instantly give up to protect their exquisitely tender hooves. If the surface is too smooth, they refuse to take a step because this might deform their hooves and the walking would be too painful. A truly challenging animal, indeed!"

The only possible route to Vienna is a road covered with rocks, rugged and very sharp. The woods are thick, the mountains steep, and the rivers treacherous. The giraffe will, simply, not walk over or through any of it, and no appropriate vehicle is available at the time. Which is only natural, since all of this is happening in the mid-eighteenth century.

The Emperor's birthday draws closer, and Vienna seems to be farther away by the day.

Captain Koenigsmark comes, however, upon a revolutionary idea while out shopping for shoes. He orders giant slippers made. It takes a cobbler several days to make them. They put the slippers on the giraffe's feet, and finally it can walk.

Koenigsmark hires the cobbler straight away; he has a special cart made for the man and his apprentices, and the caravan departs.

Journey to Vienna, 1752–53

The slippers wear out every two to three days. The cobbler and his apprentices have to be working on new ones day and night. Slowly but surely, cutting through the woods where necessary, over bridges that are only barely able to sustain the weight, avoiding the peaks of the Alps and forging through blizzards, the caravan finally approaches Vienna.

Vienna, 1753

The Empress heaves a sigh of relief. The Emperor's birthday will be celebrated with dignity. Half of Europe comes to Vienna. They come, of course, to see the Emperor, but the strange giraffe and Captain Koenigsmark are the main attraction.

That day is celebrated in all relevant documents as the birth of the first zoo.

The giraffe is cared for at the zoo by Captain Koenigsmark only. Only he can come near it. He is said to have spent hours talking to it in a language only the two of them understand.

The Emperor observes all of this from his glass palace and is overjoyed. The Empress is finally reassured.

London, 1993

Pippa Cross, a producer at Granada in London, optioned the story. I wrote the first draft with Clare Foster in Los Angeles at an old MGM studio, in the scriptwriter's apartment where Charles Chaplin used to work. In London, in the Film TV Granada offices, I wrote the second draft two years later.

My lawyer, Susan H. Bodine, offered the project to Ted Hope and James Schamus from the Good Machine production company in New York. They had a first-look deal with Columbia, so they offered Columbia this project, and Columbia showed serious interest. So serious that they went into preproduction. With the English and Austrian producers and set designer Željko Senečić, I scouted locations. We spent days traveling between Istria and Vienna. In London, the giraffes we chose had to undergo at least six months of preparations. At that point, Columbia's management changed. The new management decided not to take up "children's movies" for the next three years. The preparations were discontinued.

Over the next eight years, Pippa promoted the project. She kept extending her option. Those funds paid for Olga's studies in New York. A story made for Olga financed her schooling. There was justice in that.

Anticlimax

An anticlimax is when an almost unresolvable plot is resolved in a trivial way.

Zagreb, 1972

Sulejman Kapić, the general manager of Jadran Film, the first production house in Yugoslavia at the time, read film scripts while being driven from home to the studio in a light-blue Mercedes. So I heard from his driver, Ivica, that, having read only a few pages of my first feature film script, *If It Kills Me* (*Kud puklo da puklo*), he tossed it from the speeding car.

Zagreb, 1973

A month before shooting is supposed to begin, I gave the shooting script to Jadran Film, as was customary back then. It covers every frame and the information about its exact duration, the type of lens, the camera movement . . . Almost 350 pages describing over 700 shots in detail.

For my closest associates, though, the cameraman, the directing assistant, the set designer and the two lead actors, I secretly draw up a script that was some fifteen pages long. I had decided to shoot the film in shot-sequences, and finish it in some thirty sequences. Knowing that Jadran Film will never allow this, we go for the guerrilla approach.

On the third day of shooting—and we are in a backyard on Ilica Street, close to Britanski Square, one of Zagreb's main squares—two production directors from Jadran Film come and put our work on hold. According to reports filed by the laboratories and the script supervisor, they have calculated that we shot two shots over the first two days, so at that rate, we'll only shoot only thirty-four shots over the thirty-four days allotted to us for making the movie. Which means that for the seven hundred frames outlined in the shooting script we will need almost two years.

It takes me forty-eight hours to explain. The film is in peril. Eventually, Jadran Film agrees to let us continue as we'd started.

Zagreb, 1974

In the sound-stage studio at Nova Ves, where the film was also mixed, the first screening is attended by the entire board of directors of Jadran Film, a dozen of them, led by Kapić. His driver Ivica sits right next to him.

As the screening ended, they all look at Kapić. The movie depends on his opinion.

He turns to Ivica and asks: "So, Ivica what do you say? Did you like it?"

Ivica is a little startled but finally he smiles timidly and says: "Yes, I do!" That *Yes* of his more or less determined my fate. Had Ivica said *No*, I would probably not be doing what I have been doing ever since.

Trapani–Sicily, 1982

In Sicily, I am given the *Trinacria*, the biggest Sicilian art award, for *You Love Only Once* (*Samo jednom se ljubi*). Monica Vitti hands it to me.

Kapić comes to the ceremony too, although he rarely, almost never, attends openings or festivals. One evening, I ask him why he decided to produce *If It Kills Me* even after throwing the script out the car window. "Well it didn't cost much, and you were so persistent. And I thought you'd fuck it up and I'd be rid of you once and for all!"

The two us end up making seven films together.

Zagreb, 2009

Rearranging my library, in one of my mother's books I come across a letter from Kalajdžić, a family friend and colleague of my parents, a journalist at *Vjesnik*, the Zagreb newspaper.

> Dear Eva,
> Last night, the holy family watched your son's movie on television with bated breath; this is how the viewing ended: says my son:
> "That Auntie Eva, she sure does have a genius of a son"; says my son's mother (my Comrade Ilse): "That Rajko, he's more Eva's son than he is Professor Grlić's." I didn't say a word, I was choking back the tears, but it's unseemly to cry . . .
> My dear Eva, you can now die and rest in peace! I mean, a glance at children tells you all you need to know about their parents (Comrade Professor's role is minor, insignificant, I know all about that, I've been married for almost 20 years!). And, another thing, and I mean this: if I gave birth, I'd be saved!
> God knows I don't know the first thing about movies, but *truth* I can spot no matter what kind of skirt it's wearing or how drunk I am. Tell your boy Rajko I kiss his ruddy locks twice, Russian-style! I remember the year, 1974 unless I'm mistaken; we were at work and we started talking about the Pula Film Festival and I said something like: "Well, it's not a children's festival, for f . . . sake!" So, even back then I was an old codger . . .
> Watching Rajko's movie last night, I understood what comrade T . . . once meant by "the continuity of the revolution": there is, between the

images in the movie—*image* is an ignorant form of expression—there is a kind of damned rhythm, as musicians would put it, a fugue, and the rhythm is the only thing I remember, even from the Partisans (do forgive me). For example, the image of the train windows—not the wheels but the windows!—that image probably belongs in the anthology of Yugoslav cinema; is Rajko familiar with the train windows by that crazy painter, M. Popović? So, there you go: his is a movie the son of the queen of England wouldn't be able to make! Only children whose parents sweated their butts off "in the woods and over the hills" (and whose pistols were stolen on trucks after liberation), only they are capable of thinking things through like THIS! See, my dear Eva, no matter how angry we may be about the shit we flounder in like blind puppies, there has been a wonderful sense to our lives—Your son is proof of this! I'm sick to death of life but I bow down low before the times when we had nothing more than "boots, a rucksack, and a machine gun." You, too, bow to them and if there really is a life UP THERE, rest assured—go THERE and all you have to say is: I was a Partisan in World War II, I was the wife of D.G. and I gave birth to a son, Rajko! And if Mr. Saint Peter doesn't drop at your feet, go ahead and shout at him: "My friend D. K. told me to tell you he f . . . your holy head!"

This is night a real Croatian night—not a star in the sky, the autumn rains are falling, the neighbors are snoring . . .

We were—over the holidays—in Europe. Tell Danko there are wonderful books, all expensive. And many newspapers, all silly. There are some roomy taverns, all sad. (In Vienna, there was a huge sale of mountaineering gear, but neither me nor my family are . . . psychopaths.) It's so wonderful that we never see each other (some nutty globetrotter you are!).

Say hello to your family and I kiss your hand

Kalajdžić

Zagreb, February 1, 1977
<u>Coming to you from: Ravnice 106/6 entrance 1</u>!!!

The Beginning & The End

Writing about the three-act structure in his Poetics, Aristotle says: "The beginning—nothing particular before it, everything after ... The end—everything before, nothing after ..."

The Beginning–Prague, 1968

It is an early afternoon in the beginning of April. A large crowd has gathered at Staroměstské náměstí, the central square in the Old Town quarter of Prague. All eyes are on the balcony at the northern end of the square. This is where Dubček, the leader of the Prague Spring, is to appear and hold his first speech.

Meanwhile, across the square on its southern side there is a smallish group of writers, actors, painters, and directors. They are looking at another balcony, where stands a Prague tramp.

Dubček starts speaking, followed by the crowd's enthusiastic approval.

Across the square, the tramp starts uttering garbled phrases. He is having a grand old time, and so is his audience, who show him their undivided support.

This is Prague '68. These are the Czechs. At a great historical moment, in the irresistibly pathos-laden atmosphere, they are mocking themselves.

The End–Prague, 1968

Six months later, after the Russian tanks have already buried the Prague Spring, and Dubček, now retired, is living in a small Slovakian village, I am again on the same square. In a somewhat smaller, but equally impressive crowd.

This is the day of the traditional annual military parade in Prague, marking the anniversary of the October Revolution. The new state government hasn't dared to organize a military parade, but they do decide to renew the custom of adorning all public buildings not only with the flags of Czechoslovakia, but with the flags of the USSR as well. This is the first time since the occupation that red flags wave on the façades of Prague buildings.

Elmar Klos is teaching a class on directing. It is dusk. Drizzling. When we hear a murmur from the street below, we look out the window and see a small group of people in front of the National Theater. There are two Soviet flags, twenty meters long, draped on its façade. Several young men grab ahold of the first and yank it down with great effort. The street echoes with a round of applause. Soon, the second flag, too, is down.

We interrupt the lecture and join the people out in front of the theater. The group starts moving. It is led by two men holding an orange traffic cone, the kind used for road work. A yellow rotating light flashes on it. They follow the same route the military parades take. In front of every building with a Russian flag on it they stop, perform the ritual of tearing it down, and move on.

The police do not appear. Not even the Russian patrol cars that are forever cruising the city. The procession, which has grown in numbers, reaches Staroměstské náměstí, the square where, less than six months before, the Prague Spring was officially celebrated for the first time.

This is when the police decide to intervene. They surround the square, closing us in. Tensions mount. Armored buses arrive with the intention of taking away the protesters the police arrest. A skirmish might break out at any moment.

I happen to be among the protesters at the head of the crowd. The police officer who is right in front of me, a mild-looking middle-aged man with a beer belly, implores us: "Kids, go home. You think I feel like standing here? Please, go home."

The crowd soon disperses.

As someone born in the south of Europe, in a region where people easily fall for pathos and where blood boils at much lower temperatures, I saw these two scenes, the one at the beginning, the other at the end of the Prague Spring, as the opening and shutting of an entire world.

Between these two points, the rise and fall of a great social utopia took place before my very eyes. It was a utopia in which I believed, in which I took part, and the fall of which determined my "political destiny" once and for all. Never again have I trusted politics, or any movement led by politics. For me, this was when politics lost its utopian dimension forever.

Biopic

The biographical movie or biopic (biographical motion picture) deals with the life of a real person or group of people.

Prague, 1970

My final project in Scriptwriting, assigned by my professor, Elmar Klos, was the story of Jaroslav Čermák, a nineteenth-century Czech painter. The artist's life represented a link between Klos's two loves: Prague and Montenegro, the north and the south. The only thing I knew about Čermák at this point was that he had painted *The Wounded Montenegrin*, a famous painting reproduced in all the literature textbooks of my youth.

I roamed through the libraries, galleries, antique shops. A story started taking shape, the story of a kid from Prague who broke his leg and was lame for the rest of his life. A kid whose effortless ability to draw helped him compensate for the effort of walking. And whose life, as usually happens in the compensation game, became, thanks to drawing, one that was in a constant state of motion.

Čermák begins his study of painting in Prague and continues in Antwerp. There, he falls in love with the wife of a professor and elopes with her to Paris. The infuriated professor hires detectives, they locate the lovers, who only barely elude capture. Several months later they are tracked down again, this time in Dubrovnik. Backed into a corner, the lovers escape to Montenegro, which, at that time, is at war with Turkey. They are safe, no one will ever search for them there.

In Cetinje, King Nikola I offers them refuge. Čermák becomes a court painter. Day and night, he paints portraits of court ladies and Montenegrin heroes whom he occasionally joins in battle. After their victories, he makes paper balloons, draws the heads of Turks on them, and uses candles to float them up into the air. Montenegrin heroes shoot them down with their muskets. For his valor in war, he is decorated by King Nikola I.

Cetinje, 1862

In Čermák's diaries there are a few more scenes like these.

Čermák writes how he spends a long time working on a portrait of a gaunt hero and his bony face. The man poses for days, dressed in apparel bristling with guns and daggers. He stands there completely still. Only his eyes are restless. "I had trouble painting them," writes Čermák.

And then, the hero suddenly stirs, runs to the window, flings it open, grabs one of his firearms and shoots. Across the street, a man falls to the ground, hit. The hero calmly closes the window, tucks the gun back into his sash and apologizes for the interruption. He was compelled to, he says, because the goddamn Turkish spy had been tailing him for days. He assumes exactly the same pose, as if nothing happened. From then on, his eyes are still.

Čermák's life story is, however, in for a new twist. He'd come to Cetinje to escape the jealous husband and his posse. While in Cetinje, however, he does what he can to escape the woman he has eloped with—without success.

As I remember it, this is where his true story begins. The story of a younger man and an older woman, and the torment their love has become.

Italy, 1865–67

They travel through Tuscany and Umbria, hoping the new destinations will bring them peace. But her fear of losing him grows instead of ebbing. There are frequent dramatic clashes between them after which he leaves her forever, only to return either out of pity or fear, he himself is not sure which.

Roscoff, 1869

After two years of roaming the French Riviera, they settle in Brittany. While there he receives an offer from the Prague Academy to become dean. She refuses to go to Prague, so he declines.

Eventually, he does break things off with her and runs off to Paris where, several months later, he dies, alone, at the age of forty-six.

Prague, 1971

If it hadn't been for the Russian occupation of Czechoslovakia, if Barrandov Studios hadn't been so meticulously cleansed of the "non-national elements," if Klos had been able to keep his production group (*Tvorčni skupina*) afloat, this story would have been my directorial debut.

But, since everything unfolded as it did, I slowly forgot about it and misplaced the script.

The only thing that lingered was my quiet sadness about the man for whom the woman he loved became the end of him, about a Czech who was delivered to his resting place in Prague by an escort of one hundred Montenegrin horsemen in dress uniforms, as their national hero, and accompanied by the roar of muskets.

Cetinje, 1990

Prince Nikola Petrović-Njegoš, the great-grandson of Montenegrin King Nikola, an architect from Paris who claims to harbor no ambitions for the

Montenegrin throne, organizes the Cetinje Biennale, the first gathering for the fine arts in Cetinje. I have no idea why, but the French Minister of Culture names me to serve on the honorary board of the Biennale. I set off from Zagreb to Montenegro with a Croatian team of painters and sculptors: Kožarić, Knifer…

For the first time I set foot in the court of King Nikola I. The walls are hung with Čermák's portraits.

Black Wave

The "Black Wave" was an expression used by Serbian politicians in the late 1960s to refer to "unacceptable phenomena in culture," predominantly in film. Their witch hunt persecuted the most relevant Serbian directors of the time: Dušan Makavejev, Žika Pavlović, and Aleksandar Petrović.

Pesaro, 1981

Pesaro Film Festival organized a retrospective of Yugoslav cinema. Snežana and Žika Pavlović, Alenka and Tomislav Pinter, and Ana and I were among the guests.

Belgrade, 1969

The witch hunt for "black wave" members stymied the flourishing careers of several directors who, at the time, were making their best movies. Makavejev and Žilnik left the country; Pavlović and Petrović stayed. The vacuum caused by their absence was filled by the production of "cheerful B movies." Several years later, we, the "Prague students" returned to Yugoslavia, and slowly, one by one, started making our movies.

From that moment on, though we'd grown up watching their films and swearing by them and truly loving them, Mak and Žika regarded us with a dose of suspicion. In interviews they were asked to comment on us and our movies, and though never directly, but clearly enough, they said that the same politics that destroyed them was using us to assuage its conscience. In short, the politicians allowed us to make our films so that we would take their place, because our attitude toward the regime was more conciliatory than theirs.

I used to find this theory intensely irritating, and whenever I met any of them, I said so. But we were always in a crowd of people and they'd shrug off my words and laugh, saying I'd gotten it all wrong, they really did love my work.

Pesaro, 1981

One spring evening, at this Italian summer resort, I had a chance to really talk with Žika for the first time. We were at a disco-club, and while others were dancing, we began, emboldened by alcohol, to talk. I felt a burning need to disperse the fog. Witnesses say this went on from nine in the evening to four in the morning.

My premise was: "You were children of the revolution. You believed in it heart and soul. And then you realized your revolution had sold you short. So, like anyone who had been betrayed, you wanted revenge. Your movies, which I truly love, can be interpreted through the prism of Freudian theory as revenge against the betraying father."

"I was never a believer, I never caught my beloved Stalin or Tito in flagrante. I was not one for revenge or, to be more precise, although I had quite a few family reasons for something of the kind, I realized early on that hatred devours my energy and kills the joy of filmmaking for me. I cannot make a movie that is pitted against someone, about someone I don't like, someone I despise, someone against whom I would use my movie as a weapon."

"On the other hand, I do make what we call 'political movies.' I know where I am, what kind of stories I tell, and I'm aware of the context in which my characters live. Moreover, many of my movies have been banned. I have never tried to run away from that, nor have I ever sugarcoated the destinies of my characters. But I have also learned that political opinion isn't the only thing that determines people—people consist of more delicate layers that can, in terms of filmmaking, also turn out to be more interesting."

"I believe, therefore, that those movies, which have achieved ratings far higher than yours, speak not only against politics, but very often in a more direct and a more detrimental way than yours have."

The next day, quite hungover, we tried to reconstruct our conversation. Everyone else remembered it better than we two did.

Zagreb, 1985

The League of Communists of Croatia published a diatribe called the *White Book* about negative phenomena in culture. And in it, the film section, alongside Makavejev, Petrović, Pavlović, and Žilnik, was also included my name, as the fifth in the honorable group of antiheroes from Yugoslavia. The rest of the world was represented by Ernst Lubitsch and his "anticommunist" *Ninotchka*.

Athens, Ohio, 1997

I had that conversation with Makavejev years later. Bojana and he visited us. Infinitely pleasant, smart, unassuming, and so witty.

The talk with Makavejev was far more peaceful. Years had passed and a foreign country had become home for each of us.

From that conversation, which went on for days, there is one sentence of Makavejev's that still rings in my ears: "It was easy for you, you were the beloved children."

Bollywood

A portmanteau of "Bombay"—the most populous Indian city, today Mumbai—and "Hollywood." The term refers to Hindi-language movies, typically very long, where dialogue scenes alternate with scenes of singing and dancing.

Athens, Ohio, 2017

Bilal Sami, a Pakistani student, brought me his first Bollywood film that had enjoyed great success in Pakistan and India. He told me how the producer—as any other Bollywood producer would—urged him to stick to the five cardinal rules: 1) music from the beginning to the very end, with at least five original scores sung and danced by the actors; 2) no kissing or any other physical contact; 3) an obligatory scene of a rich wedding replete with dances; 4) no alcohol; 5) obligatory minimum running time of two hours, preferably three or more.

"Now, just you try and make a romantic movie following those rules!" said Bilal laughing.

Mostar, 2005

We are scouting locations for *The Border Post* (*Karaula*) amid the barren rocky terrain of Hercegovina. We are looking for a backup in case the hills overlooking Ohrid Lake in Macedonia are snowed under longer than expected. The late Kemal Hrustanović, the set designer, suggests that we spend the night at his friend's hotel in Međugorje, a place of Catholic pilgrimages since the Virgin Mary allegedly appeared on Apparition Hill in 1981.

Međugorje, 2005

We enter the hotel. The interior is mostly done in marble. The tables and walls are covered with sculptures of the Virgin Mary in all sizes and materials: wood, stone, plaster, plastic. They are lit-up, revolving, flashing.

A tall woman in a sari comes over. On her forehead she has the red tilaka, the mark worn by married women in India. Shouting joyfully, she throws her arms wide: "Welcome, Kemo, you motherfucker!"

A few hours later, we hear her story. She was happily married to a Yugoslav military pilot. He died in the 1980s at an air show in Paris.

When the war broke out, she became Tuta's mistress. He, one of the most brutal warlords, helped her build the hotel. But, Tuta was handed over to the War Crimes Tribunal in The Hague and convicted of war crimes.

UNPROFOR peacekeeping forces came to Hercegovina, led by a Pakistani general. The two of them met and soon they married. Out of love for her, the general left the military and moved to Međugorje. A year later, he organized the manufacture of Virgin Mary figurines in Pakistan and opened a shop in the hotel.

Toward the end of dinner, the general joined us, too, a tall man with striking features and a black beard in a turban. His whole body radiated love for the woman in the sari.

I wait, poised to hear the strains of the sarangi, and see the loving couple burst into song and dance.

Box Office

A booth from which tickets are sold, placed in front of the cinema. Weekend Box Office Results *is the report published weekly with information on ticket sales.*

Where I come from there is a custom, honed during the 1990s when nationalism was the main weapon in the lead-up to the civil war that was about to erupt: the counting of your blood cells and the evaluation of your personality accordingly. Since the "purity" of my blood has always been highly suspect, I have been asked many times, both publicly and privately: "What are you, exactly?"

So, here is my answer:

A. Religion
I am an atheist. A Jew, hence a secular Jew. Atheism is my choice, and Judaism is not, it is something you automatically become when born to a mother whose maiden name is Izrael.

Or, to be specific:

My grandfather, Osias J. Daniel Izrael was a Sephardi Jew, meaning that his Jewish ancestors from both his mother's and father's sides came from Toledo (Spain) to Sarajevo (Bosnia and Herzegovina) via Istanbul (Turkey) and Novi Pazar (Serbia), and thereafter he moved from Sarajevo via Budapest (Hungary) and Split (Croatia) to Zagreb.

My grandmother, Katarina Klingerberg, was an Ashkenazi Jew, that is a Jew whose ancestors, on both her parents' sides, came from southern Austria to Hungary, first to Orkeny and then to Budapest.

My other grandmother, Olga Cekić, was an Orthodox Christian. The Cekić family came to Zagreb from Karlovac, their ancestors having moved to Karlovac many generations earlier from Serbia. Her mother was Schwarz, a Catholic whose ancestors came to Zagreb from the south of Germany some three hundred years ago.

My other grandfather, Aleksander Grlić was from a Catholic family. His father, Stjepan Grlić, came from a family which used the name Görlich, changed to Grlić by a Zagreb priest in the nineteenth century. They came to Zagreb from Schwarzwald, but, as Donauschwaben, through Banat. His mother was Maria Hühn, and the Hühn family also came from Schwartzwald, but they came directly to Zagreb.

So, religion-wise, mathematically speaking, this is my blood cell count:

    25% Sephardi Jew
    25% Ashkenazi Jew
    37.5% Christian, Catholic
    12.5% Christian, Orthodox

B. *Nationality*
My birth certificate, issued on September 2, 1947 in the municipality of Medveščak, Zagreb, declares me and both my mother and father to be Croats. While, actually—and there is no document which declares this—I'm a "Zagrepčanin" (a citizen of Zagreb) through and through. Anything broader than that, I see as pure abstraction.

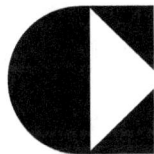

Cameo

When a famous person, usually the director, appears briefly in a scene of their own movie.

Zagreb, 1978

My dad used to tell a story about a knowledgeable history professor from Zagreb who presented history with the passion of a witness, from a first-person perspective.

Talking about an armored train which transferred banished Russian revolutionaries from Berlin to Saint Petersburg, he'd say: "So, Lenin says: Yes, Stalin is right! And I respond: How can you trust Stalin? He will be the end of you . . ."

In short, he would slip himself unobtrusively into every event, and then, as if nothing had happened, go on with the story.

Zagreb, 2010

Former Prague student, Lordan Zafranović, my Prague Film Academy classmate, spoke yesterday about Prague, the year of 1968, the Soviet occupation, and the student strike at FAMU, while he was a guest on the Goran Milić Show, on Croatian National Television. Interviewed at the entrance to the Academy, he held a microphone while he spoke in a very persuasive, almost dramatic manner about a Russian soldier smashing the door, an enormous tank appearing right behind his back, and how, just then, the soldier drove us out of the Academy, shouting: "Out!"

I watched Lordan and I could see him speaking with the passion of a true witness.

The only problem was that Lordan was neither in Prague nor at the Academy at the time. He was in Split, making his first feature film, *Sunday* (*Nedjelja*), with Goran Marković, yet another Prague classmate of ours, in the leading role.

While I was watching him, not for a second did I think he might be deliberately lying or fabulizing, that he was senile, or that he was bragging about something he'd never experienced. In fact I am certain that he truly believed that this all happened exactly as he told it, and that he was one of the participants.

Over the past forty years or so, all of us "Prague survivors" have talked about the Prague of our youth so much and so often that it has become very difficult, impossible even, to tease out fiction from fact, to separate someone else's experience from your own.

And there we were, once upon a time, laughing at Partisans and their squabbles about who was shooting whom, when, and from which position in World War II.

Camera Angle

There are three basic angles between the camera and the subject: the high-angle, the low-angle, and the eye-level angle.

Unless the technicians are instructed otherwise, they adjust the camera to the director's eye level, once the director has chosen their position. This is how movies show that Huston was tall and Polanski very short.

Gorjani, 2012

Around the time of my sixty-fifth birthday, I become aware of my own mortality. No panic, no great fear. The only thing irrevocably shifting was my point of view; it disrupted the hierarchy of relevance, made me discard things I used to think were of great importance.

Gorjani, 2017

I turned seventy. A glass of wine and the Istrian landscape. "Dolce far niente."

In my youth, I would have immersed myself in the "pleasure of work" far easier than I do now that I've abandoned myself to "sweet idleness." So that is why, from time to time, sneakily, I cheat on laziness, and work.

P.S. Pero Močibob, a former professional soccer player, warns me: "Be careful, old man, don't overdo it, at your age this is an elimination game."

Character Arc

An arc which denotes the transformation the main protagonist undergoes from the beginning of the story to its end.

Kurili, 1995

Ivica Matošević, Moreno Degrassi, and Gianfranco Kozlović are young winemakers, more or less beginners. I meet them through Slavica and Vlado Borošić, wine traders without whom the wines of Istria wouldn't have become what they are today. I watch them learn the ropes from Slovenes, especially Sčurek and Krstančič, I taste their beginner's Malvasia, I witness their family squabbles over the introduction of stainless-steel wine barrels . . .

Motovun, 1999

At the end of the spring, I explain to them that we are preparing a film festival, that we are hopelessly poor, and that if they could bring some of their wine and treat the audience to one of Istria's finest products, that would be fantastic.

So they come, all three of them: Matošević, Degrassi, and Kozlović, with their wives. They carry in the crates themselves, set out the glasses, and open the bottles. A moment before they start serving the wine, they all put on yellow T-shirts which read, in Istrian dialect: *Free Wine*. They grin, relaxed amid the crowd milling around them and I can't tell who is enjoying it more—the ones pouring or the ones they are pouring for. But wine, no matter how much of it they'd brought—and they were very generous—has a way of disappearing fast. Once the last bottle is empty, they take off the yellow T-shirts and proudly don black ones which read, also in the local dialect: *All gone!*

Motovun, 2003

Five years later. The festival lives on. Merrier than ever. I suggest to the winemakers that they might celebrate this fact by repeating the wine party. All three of them come. They bring plenty of wine and T-shirts that read, again in Istrian dialect: *A drinking T-shirt—divine free wine—to help the festival for the fifth time—degrassi, kozlović, matošević—motovun, July 28, 2003*. This time, however, the crates are brought in by their assistants who also tend to the wine, open the bottles, pour. The three of them supervise. The wines are different, too: more refined, purer, clearer.

Motovun, 2009

Over the past ten years, all three of them have become Istrian brands. They have planted large vineyards, have major wineries, and they travel the world, winning medals. Their wines are on the shelves of famous restaurants and wine cellars worldwide. Sometimes, I find them in the United States and, bragging that know the makers personally, I offer them to my guests.

For the tenth anniversary of Motovun, my last Festival before I went into my "honorable retirement," all three of them came with their wives, and some of these wives were new. They arrived in fancy cars, with plenty of wine, and sommeliers and assistants. Elegantly dressed, aware of their status in the world of wines, they stood to the side, enjoying the sight of the crowds jostling around their wines.

Motovun, 2015

I am given the Festival award for my fifty years of filmmaking. The three winemakers throw a surprise wine party for me. I watch them wearing replicas of their 2003 T-shirts, pouring their wines, carrying the glasses, opening the bottles. Once again, they are simple and upbeat. The fame, probably also the money, has allowed them to drop the sophisticated airs they have been cultivating for years and return to where they started. The only thing that has never returned to the starting point is the wine—they have gone much, much further than any of them ever dreamed possible.

Chase Movies

A movie about a chase after a single character or group. One of the most popular film genres that touches upon the very essence of the media: live, moving pictures.

Zagreb, 1953

A soccer ball, a proper leather one, size 5, was a true rarity in my childhood. One came to my family as a prize my father won at a table tennis tournament for journalists, just a few months before he was sent off to Goli Otok, a prison camp on an Adriatic island. Family legend has it that, at the tournament, he won a whole set against Žarko Dolinar, one of the finest players in the history of the game. Because of this, our soccer ball was a family treasure, and it left the room only on Sundays when my dad, with his colleagues and fellow philosophers, Kangrga and Kalin, went to Maksimir, and there, above the second lake, they would play five-a-side with other colleagues from the Faculty of Humanities and Social Sciences.

One day, I sneaked the ball out of our apartment on Kulušićeva Street. We quickly pulled together a pick-up game in the field behind the high school. I was the youngest in the group, but since I was the one who brought the ball, I was not only allowed to play but could also pick my team.

We had only just begun when a tall boy came dashing over, snatched the ball, and laughed: "'Find your way out, comrade,' as Comrade Tito used to say!" and broke into a run. Another ran with him. Obviously, they were both in on it. A few of us gave chase. We ran along the school building, but they were bigger and faster, and clearly we wouldn't be able to catch up. One by one, my team players dropped out, but I kept running as fast as I could. We reached Trg žrtava fašizma, a square where the two of them hopped onto an old number ten tram with its open section in the middle. When the tram turned onto Socijalističke revolucije Street, I was still doggedly running after it.

The last thing I remember was the sight of the two of them at the open rear window, guffawing and waving.

Zagreb, 1998

Croatian Television was filming a biopic of Žarko Dolinar. He was the person who won eight medals at world championships in table tennis, but was also named a Righteous Among the Nations, as someone who, with his brother, saved three hundred Jews from certain death during World War II.

The television crew approached me in the street and asked me to say something about him. Dolinar was with them. I asked him: "Is it true that my dad once won a set against you?" Dolinar laughed, shrugged: "Maybe. I might have been drunk. Don't know."

Children's Movies

Movies for children, and family movies about children.

Zagreb, 1952

My parents enrolled me in a Jewish kindergarten on King Tomislav Square. It was on the third floor of a house across from the Art Pavilion. It was, or at least as I remember it, wonderfully equipped: watercolors, pencils, easels, sculpting material . . . a dreamlike space in the black-and-white Zagreb of the time.

My dad took me there every morning. We always parted in the same way—he'd say: "Šani," and I would respond: "Šani Ujheli." Years later, my sister explained that this was the name of a conductor at a Zagreb cabaret, and this was always a source of laughter in our family.

One day, I came home, excited. We were preparing a performance for Hanukkah, and I was going to play one of the candles. My father, however, was none too thrilled with the poem I recited in Yiddish. He said: "Had I wanted my son to become a religious fanatic, I could have enrolled him in the Catholic Church kindergarten on Kaptol."

That sentence put an end to my early-Jewish colorful phase. Soon I found myself in a proper socialist kindergarten at the intersection of streets that now bear the names of two heroes from Croatian mythology: Duke Borna and Duke Domagoj. The only thing I remember is a floor made of planks coated with a horribly smelling black liquid.

Zagreb, 1984

We lived in Zapruđe, in New Zagreb. Olga attended a well-equipped kindergarten. Ana and I came to the final performance. At the very beginning, holding hands, the children danced around and sang: ". . . I love Tito more than my mommy and daddy . . ."

That summer we moved back to the center of town. Olga started school on Gundulićeva Street in the fall. Because of this, I didn't have to put her through what I was put through by my father.

Cineaste

A filmmaker, but also someone devoted to movies.

New York, 1993

They called me from *Cineaste*, one of the oldest American cinematic journals, asking for an interview. I suggested a meeting at *La Lanterna*, an Italian café in the Village, close to where we were living. A few days earlier it had caught my eye and seemed appealing.

A middle-aged woman appeared. We introduced ourselves, took seats. A waiter came over, a young man of thirty or so. He addressed me in Croatian, he was glad to see me, he liked my movies. The woman asked me what he was saying. I translated and she smiled. "So, you chose this place to show me how your people like you?" I failed to convince her that I was here for the first time and didn't know this man. Some ten minutes later, another waiter came to our table. He, too, greeted me in Croatian.

The next day, I went to *La Lanterna*. There were four waiters from Zagreb and, if I remember correctly, all or most of them had PhDs. They used to work at the Ruđer Bošković Institute, a Zagreb-based research center, but were disgusted by the political atmosphere in Croatia. This was their first job in America.

They inquired about journalist Jelena Lovrić. They'd heard she was out of favor. They had collected money among them and wanted to send it to her.

Within a year, three of them found academic jobs. The fourth stayed in New York, so he could start his own business in Queens, and he was in no hurry.

It was highly unlikely that any of them would ever return to Croatia. But they also would never become a part of what our politicians refer to as the "Croatian diaspora." They would not be gathering in churches, glorifying Ante Pavelić, the governor of the fascist state of Croatia during World War II, or waving flags, they would not be attending picnics or strumming folk tamburitzas.

Cinema's Exiles

Filmmakers: directors, scriptwriters, actors . . . who had to leave their homeland for various political reasons.

Prague, 1968

Venclik was a skinny young man with a fair complexion and thinning hair. Just like a character from Forman's *Black Peter* (*Cerný Petr*).

We were students of directing together.

Right after the Soviet occupation he joined the *V. I. Lenin's Friends Society*. The entire Academy was appalled. We despised him and stopped speaking to him.

Prague, 1969

The *V. I. Lenin's Friends Society* organized their first field trip: *Lenin's Path Before the October Revolution*. They set off on five buses. Helsinki was their first stop. The morning after they arrived, the five buses stood empty in the hotel parking lot and all the passengers, including the drivers, petitioned for political asylum.

We were horribly embarrassed when we heard this; we realized what he had suffered through in order to escape.

Prague, 1999

I was casting *Josephine*.

Venclik came as one of the actors, recommended for one of the smaller parts. He hadn't changed. He laughed like he used to and had the same walk. He told me he came back right after the Velvet Revolution, he had been acting and directing, sometimes he appeared in movies as an extra. I could see he was having a rough time. I tried to apologize somehow for my stupid behavior in '68, but he waved my apology aside. He didn't want to talk about it.

Cinema's Exiles II

Goa, 2016

We sit on the porch of a Portuguese colonial villa. We are visiting Tom, an Indian producer and waiting for dinner. Over a glass of wine, Ivan Passer tells Ana and me how he and Miloš Forman escaped from Czechoslovakia.

Prague, 1969

Ivan heard that the Russians had started arresting people. He called Miloš and told him to pack his things.

Mikulov, 1969

Around four a.m., they reached the Czech-Austrian border. They stopped, turned off the engine, and waited. A few minutes later, two soldiers emerged from the dark. Ivan rolled down the window and handed over their passports. The soldier flipped through them, stopped, and asked for their exit visas, without which Czechoslovakian citizens couldn't leave the country. They had no visas, but Ivan, in an effort to buy them time, told the soldier the visas were in the suitcase. He got out of the car, popped open the trunk and started rummaging through his things.

Meanwhile, the officer approached Miloš. He asked him if he was the film director Miloš Forman. Miloš affirmed in his deep voice, adding that he knew the officer probably didn't like his movies. Ivan had been about to tell Forman that this was the wrong thing to say at the wrong time, but—Forman had already said it. The soldier didn't mind at all; he said he loved Forman's movies and that his favorite scene was the one from *Loves of a Blonde* (*Lásky jedné plavovlásky*), which involves a ring rolling over the floor. Ivan stopped rummaging through his suitcase and watched the officer, bent down at Miloš's window, acting the scene, laughing all the while. When he saw Ivan watching him, he waved at him to stop searching, they could pass through.

They were both in the car again, but just as they were about to go, the soldier leaned into the window and said: "S panem Bohem panove" (Go in peace). Ivan says that this, like "farewell," is said only when you are seeing off someone you don't expect will be coming back.

And so, Ivan and Miloš moved to the West together. They had grown up together in a postwar orphanage, they had begun making movies together. Ivan wrote the scripts for all of Forman's Czech movies and directed what is quite possibly my favorite new-wave Czech movie, *Intimate Lighting* (*Intimní osvetlení*). Ivan is eighty-three and lives in Los Angeles. Miloš is eighty-four and lives in New York. They talk to each other on the phone once a week, every Saturday.

Cinematography

A word which refers to all film-related jobs, from the production and distribution to the care and storage of films.

Novi Sad, 1982

Dejan Obradović was the director of Yugoslavia Film, a state-owned company in charge of the whole process of placement of Yugoslav films on foreign markets, from festivals to distribution. He was an orderly, charming gentleman whose credibility was reinforced by his age and the powers entrusted to him.

One day, he took Điđa (Srđan Karanović), a classmate of mine from the Prague Film Academy, and me to dinner in Novi Sad, to see Draško Ređep, the director of Neoplanta Film. He said: "Now that you've entered cinematography, it's time to taste it."

At the dinner, which really was amazing and lasted well into the night, accompanied with a thousand and one stories, Dejan told us about the birthing of Yugoslav cinema.

Belgrade, 1945

He was a Partisan intelligence officer. Several days after the Partisans had entered Belgrade, he was informed that he was to report to Mitra Đilas, who was the Minister of Education and the first wife of Tito's vice president, Milovan Đilas. He was puzzled by why such a powerful woman would want to see him, he, who was a totally anonymous officer in Belgrade for the first time. On top of this, he had nothing to do with education. In short, he was feeling awkward about going to see her. He knew, he said, he could expect nothing good.

He entered her office, a long empty room with a desk at the far end, and reported in a military manner. Without standing on ceremony, she shouted down the office: "You, Obradović, you'll organize the cinematography!" After a moment of confusion, he responded, in shock and fear: "But I know nothing about that!" "That's exactly why I want you to do it!" she shot back calmly and started listing all the things he would have to do. As his first task, he was given a seven-day deadline to find a location in Belgrade where a film city could be built.

He didn't dare ask what a "film city" was. A place where filmmakers lived or where films were made? And even worse, he had no one in Belgrade to turn to.

Seven days later, Milovan Đilas checked in for a progress report. "Have you found a location yet?" "Still looking," answered Dejan. Đilas explained that a meeting of the Yugoslav League of Communists would be held that very afternoon and Dejan was expected to report on cinematography. With no further ado, Djilas picked up Dejan in his army jeep and off they went in search of a proper location. They stopped at various places, as Đilas's nervousness increased. Finally, he stopped in Košutnjak, a forest by the side of the road, and said: "Got to go now. And here, for example, is a good place where you could start building your film city."

This is how Košutnjak, that is Avala Film was built—the first bona fide film studio in the new Yugoslavia.

Belgrade, 1970

This was the very same Košutnjak, that is Avala Film, where Điđa and I took the script for his first feature film, *Party Game (Društvena igra)*. This was also the first proper production company the two of us ever entered.

Zagreb, 1991

It was clear the war was about to begin. This is probably why, as if spurred by an unspoken sentiment, the people who were in charge of the production of Croatian, Serbian, Slovenian cinema, in other words, Yugoslav film, came to the opening of *Charuga*, though they almost never attended openings. More or less everyone was there: Sulejman Kapić, director of Jadran Film, the most powerful production company at the time and his greatest Serbian rival from Belgrade; producer Dušan Perković, director of Centar Film; Vladimir Terešak, director of the foremost Yugoslav distributor, Croatia Film; and Dejan Obradović, director of once powerful Yugoslavia Film; and Josip Košuta, director of Slovenian production company Viba Film . . .

Cliché

A phrase or expression which has been overused to the point of losing its original meaning. In movies, this usually denotes something already seen, something trite or hackneyed.

Zagreb, 1987

Peter Brook was our guest. He was preparing an English version of *Mahabharata* and was assembling an international cast. He planned to stage it at his Théâtre des Bouffes du Nord in Paris and wanted the leading actor to be from Yugoslavia. He asked me to pick two of the best actors from my generation, and to let him spend, incognito, a few days with them at our Zagreb apartment.

On the second day of the actors' bravados, long talks, and Ana's dinners, I went out for a walk with Brook. He stopped in front of a theater and asked me if this was the Croatian National Theater. I nodded, he sat down on the sidewalk, gesturing for me to join him.

Zagreb, 1956

For the first time since World War II, a theater troupe from the West is visiting a country on the other side of the "Iron curtain." As "something in between," Yugoslavia is the first stopover on the Royal Shakespeare Company's tour with *Titus Andronicus*, directed by Peter Brook, and with Sir Laurence Olivier and Lady Olivier—Vivien Leigh—in the leading roles.

Those are the days when Sir Winston Churchill, at the peak of the Cold War, sends his old friend Marshal Tito a small token of his appreciation in the form of Scarlett O'Hara.

Both sides are apprehensive and suspicious. Police officers are ordered to prevent anything unexpected. "The country's reputation is at stake. The whole world is watching." Preparations last for months. The English ambassador is duly informed that the respected guests will have police protection, security officers will be everywhere, and the guests' absolute safety is guaranteed.

It is early spring when the troupe arrives in Zagreb, their first stop. After a grand welcome, the national anthems, the diplomatic fanfare, the speeches by the statesmen, and a ride around the town, they settle in at Hotel Esplanade and the performance takes place that evening at the Croatian National Theater.

Vivien Leigh and Laurence Olivier were, at the time, the world's most famous actor-spouses. In reality, however, their intimate relationship had been a formality for a long time. She was drinking heavily. He was in a relationship with a younger actress. And furthermore, they were unbearably jealous of each other. The tour was the only reason why their imminent divorce hadn't yet been announced.

During the performance, which is to be followed by a presidential reception and a dinner party for a small number of guests, Laurence and Vivien have several fights. He makes sure that not a single drop of alcohol is to be found anywhere in her vicinity, and she recognizes his hand in the alcohol shortage.

After all the curtain calls, rounds of applause, and tons of flowers, while everyone is waiting for the presidential reception to begin, Vivien Leigh sneaks out of the theater. Disguised, in a wig she finds in the dressing room, she passes all the security points without anyone noticing her; no one but a young twenty-year-old police officer.

She is just going out for a drink, but once he realizes she has sneaked out, there is no time to notify his superiors. He goes out after her.

The following day, at about eleven o'clock in the morning, someone knocks on Brook's door at the theater. When he opens it, he sees the young police officer carrying Vivien Leigh in his arms. Her hair is disheveled, she is asleep. The young police officer carefully sets her down on the sofa and leaves without a word.

At the main train station that same afternoon, during the grand send-off, Vivien Leigh stands at the train window, her eyes searching for just one person. She sees him as the train is pulling away. The young police officer is standing to the side at the corner. Brook said that at that moment he sees tears in her eyes.

Zagreb, 1987

Vivien admits to Brook that she had slipped out of the theater and she truly did like the young police officer, but he refused to have anything to do with her. If he is afraid to lose his job, or simply stunned by the fact that he has Scarlett O'Hara right there in front of him, she can't tell. She also can't tell what happens later; she can't or won't. And Brook told me he could still remember the officer's name. "He was Ivan and he'd be about fifty now, no more. Try to find him and hear him out. Make a film. This story is my gift to you."

During my research, as I read and explored the memories of the participants in this story, I slowly discovered the reality of that one night which brought together a grand movie star from the West, and a young police officer from the East, two prototypes, two clichés of split and opposing halves. The ensuing adventure, although brief, changed the lives of them both. And, the more I dug, the more I began to think that the least relevant aspect of the encounter was the fact that she was the great Vivien Leigh, and he, Ivan, a small-time communist cop. What mattered was that these two completely different people, despite all the prejudices that separated them, coupled up for the night through a unique attraction.

Los Angeles, 1992

Clare Foster, the English scriptwriter, wrote a script based on this story. I cooperated on the first draft, but then I left Los Angeles and she wrote the second and third drafts on her own.

Some ten years later, she contacted me to ask if I'd be willing to sell the option on the story. After a long search, she'd obviously found someone interested in the script.

Close-Up

The Merriam-Webster dictionary gives two entries: a photograph or a movie shot taken at close range, and an intimate view or examination of something.

Hollywood, 1913

D. W. Griffith is considered the first to use a close-up in a movie. This fact is often illustrated in film-history books with an anecdote from actress Lillian Gish: "The front office was upset. They came down and said: 'The audience doesn't pay for the head or the arms or the shoulders of the actor. They want the whole body. Let's give them their money's worth.' Griffith stood very close and said: 'Can you see my feet?' When they said, No, he replied: 'That's what I'm doing. I am using what the eyes can see.'"

Hollywood, 1940

Hollywood forgot its greatest director-star. Griffith had financial troubles. He lived alone at the Knickerbocker Hotel in Los Angeles and died there in 1948.

Someone's memoirs, I believe it was Chaplin's, described Griffith as an old man sitting at the hotel bar, telling strangers he'd invented the close-up. Had he been wise, Griffith used to tell them, and filed a patent and earned just a penny for each use of any close-up in any film, he'd have been a rich man.

Grožnjan, 1998

I talked with Branko Bauer, one of the finest Croatian film directors. He leaned forward suddenly, paused briefly, looked at me, and in a hushed, secretive voice, said: "You know, whenever I had trouble with a scene, when I was unsure of how to approach it, I'd go for a close- up."

Cold Open

The first movie scene, before the opening credits, which takes us directly into the story and serves as the key to the story.

Crna Mlaka, 1990

We are filming *Charuga*. It's lunch time. The production accountant enters the dining room. A short, silent, middle-aged man. He sits down, doffs his hat, reaches into his inside coat pocket and takes out a gun. "I was at a meeting of the Croatian Democratic Union. They gave us this, just in case," he says, turning to check our reactions, and then smugly puts the gun away.

Zagreb, 1990

The Croatian Democratic Union (a right-wing nationalist political party led by Franjo Tuđman, a former general in Tito's Yugoslav People's Army) wins the election.

Completion Guarantee

A form of insurance offered by financial institutions to guarantee that the producer will complete and deliver the film, in return for a percentage fee based on the budget. Banks will not make loans and big productions will not embark on projects which do not have a completion guarantee.

Zagreb, 1990

Zoran Pusić, a professor of mathematics and a peace activist, assembled seven "intellectuals" or "academic citizens," or whichever term might best apply, to join him on his visit to the president of the republic, Franjo Tuđman, in an attempt to persuade him to stop preparing for war against the Serbs in Knin, but to begin a dialogue instead. And to tell him that we could, if he agreed, serve as go-betweens. Most of the people in the group were strangers as far as I was concerned; I had no idea who they were or what their jobs were. By their accents, I could tell that some of them were from Istria, some from Dalmatia, and one or two from Zagreb.

Tuđman agreed to meet us and invited television and the newspapers, and only after the cameras left the room did he become a little less tense.

One of the first things he said to us was: "I am delighted to welcome you as a delegation of Serbs..." I interrupted him: "Excuse me, Mr. President, you must have misunderstood. We are not a delegation of Serbs. I don't know the nationalities of the people here, but I don't think that is what matters at this moment. We have come as a group of people who would like to help initiate a dialogue between you and Knin. Nothing more, nothing less." Tuđman apologized, explained that he must have been misinformed, and the conversation proceeded.

After half an hour, when the conversation was drawing to a close, Tuđman said once again: "I'm delighted that you, a delegation of Serbs ..." Once again, I asked to speak and repeated the same thing I had said at the beginning. And once again, he apologized for the misunderstanding, in almost exactly the same words, and our meeting with him was soon over.

It was pretty clear that, from his point of view, war was the only option.

The next day, all the newspapers, even *Vjesnik* on its front page, published a picture of us with Tuđman and the caption, "President Tuđman Receives a Delegation of Serbs."

So, not only did I become a Serb, but an official representative of the Serbs. And at that time in Croatia, there was no greater curse.

A few days later, my uncle Ljubiša sent me a photocopy of my grandfather's birth certificate to show he'd been baptized in St. Mark's Church in the Zagreb Upper Town. He also sent my great-grandfather Stjepan's high school certificate, and my great-great-grandfather Leopold Görlich's birth certificate so in case someone gave me any trouble me or showed up at my door, I could bring out the documents as the evidence of our centuries-old Croatian origins.

I laughed and remembered a story about how the wife of writer Branko Ćopić, who had been facing the threat of arrest for years, pasted an article on the door of their Belgrade apartment, an excerpt from one of Tito's interviews with foreign journalists that had been published in *Borba*. Asked about Ćopić and his destiny, Tito said: "Nobody will arrest Ćopić."

Rajko,
I'm sending you these, just in case:
1) Your grandfather Šandor's birth certificate;
2) Your great-grandfather Stjepan's high school certificate;
3) The birth certificate of your great-great-grandfather's Leopold Görlich (born 1839), son of Leopold and Barbara.
Phone me to let me know you've received them!
                                             Sincerely, Ljubiša

Continuity

Uninterrupted connection or succession; a meaningful whole.

Brela, 1947

The year I was born, my grandmother, Olga, planted four cypresses next to our summer house in Brela. The locals warned her that cypresses should be planted only at cemeteries and bring death to whoever breaks the rule.

Zagreb, 1948

Grandma died that spring.

Grandpa brought one of her four cypresses to Zagreb and planted it behind her grave in Mirogoj cemetery.

Over the years, the cypress grew and overshadowed the grave.

Zagreb, 1984

That spring, my father and my grandfather died in the same month.

Less than six months later, next to Grandma's cypress sprouted two new, almost identical ones.

Zagreb, 1994

Ljubiša, my father's elder brother, died. He was buried in the same grave. Then there were four cypresses behind the granite grave at Mirogoj, the Zagreb cemetery. The exact number my grandma Olga planted in Brela.

Zagreb, 2008

The urn with my mother's ashes, and, a bit later, the urn with the ashes of my father's youngest brother, Saša, are buried in the family tomb. Soon, another two sprouts of cypresses from Brela appeared behind the tombstone.

Now there are six.

Courtroom Movies

Movies that focus on narratives based on legal practice and the judicial system: Tell It to the Judge *(1928),* The Judge Steps Out *(1948),* Paths of Glory *(1957),* The Life and Times of Judge Roy Bean *(1972),* The Devil's Advocate *(1997),* The Lincoln Lawyer *(2013),* The Judge *(2014) . . .*

Los Angeles, 1991

At each intersection in Beverly Hills, there stands a stop sign. Drivers are expected to bring the car to a full stop, let the vehicle in front of them go through or if no one's there, look to the left and to the right, and only then move on. The phrase "California stop" describes the act of not completely stopping, but rather "rolling" through an intersection, while slowing down ever so slightly. To stop at a stop sign is mandatory, while the "California stop" is a traffic offense. Police officers can tell the difference by observing the driver's physical position: when putting on the brakes the driver has to lean forward, whereas when rolling through a stop sign the driver doesn't lean.

I am pulled over and the police officer, despite my efforts to explain that I had, indeed, stopped, calmly writes out a ticket. When he says the fine is $85, I look at him with such surprise that he smiles and explains that I don't have to pay straight away, though, in that case, I'll have to see the judge. And the magistrate, if I am able to justify my offense, is allowed to reduce the fine or cancel it altogether.

There are about one hundred people in an impressively large room of the Los Angeles City Hall. The magistrate is on the stage, and by his side, at the same table, an elderly woman, probably the treasurer. I am holding a number, and as the screen indicates that my number is drawing near, I get up, join the line, and wait.

In front of me is a taxi driver, Russian. He goes up onto the stage and launches passionately into his defense: "Your honor, the officer claimed I was driving at 67 mph down Sunset Boulevard. But trust me, that's impossible. I went out yesterday to check, and I could barely reach 56." The judge listens to him calmly and says: "Sunset Boulevard is a major class II highway, and the speed limit is 35 mph. So, for the first offense, you are fined $180, and for the second one, the one that you committed yesterday, the same. Altogether $360." The taxi driver tries to say something but the magistrate gestures that his defense is over, that he should go and pay the woman who is sitting next to him, and then says, "Next."

As I climb onto the stage, it hits me that after this, all my excuses are pointless. The magistrate asks me if there's something I'd like to say in my defense and after a long pause, I say: "Nothing!" He looks at me, surprised, and then says: "So, it'll be $85, but for taking up my time I sentence you to watching the movies."

I pay up and, with another fifty offenders, I spend eight hours the following weekend watching documentaries about traffic accidents. For three days after that, I dream of bloody faces, severed arms, and mutilated bodies.

Courtroom Movies II

Athens, Ohio 2001

It's early on a Sunday morning. I'm on my way to pick up a copy of the *New York Times*. A police siren suddenly wails behind me. I pull over.

"You were driving at 37 mph, and the speed limit here is 25. Do you want to pay the $90, or go to court?"

There are fifty people in the grand hall of the Athens City Hall. Most of them are wearing orange overalls, meaning they spent the night in jail. Over the weekend, they were caught either very drunk or with a certain amount of drugs for personal, or sometimes someone else's, use.

A tall, dignified judge with a white moustache, reminiscent of a character from the 50s black-and-white movies, is up on stage, calling out names.

When my turn comes, I stand and, when asked if I have something to say in my defense, I say: "Yes, your honor. I was driving at 37 mph in what for years was a 35 mph zone. I didn't see the new sign." The magistrate nods and says: "Fair enough. The new sign was posted only a few days ago. I hereby reduce the fine from $90 to $60." I thank him and ask with a smile: "Can I continue with my defense to have it reduced even more?" He smiles too and, in a meaningful tone, says: "Of course you can, but in that case, I recommend that you hire a lawyer!"

Courtroom Movies III

Athens, Ohio, 2014

I receive a jury summons with the following explanation: "A jury summons is a court order. It means you must attend at this time and place so a jury can be selected, unless you have been excused. Although you may not be chosen as a juror, you do have to show up. Serving on a jury in our society is both a privilege and a legal duty. If you do not appear, you may be subject to severe penalties provided by law."

It is early in the morning. There are about one hundred people in the courtroom foyer. A court clerk calls out names. As one of the twelve people who are first called, I enter the courtroom and sit in the jury box. Before the selection process begins, the judge asks for all those to step down who have committed a criminal offence or are related in some way to the defendants, the local police, or the court. Once these people have left and other candidates have taken their seats, the selection begins. The potential jurors are questioned by both the defense attorney and the prosecutor. As soon as one of them is not satisfied with a candidate, the candidate is excused and a new one takes their place.

The jury selection has been going on for over two hours. Worried that, at this pace, it might last for days, I address the judge. I explain that my English might not be good enough to understand all the legal subtleties and perhaps a native speaker should take my place. The judge smiles and refuses my plea, adding that my English is just fine. I'm surprised that no one else is trying to bail out. On the contrary, everyone seems truly eager to be chosen.

Four hours later, I am selected as one of twelve jurors. A few spare ones stay in the courtroom, and then we have a lunch break.

The trial finally begins. Having seen numerous courtroom movies, I expect a tough murder case, or at least an attempted crime. Hardly. The defendant, a young man, and his friends had a clash with another group of local guys. He snatched a cell phone from one of them and ran off with it.

The friends of the man who was robbed went after him and, after a long chase through town, they found the phone in a garbage container right in front of the pub where they'd been drinking. No battery. Since the two groups knew each other, the police quickly located the accused.

All of them had come down that evening from the Appalachian Mountains near the town. That's when the clashes usually happen: when the students leave town for the holidays, the boisterous, burly young rowdies muster the courage to venture into the local student bars.

It is already dark outside when the jury withdraws to deliberate over our verdict in the well-guarded chambers. I am familiar with the ritual from the movies I've seen, but nothing prepares me for all the people who, so easily and vehemently, welcome the task of punishing someone. To my greatest surprise, the women are the leaders. They really enjoy having someone's destiny in their hands.

Since the young man is facing two charges, we are asked to make two separate decisions. After almost two hours of heated argument, I am addressed by the elderly and somewhat anxious man sitting next to me. By his accent, I can tell he is from the same parts as the defendant. He asks me to try and convince the jury to drop the first of the two charges. Namely, it could have damaging consequences, it will remain on the young man's record, and might make getting a job virtually impossible for him. The second charge is less serious since it won't go onto his record.

Convinced that we shouldn't let a phone battery ruin someone's life, I start in steadily and carefully. This is far from easy. Especially since some of them are seeing this as an opportunity to extend the deliberations to the next day, which will mean an additional $30 of juror compensation.

More than three hours later, the jury has reached a verdict. He is found innocent of the first charge, guilty of the second one.

We leave the courtroom. I get into the elevator. There's the judge. I ask him if I may have a word now that the trial is over. He nods. "How is it possible to have about one hundred people miss a day of work, to involve prosecutors and expensive lawyers, to have the whole court, including yourself, waste an entire day, all over an old phone battery?" He laughs. It is not up to him but to the pre-trial chamber to decide which cases go to court. Justice, no matter the size of the crime, must be served.

On my way home, I muse over Croatia, where not even people who have stolen whole battery factories, and thieves even bigger than that, end up in court or, if they do, the trials go on for decades until they are indefinitely postponed. A country where the judges are completely controlled by politics, and where almost nobody believes in the objectivity of the court, its incorruptibility, or, in fact, in justice.

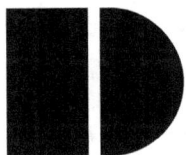

Damnatio memoriae

In ancient Rome—the erasure of the name of someone who is deceased from all written documents and public discourse going forward. In scriptwriting, it sometimes refers to the elimination of an unnecessary character.

Zagreb, 1964

A month before our final exams, the last issue of *Thicket* (*Šikara*), the student newspaper of the Seventh Zagreb High School, was banned. At the very end of our high-school days, we had decided to speak up and publish our opinions of certain professors. That same day, the school janitor burned all the copies of the last issue. The four editors were summoned for an impromptu meeting. After a heated discussion, we were given our final warning before expulsion.

Zagreb, 1970

For television editor Angel Miladinov and TV Zagreb, I made *All Men Are Good Men in Bad Society* (*Svaki je čovjek dobar čovjek u rđavom svijetu*) a documentary about people who live on the streets of Zagreb, obsessed by the idea of changing society and fomenting revolution. It was banned and had to wait almost forty years for its first public screening.

    I made *Praises* (*Pohvale*), a television documentary series of six movies, also about the people living on the margins of society. It, too, was banned or, as they explained it back then: "Postponed for a better time." "Postponement" was a decision made by the general director and the production manager. They thought the documentaries contained more "real life" than the small, strictly controlled screen could bear.

Angel told me: "Keep on filming and I will, within my limits, fight to have it shown." And so, I did keep on filming, since that was what mattered to me most, Angel kept fighting, and TV Zagreb "postponed for a better time" almost everything I did.

Beram, 1974

I made *Drinkable Water and Freedom* (*Pitka Voda i Sloboda*), a one-minute documentary filmed in a single take. This was a movie about a village fountain that had been tapped out, and it bore an inscription that drinkable water and freedom were won after a long struggle and that the freedom had been paid for in blood. I sent a release print to the Film Committee, as they used to call censorship back then. They sent me a green card crossed out in red pen. The movie was banned from public screening because "it insults the tradition of the national struggle for liberation in World War II" and for "corrupting the youth."

Throughout Istria, Associations of the Veterans held meetings in which they passionately discussed and assumed things about the movie though none of them had actually seen it. They invited me to come and "explain myself." Cunning old devil Dušan Makavejev advised me to skip the meeting, and refrain from responding to the various newspaper articles. His suggestion: wait it out. "This will blow over," he says.

Zagreb, 1981

The Jadran Film lab produced a copy of *You Love Only Once*, a love story about an encounter between the revolution and the reality of the first postwar years. The same day, at the demand of the Croatian secret police, seven of their top officers watch it at a special screening.

After the screening, which took place in complete silence, the youngest officer was the first to turn to look at me and the producer, Sulejman Kapić. He was wearing a tight beige suit, one of those slick suits from Trieste. After a long pause he frowned: "Had we asked the Ustasha emigration to make a movie about the Service (as they called themselves), what they made wouldn't be as bad as this."

The talk lasted for over an hour. They talked. We listened. One by one, in a benevolent tone, they kept suggesting what should be discarded.

In the end, they asked Kapić and me not to leave Zagreb, take no trips. Because we might be asked to come back.

After they had left, we stayed in the theater. We sat there in silence. Shrugging with helplessness and disbelief, Kapić muttered: "If we jettison all they've suggested, the movie will last for less than five minutes."

The next day, the police locked away the negative of the film. They were unaware of the fact that we had taken the precaution of making two prints and that the same morning I had sent one of them to my sister in Paris via a stewardess on JAT, the Yugoslav national airline. That print got *You Love Only Once* into the official selection of the Cannes Film Festival, thus saving the movie.

Zagreb, 1987

Jadran Film decided to produce *Charuga*. To finalize the funding, they asked TV Zagreb to join the coproduction. At the management meeting while they were discussing the offer, the manager of the culture section said that the scriptwriters were actually trying to depict Comrade Tito, using the character of Čaruga as a disguise. This "kiss of death" was supposed to kill the project once and for all.

Zagreb, 1991

Four years later, after we had filmed *Charuga*, a film about a beloved leader, which we, ourselves, produced, I once again heard the sentence that had been supposed to seal the fate of *You Love Only Once*.

"Had we ordered a movie from the Serbian Chetniks from Knin, it would be less appalling than this!" said Slaven Letica, President Franjo Tuđman's political advisor, after the movie opened. The next day, his words were published in the newspaper in bold italics.

Pula, 1991

The last evening of the Pula Film Festival, after *Charuga* was screened, Darko Zubčević, an official film critic for Croatian Radio Television, asked me on live TV: "What are you going to do now that you've made this Chetnik film?" I looked at him and walked out.

I had several interviews in which I said what I thought of it all.

Over the next ten years, not a single frame of any movie I'd ever made was screened in Croatia on either the big or the small screen. My name was removed from the encyclopedias, I was erased from the roster of freelance artists, I was expunged from the pension plan, various newspapers dragged me through the mud...

And not a single person from the local cinematography or affiliated with it, not a single colleague or critic, has ever written or said a word about any of this.

The only exception was the writer Slobodan Šnajder who dedicated one of his columns in *Novi list*, the newspaper in Rijeka, to this "case."

Defining Premise

The process of choosing and articulating the initial state of affairs that drives the plot.

Rocky Mountains, 1993

I'm standing in front of Buffalo Bill's grave. He was buried at a high elevation, halfway between the small town where he was born and the one where he grew up. Both towns claimed his grave, so this location is their "historical compromise."

He died on almost the same day that Lenin started the October Revolution in Saint Petersburg.

Paris, 1911

Legend has it that Nadezhda Krupskaya and Vladimir Ilyich Lenin had tickets for a Buffalo Bill circus performance, but Nadezhda caught a cold so they never went.

Denver, 1993

"Western civilization has won its ultimate victory over communism!" states George Bush senior, victoriously announcing the end of the Cold War.

While I watch him, I think: "Wrong. It's not your victory. It's the inner hunger for life that has overpowered the idea of life!"

Deliverance

A John Boorman movie from 1973 about four friends who spend a weekend in the Georgia backwaters.

Dublin, 1978

I come to the opening night of *Bravo Maestro*.

The sound designer, who worked on *Deliverance*, shows me how he makes sounds. He screens the movie without sound and, with several small planks in a bathtub set in the middle of the sound studio he creates the sounds of a rushing river.

Los Angeles, 1979

Bravo Maestro is shown at Filmex, the greatest American film festival at the time.

The *Deliverance* soundtrack was the first LP I bought during my first visit to America. Tom Waits's *Small Change* was the second one.

Athens, Ohio, 1994

A local film association is screening the movies based on the cliché that the people of Appalachia are primitive, dirty, and evil creatures. *Deliverance* is the first in the series. In the follow-up discussion, almost everyone agrees that this very movie has done them the greatest harm in the eyes of the world.

Telluride, 1999

I'm sitting with Boorman, the director of *Deliverance*, in the garden of a Main Street saloon. He is playing with *How to Make Your Movie*, my interactive CD, on his laptop. He wants to include it in the new issue of *Projections*, a journal dedicated to film education. I tell him about the Athens screening. I ask if he'd come and talk those people. "I'm not that brave!" he says.

Dialogue

A conversation between two or more people.

Hvar, 1970

My friend, Belgrade actor Branko Cvejić, is marrying Vesna. His father Žarko, a famous Belgrade opera singer, a bass, is also there. A stout old man with a wide benevolent face. During the lunch, he asks me in his deep voice:
 "You're a Serb?"
 "No, I am not!"
 "So, you're a communist!"
 "No!"
 "So, what are you, son?" Žarko asks, his eyes filling with worry.

Director

The person who creates and makes a movie.

Athens, Ohio, 1999

I have a dream in which I watch the thing I'm dreaming about. And in my dream, I'm irritated by actors for being too slow, off the mark, too soft-spoken. And then I . . .

I direct my own dream within the dream.

Maybe the time has come to put an end to my ten-year abstinence and go back to making films.

Director's Cut

An edited version of a film which represents the director's own approved edit. If the contract does not grant the director the right to the final cut, this right goes to the producer. In that case, the director's version sometimes appears after distribution and differs from the version screened in theaters.

New York, 1984

With our friends, we went to the movie theater on the corner of 3rd Avenue and 59th Street to see *Once Upon a Time in America*, Sergio Leone's new movie. At the entrance, we were given yellow pens and a survey with a dozen questions. This was a test screening organized by the producers, who often determine the fate of a movie. People were smoking up on the balcony, mostly marijuana. The light from the projector illuminated clouds of smoke.

Salsomaggiore–Parma, 1987

My movie *Three for Happiness* (*Za sreću je potrebno troje*) won the festival Grand Prix. Sergio Leone headed the jury. After the awards had been announced, he invited us to lunch.

Ana, Olga, and I had lunch with him and his assistant. He talked about the problems he had while making *Once Upon a Time in America*. He was still trying to raise the money to buy out the footage and show his version of the movie. It was almost twice as long as the one released by the producers. While talking, he poured us champagne. He served a little to ten-year-old Olga. She shook her head firmly. No, she did not drink alcohol. Sergio Leone winked at her, coaxing her to have a taste. I did, too. Eventually, she reluctantly raised her glass, clinked it with Sergio Leone, licked a drop of the champagne and quickly set the glass down with a grimace.

Rome, 1989

Sergio Leone died. A newspaper article said he died at home, while watching *Once Upon a Time in America* on television. The same article said that his sons had pledged to buy out the footage and show their father's version to the world.

New York, 1999

Olga was a student in New York. She phoned to tell us she'd been at a party the day before, where they were watching Sergio Leone's movies. While they were preparing the screening and talking about him, she casually remarked: "He's the man with whom I drank my first glass of champagne!"

Athens, Ohio, 2010

I searched the internet for a "director's cut" of Once Upon a Time in America. It was never released.

Cannes, 2012

Martin Scorsese reintroduced Leone's 229-minute version. Leone's children were still trying to gain back the rights to the more than twenty-nine missing minutes of the film to show his almost complete 269-minute 1984 Cannes version.

Athens, Ohio, 2015

Twentieth Century Fox released a Blu-ray two-disc set featuring a longer theatrical cut and an extended director's cut with the note: "The added 22 minutes of extended scenes bring us closer to Leone's original vision of the film."

Leone's real director's cut has never been released.

Director's Language

"As a film director, you want to make sure that your commands are understood when directing film talent. For this to happen, using the proper terminology is crucial" (videomaker.com).

Karlovac, 1986

The first time I worked with actors whose first language is English, it took me some time to realize that the comments I was making, such as "fine," they took to mean "bad," "good" as "not so bad," "very good" as "you can do better," "perfect" as "decent," and "excellent" as "good."

Athens, Ohio, 1994

Ana showed me an American magazine that published a number of phrases suggested by education experts to young mothers when they want to encourage their children. Inspired by this, I compile a list of exclamations and phrases for my CD, *How to Make Your Movie*, which I urge young directors to use when they want to encourage their actors. Use these seventy-seven phrases to inspire your cast:

Wow
Super
Outstanding
Excellent
Great
Good
Neat
Well done
Remarkable
I knew you could do it
I'm proud of you
Fantastic
Superstar
Nice work
Looking good
You're on top of it
Beautiful
Now you're flying
You're catching on
Now you've got it
You're incredible
Bravo
You're fantastic
Hurray
You're on target
You're on your way
That's the way we do it
How smart
Good job
That's incredible
Hot dog
Dynamite
You're unique
Nothing can stop you
Good for you
That was clever
You're a winner
Remarkable job
Beautiful work
Spectacular
Great discovery
You've discovered the secret
You figured it out
Fantastic job
Hip, hip hurray
Bingo
Magnificent
Marvelous
Terrific
Phenomenal
You're sensational
Creative job
Super job
Fantastic job
Exceptional performance
You're a real trooper
You are exciting
What an imagination
You're spectacular
You tried hard
Outstanding performance
You're a good friend
I trust you
You're important
You mean a lot to me
You make me happy
You belong
You've got a friend
You make me laugh
You brighten my day
I respect you
You're wonderful
You're perfect
A-plus job
My buddy
You made my day
That's the best

Istria, 2017

When I ask a local peasant, "how's it going?" and he scowls, shrugs, and says, "what can I say?" I translate this as "not bad." The answer "so-so," I translate as "good," and "it's going, it's going!" as "never better."

Documentary (Autobiographical)

Movies in which authors tell their personal stories using footage from the past and the present, as well as stories and accounts told by their friends and relatives.

An unfinished and partially lost letter to Olga.

> Cannes, May 12, 1994
>
> Dear Ogac,
> The journey from our house in Athens to this hotel took a full twenty-four hours. Worn out from the travel and dead tired I went to bed at about nine this evening and woke up a few hours later. So, now it's the dead of night here in Cannes, three, three-thirty in the morning, and I'm well-slept and ready to go. The only trouble is that even hopping Cannes is fast asleep at this hour. Everything has shut down, people are sleeping.
>   That is actually what I want to write about. Not about sleeping, of course, but about how hard it is to synchronize all the different times, the different places, and the different lives. To write to you about what you wrote to me in your letter "for reading on the plane." In your wise, smart, sad letter about where you are, what you are, and how you are in the midst of it all.
>   I read it carefully, very carefully. My first reading made me incredibly sad. After the second reading, I promised myself I would respond.
>   Of course, what I'll write has no "instructional" aspirations. Nothing "educational." Nothing ... in short, of what a father should be aiming for when having a heart-to-heart with his daughter. Whenever I try on any of these roles during our talks, I feel like someone who is acting in a way he doesn't believe. In short: stupid and bad. So I'll skip all that as far as my silly parental position allows.
>   Your question, which you've asked like a real grown-up, without accusing anyone of anything, is: "Where am I, where do I belong, and why am I here and not there?"
>   Something along those lines. I hope I haven't trivialized it with my simplification.

It has been more than two, almost three years, since you and Anek came to LA. Which makes this, with short breaks and trips to and from Zagreb, our third "school" year in the United States. I call it a school year not only because you're in school, but because this has been a "school" year for all three of us, in a much broader sense. But, we'll get to that.

Three years ago, you were a little girl who found herself, against her will, faced with a strange and unanswerable question: why did we so abruptly, with no preparation or intention, leave our nice, comfy life, for a life which, at least at first, was not as comfortable and was endlessly uncertain, hectic and sad?

I didn't have the right answer then and I don't have it now. The only difference is that back then I had a good alibi for no response, you were still too young and wouldn't understand. Not so anymore. You are now a big, smart, talented, and beautiful girl. I have no alibi. The time has come for me to answer the question you are rightly asking: "Why are we here and not there?"

In all good novels and dramatic human histories, for one life to come to an end and another to begin there is always a single basic, hard-and-fast, firm and unshakeable reason. In our case, there wasn't. The war could have been that, the war could have been used for that, but the war, as you know, wasn't directly what drove us away. We did live with it for a while, and maybe we could have survived in Zagreb without ever feeling it on our own skin. No one in our family was killed, nobody's home burned down.

And yet it was the war that turned our lives upside down. Not directly, which, no matter how stupid and cruel that may sound, might be easier to survive. They torch your house, destroy your past, and if you're lucky, you survive, you leave. You know, no matter how painful it might be, that your past life no longer exists and you have to start anew. In our case, none of that happened. The war, for us and our decision, had only an indirect and far more insidious impact, which was therefore harder to see.

I am worried that I'll go into too much breadth with this. That's why I'm simplifying. I'm groping. I'm trying to find a sentence that could at least be somewhat true.

(I found this letter on my computer, to which I haven't add or remove a word, with this "document error" fragment in it. As if these sentences were crossed out by an invisible censor's hand. It's nice, though, that the computer at least left the final words: "pieces of shit.")

When the war began, it didn't seem to be about a struggle, though this was how they tried to sell it to us, a struggle e$P^^^Document Error^^^

LH"^^^Document Error^^^c^^^Document Error^^^S"^^^Document Error^^^(^^^Document Error^^^|m^^^Document Error^^^<X^^^Document Error^^^JG^^^Document Error^^^w^^^Document Error^^^+1^^^Document Error^^^U`k.Z^^^Document Error^^^7X^^^Document Error^^^e_^^^Document Error^^^/b^^^Document Error^^^{me^^^Document Error^^^|H^^^Document Error^^^3^^^Document Error^^^$S^^^Document Error^^^`K
^^^Document Error^^^|3^^^Document Error^^^Ni^^^Document Error^^^L^^^Document Error^^^o^^^Document Error^^^b^^^Document Error^^^ DnN^^^Document Error^^^`^^^Document Error^^^6^^^Document Error^^^s(^^^Document Error^^^`M$^^^Document Error^^^`^^^Document Error^^^jV
;^^^Document Error^^^t^^^Document Error^^^}K{uE `^^^Document Error^^^F^^^Document Error^^^b"^^^Document Error^^^W^^^Document Error^^^?^^^Document Error^^^:^^^Document Error^^^Y6*w ^^^Document Error^^^S^^^Document Error^^^gq^^^Document Error^^^;^^^Document Error^^^+^^^Document Error^^^T}^^^Document Error^^^W^^^Document Error^^^~^^^Document Error^^^{^^^Document Error^^^fU9t^^^Document Error^^^.6W^^^Document Error^^^ecu^^^Document Error^^^ }F^^^Document Error^^^ pieces of shit.

As you know, this kind of opinion wasn't too popular among Croats then. And something more important. The milieu there is very narrow-minded, especially after Yugoslavia fell apart and Croatia was reduced to Zagreb. There, if the authorities don't like you, and you are involved in working for the "public," as your father is, life is not exactly a rose garden. That's how things used to be under communism, and that is what they were, just a little worse, under the new nationalists.

I made movies under these conditions for more than twenty years, and, no matter what, I worked to stay true to the principle of individuality, to remain independent of any power structures, to keep doing what I thought I should be doing and how I thought it should be done. So I was trying, sometimes with considerable difficulty, to hold on to the right of the individual to their own opinion and their own work. In a collective that has functioned, more or less, like a lynch mob, I was trying to be an individual.

All of this sounds way too pathetic and tedious, but I have to talk about it, too, if I'm going to tell you some of the basic thoughts that have been troubling me and which I have been living with these last three years, and which are, perhaps, a small piece of my answer to your question.

It's dawn. Under my window is the blue Mediterranean Sea. The scent of rosemary. I'm sleepy. Off to bed.

Six days later.

I'm on the plane for NY. I'll try to write faster because it looks as if my battery is close to empty. That's good. At least I won't digress as much.

Where were we . . .

When the new government came into power, a new, even more violent rape of the individual began. At the same time, the maneuvering space had shrunk drastically and there would be respite from the government, where you could work without having the government watching your plate or your bed, or listening in on your phone.

And, again, I'll keep this brief. When it came to my profession, this meant I couldn't do anything unless I started sucking up, unconditionally and without restraint, to the people in power. Or, more simply put, this meant we'd have nothing to eat if I held to my basic principles, the basic ethical values I'd cared deeply about for the past twenty years. In small, closed communities, in snake pits, this is how the government intimidates people into obedience. And this is what happened in Croatia, along with all the tragedies of the war and a monstrous flourishing of thieves and murderers.

And so, I felt cornered, caught in a mousetrap. Night after night Anek and I talked about all this, looking for a sensible way out.

Meanwhile, I was producing Điđa's movie, and in Knin, no less. That's how I was proclaimed a Chetnik (later on, the same newspapers "promoted" me to Jew and used that to harass me), that's how the anonymous phone calls and threats began. That is how the mousetrap feeling grew.

So, there, those were a few of the basic issues.

Listed like this, they sound like a heap of selfish reasons. But it was more than that. I kept thinking about it all. Anek and I talked and talked. And it was mostly you we talked about. Because, this really was about you, in the end. I could have stopped making movies. I've always joked that I only ever wanted to make seven movies anyway. The way Anek lived and how she lived for us, she could have done much more easily and nicely in Zagreb. You, too. You had a whole crowd of friends and all of them loved you. You had your community and your safety. And yet, we felt none of this had a future. It seemed as if unhappiness, a greyness of the soul, would slowly but surely consume everything and it would be horrifying to watch you grow up in that.

We have given you the chance, by leaving, and we still hope our time away will be temporary, to have two equal opportunities one day when you start making decisions about your own life. We have given you the option to decide after high school, or even better, after your studies, whether you want to go there or stay here. Had we stayed in Zagreb, you wouldn't have had that, and you would have been confined to a small community with very few possibilities.

This, of course, is extremely simplified (I've mentioned that eight hundred and fourteen times, but I have to).

So, when I went to America at the end of that summer, we were still certain it would be for just three months, that you'd join me before Christmas and at some point after New Year's we'd be back. But that's when the air raids started in Zagreb, the sheltering in basements, the alarms. That's something you know much more about than I do, I wasn't there.

That's when you came to LA, and we were still hoping that at the end of the fall semester, or at least at the end of the school year, we'd go back.

And we did.

In Zagreb, we felt again how viciously the war scars the soul. How hatred twists the psyche and how difficult, impossible even, it would be to live there without feeling the hatred. And that alarmed us.

We went to New York. Once there, we realized a decision had to be made. At least for the next four years for your high school. You needed that basic stability, to know which continent you'd be going to school on.

And then, there was Ohio.

Over the three years, you grew up much faster than you would have in Zagreb. You became savvy (after your dad, we hope) and beautiful (after your mom, we hope).

And this has been and still is, though a little bit less, hellishly rough on you.

You have been under double pressure. On the one hand, school, new people, new rules. You started living among kids whose childhood had been different, whose experiences and habits had been different from yours. And it was awfully difficult, especially starting it all over again each year.

On the other hand, you had the bad luck of having Anek and me with too much time on our hands, and you were the easiest victim of this surplus. We were constantly right there, in your face, behind you, over you. We worried a lot and, while you were busy dealing with your new surroundings, we burdened you even more with our love which was like a weight that smothered you, pestered you, dogged you. You alone against the two of us. Totally unfair, I admit. And it would be silly to try and explain that this was all for your good, when that's not how you felt.

They've just brought me lunch. The battery is almost gone. So, I'll stop. Later I'll try to finish this "letter–novel–sausage–soap opera."

The lunch wasn't bad.

The machine is warning me it's out of patience. The batteries are empty.

New York, 2017

P.S. Olga is creative art director at one of the largest publishing houses in the United States. She has a daughter Rubi and a son Lou, and lives, with art director James Iacobelli, in Manhattan.

Double Feature

A film program offering two feature films for the price of one. During the 1930s, the double feature was a common practice in America. The first one in the package was always a high-budget film, the A-movie, while the other, low-budget and less ambitious, the B-movie. The practice was discontinued a long time ago, but the division into A and B categories has remained to this day.

Prague, 1966

To study in Prague, foreign students had to be given temporary Czechoslovakian citizenship. Technically, this meant we had two citizenships and we had to have an exit visa issued every time we wanted to go home. The visas were issued on Bartolomějská Street. That street, just like Petrinjska Street in Zagreb, and like many other similar streets in Central European towns, was marked by a peculiar symbiosis of whores and police officers.

The visas were issued on the ground floor. There were two offices: one for citizens of capitalist countries, and the other one for citizens of Communist ones. Each time we went there for a visa, we had to check both doors, to see where the flag of Yugoslavia was. The flags indicated which office dealt with which countries, and the Yugoslav flag was often, depending on the political relations of the moment, moved from one door to the other.

Prague, 1968

With my classmates Agnieszka Holland and Srđan Karanović, I ran the "culture" department on the strike board at the FAMU (Film Academy of Performing Arts). We spent those two weeks, meaning the entire student strike, holed up at the Palác Lažanských. The whole situation was a wonderful combination of Hašek and Kafka. There was a kind of bittersweet *Mitteleuropa* irony to it, used by that part of the world instinctively as a shield against the merciless steam roller of history.

Among other things, we were put in charge of the cinematheque. Every night we played double features, making sure not to disturb the "bloc balance." So, for example, one night we presented the American underground *Miss Gay America*, and the Russian musical, *Moscow Laughs* (*Vesyolye rebyata*).

Prague, 1969

The "double feature" went on after the strike.

Agnieszka, being from Poland (a country that was part of the Warsaw Pact), ended up in Prague Pankrác Prison. The same place where Good Soldier Schweik did time. She was held there for over a month.

Điđa and I were told at the embassy that, because of the relationship with Yugoslavia, we would probably not be arrested for the time being. But, we were advised to always carry our passports and one hundred korunas. That was the price of a cab ride to the border. And, in case we noticed something suspicious, we were to hail a cab immediately, go to the border, and cross over into Austria.

Dream Sequence

A sequence which interrupts the main plot in order to present a character's dream, in order to illustrate his or her mental state, past or future actions.

Zagreb, 1994

Among actors, I had a particular soft spot for Mladen Budiščak (nicknamed "Budilica"—or "alarm clock"—in Croatian). We made five movies together. If one can talk about a "gift" when it comes to actors, he was the actor who was the most "gifted" at staying true to his real self while on screen. Not even the Academy of Dramatic Art in Zagreb managed to destroy that gift or his Zagreb twang.

Once when he was seriously ill, he told me his dream:

Zagreb, Belgrade, Okučani, 1992. It's war. He is sick of it all. He goes to Belgrade to see Serbian actor Miki Manojlović. He tells him: "Listen, Miki, you go talk Serbian President Slobodan Milošević into meeting Tuđman, and I'll convince Tuđman to meet Milošević. Okay?" Miki listens and nods.

The next day, Miki brings Milošević and he brings Tuđman. They put them in an improvised tent by the highway near the Croatia-Serbia border. Budilica and Miki wait outside. The presidential talk doesn't take long. Out come the presidents, smiling. They've solved everything. The war is over.

Budilica and Miki are happy. They kiss. Budilica tells Miki: "See? That wasn't so hard." Miki nods.

Budilica wakes.

Dream Sequence II

Paris, 1978

Mara Rankov used to run BITEF (Belgrade International Theater Festival), with its founder, Mira Trailović. During the 1970s she moved to Paris where she still lives and works as a music agent.

Melbourne–Brisbane, 1993

This is the letter she sent to us in New York:

> July 28, 1993
> On the plane, somewhere between Melbourne and Brisbane.
>
> My dear Rajac and Ana and Olga,
> I hope this letter reaches you—I've heard you went back to Zagreb. Even if it doesn't, I need to write it.
>   You'll probably wonder why I'm writing from here, I myself am not sure why now and why from here. Actually, I do; a dream made me do it, but why that dream, and why here and now . . .
>   I woke up this morning in a hotel after three–four hours of sleep, right before the wake-up call, dizzy with nausea and grief. I dream we're somewhere high up, there are people, two or three irrelevant people, faceless. Like, on a mountaintop where Serbia meets Croatia. It's so peaceful all around us, the clouds are white, and then they float up on the right like a white fog. We aren't talking and the grief weighs heavy—it's only you, Rajko, and I, who are there. I'm feeling guilty, because the very fact that we're there at the border might mean trouble for you. We're not allowed to cross the line that separates the two countries so we lie on the ground on our respective sides, faces up, only the tops of our heads touching. And then, tears spray up into the air as if from a water pistol.
> RAJKO CRIES INTO THE SKY
> AND I CRY INSIDE
> I've been here in the middle of nowhere for two or three days, and, on purpose I haven't opened a newspaper or watched television, to give my mind and soul a rest. I'm here with a quartet—I've arranged for a concert in Melbourne, a concert in Sydney and a "residency" in Brisbane (five concerts). And yet, despite the distance, despite the context, the soul pulls its strings. In dreams.
>   Apart from that, I'm fine. I don't remember if you've met Roland. I've been with him for five years now. It's easier this way—only when I started living with him did I realize how hard it used to be before. Marko is great and he's doing fine. He's up to my eyebrows. Roland and

he and a schoolmate of his will join me once the tour is over (June 7th) and then we'll spend seven weeks traveling across North Australia. To check on those koalas and the kangaroos, to make sure they, too, don't make a mess of things.
I'D LIKE TO HEAR WHERE YOU ARE AND HOW YOU ARE.
There isn't any address on the card you sent me, so I couldn't write back. DO MAKE IT THROUGH—by letter, fax or dream . . .
    I'm thinking of you and I love you so much.

Marija Rankov

DVD

"Stands for 'Digital Versatile Disc.' A DVD is a type of optical media used for storing digital data. It is the same size as a CD but has a larger storage capacity" (techterms.com).

A wind ensemble from Šibenik called Šibenik Folk Music (Šibenska narodna glazba), founded in 1848, is one of the finest in Croatia, and over its 170 years they have held over 12,500 performances.
    Toni Gojanović, an actor from Šibenik, made his acting debut in 2006, in the leading role of my movie *The Border Post*.

Šibenik, 2018

In her article for the *Slobodna Dalmacija* daily about the beginning of the HBO series *Success*, journalist Jordanka Grubac writes about Toni Gojanović, one of the lead actors in the series:

> . . . In case there's someone out there who hasn't (yet) seen *The Border Post*, I suggest they get in touch with the orchestra. When the Šibenik musicians go on tour, they always ask the bus dispatcher if they have a television set on the bus. The next question is if they have a DVD of *The Border Post*. If they have a TV but not the DVD, that's fine. The orchestra has its own copy. It's well-worn but still works. As soon as the bus goes, *The Border Post* begins. The orchestra members know all the lines from the movie by heart. You don't have to listen to the protagonists at all. The bus echoes with the dialogues, including the sighs and other sound effects. All of them know it inside out. The roles, the situations, the sounds . . .

Athens, Ohio, 2018

While I'm reading this on the web, I think: I cannot imagine any of my movies aging better than this.

Editor

Each film story is told three times: during the writing, the filming, and the editing. The role of the editor, the director's coplayer in the finale, is very often crucial in the shaping of a film story.

Zagreb, 1968–91

I was a twenty-year-old Prague student, making the feature documentary *All Men Are Good Men in Bad Society* in Zagreb. The first day of editing, I came to the studio on Dežmanova Street and there, at the editing board, I saw a woman looking over at me, puzzled. A little huffy, she asked: "And, when is the director coming?" "That's me," I answered, noticing a shade of disappointment cross her face.

This was Živka Toplak, a really nice woman, with whom I edited five fiction feature films, two feature documentaries, and two docuseries, six episodes each. She was merciless with footage, unerringly capable of telling the right shot from the wrong one.

We worked together until she retired, yet we were never on a first-name basis. Our final project, a documentary about Čaruga, remained unfinished because, in its final stage, we were banned from the editing room by the director of Croatian Radio and Television.

Zagreb, 1990

This same Croatian National Television director marked the beginning of my cooperation with Andrija Zafranović, a classmate of mine from Prague, a man who has edited over one hundred films and is quite possibly the most important editor in Yugoslavia.

The first movie Andrija and I worked on together, *Charuga*, was edited at Jadran Film. The huge studio was almost empty. It was being prepared for the free-for-all known as privatization.

At the time, I was attacked by a journalist of the *Večernji list* newspaper—if I remember correctly, the reason for the attack was that I was producing *Virgina*, directed by my friend Điđa (Serbian director Srđan Karanović), and I told him I had no intention of talking to messengers. He should tell his boss that if his boss had something to tell me, he could tell me to my face. The problem was, however, that the Parliament had just chosen this very person, who was an actor, a film director, the head of Croatian National Television and of the Croatian Olympic Committee, to be the country's vice president.

We had only started the editing and were taking our coffee breaks at the Jadran Film cafeteria. One morning, while we were sitting by the window overlooking the courtyard, we saw a black limo pull into the courtyard and head straight for the cafeteria. A tall man in an overcoat jumped out and opened the back door. The vice president of the Republic, Antun Vrdoljak, stepped out of the limo and headed straight for me and Andrija. A bodyguard right behind him. As he came nearer, he started bellowing: "Don't you dare send messages to me. Hear? Because, feathers will fly, feathers will fly once I get my hands on you. Mark my words!" Shouting all the way, he came right over to me, glowering, and shouted once more: "Feathers will fly!" then he spun around and made for the exit. Looking after him, stunned, I said: "Cool it, stop shouting. You're the vice president of the Republic. Behave yourself." He turned, glared at me and, repeating: "Feathers will fly!" louder and louder, strode out of the courtyard, the bodyguard at his heels.

They left as they'd come. The entire show lasted all of two or three minutes. The cafeteria sank into silence. The Jadran Film staffers dropped their heads and left without a goodbye.

We decided to put that sentence "Feathers will fly!" into Čaruga's mouth during a robbery.

A week later, as we were leaving the sound stage, we bumped into him and editor Damir German. There we stood and stared at each other. We stepped aside to let them pass us and they gestured for us to leave. Just then, Vrdoljak addressed me in an unctuously cloying voice: "Rajko, why are we arguing? We can agree on everything!" I looked at him and said: "You are insane!" and walked out with Andrija. This was my last encounter with the man who would inflict a lot of misery on Croatian cinema over the next twenty years.

By the time we finished the editing, people were treating us like lepers. Having been stigmatized by the authorities, we were literally, to the point of caricature, being avoided.

Zagreb, Munich, Prague, Ohrid, Ljubljana . . . 1990–2017
Since then, I've worked with Andrija on almost everything.

We always have the same approach. He reads most of the drafts of the script and comes to the editing room a few days after the shooting has begun. I mark the best take of every shot and he goes to work on them. We talk almost every evening, and every three to four days I come to the editing room. Andrija never comes to the set. That allows for his sensible approach to the actors' continuity, internal rhythm, clarity of scenes . . . With the script supervisor—Ivanka Forenbacher earlier, and Nada Pinter for the last twenty years—Andrija has always been my abiding "lie detector." And, without someone who tells you the truth, no matter how painful the truth might be, making a movie would be almost impossible.

Several days after the shooting ends, the film is already edited. We watch it, pinpoint the weak points, and only then does the real editing begin, which, depending on the movie, lasts three to four months.

Over those months, the two of us and the assistant at the computer share the dark chamber known as the editing room. We do this ten hours a day. A person you can sit with for that long in such a small space and continue to be normal with must be someone you're fond of. And I am fond of him: Andrija is a quiet, wise man who finds childlike glee in the process of combining, arranging, and rearranging, in searching for the pivotal emotional points which he finds to be more important than any narrative logic.

While he is working on a movie, he is one hundred percent there, day or night, while eating and drinking. Nothing else exists for him then. He dives in and resurfaces only after it is completely done.

In his old age, he has become a loner who spends his time, when he's not editing, in the north of Serbia in his house along the Danube River, restoring porcelain figurines. I hereby leave him in that peaceful setting, doing what most closely defines who he is.

Entertainment Trade Magazine

Magazines about the new and ongoing deals in film production, representation, and project development.

Cologne, 1985
At a conference on European coproductions, I met Mike Downey, an Englishman of clearly Irish origins. He was living in Munich at the time, directing plays, and writing as a correspondent for *Screen International*. He spent a year in Belgrade on a Fulbright scholarship, where he became friends with my partner in scriptwriting, director Srđan Karanović.

London, 1990

"*Moving Pictures International* was established in 1990 and became one of the key international trade papers serving the global film industry, alongside Variety, The Hollywood Reporter, and Screen International. John Campbell was a Managing Director and Mike Downey the Publisher," or so says the internet.

At big festivals, such as Cannes, Berlin, Venice . . . they beat *Variety and Hollywood Reporter* both in terms of circulation and ads. The offices were in the heart of Soho, where John had a huge pool table in his office. When I was in London, I sometimes went with Mike to a Thai restaurant, or we'd have Indian dinners at John's. They were full of life, always on the move, incredibly funny. They did what they liked, and they were great at it. Two working-class kids grabbed their slice of the English dream and enjoyed it tremendously.

Zagreb, 1991

My movie, *Charuga*, was also Mike's first step away from journalism and into production. His name appeared for first time as associate producer in the opening credits. We worked together later on three more movies: *Josephine, The Border Post,* and *The Constitution* (*Ustav Republike Hrvatske*).

Athens, Ohio, 1994

I enter the office of the secretary of the School of Film, Jeanette Sullivan, a genteel Englishwoman, a real lady. She holds the telephone away of her ear and stares at me, appalled. From the phone I hear a voice shouting: "Fuck you idiot, fuck you . . . ." Jeanette hands me the receiver, disgusted. "This is for you!" I recognize John's voice. "Mike and I are in New York, we have the day off so we're coming to visit!" I try to explain this might not be the best of times, we've just moved into a new house, everything's still in boxes . . . "We're on our way!"

They arrive in a shiny new white Mustang they rented at the Columbus airport. They nibble a bit and are ready for action: a brief walk around town, with a slightly longer stopover at a bar.

The spring evening is warm. The last day of school. Probably two-thirds of the twenty thousand students are out in the streets, or in some of the twenty-odd bars on Court Street, the main and only street in town. In short: everything looks a lot more like the Carnival in Rio than a sleepy university town.

They walk along Court Street, which was full of noisy students. John moans: "Fuck you! You never said Athens looked like this. If we'd known, we'd have moved the magazine here." I try to explain that the town isn't like this every day, but they wave this away.

About three a.m., after five or six bars, we walk into one that is slowly emptying. The two of them down vodkas as fast as ever. I'm trying to keep up.

At some point, sitting at the bar, John turns to me: "Fuck you! It's all lies that you teach here. We've seen hundreds, thousands of kids tonight and not one, not a single one, addressed you as professor. What are you actually doing here?"

I turn from the bar and at the far back corner, among the pool players, I spot Tania, a beautiful student from Norway. I call, "Tania!" and wave to her to come over. "Would you, please, tell these gentlemen what I am to you!" "Professor," smiles Tania without a blink, and goes back to the pool table. John watches her as she goes and, when he finally looks back at me, he raises both arms, gesturing surrender, and bows deeply. Mike does the same.

Grožnjan, 1998

Mike comes to Istria for the first time in 1998, when I invite him to the Imaginary Academy in Grožnjan, to teach a series of lectures on European coproduction. That summer proves to be fatal: Ana introduces him to Marijana with whom he has been ever since. Moreover, through no fault of his own, he becomes involved in founding the Motovun Film Festival. To make a long story short, he falls so deeply in love with Istria that he builds a house and moves there.

For twenty years now, Mike has been running F&ME Film and Music Entertainment Ltd. in London with Sam Taylor, doing coproduction all over the world, he is vice president of the European Film Academy, and spends most of the year in Grimalda, Istria.

Motovun, 2008

After they sold *Moving Pictures* to the owners of *Variety*, John went in a different direction, into a new, non-film life. He visited us only once in Istria. Although his eyes revealed he'd been through troubled times, his smile was as wide and cheeky, as "fuck you," as I remembered it from the 1990s.

Epic Movies

Movies which, through grand gestures and spectacular imagery, follow a character over time. The genre consists of several subgenres: the romantic epic movie, the war epic movie, the epic western, etc.

Farska, 1984

Farska is a small cove on the northwest side of Brač, the highest Adriatic island. A forest of pine trees, crickets, a pebbled beach, calm seas in the morning, a cool breeze in the afternoon.

We reach Farska via Bol, by boat, the only possible way to get there. We are accommodated in a two-story house at the east end of the beach. At the other end stands an old stone house. The owners of once-upon-a time rich vineyards built the stone house as a summer retreat and a place for undisturbed wine storage. The stone house and the white two-story house where we're staying are the only buildings on the cove by the beach.

A few days after we arrive, the owner, Niko, asks me to go with him to pull up his fishing net. I wonder why he'd do this at night. Why doesn't he wait till morning? But I don't ask. I crave the sea and fish.

We leave the cove in his boat. Gesturing for me to row westward, Niko whispers: "The net is over on the other side, but this is to fool him!" Who? Why? I'm baffled. About ten minutes later, he gestures for me to turn the boat and go back. We pass through the cove and head eastward. Standing there, silent, Niko stares toward the shore. Pitch-black, you can't see a thing. Soon, we reach the buoy marking the net. I pull up a *poplunica*, a double net with big and small holes, which is banned in summertime. Several black scorpionfish, two or three stray seabreams, starfish, and urchins. Niko seems nervous. Instead of taking the fish out of the net, he swiftly shoves the whole net into a sack. Then, he takes the oars and makes for the shore. Pricking up his ears in the dark, he slows the boat by a large rock, hands me the bag with the net in it, whispering: "Hide it up there!" Still baffled, I take the net, clamber up the rock and wedge it between two stones.

We return to Farska. Niko is still standing, peering into the dark, listening tensely. Suddenly, he gestures to me to stop. I spin the boat, raise the oars, we hold our breath. Silence. Niko whispers in fear: "He saw us!" I can neither hear nor see a thing. Niko sits down and gloomily beckons me to keep on rowing.

Half an hour after we return, Niko takes a wheelbarrow and asks me to join him to retrieve the net. I follow along, lighting his way through the shrubs with a flashlight. He stops, listens. Someone is coming toward us; I hear branches cracking. Niko whispers: "I'll kill him! I'll kill him!" I hold the flashlight up high. Out of the shrubs appears a short, hunchback, stunted creature. He lifts his hand to block the light. His face is ugly, his mouth twisted, one eye totally white, no pupil. Niko freezes and stares at the man, muttering something. The hunchback runs off into the dark. "I told you he saw us!"

The net I'd wedged between two rocks less than an hour before is now heaped with trash. The next morning I get up very early. I go down to the terrace. Through binoculars, Niko is watching the stone house at the other end of the cove. The hunchback comes out. An old woman by his side.

It takes me ten days to piece the story together. It is obvious that some immense, almost pathological hatred is seething between the owner of the house where we're staying and the people in the stone house. The guests of both houses are expected to share the ill will. An invisible line runs across the common beach, and on no account is it to be crossed by the guests on either side. Moreover, the guests on either side are resented if they greet the people across the line. And, another tiny detail: both houses are armed with guns. And furthermore, the owners of the stone house also have a radio transmitter, provided by the police. I choose not to ask anything, knowing that sooner or later the story will unfold.

At the end of the second week, Niko invites me for a boat ride. I don't ask why. We set off and sail off far from the coast. We stop. Silence. Just in case, Niko surveys the seascape. And then he tells the story.

Brač, Biokovo, 1942

It is wartime. Niko is a young Partisan. Since he was born on Brač, he is sent from the Biokovo Mountain to Brač to bring back salt. He organizes the collecting in improvised salt fields. Couriers take the sacks of salt across the island to the Partisan boats. But, more and more couriers don't make it to the boats. For a few days, Niko struggles to figure out what's going on.

And then he realizes: three brothers from one of the poorest families on the island are ambushing the couriers, jumping them from behind boulders and bashing their heads in with rocks. Then the bodies and the bags disappear. It is wartime, and salt is worth more than gold. Niko tries to stop them but fails. The local authorities are protecting them. The fact that the Partisan couriers are being murdered is not their concern. In return, the brothers inform the authorities about what is going on all over the island—who is saying what, meeting with whom.

Brač, 1945

The war is over. Niko is now a Yugoslav People's Army officer and he returns to Brač. He is sent to preside over a court martial. The first three defendants to appear before the bench are sentenced to death and shot; they are the three brothers who were killing the couriers and stealing the salt.

Brač, 1947

Their fourth brother and one sister, with the rest of the family, become a problem for the entire municipality. They have nothing to eat, no place to live, no way to eke out a living, and cannot seem to break their habit of stealing. A local disgrace, they must be pushed out of the healthy socialist community as soon as possible. A member of the local authority remembers the old stone house in Farska, two hours' walk away. The owners have moved to Italy. The municipality has taken possession of the abandoned house. The poor family soon moves into the house.

Moscow, 1948

The ten most trusted officers of the Yugoslav People's Army are sent to M. V. Frunze Military Academy in Moscow. Niko is among them. The Academy is training the future elite of the fraternal socialist armed forces. That fall, the Informbiro clash erupts when Tito and Stalin sever relations and Yugoslavia breaks off from the Soviet Union bloc. Yugoslavia expects an attack from the Russians. Tito's officers are required to declare their allegiance. Some of them stay true to Stalin and remain in Moscow. A handful of them, among them Niko, return to their homeland.

Novi Sad, 1950

Niko is the political commissar of the Fifth Army corps. The Korean War breaks out and, again, the officers are required to take sides. Niko chooses the wrong side. His punishment is a place called Goli Otok (Bare Island)—a sort of Yugoslav Alcatraz on an Adriatic island. The prison has three sectors: for men, for women, and the harshest one—for army officers. During the coldest winter storms, they are forced to stand waist-deep in the sea. The torment is horrible, death is usually the only dignified way out.

Goli Otok, 1956

After he reconciles with Khrushchev, Tito frees all political prisoners.

Rijeka, 1958

Niko finds employment at a warehouse in the port. There he stays until his retirement. His health is poor, he has breathing problems.

Brač, 1974

Niko inherits his grandfather's tavern and a remote patch of land. His son has moved off-island for his studies. With his wife, he returns to Brač. In the beautiful cove known as Farska he expands his grandfather's tavern. All would be fine if his idyllic life weren't spoiled by one tiny detail. At the other end of the pebbled cove stands the old stone house. And in it, the brother and the sister of the three men Niko sentenced to death right after the war.

Brač, 1987

As a former Goli Otok prisoner, in the eyes of the authorities, Niko is forever stigmatized as a traitor and public enemy. So, no wonder that upon his arrival in Farska, the police supply the brother and sister across the cove with a radio transmitter. Although they have, officially, been asked to report any suspicious ships, their real task is to keep an eye on Niko and his guests.

The former "public enemies" diligently spy on the new "public enemy." Niko, like everyone else, fishes furtively, without a permit and the hunchback reports on him. When he does, the police come in a speedboat, catch Niko out in his boat, confiscate his net, and give the fish to the hunchback as a reward. His sister then sells the fish to tourists.

Zagreb, Summer 1993

I hear the brother and the sister from the manor have died. And since then, Niko's health has rapidly deteriorated.

The tourists are gone. A new war is raging on the mainland.

Epiphany

In scriptwriting, the term is used to describe an unexpected event which seems shocking but assumes its full importance when perceived within the larger context.

Prague, 1968

I've heard many stories about how Czechs and Slovaks heard they had been occupied by Warsaw Pact troops. The one I heard from my friend, Alex Koenigsmark, a writer with whom I wrote four scripts, was by far the closest to something that could have written by Jaroslav Hašek, the author of *The Good Soldier Schweik*.

Plzeň, 1968

It's the end of summer. Alex is visiting his parents. He gets home pretty late, about two a.m. Just as he is about to go to bed, the phone rings. It is his father's old colleague, a fellow doctor. He sounds agitated and shouts that Alex must tell his father that the Russians have come and this is the end. Alex listens and tries to say something, but since he can't get a word in edgewise, he hangs up.

At breakfast, Alex tells this to his dad, laughing: "This friend of yours, Dr. Jan, called last night. Drunk again. He said something about the Russians, some sort of occupation..."

His father interrupts him: "Doctor Jan has been sober for seven years."

Alex turns on the radio. The announcer is finishing the news, reporting that, during the night, the troops of the Warsaw pact, led by the Soviet armed forces...

Escape Movies

A subgenre of adventure movies which covers prison breaks, escapes from concentration camps, fleeing across borders or any other forbidden lines. The most famous ones are: The Loneliness of the Long-Distance Runner *(1962),* The Hill *(1965),* Papillon *(1973),* Midnight Express *(1978),* Down by Law *(1986),* The Shawshank Redemption *(1994),* O Brother, Where Art Thou? *(2000)...*

Lastovo, 1953

On the most remote island in the Adriatic, a special law was passed ordering that all oars were to be stowed at the police station after fishing was done. This is how the authorities prevented the islanders from escaping to Italy in their fishing boats.

At the time, Kruno was nineteen. He and his five friends had been working on making oars for months. They swore a pledge of silence and waited for the right night to row over to Italy, toward a better and happier life.

But when the night finally came, Kruno got cold feet. His friends waited till dawn and then left without him.

Lastovo, 1984

Kruno was a tall, handsome man, surprisingly quiet and withdrawn. He had spent his life working as a cook for the merchant marines and retired early. He, his wife, son, and daughter opened one of the first bed and breakfasts on the island, in Lučica, on a cove where the inhabitants of Lastovo used to keep their fishing boats.

With the Kušan and Magelli families, we spent many summers there, fishing, enjoying the hospitality, the food, the wine, and the sea below the terrace. Lobster stew was Kruno's specialty.

One day, while other guests were still at the beach, I found Kruno on the terrace, staring across the cove, where an adept middle-aged couple were restoring a small fisherman's cottage.

This was the first time he told me, in no more than a few dry sentences, the story of what had happened thirty years before. "Not a day or night goes by that I don't think of it," said Kruno. He went on to explain that the man working on the house across the cove was one of the five friends who had left that night. And the first one to return to Croatia. Village rumor had it that he'd spent his life in Australia working in construction, that he'd saved his money and decided to return to Lučica with his wife to live out his remaining years in his father's old cottage.

Since he'd arrived, and it had been a few weeks, he had not come by to say hello to Kruno. And Kruno didn't have the courage to go to him.

Over yet another glass of *bevanda* (red wine mixed with water), we watched the people on the other side of the cove stripping roof tiles and pushing wheelbarrows full of plaster. Just then Kruno broke the silence and asked if I could go over to the man and invite him to the terrace for a glass of wine. I looked at Kruno and realized that asking him to do this himself would be all wrong.

So, I did. I introduced myself and explained why I was there. He gave it some thought, and then, in Croatian with a strong Australian accent, said he would, as soon as he washed his hands.

And indeed, after half an hour, he stopped by. They shook hands, sat down, exchanged a few formal sentences. The conversation didn't seem to be making progress. I withdrew, realizing that witnesses were unnecessary.

What they talked about I'll never know. What I do know is that they only met once or possibly twice after that. All I remember is that, after they had put in two years of work on the house, the people decided to sell everything and go back to Australia. Kruno told me they'd had so much trouble with the local islanders that they couldn't take it any longer. They felt they were unwanted and said they'd never return.

I never asked Kruno what the two of them spoke of that day. But, at each mention of the topic, the expression on his face made it clear that the old wounds had never healed. Just like the fisherman's cottage which stands there, unfinished.

Escape Movies II

New York, 1985

The movie director, Dejan Karaklajić, takes me to his Romanian friend's architectural bureau. Over a glass of wine the man tells us how he fled to

Yugoslavia, somewhere near Đerdap Gorge, propelled by a propane gas tank. He released the gas and the pressure torpedoed him from one bank of the Danube River to the other. Many Romanians opted for this form of escape, but quite a few lost their lives in the process.

Several months later, I read an article in the *New York Times* about East European borders and the methods the authorities use to catch the fugitives.

Bucharest, 1980–85

Bogdan spends five years planning his trip. For five years he is careful about everything he does, where he has a drink, how he talks, and to whom.

Salonta, 1985

His troubles are about to end. He is only a few hours from freedom. There it is, almost within reach, he is one hundred meters from the border crossing, below the forest where he has been hiding for three nights.

The open ground along the border between Romania and Hungary is fenced in with barbed wire. No man's land is a muddy path, illuminated by searchlights. The first checkpoint is on the Romanian side, the second somewhere in the middle. The third one stands at the end by the Hungarian border post, and over it flies a large Hungarian flag.

Waiting for the next change of the Romanian guard, what he thinks will be the best possible moment for escape, Bogdan thinks about his life in freedom. One thing he knows for sure is that he'll get drunk as soon as he makes it over.

At 4:13 a.m., exactly two minutes before the next guard is supposed to come on duty, Bogdan makes a run for it. He sprints downhill, through the forest, and then along the road.

The change of the Romanian guard is underway. Soldiers pay no attention to the road.

Bogdan speeds up, zigging and zagging. He has been practicing the technique for years; four steps to the left, five to the right, seven to the left, then two to the right. He reaches the first barrier, jumps it. He keeps on running. He reaches the second barrier. He hears a soldier commanding him to stop.

The first bullets whiz by his leg. More by his head. The third checkpoint is only a few meters away. Another round of gunfire. Bogdan jumps the barrier, rolls over the ground. He crawls to the Hungarian border post and slips behind it. Then stops.

He is surrounded by soldiers in Hungarian uniforms. Smeared in mud, Bogdan's face is wreathed in happy smiles.

At that moment, the closest soldier kicks him as hard as he can. Bogdan groans.

He was interrogated for two days by the Hungarian soldiers: where was he going, who helped him, which route did he take. Happy to finally be over the border, he talked, revealing names and secret passageways.

When the interrogation was over, they threw him into a dark room. It took him twenty-four hours to realize that he, as well as the fifty other men he shared the floor with at the fake border post, had fallen into a trap set by the Romanian police.

The real border between Romania and Hungary border was exactly like this one, except that it was some two and a half kilometers to the west.

Establishing Shot

The shot, usually the first one, which signals the geography of the space, the location where a scene or the entire film will take place.

Edo Murtić, whose works now hang in the permanent collections of many major museums, including the Tate in London and MoMA in New York, was a remarkable painter. Remarkable in gesture, in painting, in personality. Every Sunday, for over half a century, his studio at Tomislav Square, which had earlier been the studio of painter Vlaho Bukovac, became a meeting place for painters, sculptors, writers, philosophers, politicians, accidental visitors. From the great writer Miroslav Krleža, and on. I joined these gatherings in the late 1980s and went whenever I was in Zagreb, almost till the end of Edo's life.

The studio was where, one Sunday morning in 1999, Edo, attorney Čedo Prodanović, theater manager Vjeran Zuppa, and I came up with the slogan "Change Is Victory" which—after it was signed by some twenty people and with the help of publisher Nino Pavić—we published on a full page of the *Jutarnji list* daily. Later, the phrase was appropriated by Social Democrat Ivica Račan who won the election in 2000 against the Croatian Democratic Union, the nationalist right-wing party.

Zagreb, 1993

We were leaving for America in two days. Edo called. He asked me to come to his studio. A large package—over a meter wide and just as high—was waiting for me there. "How do you expect me to get this on the plane?" I was overwhelmed. "That's your problem," laughed Edo. "There are prints inside. Take them to your university, they're a gift from me. That way they'll know you're not coming from some godforsaken place. They'll know who you are and where you're from."

Athens, Ohio, 1994

Ohio University's Kennedy Museum of Art, which owns one of the largest print collections in the United States, accepted the gift with gratitude and organized a show of Edo's work, ten prints dedicated to wartime Dubrovnik.

Extras

The performers in a movie who appear in the background, crossing the street, buying newspapers, sitting in restaurants, repeating the same movements twenty or fifty times a day. Those with more to do are called bit parts. In his autobiography, Still Foolin' 'Em, *Billy Crystal gives them a much nicer name: background artists.*

Zagreb, 1977

In a villa in Tuškanac, we are filming *Bravo Maestro*. In the house party scene, Vitomir, played by Rade Šerbedžija, goes to his bedroom to get something, opens the door, sees two strangers having sex on his bed, and shuts the door without a word. In short, it is a very simple cutscene made of two reverse shots.

The first thing we do is Rade's "over the shoulder" shot, in which he opens the door, sees the people on the bed, and shuts the door. The person in charge of extras, the famous Tonkica, brings the background artists, a young man and a young woman. After a few minutes, I am called in. They are in bed, naked. I explain what they are supposed to do. On my way out, I hear Tonkica whisper to the young man: "If you get a hard-on, don't hesitate, just slip it in. They're short on film."

Faces

Filmed in 1968, Faces *is the most important movie by John Cassavetes, one of the key directors of the late 1960s. He restored improvisation to both the camera and actors, thereby bringing his feature films closer to documentaries.*

The human face is the most appealing cinematic landscape, which is why it is said that "each face tells its story."

Prague, 1968

FAMU is on strike. I am on night guard duty at the entrance to Palác Lažanských. It is three a.m. A tall skinny man, all in black, comes over. He wants me to let him in. He wants to dance the *kozachok* for the students. I explain it is too late, the students are sleeping, he should come back the next day. I can see that the man in front of me has a mental disability, so I'm speaking as slowly and calmly as possible. Nevertheless, he suddenly twitches, draws a thin knife and presses its point right under my Adam's apple. "Let me dance the *kozachok*! Let me dance the *kozachok*!!! . . ." he repeats faster and faster. I catch a break when his grip loosens, and dodge. Then like a child who has lost interest in the game, he sheathes his knife, and off he goes into the dark.

Venice, 1970

Tanja and I are staying at a hotel near Piazza San Marco. On the second day of our visit, we come to the hotel only to find a group of guests in distress. The hotel is locked. No one is opening the door.

The owner's wife has run off with a guest. She hates the sea and loves the mountains. So, almost every year, she finds a lover to take her to the mountains. When that happens, the husband locks up the hotel and sets off to find her. The chase typically lasts four or five days. This is why the husband has bought a sports car—so he can be faster and more efficient at finding her and bringing her back.

A stout *carabiniere* is explaining the situation while we wait for the fire department to come by boat and bring us ladders. We will use them to climb up to our rooms to retrieve our belongings. When he hears where we've come from, he tells us he is from Sarajevo. Until World War II, his father owned a tobacco factory there.

Kaldir, 1973

Father Galo, a priest, has a large red nose. Those in the know claim he has fathered many children in the village. He lives with two young nuns in a home for the clergy across from the Church of Saint John the Baptist. His mother is Czech. We drink and speak Czech. He is happy. Finally, someone who speaks his mother tongue. His eyes fill with tears.

He dedicates Sunday Mass to us. His saviors have arrived. They will renovate the castle in Petretići.

Connemara, 1978

I come to Dublin for the premiere of *Bravo Maestro*. This is my first visit to Ireland. I have four days before the grand opening. This will be quite enough for me to make one of my childhood dreams come true—to spend a few days on a fishing boat on the North Sea. They tell me where I should go, but they also warn me that I am highly unlikely to be allowed to go out on a boat. Captains are not fond of outsiders. And also, they seldom speak English, preferring Gaelic.

I rent a car and drive across the island to Connemara. This is where *The Quiet Man* was filmed, one of my favorite movies by Ford. After a few hours' drive, I find a small port tucked deep inside a rocky harbor, with a few fishing boats. I approach one of them that is about to set sail and ask for the captain. They were right, nobody speaks English, or at least no one wants to show me they do. I keep at it. I wait.

After an hour, a man comes off the boat, looking as if he has just stepped out of one of Ford's movies. A captain's cap on his head, wearing a short coat and coarse turtleneck sweater. Of course, he has a beard and of course he is smoking a pipe. I explain I'd like to go out to sea with him. He looks at me for a long time, giving an answer. I can't tell whether he's understood me. I repeat my request. Maybe the man hasn't understood my broken English. His stern face finally melts into a smile. He welcomes me on board. And then, calmly, in English, he explains they will be setting sail that evening and will stay out at sea for seven days. Reefer ships come out to them, so they don't have to return to the harbor after every catch.

Since I have only four days to make my boyhood dream come true, I cannot join them. The captain, with his Ford-movie face, shrugs and puffs a huge cloud of smoke.

New Orleans, 1982

I have breakfast, like every tourist, at Café du Monde in the French Market. I drink a café latte and eat *beignets*. I've been brought here by the honorary consul of the Socialist Federal Republic of Yugoslavia to New Orleans. In his old-fashioned Croatian, a language found only in books written in the late nineteenth century, he talks about people from the Pelješac Peninsula who have been running oyster farms on the Mississippi delta for over a hundred and fifty years.

After breakfast, he shows me around in a big white car so I can see villas that look as if they come straight from *Gone with the Wind*. And finally, he takes me to the cemetery. This is the first time I have driven through a cemetery in a car. He talks about the Croats buried there. And every now and then, he makes an ugly remark about Black people.

Southern racism sounds ridiculous in his old-fashioned Croatian.

New York, 1993

Entering a building on the middle Upper West Side, we pass an elderly doorman who strikes us as very distinguished looking.

That evening, the hosts tell us the doorman's story. For many years he was the Afghan Minister of Foreign Affairs. The government fell, the Russians came, and he found his way to America. He lives alone in Queens. And he is always reading.

A few months later I see him on Fifth Avenue. Tall, elegant, stately, in his doorman's uniform, he is walking an equally elegant white Afghan hound with a red lipstick smudge from a woman's lips planted on its brow.

Fade to Black

The end of a scene or movie.

Zagreb, 1984

My father came back from a ski trip to Slovenia a few days earlier than he planned. He was not feeling well. My mother phoned me. I went to their place on Vrbanićeva Street. Dad was ashen, in bed. He had taken nitroglycerin but this time it hadn't helped. I called an ambulance. I asked if he wanted me to go with him. No need, he said, they would just examine him and send him home. An ambulance came and took him to the hospital, to cardiology, which was run by a friend of his.

The next day, Mom and I went to the hospital. We ran into his friend, the doctor, in the hall. He looked at us for a few moments in silence, and then asked: "No one called?"

The previous night, Dad had had a heart attack while in the ICU. He kept ringing for a nurse, but no one answered. A nurse finally appeared, and Dad said to her: "Sorry, I'm dying." Those were his last words.

False Ending

A false ending is introduced near to the end of a story, at a place where the plot might logically reach its conclusion but it doesn't; instead, it moves in an unexpected direction until it reaches the real end.

Prague, 2000

We are filming *Josephine*, a German-English coproduction. After two weeks in Hamburg and Munich, we move to Prague. The stage designers have turned an abandoned factory hall into a magnificent Hamburg cabaret-brothel.

I have a terrible backache. It has gone on for weeks but over the past few days the pain has become unbearable. Standing causes me acute discomfort. They have set up a mobile bed for me with monitors mounted on it.

About nine in the evening, a rap at my hotel door. I open it to see two orderlies with a stretcher. They explain nervously that the lab report just came in and they have been ordered to bring me immediately to the hospital. They insist that I lie down. Pushing the stretcher, they run to the elevator.

At the hospital I'm put through the tunnel of the CT scanner. I wait for the results in the basement of the hospital at Vinohrady, with the orderly who has been pushing me from place to place. It is late. The waiting room is empty. Two technicians are at the computer, speaking in hushed tones while putting together the lab reports. The door is ajar. They are speaking in Czech, assuming I don't understand. "What a pity," says the shorter of the two men. "Such a shame he's on the way out, so young," says the taller one. The results must be awful. The technicians are not hopeful. According to them: case closed. The end.

They prep me for a gastrointestinal operation to treat my perforated ulcer. The nurses say nothing. I do persuade them to let me have a mobile phone to call Ana. I can hear she's terrified. She'll be there the next day.

A young doctor walks in. He is on call. He is swearing, furious about the professor. Of course, Havel's office has been notified, which means Herr Professor will operate.

Only later do I find out that the producers had informed Alex Koenigsmark who, with the help of President Havel's office, track down the doctor renowned as the finest Czech abdominal surgeon; he operates all over the world and just happened to be in Prague at the time.

"When it's something simple, assistants will do. When it's something like this, Herr Doctor takes it all. I'll never get a chance to operate on one of these." The young doctor is so outraged that only after my second attempt to stop him and ask about my condition does he realize I'm addressing him in Czech. The swearing stops. He apologizes and leaves.

They take me to the operation room and put me under.

I wake up in the ICU. Wires of various colors hook me up to the machines around the bed. The first thing I see are the producers' worried faces. Insurance is asking them to stop the filming. Barely able to speak, I beg them, no. If we stop, I'll never be able to resume. I manage to stay awake for a minute or so.

That same day, the doctor bans the producers from coming to see me at the ICU. "You won't pull through with them around," he says. From then on, only Ana can come.

I was scheduled to have lunch that day with Mike Downey, one of the producers, and Điđa (filmmaker Srđan Karanović). He is passing through from Karlovy Vary, where he was on a film festival jury, on his way to Belgrade via Prague. The two of them have lunch, Mike tells him what has happened and persuades him to stay. Then he makes the German producers start filming again after a ten-day break, with Điđa as director.

Over those ten days, I lose sixteen kilos. People in the ICU are mostly dying. Every now and then, a body is carried out. Paradoxically, this room of death is run by a dozen of the most cheerful, flirtatious, beautiful nurses. They do their best to keep people alive.

I am transferred to a hospital room with several television sets and video players. Whenever I am awake, which is for about four to five minutes every half hour, I work on drawing up a provisional storyboard. Điđa and Trn (cameraman Slobodan Trninić) come to pick it up each morning before the filming, and the assistants bring me the footage in the evening.

As I watch it, I cry. For a long time, in silence. With and without tears.

After ten years of abstinence, I am finally making a movie again, and now, semi-conscious in a hospital room, I can see the movie slip through my fingers, evaporate, disappear. What was supposed to be a delicate watercolor painted with tea is turning into something trite. Điđa is really trying, he is doing his level best, but he has no idea what this is about, he obviously doesn't have a good rapport with the actors, the producers are pressuring him. He is miserable but he is hanging in there, for my sake.

After twenty days or so, they let me leave the hospital. Before I leave, the doctor summons me and, with Ana as his witness, makes me swear I will never again make movies. "A few days on the set, any small amount of anxiety, could cost you your life." He orders a strict diet for me in the months to come, saying I must drink at least a mug of Pilsner every day. Once a Czech always a Czech. "Beer, but not just any beer—only draft Urquell Pilsen—will rebuild the digestive fauna which, in your case, have been so savaged by the ulcer that your stomach looks like a tattered pair of jeans."

Seven days later I am on the set. I direct, if one can call it that, the last few days of the shoot. The insurance won't let Điđa leave. They're not sure I'll make it, so they insist on him sticking around just in case.

Prague, 2001

Six months later—after two more surgeries—we edit the film in Zagreb. Andrija Zafranović, without whom I probably never would have finished it, is going to Prague to visit his son, so I send a selection of wines with him to give to my doctor, a great wine lover.

As he accepts the wine, he says to Andrija: "Had I intervened only five to seven minutes later, I doubt I'd have been able to save him. I can easily say I pulled Grlić back off the gravedigger's shovel."

My doctor dies of stomach cancer a year later.

P.S. *Josephine was screened (illegally) at festivals in Asia, Europe, and the United States, nominated for the European Film Award, but never distributed.*

Indigo Filmproduktion GmbH of Germany, who produced the movie, filed for bankruptcy during postproduction. A few years later, an Australian distribution company bought the film, announced they were beginning distribution, but were unable to clear the rights through the post-bankruptcy process. To make this long administrative-nightmare story short, the movie does not exist according to the paperwork.

Festival de Cannes

Cannes Film Festival, born in 1946, is the one and only, grandest and finest film festival in the world.

Cannes, 1978

Bravo Maestro is one of twenty-three movies in the official selection. Its screening is scheduled for the last day of the festival.

Rade Šerbedžija, the lead, and I are playing tennis on the hotel court. Suddenly, we see photographers begin filling the empty stands. Then more and more come, until there are more than twenty. The cameras click. Rade and I exchange glances, startled.

At lunch, someone explains that after the press screening that morning, also attended by the jury, Liv Ullmann, actress and chair of the jury, told director Alan J. Pakula, that the lead actor was brilliant, and that they should keep him in mind. A journalist overhears, the story spreads, and soon they realize no one has a picture of this actor who might win the Palme d'Or.

Many of the journalists from Yugoslavia are so thrilled by the news that they start right away writing celebratory articles. They keep patting our backs, congratulating us in advance.

The next day, the jury has its final press conference. At the same time, all the crews in the competition are at a luncheon. And you can cut the tension with a knife. At some tables, people are singing, or laughing loudly. One of the women in the running for the Palme d'Or suddenly bursts into tears. Someone is bringing the news to almost every table. We have no one who can let us know what's happening at the press conference.

Rade and I decide to go to the Grand Palais. We arrive too late. The conference is over, and the journalists are trudging out down a long corridor. As we walk toward them, we come upon the Yugoslav journalists who pass by with barely a hello. They seem almost offended. After a few such encounters, I tell Rade: "Fuck it. You obviously didn't win it!" Rade nods, we turn around, and leave without asking anyone who won what.

On our way to the hotel, we decide to leave Cannes. As I remember it, this wasn't because either of us was disappointed or sad, or even angry, we just wanted to get out of there as fast as we could.

We pack up in less than half an hour, and Ivanka and Rade, Ana and I, are in the cars on our way to Genoa.

Genoa, 1978

We find accommodation and ask where we might have a good dinner. The fine hotel recommends a fine restaurant. On our way there, we buy a dozen Italian newspapers to see our reviews.

At the restaurant, we start opening the newspapers. Almost all of them give us at least half a page, but many of them, a full page. Rade's photos are all over them. The waiters recognize him. They started helping us translate the reviews, which turn out to be more than favorable. The manager comes too. He is thrilled that a movie star from Cannes has come to his restaurant. We enjoy the amazing food. The bill shows how thrilled they are. The sum is painful. But this is our fault, no one made us show off.

On our way back to hotel, we conclude that we were lucky Rade didn't win the Palme d'Or—that bill would definitely have been way beyond our means.

Festival Opening Speech

A speech held at the opening of a festival.

Athens, Ohio, January 20, 1995

I receive a fax from Peter Hledík, an acquaintance from my studies, who is founder and director of the Art Film Festival in Trenčianske Teplice, Slovakia.

I answer the same day.

Dear Peter,

It's Saturday evening. I just received the fax in which you let me know that the festival will be screening a dozen documentaries from Sarajevo under siege. You ask me to write something you could read as an introduction to the screening, suggesting that the text should be a response to the question: "How did the war on the territory of Yugoslavia affect my life as a person and an artist?"

Here I am among remote American mountains with your fax in my hands, I'm looking out the window and wondering: Are you screwing with me? Are you joking? Or are you seriously asking a question that has no answer? Meanwhile, the snow, which started falling two days ago, is coming down heavier.

One of the first movies from Sarajevo under siege that I saw was a documentary made by one of Kenović's students whose name, sadly, I cannot remember. He spent the first few months of the war working in a hospital. His task was to clean the operating rooms, collect the amputated arms and legs, take them to the basement and incinerate them.

When his job at the hospital finished, he took a camera and went off to visit the people whose arms and legs he had incinerated. He conducted simple interviews with them and then made the interviews into his movie. I remembered one conversation held in winter, in a barren park in Sarajevo, in deep snow, much like the snow falling here now.

In front of the camera is a young man, about eighteen or nineteen. Handsome, well-dressed, smiling. He is holding a snowball. He is pressing it to his chest to firm it up. And he is telling how he lost his other hand. No, he has not taken this all too tragically. Not at all. He used to do everything with one hand anyway. Writing, eating, drinking. Come to think of it, he has actually found the other one, blown away by a grenade, unnecessary. Maybe he does need it from time to time, but rarely. Now, for example, as he is trying to make the snowball. He has realized, he says, that one can't make a proper, solid snowball with just one hand. And this is the only reason he misses his former hand. Other than that, all's well, he's terrific, never better.

Dear Peter, All's well. I'm terrific. Never better.
For all these reasons, I'm writing to you from faraway, snowbound America, begging you to bear in mind, while you watch those moving images of death, that they represent a last-ditch effort to remind everyone that there, in the middle of the bloody war over the ex-Yugoslav territories, it's not only politicians, warlords, and criminals who are left, but people too. They are living their lives without an arm or a leg or a head, but, as the movies clearly show, not without a spirit. And for the sake of that spirit, which is exactly why some are doing all they can to destroy Sarajevo, I'm writing to you in hope that you are well, terrific, never better.

Yours,
Rajko

Festival Selector

The person who chooses the films, conceptualizes, and creatively shapes the festival.

Cannes, 1981

In the hall of Palais des Festivals, someone taps me on the shoulder and, before I have a chance to turn, the person starts talking about my movie, *You Love Only Once*, in a jumble of Czech, Russian, and Spanish.

"Honorio Rancaño, selector for the Valencia Film Festival," the man finally introduces himself, unshaven, chewing on a long, wet cigar.

Valencia, 1936–39

Valencia is the capital of Republican Spain. This is also where the Republic met its end.

Valencia, 1981

In a coup attempt in February, the army brings the tanks out onto the streets. A few months later, Valencia becomes the first town the socialists win in the elections. In early September, in Valencia, they organize their first "cultural event"—a film festival, known as the Mostra.

Over the next ten years, I come to Valencia on a regular basis, sometimes more than once a year. It is an open and cheerful town of good-natured people. That is where I meet many interesting Spanish cultural figures, many of whom later lead the country's politics. All of them are full of amazing stories about the Franco years, but none is nearly as exciting as Honorio's.

And he never tells his story at one go. To me, or, apparently, anyone else. Only occasionally does he toss out a detail or two, recount an image, and quickly move on to the next subject. Here are some pieces of the puzzle.

Valencia, Paris, Ciudad de México, Athens (Greece), 1938–47

Honorio's father is an anarchist. He is the Minister of Economy in the last Republican government. The Republic falls in 1939 and the family goes into exile. Honorio is less than a year old. First, they live in France and then, during World War II, in Mexico. After the war, they are banished to Greece and afterward then, in 1947, are deported to Russia after the fall of the Communist government.

Valencia, 2011

I check this story with Honorio's widow and daughter. But, since the two of them have also heard only bits and pieces, they can't distinguish facts from fiction.

They say the biggest problem for the family was his father's vast library. He packed it, took it with them into the exile and never parted from it. Hence this collection, and the question of how to transport it, was often the deciding factor in the choice of their next destination.

Russia, 1947–54

They are sent to the Russian Far East. As a model member of the pioneer boy scouts, Honorio becomes part of the delegation of the Spanish

Republic in exile. So once a year, on November 29th, Republic Day in Yugoslavia, he also flies to Belgrade. Straight from the airport, he is taken to Mount Avala to visit the tomb of the unknown soldier. They lay a wreath, have their pictures taken, and then, without further ado, they are put on a plane and flown back to Russia. His only memories of Yugoslavia are the airport and the memorial tomb on the nearby hill.

Prague, 1954–57

At the age of twenty-six he comes to Prague and enrolls at Charles University to study literature. A year later, he is transferred to FAMU, the film academy, and begins his studies in directing.

At the same time, over on the other side of the world, in Cuba, somewhere in Sierra Maestra, Fidel Castro is assembling an army to fight against Baptista. Honorio abandons his studies, goes to Cuba, and joins Castro's soldiers.

Sierra Maestra, Havana, 1957–65

He remains in Cuba for almost ten years. First as a soldier, then as a high state official in Havana. He marries and works for the Ministry of Culture, running the film department.

Valencia, 1985

At Vasco's restaurant, Honorio laughs and smokes while telling us about the first script he read. It was sent to him by the Russians. It was modeled after Eisenstein's never completed *Viva Mexico*. The script was full of horses and cactuses. And there were no horses or cactuses to be found anywhere in Cuba.

"So, what did you tell them?"

"Nothing. We made cactuses out of paper and brought in horses from Mexico!"

Havana, 1966

Che Guevara parts ways with Castro and goes off to Bolivia to start a revolution. He is accompanied by ten friends. Among them, Honorio and his wife. At the Havana airport, they wait for a flight to Moscow. Once there, they will, via Prague, Vienna, and Rio, make their way to Bolivia.

At the airport, Honorio confesses to his wife that he has neither the stamina nor the enthusiasm for new revolutions. He is homesick for the country of his birth, about which he knows nothing. He has decided to go to Spain. Somehow, he will cross the border, he will live there illegally. He begs her to join him. She understands what he is saying but, determined to keep her promise, she goes to Bolivia with Che.

Valencia, 1987

Honorio tells me this story while we are in a bookstore, flipping through a book about Cuba. He stops at a page with a photograph of Che Guevara's dead body surrounded by the bodies of his comrades. They were caught and killed in an action led by the CIA eleven months after they arrived in Bolivia. For a long time he gazes at the picture and then rests his finger on one of the bodies.

"There she is. I haven't seen her since that day at the airport."

Paris, Barcelona, 1966–80

On his way to Spain, he stays for seven years in Paris. He studies, writes, works on film crews. In 1973, he crosses the border illegally and, in the mountains above Barcelona, organizes the distribution of guerilla films. They use 16 mm projectors to show "revolutionary documentaries" to villagers.

Valencia, 1981

Socialists invite him to lead the film festival in Valencia with Josep Pons Grau and Vincent Garces. Pepe—a young, high school teacher who later becomes leader of the socialists in the European Parliament—becomes the director, and Honorio, the selector.

This is how actor Miki Manojlović and I come to Valencia for the first time. To present the film *You Love Only Once*. At the end of the festival, we are on the stage of the now long since closed Cine Goya; Honorio is standing next to us, while Ricardo Muñoz Suay, the writer and producer of Buñuel's *Viridiana*, hands Best Actor to Miki and the Grand Prix to me. Muñoz introduces me as a Sephardi Jew. Honorio chuckles around the cigar in his mouth. I accept the award, saying I am sorry my people were banished from there five hundred years ago. Otherwise this would now be an award for Spain. Honorio winks at me.

Valencia, 1982

He decides to stay in Valencia. He marries, his daughter is born, he writes. For ten years he is the Mostra selector and producer.

His father also returns to Spain. He has only one wish: to purchase a Basque cap in his home village, in the mountains above Gijón. Honorio takes his father there. They find the shop his father had talked about so often and buy the cap he has dreamed of for years. Several months later, his father dies.

Zagreb, 1983

Honorio visits Belgrade and Zagreb. He selects movies for a retrospective of Yugoslav film. I take him to the festival in Pula, I take him around Istria.

Valencia, 1983

In the fall, they hold the retrospective in Valencia. Josep Pons Grau and Honorio Rancaño publish *El cine Yugoslavo (Historia-filmografía crítica)*.

Valencia, 1985

Honorio and I stand in the great display window of Cine Goya at two a.m., looking out over a thousand people who are waiting to enter the screening of my movie *In the Jaws of Life* (*U raljama života*).

Valencia, 1987

I come from Madrid to Valencia only for the night. Honorio is running a newly opened art multiplex with three cinemas, a bookstore, and a bar. *Three for Happiness* won the Mostra that year and is about to enter Spanish distribution, and it is honored as one of the first movies to be screened at his movie theater.

San Sebastian, 1989

That Summer of White Roses is premiered in the official festival selection. Honorio comes. We go out for dinner. As always, we first stop at a tapas bar. We drink red wine and have a few snacks. As usually, he eats very little and drinks a lot. I eat a lot and drink a lot.

Suddenly, gunfire reverberates from the street.

Guests move away from the windows but don't stop talking. The gunfire gets louder.

A young man, drenched in blood, staggers into the bar. One of the guests hurries him into the kitchen. Outside, the noise is louder, the running, shooting, shouting. Uniformed police officers come in. They scan the bar. The guests behave as if nothing is happening. The police officers leave.

We leave the place some ten minutes after the last gunshot. A few steps away, gunshots whizz right over our heads. We drop to the ground. Honorio gestures for me to follow him. We crawl toward the closest cover.

Finally, I get a chance to see this old soldier in action. He is worried but clearly is enjoying the situation. It takes us more than half an hour to crawl our way out of the old town.

On the other side of the wide avenue, in front of the theater where the festival screenings take place, people are calmly watching the police officers, the armored vehicles, guessing where the gunshots are coming from. One of them is listening to a football match broadcast over a portable radio while watching the street clashes.

Honorio says this happens every year during the festival. The Basque separatist organization ETA uses the presence of all the journalists to organize street skirmishes to attract their attention.

Enormous speakers are set up in front of the theater. Mozart's *Don Giovanni* is thundering. Knowing what to expect, the festival was prepared for the sound duel. And really—there, on the large square close to the old town, thanks to Mozart, the gunfire is virtually inaudible.

Valencia, 1989

The Mostra celebrates its tenth anniversary. I leave the Tokyo Film Festival, probably the most expensive of the prestigious festivals at the time, three days before it ends so I can reach Valencia in time for the celebration.

Pepe takes me to a bullfight. To the mayor's box. The one from which the signal is given whether or not to cut off the bull's tail.

During the first fight, a girl enters the box and whispers that Honorio has asked me to come back to the festival immediately. My wife has called from Zagreb. It must be urgent. I know Ana never calls while I'm away. Something must have happened to Olga. I panic.

Outside the festival building, several of the administrators are waiting for me. They escort me to Honorio's room. I can see something is wrong but I'm too nervous to realize they're all smiling.

I enter the room and call Ana. They've called from Tokyo. *That Summer of White Roses* has won the Grand Prix. They are asking if I could come back.

Honorio is standing next to me. Knowing what the fuss is about, he is enjoying the commotion. At that moment, the door bursts open and almost everyone from the festival comes in carrying bottles of champagne.

Once we've heard the full report on the Tokyo awards, I accuse Honorio and his celebration of having made me miss my "Kodak moment" of a lifetime. The film won the Grand Prix, and I won the Best Director. The president of the jury was Yves Montand, and the Best Actor went to Marlon Brando, who came to the ceremony. I have missed the chance to have my picture taken with these two grand masters.

That evening, I speak with Emir Kusturica for the last time. Goran Marković is there. The conversation begins in Goran's hotel room, and we kept talking while we walk through the empty streets of the old town almost until dawn. We talk about the coming war. We do not see eye to eye.

Zagreb, 1991

Honorio calls from Valencia, he sounds worried. Vasco, the owner of the small Basque restaurant where we have celebrated many awards, where we have eaten a lot of *angulas a la bilbaína*, and drunk plenty of *vino tinto* is offering me an apartment. It is not large but it is in the center of town. Vasco doesn't need it for the time being and we can stay there until we get settled. Honorio has found me a job, too. I will teach film. And our citizenship can be easily arranged. The King has promised that all the descendants of those who were banished five hundred years ago from Spain will be granted passports. I thank him. I do what I can to reassure him.

"It's not so bad as all that."

"I know, but it will get bad!" Honorio is shouting.

Mostar, 1995

Honorio leads a Spanish TV crew which is making a movie about Mostar. He phones from Split. That is the last time we speak.

Valencia–Zagreb, 2001

After my surgery, I'm in the hospital. Honorio's daughter calls to let me know her father has died. She asks me to come and give the eulogy at his funeral. I can't even get out of bed, let alone travel. I write a few of sentences. Pepe kindly agrees to read them.

"Honorio Rancaño died while working on *My Father*, a film script," reports the Madrid daily *El Pais* in its obituary about Honorio.

San Sebastián, 2006

The Border Post has its premiere in the official festival selection. I wander through the old town. No gunfire, no Honorio.

Valencia, 2011

I return to Valencia after more than twenty years. I am at Vasco's with Pepe. We talk about Honorio; we connect the puzzle pieces of his life. Vasco laughs: "The apartment still is empty. You can still come and live a decent life here with us instead of dragging yourselves around the United States."

Honorio's widow and daughter come to the festival screening of my movie *Just Between Us* (*Neka ostane među nama*) and bring a book of his poems his friends have published posthumously. I ask them about Honorio's father's library. Did he bring it back with him to Spain? They don't know.

The night before I go back to the States, I stay at Yvone and Pepe's place. They live in the hills above Valencia, surrounded by orange and lemon plantations. Everything is in bloom. The scent is fantastic.

Pepe gives me a reprint edition of his and Honorio's book about Yugoslav film. We have dinner with Ida and Yvone's brother and listen to Morente. They talk about the disappearance of the Spain I had a chance to see some thirty years before. At the moment, Valencia is being run by the extreme right.

Athens, Ohio, 2011

Yvone lets me know that the city authorities have decided to shut down the Mostra. Students are protesting. They are asking me to write something. I write a few bitter sentences; I mention Honorio. Pepe reads it at the rally.

Valencia, 2012

I come across a news item on the internet that goes something like this:

> The streets of Valencia turned red with the blood of local students and with the disgrace of those who brutally provoked it. Peaceful demonstrations against education cuts in Valencia entered their fourth day yesterday, but this Monday, things did not end peacefully. The chief of the local police, Antonio Moreno, saw to it by literally sending a bunch of heavily armed members of special forces to hunt the students down. Everything resembled Pamplona, except for the fact that the bulls were wearing blue. The photos and footage show young people's faces smeared with blood, their heads smashed, and the police wielding batons left and right. Similar pictures of people racing through the streets have only been seen in Pamplona until now, except that this time the young men and women were not being chased by raging bulls but by even more raging heavily armed special forces . . .

Fiction & Nonfiction

Generally speaking, narrative film belongs to fiction, whereas documentary belongs to nonfiction. *Each movie, however, including documentaries, presents a selective reality which creates a new reality. Any movie, therefore, can be considered fiction which, more or less, aspires to make its reality, that is, its nonfiction, believable.*

This contrast between "true reality" and "created reality" has always existed. Jewish written documents, too, are divided into two groups:

> *Halakha*—(after the Hebrew verb *halakh*, to walk)—a collection of rules and regulations which apply to everyone, and
>
> *Aggadah*—(by the verb *aggad*, to talk, to tell a story)—exodus stories passed down from father to son.

Eugen Weber, the translator for the Otokar Keršovani edition of the *Talmud*, says, in his preface: "Reaching into every corner of life, the *Halakha* theoretically elaborated and developed legal and ritual rules, while the *Aggadah* used storytelling and other literary elements to habituate people to these same rules and regulations."

Zagreb, 1978

Ms. Ruža Jurković called me at least three times to suggest that I read her diary. Each time I told her I would be happy to read it, but she should send it to me. Or, if it was as valuable as she felt it was and couldn't be entrusted to postal delivery, I suggested she send it with a person she trusted. After she called me the third or fourth time, I realized that all I could do was to visit her myself.

I rang the doorbell of her first-floor apartment on Mažuranićev Square. The woman who opened the door had on heavy makeup and the room was dimly lit, so I couldn't tell her age. Sixty, sixty-five, maybe even seventy.

We sat in a living room thick with the scent of cologne. She offered me sweet sherry and launched into her story, while leafing through a photo album. She used to be a ballerina. She had danced everywhere. During the war, at the Cabaret Dverce in Ilica Street, and after the war at the Croatian National Theater.

We spent quite some time looking at the photographs before she finally took out the diary I had come for. It was a single folded sheet of paper. The entire text was handwritten and consisted of just one sentence with no punctuation.

While she was a ballerina at the National Theater right after the war, she met a young policeman. They fell in love and married. He was dashing, and somewhat obsessed with sex. Soon, he turned out to be pathologically jealous. He kept her locked up for days, letting her out only for her performances. After a few years, she managed to get a divorce. He remarried, had a child and was killed, one day, in a car accident.

After I had read the diary, she turned a page in the album and proudly showed me a naked photograph of herself, obviously taken some forty years earlier. She was beautiful. When I looked at her, I saw a strange flirtatious gleam in her old eyes. At that moment, I finally realized where I had already seen this scene—in Wilder's *Sunset Boulevard*. Joe Gillis, a young scriptwriter, inadvertently ends up at the apartment of Norma Desmond, a famous star of the silent films. She shows him photographs and presents her manuscript for a future movie.

Zagreb, 1980

It took me two years of work with various writers: Srđan Karanović, Alex Koenigsmark, Pero Kvesić, Nenad Burcar, and Branko Šömen, and eight or nine drafts of the script, to finish it. Although nothing from the actual diary remained in the film, apart from the fact that the leads are a policeman and a ballerina—I must admit that if it weren't for Ruža Jurković, the film *You Love Only Once* would have never happened. This is why the opening credits read: "Based on a story by Ruža Jurković."

Zagreb, 1981

The movie played in the Zagreb movie theaters for quite some time. Ms. Ruža Jurković gave several long interviews. In one of them, trying to illustrate how pleased she was with how it had turned out, she said that she had been to see it seven or eight times.

Zagreb, 1983

I was called by the editor at a prominent publishing house who asked me if I'd read *the* text by Ruža Jurković. What text? The manuscript of her book *You Love Only Once*. He explained that she had offered them an autobiographical novel which closely followed the movie, scene by scene. It was, in fact, a transcript of the movie. What should they do? I laughed and told him that wasn't up to me. It was up to them. He laughed too. He knew he couldn't publish it. He just wanted to check whether I had seen the manuscript.

And indeed, the book was never published, and I never asked Ms. Ruža Jurković what made her believe that the things on screen depicted her life.

The reason I never asked was because I feared I might transgress the fine line of the imagination that brought a life onto the screen and then moved it from the world of fiction back into reality.

Fifty-Fifty

A shot that portrays two actors sharing the frame, usually facing each other, while given equal visual weight.

Toronto, 2017

Many films about Nikola Tesla have been proposed, but very few actually made. And even those few were made as relatively modest productions: *The Secret of Nikola Tesla* (*Tajna Nikole Tesle*, 1980) by Krsto Papić, *Tower to the People* (2015) by Joseph Sikorski . . .

I have been asked on several occasions, as many other directors from the ex-Yugoslav region probably have, if I would consider a Tesla project. The last person who asked me this was Nenad Stanković, publisher of *Tesla*, a Toronto magazine. I told him I hadn't been considering it, but told him the story of Telluride, a small town in the mountains of Colorado.

Telluride, 1891

In the mid- to late-nineteenth century, the mountains around Telluride were consumed by the gold rush. About five thousand people worked there in the mines. Determined to keep the money the miners were making, the owner built a small town. Its main and only street consisted of about thirty whorehouses, several banks, and an opera house where Sarah Bernhardt dropped by from time to time.

The man who came up with this plan was Lucien Nunn, a lawyer and owner of the *Gold King* mine. At the peak of his power, he ordered the Tesla's A.C. power system. The idea was to exploit the cascades on a nearby river to produce electrical energy and replace the costly system of generators that burned coal to make steam. Enter Nikola Tesla and Ames power plant—the first power plant to produce and transmit alternating current of high voltage.

From what I've heard, Nunn invested in it for two equally relevant reasons: he needed cheap energy not only for the mines but also for lighting the only street in town to reduce the number of late-night murders and robberies.

What I found most interesting, though, was the legend of Tesla visiting Nunn. If this is true, it would be interesting to know how Tesla felt in this town of whorehouses, how Lucien thought he'd impress his guest, how long Tesla stayed, and if something nice happened during his stay in Telluride. Did Nunn offer him a young lady from his place of birth? Did she make Tesla want to stay longer than he had planned, possibly forever? Did Nunn use the lady to blackmail him, did he manage to extract from Tesla any of his secret inventions? Did Tesla, in the end, buy out the young lady from the brothel owner?

The answers to these questions could take us into Tesla's intimate world, one beyond the rules and regulations he adhered to. This would probably happen with Nunn as well. With the two of them, we would enter into a classic version of an encounter between two worlds: a cunning merchant who enjoys life, and a mystic genius, an ascetic deprived of a practical feel for everyday life.

Who knows whether we'd find anything beyond the clichés. But wherever the search took us, I believe that, for the sake of the story, the two men should be treated equally, according to the "fifty-fifty" principle.

Telluride, 1978

After some forty years of gradual decline, the mines finally close and the town is desolate.

Telluride, 1980

A group of New York lawyers buy up everything they can get their hands on. Then they impose high taxes and chase out the poor people who are still living there, and within a few years, create a wealthy town with a festival, skiing, and golf. In the end, as so usually happens, they sell everything at a much higher price.

Telluride, 1998

The only thing to remind us of the gold rush days are the plaques at the entrances to the banks. They proudly state that the banks were robbed by Jesse James, Billy the Kid, and Butch Cassidy who, in 1889, with his Wild Bunch, stole $24,000, earmarked for miners' salaries, from San Miguel National Bank.

On the main street, still the only street in town, there stands a plaque dedicated to Nikola Tesla. It expresses gratitude to the man who helped Telluride go down in history as the first town with electric street lighting.

Film Critics

In the film world, they say: "Those who can, make movies; those who can't, teach; and those who can't do either, write reviews."

Cannes, 1978

Điđa and I had two movies showing in Cannes: *Bravo Maestro* in the official competition, and *The Fragrance of Wildflowers* (*Miris poljskog cveća*) in the critics' week. We had written the scripts together and were pleased to be presenting them together. We were young, we enjoyed it all, but never took it too seriously. We had already been at Cannes with *Party Game* (*Društvena igra*), and later, again, with *You Love Only Once*.

Still, the high point for me was when Olga first kicked in Ana's belly. And, even more of a cliché, this happened while Ana was eating oysters and drinking champagne at a bar on the Croisette.

Those were strange times when we believed that movies could fight their way onto the big festivals and then the world cinemas, thanks to what they were. We believed this could be done without vast sums of money and powerful distributors. Today, when money can turn every frog into a prince, when every success can be named a failure or vice versa, this may sound utterly naïve and implausible, but back then it was true. Or—perhaps even more important—we thought it was.

And not only that. Those were times when even film critics mattered. Their judgment often determined the fate of a movie. It truly did matter what kind of review you would get in *Variety* or *Hollywood Reporter*, not to speak of the Yugoslav newspapers *Vjesnik*, *Politika*, *Oslobođenje*, *Nova Makedonija*, *Pobjeda*, *Delo*.

Gene Moskowitz (*Variety*) and Ron Holloway (*Hollywood Reporter*) were the big names among the critics. Both of them used to write truly favorable reviews of our movies. Appealing, straightforward, and completely normal people. Sadly, they were first and foremost critics—people driven by a nymphomaniac urge to identify "young meat." After all the French, Italian, Hungarian, Polish, Yugoslav (Dušan Makavejev and Žika Pavlović), Czech, and other waves, the day had dawned for a new story. We were the stars of this story and the "new Yugoslav wave." After the press conference, Moskowitz approached me, introduced himself, and told me that he and Holloway would love to interview me and Điđa.

We suggested they should also meet some of the other directors from Yugoslavia who were in Cannes. And that's how we arranged a lunch at *La Mère Besson* on Rue des Frères Pradignac, right behind the venerable Le Grand Palais, now gone.

La Mère Besson was at the time one of the best, if not the best restaurant in Cannes. I had been there only once. I still remember the taste of the entrée: baskets made of roasted sole, filled with shellfish and shrimp in a béchamel sauce. Before the main course, they brought out a big guest book. Only the directors and actors who had a movie in the main competition were invited to sign it. Each person was given a page. The entire history of cinema is in on those pages and in the drawings.

The four or five of us—I believe that Lordan Zafranović, Dejan Karaklajić, and Joca Aćim were also there besides Điđa and me—counted our cash twice, realized that together we could afford a meal at *La Mère Besson*, and decided to take the hungry critics to lunch. When you are young and from a small country, you worry that your poverty will show on your face. And so you try to disguise your fear by doing something sweeping and grand. Our gesture falls into that category.

The lunch lasted for three, possibly four, hours. Everything went better than well. An ideal French lunch over which, like layers on a cake, the stories alternated with the delicious food, the fine wines, fine cheese, and smaller cigars.

But we made just one mistake. We booked a table outside, forgetting that those tables are visible from the street, and that anyone who is in any way connected to the festival passes by. And so, over the hours we spent there, at least a dozen critics from our "region" stopped by to say hello, and use the opportunity to meet their famous American colleagues and, since they were there, have a drink and a bite.

Once Gene and Ron had left, the bill arrived. It was much, much higher than what all of us had. In our wallets or at the hotel. We sat at the table, baffled about whom to ask for help, whom we could borrow the not so insignificant amount. At the time, credit cards and ATMs had not yet entered our lives.

We sat there for nearly an hour. Desperate, we ordered another bottle of wine. And then, as if this was a *deus ex machina*, Vlado Terešak appeared. He was the director of Croatia Film, coproducer and distributor of almost all the movies I'd made. I ran over to him, stopped him, and told him our problem. He joined us at the table, had a drink, paid the bill, and left like a true gentleman, saying: "Don't worry. I'll write it off as part of your movie expenses. Have fun."

Cannes, 1997

Lisa Bruce and Bob Nixon, producers and friends from New York, suggested we go out for fish. Bob remembered *La Mère Besson* and called to book a table. They said they were fully booked for the next two weeks.

We went for a walk, planning to find another place. As we passed *La Mère Besson*, I asked Lisa and Bob to wait. I went in, explained that I needed a table for three and, before he could tell me they had none available, I told him I was in their book.

A new table was set in minutes. We had a fantastic dinner, and just as important, this time we had the money to pay for it.

Film Festival

An organized event where movies are screened.

Oprtalj, Motovun, 1969–70

With Živko Zalar, I scout locations for my student thesis film. We need a desolate town. Živko's father Slavko suggests that we go to see Oprtalj and Završje. This is my first time in the Istrian interior.

The name of the movie is *The Return* (*Povratak*), we film it in Oprtalj, and the crew stays at the newly opened Hotel Kaštel in Motovun.

Motovun, 1972

At the same hotel, Điđa and I write the script for *If It Kills Me*.

Petretići, Motovun, 1972–77

Friends start coming to Motovun. Sometimes, there are fifteen, twenty of us. We are there for New Year's Eves, we spend summers there, we run a disco club, we write, and make movies.

Jagoda Kaloper, Goran and Vesna Marković, Điđa and Vera Machiedo, Vesna and Branko Cvejić, Živko and I, get together and buy, at a public auction held in Motovun, a "castle" in Petretići, with the intention of turning it, one day, into an old people's home for us. It's a vast three-story mansion, with a large cellar built by a wealthy man from Trieste who also owned the nearby vineyards. We take out a loan, repair the roof, have windows and doors installed, to conserve the "castle." We spend two summers planting the garden with exotic plants.

We stay at a Motovun hotel that lets us use half the kitchen and a small terrace with a table under a mulberry tree. Every week, one us takes the Citroën 2CV to Trieste for food. At Motovun, we drink the Teran and Malvasia from the town cellar by the Canal, and, in Petretići, from Benvenuti's cellar in Kaldir.

A brief digression in the style of *The Good Soldier Schweik*: the "castle" in Petretići is ransacked. Whole pieces of the construction are carted off, as well as all the solid stones. The house collapses. The wine cellar at the Canal closes. On the other hand, Benvenuti's grandchildren have become the first Croatian winery to win the two most influential wine competitions in the same year: the International Wine Challenge and Decanter World Wine Awards.

Motovun, 1975

To celebrate our time spent in Motovun, one of the final scenes of the series *The Reckless Years* (*Grlom u jagode*), the wedding of the lead character, Bane Bumbar, is held in Motovun. Officiating is Vergilio Soldatić, director of Hotel Kaštel, where we have often been the only guests.

Athens, Ohio–Grožnjan, 1994

I am given $15,000 by Ohio University to start a workshop on film-directing in Prague. I persuade them to allow me to start the workshop in Croatia instead. With financial support obtained later from the George Soros–financed Open Society in Zagreb, we have the startup capital we need for the Imaginary Academy in Grožnjan. The first lecturers are Yvette Biro from New York University, Rajko Grlić and David Thomas from Ohio University, Lew Hunter from University of California, Los Angeles, and Nenad Puhovski and Vjeran Zuppa from the Academy of Dramatic Arts in Zagreb.

Grožnjan, 1997

The Imaginary Academy in Grožnjan opens an improvised "movie theater" with the screening of a Branko Bauer movie. The theater is named after him. The Academy is visited by many ostracized writers, directors, painters, journalists. Every now and then, police drop by to check on our documents.

Boris Matić, a student at the Imaginary Academy, asks me to offer a selection for a festival of debut movies he plans to start in Zagreb.

Grožnjan, 1998

Boris comes to my production class for a second year. He hasn't been able to pull together the funds for his festival.

Lack of space for evening screenings is one of our biggest problems. Sitting on a terrace with a view of Motovun, someone—I believe it was Boris—suggests: "Why don't we give Motovun a try?" The next morning, the two of us are in a car on our way to Motovun.

Motovun, 1998

The president of the municipality, Fiore Flego, listens to us with visible skepticism, and promises to help. He didn't dare tell us the municipality is facing bankruptcy, the town is run down, the walls crumbling, there are no tourists, only one store is functional and even that one is not open every day, and he had no idea how to deal with all of this.

This is the first time I approach the Governor of Istria, Stevo Žufić, for financial support for the Imaginary Academy.

He arranges a meeting in Motovun. I come and find him in the company of Ivan Jakovčić. Walking across the square, past the local movie theater which, at that point, has been shuttered for over two decades, I think I use these exact words: "If you reopen this movie theater, I will organize you a festival." They don't hesitate long before saying: "Deal!"

Back then, Croatia is a very sad and isolated country. A festival, as the word suggests, is a festivity, an event rooted in joy. And since joy is the best weapon against not only sorrow but stupidity and castration and claustrophobia, I think that such an event would most easily spread the joy of the Imaginary Academy.

Boris and I agree that, if we pull this off, he will be the festival director. Soon, "delegations" begin venturing from Grožnjan to Motovun to check it out. The two of us are sometimes joined by Mike Downey, Željko Burić, Robert Nickson, Lisa Bruce, Branko Ivanda . . .

Momjan, 1999

That winter, I get a call from Istria. "We're bringing the movie theater back to life. Where's your festival?"

Boris and I go to Momjan. For the first time we meet with "official Istria." I introduce Boris. Jakovčić pulls me aside to say that he cannot trust the kid with money. Boris is too young for something like this. I assure him that he can, that he's a truly good and ambitious producer. I am in the States and can't be in charge of organization; we need someone who is here and who knows how to do it.

Athens, Ohio, 1999

Thanks to all the bottles of Grappa, Malvasia, Pinot, Muscat, Terrano, and all the Istrian soups, prosciutto, sausages, and other cold meats, frittatas and wild asparagus, shrimps and oysters, fusi, gnocchi, chicken and boar, and black and white truffles in particular, the concept of the first festival is defined in very simple terms: we'll make a festival of five or six movies about the pleasures of food and wine. The Grand Prix will be called the "Golden Truffle," and the movies will be presented by accomplished chefs. Five. One for each evening. But, after several months of searching, I have to admit that the season of 1998/99 is, alas, found wanting in terms of this noble genre. And so, the idea of a gourmet-movie festival never goes anywhere.

Zagreb, 1999

Early that spring, Boris rents a basement room and brings Olinka Vištica. Soon, students Igor Mirković and Dana Budisavljević of the Imaginary Academy join us with many others.

Motovun, August 10, 1999

On the first day of the first Motovun Film Festival, in the early afternoon, I'm there almost alone on the square, staring up at the rainy skies, thinking: "No one will come!" That evening, when the square is already packed with people, someone beckons me with the wave of a cane. It is old man Soldatić. He asks me if I know who the last person was who filled the square like this. I shrug and he winks, and whispers: "Mussolini!"

And so it was that the Motovun Film Festival, the bastard child of Croatian cinema, was born.

Motovun, 2009

Right from the start, from day one, I see this as an event rather than as a classic film festival. This is why I appreciate and enjoy it so much, like it is a toy free of all constraints. All the ideas that have been dormant in me for years—in my inner unrealized conceptual artist—finally surface in Motovun. At the same time, though, I firmly believed and still do, that after its tenth year we should thank everyone, wrap it up, and end it. That we should reach its peak and then stop while all the reasons for starting it are still alive, while it is still more than just another film festival. In short: that we should walk away with our heads held high.

Igor Mirković asks me not to close the festival, saying there are too many people who want to keep it going. I agree and withdraw as quietly as possible.

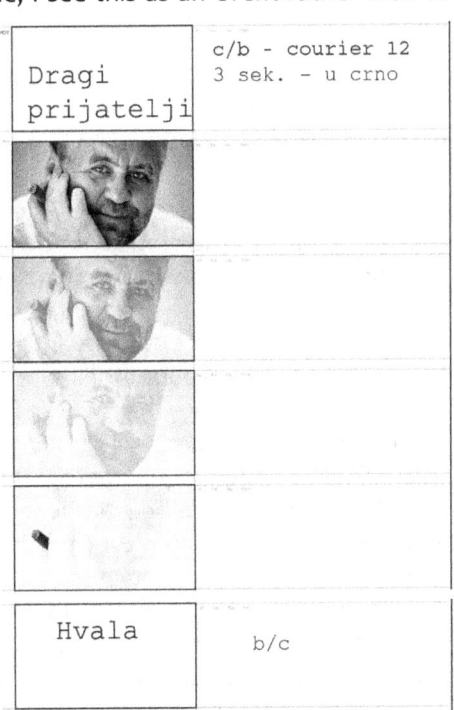

Grlic's farewell to the Motovun Film Festival, published in the festival catalogue, used with permission.

Instead of the usual foreword, I have this published in the festival catalogue:

"Dear friends, Thank You" and from there gently fade out with the Monty-Pythonesque title "honorably retired artistic director."

Motovun, 2017

The festival is still alive and well. More than alive. Igor is managing it bravely despite all their financial woes, despite the growing aggression by the "associations of widows and veterans" which have been flexing their muscles over Croatian culture.

Film History

A branch of film theory focused on the development and historical context of all the data about movies and the people who made them.

Athens, Ohio, 2010

I am reading Who the Devil Made It, conversations Peter Bogdanovich had with old-school American directors, and think about the egregious disregard for the people who work in film in our part of the world.

The fourth generation of film directors is slowly leaving us and, once again, almost nobody has made an effort to record their experience or to ask them to tell the stories of how they lived, how they did what they did, and why. The ones who are gone, to mention just a few, are Oktavijan Miletić and Branko Marjanović, Krešo Golik and Obrad Gluščević, Fedor Škubonja and Zvonimir Berković, and no one ever had a detailed conversation with any of them about their work, no one heard them out, recorded what they said to leave their words for the generations to come. Apart from Branko Bauer and Tomislav Pinter, all the others, dozens of exquisite masters—directors, cinematographers, actors, set designers, editors, sound designers—have been unheard, withdrawn, forgotten. Their craft and their experience are irrevocably lost. Only their obituary grants them dignity for a day, but the very next day both they and their movies are relegated to oblivion. Despite the fact that we are surrounded by people who boast of a national consciousness, both in filmmaking and around it. They seem to have forgotten that experience should be recorded and utilized if we are to create the collective memory pompously known as "national culture."

Motovun, 1999–2010

What we were doing in Motovun for years, giving the veterans of filmmaking a symbolic award for their fifty years of work in the film industry, was my small attempt at drawing them out of isolation and oblivion while they were still alive. To use the opportunity to give back to them, at least for a few days, what their work has earned for them. And I felt genuinely happy to have had the opportunity to sit with all these people on the square in Motovun, to drink wine and watch their faces light up with a youthful glow, listen to their wonderful stories, and travel with them through time.

I read Bogdanovich's conversations and think what a mistake it was that I didn't have serious conversations with each of the Motovun laureates, from Branko Bauer onwards. Unforgivable.

Film Library

A collection of books about films, and a collection of films in one place.

My father had a huge library. It was an important part of his life. He read a lot and wrote a lot. He published twenty-three books, translated several capital works in philosophy, his writings were translated into many languages, he lived among books, he was friends with men of letters.

Zagreb, 1963

This is a handwritten message which my dad, knowing we would throw parties while they were away on a trip, left in his library:

> Children, listen up
> EVERYTHING can be stolen, sold, thrown out of the window, "lent,"
> used to wipe your asses, crumbled, used to wipe your noses, spit,
> trampled upon, shat on, pissed on, covered in stuff, smudged, stunk
> up, burned, blown up, painted over, given away to friends, pillaged,
> etc., etc.
> EXCEPT THE BOOKS

Zagreb, 2009

When my mother died, we catalogued every book, and moved his entire library into my study. It took me two years to reconstruct, slowly clean each book, and put it back in its former place.

It took me this long because each book brought back memories of how and why it came into our household, what Dad told us about it, and what it meant to him. In many of them I found his notes, newspaper clippings, photos, letters, underlined sentences, and handwritten notes. And so, this reorganization of Dad's library turned into a great sentimental stroll through his and my mother's life.

His "note to the children," written a long time ago, is framed today and displayed in his library, now mine.

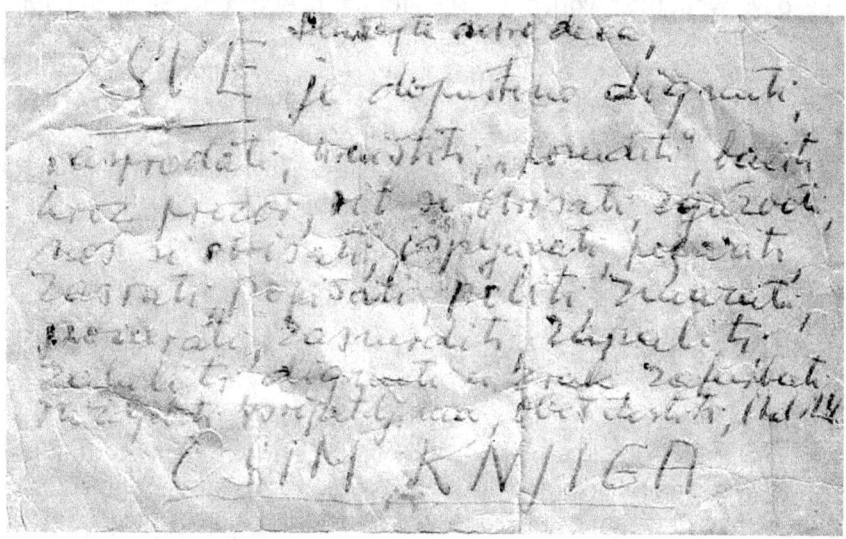

Grlic's father's "note to the children," author image.

Film Manifesto

Program manifesto by film authors.

Oakland, 2014

The University of California Press releases *Film Manifestos and Global Cinema Cultures—A Critical Anthology*, a collection of film manifestos published by various groups and individuals over the past hundred years or so.

Copenhagen, 1995

Dogme 95 Manifesto, one of the most famous film manifestos, was signed by a group of directors who graduated from the National Film School of Denmark. Most of them came to Motovun for years to screen their new movies.

"The goal of the Dogme collective is to purify filmmaking by refusing expensive and spectacular special effects, postproduction modifications and other technical gimmicks. The filmmakers concentrate on the story and the actors' performances."

Zagreb, 1972

Five directors and three cameramen, students of the Master's program at FAMU in Prague, published their Manifesto in *Omladinski list*, a Zagreb youth paper.

Several days later, Vladimir Vuković, a prominent film critic, after whom the Croatian Film Critics Award was named, said, during his "office hours" at the Corso Café, "I listened to you on the radio the other day. You speak with such a beautiful Zagreb accent. Whatever drives you to sign manifestos with those Serbs, Rajko? You really don't need that."

Film Stock

Unexposed film, raw material.

Zagreb, 1964

I made my first movie using 8 mm film. We used to make it by cutting 16 mm Ferrania in half with a razor.

Prague, 1966

East German black-and-white negative ORWO NP 7 was the first 35 mm film I used. In the editing room, on wooden presses, I taped the positive, cleaning the splice with a razor and coating it with acetone.

Zagreb, 1971–2010

Kodak entered my life with my first short movie after the Academy. After that, I shot all my feature films on Kodak. Two of them on 16 mm film, and the rest, on 35 mm. But when I first started out, Kodak was very expensive for us. And, no matter how badly I whined and begged, I was never able to obtain more than twenty thousand meters of negative for a feature film.

The first time I overshot that magic number was with my sixth movie, *That Summer of White Roses*. I reached fifty thousand meters and beyond that, and ever since this has been the number I have dealt with for my movies.

Charuga, filmed in 1990, was the last movie for which I still handled the film physically in the editing room. Afterward, the entire process moved over to the digital sphere.

Piran, Slovenia, 1976

Sam Peckinpah filmed much of his movie *Cross of Iron* in Piran, at the Viba Film studio, a state-owned Slovenian film company from Ljubljana. I watched him do the bunker scene with James Coburn and Maximilian Schell. He used five cameras. The first assistant called for the cameras, and then, after the other assistants said, one by one, that they were ready, the cameras started rolling, and finally they called out: *Action*. The actors began. After less than a minute, Sam Peckinpah stood, walked into his own shot while the cameras were still rolling, and spoke to the actors. This lasted a minute or two—an eternity for me—then walked out of the shot, sat back down in his chair, and once again said: *Action*. Mouth agape, I watched this immeasurable luxury and thought to myself: he has just spent more film on this shot than I do on a whole movie.

Generalski Stol, 1987

That scene nested in my subconsciousness like a quiet nightmare, like the sight of a sumptuous pastry shop in the eyes of a hungry child. Working on my first movie in English, when we were filming the final scene with Rod Steiger, I finally had the opportunity to face this Freudian "ghost from the past." I walked into my own shot without stopping the four cameras, talked to Steiger, walked out, and started the scene anew.

When I saw Peckinpah do that, I thought how wonderful it would be if I could afford such a luxury myself some day. But no miracle came of it. I didn't enjoy it all that much. Moreover, as a child born to poverty who had spent his entire life using the toy called Kodak with care and respect, I actually felt quite silly.

Zagreb, 1999

The documentary *Croatia 2000—Who Wants To Be a President* (*Novo novo vrijeme*), which I made with Igor Mirković and Boris Matić, was my first movie shot on video. We did this out of necessity, for lack of funds. We used many small amateur video cameras which record onto mini tapes. The final cut was transferred to a 35 mm negative, and the film copies were made from the negative for cinema distribution.

Athens, Ohio, 2011

This summer, 35 mm movie projectors were removed from all the multiplex cinemas in the United States. As many as eighteen thousand of them. I heard that most have been sold to China. They were replaced by digital ones. Small art cinemas were warned to do the same over the following year or two, as 35 mm movie copies would be gone by then. Europe is following the lead.

    I went to a multiplex to see how it came across. And sure enough—the image was perfectly sharp across the whole surface of the screen. No scratches, no bits and pieces stuck inside the projector. Solid, immutable, it couldn't breathe. I went to the multiplex three days in a row, I saw a number of different films. I didn't care what, all I was interested in was the image. I stared at it, almost alone in the big-screen theaters. I had always longed for such an image but now that I finally had it, uneasiness set in, I may have dreamed the wrong dream. Or, as usually happens, once my dream came true, it turned out to be a nightmare. The imperfect image, the 35 mm copy that breathes and wears out over time, with all its scratches and imperfections, might actually be better suited to the soul of the movie.

Zagreb, 2011

The producers asked if we were planning to film *The Viper's Glen Miracle* using a film camera or a digital one. What was I to tell them? I knew there was no money for 35 mm. They knew it too. They were simply asking out of respect for the aging director.

Athens, Ohio, 2012

Kodak declared bankruptcy. I feel as if somebody close to me has died.

Zagreb, 2015

I'm shooting *The Constitution*. We're using Alexa, an Arriflex digital camera. Thanks to cameraman Branko Linta, I feel unexpectedly great in the digital world.

Film Style

A recognizable set of conventions used by directors to give their movies a personal touch, enhancing the narration, character, and meaning.

Zagreb, 2011

I am asked about my "film style." I try to come up with a rational answer to what is a metaphysical question.

    How to tell a film story? How to shape a story so that it grows organically from the way it is told and not out of a previously devised plan? To solve this puzzle, I usually start from the main protagonist. I ask myself: if he or she were to make a movie about themselves, how would they do it? In what kind of breath, what cadences, what images, color, sound? I search for a way to tell the story from within the mindset of the lead, in their life rhythm, in short—as their story.

This approach has allowed me to avoid repeating myself, so I can make each movie in a different way and enjoy the discovery of the new.

Textbooks on film directing explain that one builds one's style by developing a more or less similar attitude toward a range of different materials. But, style is not a category so easily perceived. True "film style" is actually an "inner style," based on a unity of the diverse, and can be discerned only in a director's full opus. For, eventually, no matter how hard we try, we cannot hide in our own movies. With just a bit of effort, anyone can read us from them.

Translated into movies: I made three films that examine three pivotal moments in the utopia where we see ourselves as having lived: *Charuga*, a story about the beginnings of the utopia; *You Love Only Once*, about the clash between that utopia and real life; and *The Border Post*, about the moment when the "Yugoslav" version of the utopia came to an end. In some way, all three movies tackle the same topic. I approached each of them in a completely different way because, told through three different characters, these were three distinct stories.

As Sidney Lumet says in *Making Movies*: "But he meant beauty in the sense of its organic connection to the material. And this is the connection that, for me, separates true stylists from decorators. The decorators are easy to recognize. That's why critics love them so."

Filming Permit

In the United States, one must obtain a permit for every professional film shoot. This document, issued by the local authorities, includes all the details—the number of shooting days, locations, detailed technical information. This why all the US states, as well as every big city, have specialized film agencies: the California Film Commission *in California, the* Mayor's Office of Film, Theater & Broadcasting *in New York, the* Ohio Film Office *in Ohio . . .*

The following story is a factual description of all the stages one has to go through in order to obtain a permit for life in the United States. The list is, as much as possible, stripped of the emotions, fears, dilemmas, and everything else that make the beginning of any emigration so painful. In short: it describes the process, untainted by real life.

Zagreb, Spring, 1988

I am granted a Fulbright Artist in Residence Scholarship. I choose UCLA, with Lew Hunter, a professor of scriptwriting, as my host.

At the exact same time, however, after five years of futile attempts, the opportunity arises to make the movie *Charuga*.

Zagreb, Fall 1989

I am hired to teach at the ADU (Academy of Dramatic Arts) in Zagreb. Krešo Golik, a scriptwriter and director, persuades me to pursue the position. We have known each other a long time but not well, which is why I am somewhat surprised by his determination that I should be the one to take his place teaching senior-year film directing.

For the next two years, I teach, work on *Charuga*, and postpone the Fulbright. At the beginning of the third year, I ask for a yet another delay, but am told that unless I come that fall, I will lose my right to the scholarship.

Zagreb, Spring–Summer–Fall, 1991

Charuga premieres in the spring.

Meanwhile, the scattered conflicts are becoming more frequent in Knin, a small Croatian town with a predominantly Serbian population, and these will soon develop into the war. Under these circumstances, the shooting of Srđan Karanović's *Virgina* (*Virdžina*), which I coproduce, turns slowly into a nightmare.

I receive threatening phone calls more often, cursing and howling that I should leave, disappear, or else . . . Various right-leaning magazines publish articles claiming I am a Serbian Chetnik who is producing the movie in Knin in order to launder funds I have been given by the then Serbian president, Slobodan Milošević, and that I owe my international reputation only to the fact that I am Jewish . . .

My mother supports me to leave, never to return to this madness. Though she never says this, I see what's on her mind.

I arrange with ADU to take a sabbatical for "scholarship and professional development." The Fulbright Foundation sends me the paperwork for a one-year visa. The visa marks the beginning of this story of documents and permits.

I set off at the end of that summer so I can be there at the beginning of the academic year. Zagreb airport is closed. Ana and Olga see me off on a bus to the Ljubljana airport. The plan is that the two of them will come right before the New Year, we'll travel around the United States and then come home to Zagreb. That way, Olga won't miss more than a month of school.

Ana and Olga come much earlier. Air raid sirens echo through Zagreb that fall. I am not able to speak with them for days. They are mostly sheltered in the basement.

Bohinjska Bela, Slovenia, Fall, 1991

During one of the air raids, Ana takes twelve-year-old Olga and drives in a Renault 4 to Bohinjska Bela, to stay with our friends, leading Slovenian actress, Milena Zupančič, and her husband, writer and director Dušan Jovanović. Milena and Dušan welcome them, take care of them, soothe them, and prepare them for the trip.

Via Graz, Vienna, Amsterdam, and New York, after almost three days, Ana and Olga arrive in Los Angeles.

Los Angeles, Winter 1992

Olga starts school. Croatia has declared its independence from Yugoslavia, which automatically means that I am now a foreign citizen, so my Fulbright scholarship is revoked by Belgrade, the capital of Yugoslavia. Moreover, the Yugoslav passports on which we came to the United States are no longer valid.

Ana returns to Zagreb and manages to obtain all the necessary documents, and to have our Croatian passports issued.

Los Angeles, Winter 1991

At a picnic, we meet a group of lawyers who deal with immigration documents. They inquire about my "visa status," and offer, straight away and at half price, to request a green card for me. My family members will get it automatically.

They explain that a few weeks earlier a law for "Extraordinary Ability" was passed, which makes scientists and artists with an international reputation eligible for a high-priority green card. They see me as the ideal guinea pig—they hope to use my case to explore the meaning of "international reputation." I explain that we are going back, that I don't need a work permit and that, furthermore, I have nothing in Los Angeles with which I could prove my "international reputation." "Easy," they say. "Contact a few of the festivals where you've received prizes and ask them to fax you a document. And find a book that mentions your name. It's silly not to try. Maybe you don't need it now, but you never know."

Ana and I spend a morning at the Samuel Hollywood Bookshop on Sunset Boulevard, the biggest film bookstore in Los Angeles. In the International Film section, we take book by book and go through name indexes. We find a dozen books. "That should do it," smiles the lawyer.

New York, Winter 1992

New York University—the Graduate Film Division of the Tisch School of the Arts—invites me, in response to initiative undertaken by their student Arsen Ostojić, to screen *Charuga* in their "Director Serial" program. I borrow a coat, a pair of gloves, and a cap . . . and off I go to chilly New York. After the screening, I stay for a long conversation with the students.

Dick Ross, the director of the Graduate Film program, takes me out to dinner afterward. He offers me a professorship at New York University. As of tomorrow, if possible. I thank him. We have already booked our return tickets. And our visas are about to expire. No problem, the university can arrange everything. "Thank you, but we really want to go home. We never meant to stay longer in the United States anyway." He smiles and says he'll wait for me until the fall.

Zagreb, Summer 1992

Various right-wing newspapers publish articles about this poor Jew who is bartering his homeland around the world for breadcrumbs, and they also publish articles saying that this rich Jew is selling his homeland out of vanity, not to mention articles claiming that I'm at my best among the Serbian Chetniks in Knin . . . and all of these hurt me. An actress from a recent movie crosses the street to avoid me, unknown passersby jeer at me, wondering why I do such things, a drunken journalist for the *Nacional* weekly, who is himself an unfulfilled film director, sits in a café wearing a uniform, waving his Kalashnikov at my friend, lawyer Čedo Prodanović and me, yelling that he'll shoot us if we don't leave Croatia immediately . . .

It becomes more than obvious that I won't be able to do anything amid all the hysteria. The black-and-white world is verging on madness. At the same time, I am being notified by various "well-informed sources" that I am on all the blacklists—from the one drawn up by Croatian National Television, to the roster at the Ministry of Culture, which is also in charge of filmmaking.

Mike Miller, the associate dean at the Tisch School of Art New York phones every two weeks, asking if I have made up my mind. They are waiting. By the way, they have found a wonderful apartment. And two possible schools for Olga. She can choose which one she likes better.

We decide: we're going.

New York University sends me an invitation letter. It includes a one-year visa.

New York, Fall 1992

I teach the Master Class in Film Directing for the first-year students in the Graduate Film program at the Tisch School of the Arts at NYU. Spike Lee teaches second year, and Arthur Penn, third. First-rate teachers, exceptional students. I have never had better and probably never will. NYU gives us a three-bedroom apartment on Bleecker Street, in the heart of the Village, and a one-year work permit.

New York, Winter 1993

The lawyers from Los Angeles let me know that I can apply for my green card. I need to complete all the formalities in my place of residence, i.e., New York. They cannot help with that.

I go downtown to wait in line starting early in the morning, and do this more than once. They make me revise the application twice—first, the photos are not good enough, and the second time, the University has not properly filled out the form. A large Black man who is in charge spots me from afar and shouts: "Hey, professor!" laughing cheerfully. Obviously, obtaining papers is a question of self-control, a game you lose if you let an excess of pride override your lack of patience.

I learn from him that while the green card process is underway, we must stay in the country. Which means, no Zagreb this summer.

New York, Spring 1993

Since arriving in New York, I have been receiving offers from other universities. I feel like a first-string soccer star.

The first offer comes from the Columbia College, Chicago. They phone offering me the position of director of their undergraduate program with almost one thousand students. When they say how much more than New York University they were willing to pay, I calmly add another $10,000 to the sum. I am convinced that this is a colleague of mind calling from the office next to mine as a practical joke. When they accept and go on talking, I realize they really are calling from Chicago. I thank them and say I have no ambition to become director of anything.

I ask Mike how a person gets a raise. He laughs and says something I have quoted many times since then: "There has to be someone, apart from you and your mother, who thinks you're underpaid." In short, when you receive a job offer, ask them to confirm it by fax or letter. Bring the document to me, and then I have two options—I can either meet their offer or tell you to accept it.

A few weeks later, I bring him a letter from Ohio University. What they are offering is twice as much as New York University is paying and, more importantly, they promise to finance a project of mine. And, most importantly, they will allow me as much time as I need for my own work.

Puzzled, he tells me I have to go and see what that is all about. "You don't receive this kind of letter twice," says Mike.

Athens, Ohio, Spring, 1993

We drive southward—from the Columbus airport to Athens and the campus of Ohio University. A strange landscape of an America I don't know. One of the first questions by David Thomas, the School of Film director, the man who has convinced me to come, was: "Do you have a green card or US citizenship?" I explain that my papers are in process and I should have a green card in two to three months. He's not too thrilled with the answer. He explains that the Eminent Scholar position is appointed and paid for by the Governor of Ohio and that, by law, it can be held only by a US citizen or a green-card holder.

New York, Spring 1993

Just like all major US universities, NYU is opening European branches for theater and film graduate studies. Mike asks me to join him on his trip to Warsaw, Krakow, Prague, and Budapest. The only problem is that, while waiting for the green card, I am not allowed to leave the country. NYU approaches a New York state senator, and they are given his recommendation to the immigration office to grant me a temporary absence. The recommendation allows Ana and Olga to travel, too.

Zagreb, Summer 1993

After two weeks' journey through the north and east of Europe, Mike and I come to Zagreb. We organize a party for friends we haven't seen for a long time. During the 1980s, we used to do this often. Ana was at the prime of her skill as a cook. Twenty guests or even more would come to our apartment on Osmog Maja Street.

In the middle of the party, the phone rings. Athens, Ohio. David Thomas tells me he is in the office of the university president, that we are having a conference call and they wish to congratulate me on being named an Ohio Eminent Scholar in Film. I hush the guests; I can barely hear him. I ask him to fax me the letter.

Half an hour later, the fax arrives. Someone reads it out loud. What everyone finds most impressive is the section which states that I have university airplanes at my disposal.

After a few days, I phone David to tell him that I will respond as soon as I return to New York.

My visa has expired. I go to the US Embassy. The cultural attaché, a middle-aged woman who speaks what she calls "our language" very well, and who has obviously worked at the Embassy in Belgrade for a long time, tells me she has both good news and bad news. The good news is that I have been issued a green card, the bad news is that I cannot go to America. According to an international law imposed on the United States by the UN in the 1970s, Fulbright scholars cannot obtain a green card nor any other kind of American visa for two years after the scholarship, in order to prevent the United States from selectively grabbing the best world scholars and scientists. She has my green card, she says, and she will keep it for me. "Your wife and daughter are free to go back to America."

Saying all that, she smiles, obviously relishing my torment. She knows of the blacklists; she knows of my conflict with the vice president of the Republic. She cheerfully tells me that I will not miss out on anything for two years. "You'll be making films with Vrdoljak, and the two years will go by quickly."

Gloating, she makes a careless remark that there is an exception but it's a mission impossible. I insist on hearing about the exception. "If your country denounces you." What does that mean?

"What it means is that you must receive a letter in which your country states that they do not want you around anymore so you're free to leave." And who issues that? "The Ministry of Science, which is now in charge of the Fulbright Program in Croatia."

I phone my friend Dražen Juračić, an architect. I ask him if he knows someone at the Ministry of Science. He tells me he knows the deputy minister who has been bugging him for six months to design a house for him.

He phones me after midnight to let me know that I have an appointment at the Ministry of Science in the morning.

I sit down with the deputy minister and his assistant. Both of them are wearing the same black suit by Boss; they are both young and speak equally poor Croatian and good English. They have both obviously just arrived in Croatia.

I explain the situation. I cut to the chase. They are smart, they understand the catch and get down to writing the letter straight away. They need to formulate it so that it says I can leave, while at the same time they are careful not to blunder so the same Embassy woman doesn't accuse them of denouncing their own people. We spend more than an hour cobbling together a few sentences. Eventually they tell me to come at noon and that the letter, signed by the minister, will be with the secretary.

I come at noon. The letter hasn't yet been finished. The secretary asks me to come back the next day. There's obviously a complication.

That afternoon, I run into television director Branko Ivanda on the street. He tells me he has just received a call from the Ministry of Science, and they've asked if he thinks I will, if given the letter, work against Croatia abroad. And he thinks he's not the only one they've called.

The next day I am given the letter. I take it to the US Embassy. The lady who'd gloated over my helplessness before, reads through it several times. She is flustered. She tries to claim this is not what she had asked for. Eventually, she gives in and issues the visa. Your green card, she says, will be delivered by mail.

New York, Summer 1993

Ana and Olga enter the United States through the "US Citizens and Green Card Holders" entrance, I enter the one which reads "Others." Olga waves to me. Their line is short and fast. Mine, long and slow.

NYU offers me a fifty per cent raise and a change of status from visiting to tenure-track professor. Moreover, they offer to hold my apartment and the professorship for a full year, even if I go to Ohio. They believe I won't last more than a few months there. In return, they want me to write a letter to the students, who heard I might leave and are threatening not to pay their tuition if I do, to tell them that I am going so I can make a movie and that I'll return as soon as I finish. I write the letter, stating that I am going to Ohio and that I will see if I will be back next year. Still, NYU keeps their word—they hold both the position and the apartment. I even find them a temporary replacement—Vojtěch Jasný, a great Czech director, though getting on in years.

I'm still waiting for the green card. NYU helps me prolong my work permit for another year. So at least I have something.

Mike Miller and I are at a restaurant near NYU, talking about the pros and cons of leaving for Ohio. He takes a pen and draws a line on the place mat. Pros in one column, cons in the other. Two hours and a few glasses of wine later, both columns are equally full. The one in favor of leaving is a bit longer. Finally, Mike asks me if I play golf. No, I don't. Well, why go to Ohio, then? What are you going to do there?

The following week, he takes me to his favorite golf course in Upstate New York, and teaches me how to hold a club, how to stand, some basic swings.

New York, Summer 1993

With my friend, Shawn Cunningham, the man who used to lead Carnegie Hall Cinema, I load three beds, a table and a few chairs—everything we own—onto a U-Hall truck. We set off for Ohio. Ana and Olga come by plane.

Athens, Ohio, Summer 1993

It's terribly hot. Humid. The roof leaks on the house we rented over the phone. My green card has not arrived yet. After a week, we are contemplating going back.

Two days before the beginning of the school year, I get a fax that I can come and pick up my green card. I can finally sign my contract.

Cincinnati, Fall 1999

At the check-in at Cincinnati airport, the officer takes his time inspecting our Croatian passports and green cards. In the end, he asks if I know that I could have applied for American citizenship a year before. I say that I do, but that I do not need it because with the green card I can do almost everything I could do with citizenship. He sets the passport and cards aside, leans toward me and after a short pause asks me in an almost offended voice: "Could you please explain what you mean by saying you *don't need* US citizenship?"

Dublin Airport, Fall 1999

I fly to Dublin from the United States. They stop me at passport control. I need an Irish visa. I tell them that the last time I checked, a month ago, Croatian citizens didn't need one. An older man apologizes and tells me that new rules were put in place and now we do. It is Saturday, and I can't obtain a visa at the airport. I'll have to wait till Monday. He gestures toward a bench where I can sit.

We spend the next hour in silence, he in his office, I on the bench. At one point he waves for me to approach. He tells me he will let me in if I promise to go to the police on Monday and get the visa. I give my word and enter Ireland.

I explain to the producer who is waiting for me that I promised the man and we must go get the visa on Monday. He waves this off. Forget the visa, it is ridiculous.

We never go to get it, of course. During the departure, I fear I might have problems, but no one asks anything.

Schiphol Airport, Amsterdam, Winter 1999

Leo Hannewijk, head of a Rotterdam cinema, organizes one of the first European retrospectives of Croatian film, and includes *You Love Only Once* and *In the Jaws of Life* in his selection. Because of this, he has problems with the Ministry of Culture and Minister Božo Biškupić. They inform him these are not Croatian films because they feature Serbian actors. But he does not give way. He pressures them by telling them that the retrospective will not happen unless these films are included. The Ministry officials care about presenting Croatia well in the world, so they give in. Leo retells the not-so-pleasant exchange in the catalogue.

The entire Dublin situation repeats itself. Even more absurd this time. Less than a month earlier I passed through the same airport with my Croatian passport on my way to the United States. But the rules have changed. Now, Croatian citizens need a visa to enter the Netherlands. Two policemen take me to a special enclosed area. There are a dozen equally "suspicious" people from all over the world. I phone Leo who is waiting for me at the airport to tell him what's happening.

They take me in for questioning. A rude policeman will not listen to why I'm there and why I have no valid visa.

The airport saga drags on for nearly five hours. Meanwhile, airport police come with a return ticket to Detroit, and Leo, with superhuman effort, via the Dutch Ministry of Foreign Affairs, and the Embassy of the Netherlands in Zagreb, manages to secure a visa for me.

The police who, eventually, have to let me go, never bother to hide their disgust at the filthy Balkan brute.

Athens, Ohio, 1999

I'm sick of airport policemen. We apply for citizenship. We fill in vast forms. I don't remember the exact order, but out of a hundred questions, the tenth one or so reads, "Are you or were you ever a member of the Communist Party?" The twentieth one: "Have you ever killed anyone?" And the thirtieth one goes back to communism asking: "Do you know anyone who is or who was a member of the Communist Party?" I was very close to writing: "Yes, roughly twenty million people."

Columbus, Ohio, 1999

We are invited to the immigration office for an interview. The written part contains fifty questions and fifty answers. We have to memorize them. The oral exam consists of a short dictation and an interview with an official who asks a few private questions as well. My interview goes like this: "Do you have any children?" "Yes, a daughter." "Okay. Any other children?" "No." "You're sure?" "Yes." "Possibly somewhere you don't know about? Try to remember." "No, I don't." "You're positive?" "Yes!"

I can understand why he had asked me this and dwelled on it. I might not know as much as they do. But why ask Ana the same thing?

Olga goes through the procedure in New York.

(Years later, I saw a sentence on the front page of the *New York Times*: "James Brown's will divides his property, including several costumes, among the six children he recognized.")

Columbus, Ohio, 1999

We are given a date for the citizenship ceremony.

Unfortunately, I won't be in the United States. I will be in Munich, preparing *Josephine*. I go to Columbus and try to explain this to the immigration official. I ask him to give me another date. He is taken aback. He says he can't remember anyone ever coming to him with such a strange request.

A week later, I am given another date. But, again, I won't be in the United States that day either. Again I go to Columbus. The immigration official is bewildered. He has never seen anything like this. What in the world could be more important than American citizenship? "A movie," I tell him. I am preparing it in Germany, and I have to be there. "You're a filmmaker?" "Yes, a director." "Very well. Send me your movies, I will see them and decide what to do with you." I think he's pulling my leg. Nope, he is dead serious. He gives me his name and address. I send him three movies. After a week, I get another date for taking the oath of allegiance. Before the ceremony, there is yet another interview to make sure nothing has changed in the meanwhile. Out of five or six questions, the most interesting one is: "Have you become a member of the Communist Party in the meantime?"

That question and the oath mark the end of the six-year-long trek through paperwork.

Filmmaking

The process of making a movie. A general term for film production.

Athens, Ohio, 2008

There are two trees in front of our Athens house: a magnolia and an oak.

The magnolia buds late in the fall, poised to blossom in early spring. As if it is anxious to be the first to display its beauty and abundance of white-violet flowers. In its hurry, it is often surprised by frost. When this happens, the flowers brown and drop in a few days. While it was still a sapling, Olga and I covered the tree with newspapers. Seldom do the flowers survive. And yet, despite all its harrowing experiences, it is forever in a hurry, year after year, to show off and be the first to bring out its flowers.

The oak stands across from it. Tall, straight, orderly. Like someone who knows what they're up to and proceeds with care. In the fall, when all the other trees have shed their leaves, the oak still holds on, its leaves turn first yellow, then red, and—once the winter has set in—a grayish-brown. In spring, when almost everything else is already blooming, the oak takes its time. It lets the rest of the trees rush forward and show off, and only then, certain that there is no more risk, does it let its leaves drop and the buds appear.

Year after year, I watch them and cannot help but think that filmmaking is actually a link between life as marked by Dionysus and life as marked by Apollo, epitomized in these two trees.

Flashback

A scene or part of a scene from the past. In most cases, a sudden, disturbing moment that happens before the main story line.

Zagreb, 1995

I receive a phone call from Branka Šömen, the film critic. The Minister of Culture, actor Zlatko Vitez, has asked her to arrange a meeting for us. I barely know the man. We have never worked together; I have never even invited him to read for a part.

A few days later, I'm at his office. Zlatko tells me he has huge respect for my movies, in his opinion I am the best movie director this country has, and he would like me to work in Croatia. I am shocked by his courtesy and candor. I thank him. I explain, as politely as I can, that I don't have a project I can make here at the moment.

Los Angeles, 1998

I am invited to UCLA, to a conference about new forms of film education, and to present *How To Make Your Movie—An Interactive Film School*.

I phone Branko Lustig, the producer of *Schindler's List*. He invites me over. "We have to talk," he tells me mysteriously. I go to his place. He takes me to the hills above Bel Air where he walks his dog.

"I've talked with Tuđman," Branko starts in an undertone, as if worried someone might overhear us. "He told me to tell you not to be silly and wander around the world, but come back. You can make whatever movies you like." I look at him, he smiles. He knows my answer. "I'm just the messenger," he says with a wave of the hand.

Jerusalem, 1999

I am a guest of Tel Aviv Cinematheque. I'm presenting *How To Make Your Movie—An Interactive Film School*. Meanwhile, a student film festival is in progress. The Croatian delegation is led by Enes Midžić, dean at the Zagreb Academy of Dramatic Arts. He started his career in film as a photographer in my movie, *If It Kills Me*.

Every day they drive me around to show me Israel. On one of these days I ask Enes to join me, thinking he'd rather be in a comfortable car than on the student bus. So it is that the two of us end up in Jerusalem in front of the Wailing Wall. I barely persuade him to don a paper *yarmulke*, come up to the wall, and take a few of pictures for me.

And there, while both of us face the wall, Enes tells me he was called in 1994 by the Minister of Culture, Vesna Girardi Jurkić, who ordered him to bring me and Lordan Zafranović back to Croatian cinema. When he protested that he had no idea how to even go about such a thing, she said she didn't care. This wasn't her idea. She was just the messenger.

Grožnjan, 2017

I bump into Enes. After a few sentences, we jump to the story he'd told me in Jerusalem. He corrects me. I have remembered it wrong. He was not summoned by the minister. When Minister Girardi told him to bring me and Lordan back, they were in a box at the Croatian National Theater, while writer Ranko Marinković and Franjo Tuđman, President of the Republic, stood right next to her. She spoke, they said nothing.

Flash Cutting

A film-editing technique referring to brief shots in quick succession.

Brela, 1953

Daddy,
Mommy.
Guga,
and Vesna.

The scent of pines

and an almond tree behind the house.

Miška,
Ognjen,
Lukeša,
and Grandma Ljuba.
Loznica
and the sound of the mistral.

When things are the most beautiful
I'm consumed by fear.

Foley

Sound effects such as footsteps, wind noise, or squeaky doors are sometimes recorded in a studio and synchronized in postproduction.

In England and the United States, reproduced sounds are called *Foley*, after the pioneer of that profession, Jack Donovan Foley, who produced the sounds for the first sound film, *The Jazz Singer*.

In the Czech Republic they are called *Bruncliki*, after Bohumír Brunclík, who produced the sound for a number of famous Czech movies. I watched him at Barrandovo Studio, while he was prepping for the Klos and Kadár movie, *Adrift* (*Touha zvaná Anada*).

There he was in the spacious sound studio surrounded by mics. At some distance from him, his assistants were noting down everything he did. The movie rolled on without sound. Brunclík produced almost all the sounds without using any tools. Some he made with his voice, but most of them were by pounding his foot, scratching his shirt sleeve, crinkling the fabric of his pants, waving his hands in front of the microphones ... After the screening, the assistants, one by one, told him what they were going to do. I realized, then, that one of them was specialized in footsteps, a second in punching, a third in nature sounds ...

In Croatia, there is no special name for these sounds, but they should be called *Dörrs*, after Miljenko Dörr, our greatest master of the trade, who produced sounds for the majority of the cartoons made by the Zagreb School of Animation. I worked with him on my first short film, *All Eat Each Other* (*Sve jedno drugo pojede*, 1970). He was a tall, thin man with a tragically serious face. When he produced the sounds for a love scene, he'd take a pillow, hug it, and ask for the lights to be turned off. And then the sounds would start coming from the darkness of the studio: sheets, a man's sighs and a woman's sighs, a squeaky bed.

Venice, 1982

On the way back from Pesaro, we stayed with the Pinters in Venice. I'd won a prize and was taking everyone out for dinner. Pičo—Tomislav Pinter—suggested *La Colomba*, where Orson Welles once took him.

It was the end of summer. The sun shone in Venice in a golden-yellow sepia, yet another Kodak moment.

On our way to the restaurant, we walked past Teatro La Fenice, where Donizetti and Verdi held their premieres. A crowd was gathered on the stone steps in front of the theater. An intermission was underway, and they were sipping champagne. Black tuxedos, white and red gowns. Suddenly, the buzz subsided. Someone had dropped a glass that didn't shatter but rolled down the steps. The high-pitched sound produced by the contact between the glass and the stone hushed the crowd. The glass reached the ground and rolled on for another few feet. Once it stopped and silence reigned, all those standing on the square broke into applause.

Food Movies

Movies having to do with food. Among the fiction movies, my favorites are The Big Feast (La Grande Bouffe, 1973), *a French-Italian movie by Marco Ferreri; the Danish* Babette's Feast (Babettes gæstebud, 1987) *by Gabriel Axel; the Mexican* Like Water for Chocolate (Como agua para chocolate, 1992) *by Alfonso Arau, based on Laura Esquivel's novel (Ana and I were Esquivel's guests in Mexico City and ate, as in the movie, the food her mother cooks); the Taiwanese* Eat Drink Man Woman (1994) *by Ang Lee; the American* Big Night (1996) *by Campbell Scott and Stanley Tucci . . . Of cartoons, there is* Ratatouille (2007), *and of the documentaries,* Jiro Dreams of Sushi (2011) . . .

When we moved to Athens, Ohio University had many students from ex-Yugoslavia, but no professors.

Athens, Ohio, 1995

After we came, Nađa and Hajrudin Pašić with their younger son Mirza came as well, while their elder son, Faruk, went off to study in San Francisco. Nađa was a journalist and, before the war, director of Radio Sarajevo, while Hajrudin had taught at the University of Sarajevo. He had earned his PhD at Stanford, returned to Sarajevo where he spent two years during the war before he was able to leave. Their pathway to Athens was littered with the worst refugee hardships—war, family separation, a Danish refugee camp.

We got to know each other and occasionally went out to eat at *Casa Nueva* or into the hills for a walk. Any talk of politics, of what we had left behind, was a painful poke at still open wounds, and best avoided, if possible—though it was not possible.

As a full-time professor at the College of Engineering and Technology, he worked on research and soon developed important patents for cleaning polluted fumes, which American thermal power plants tested and incorporated.

Athens, Ohio, 2002

After them, Slađa and Srđan Nešić came with their son Marko. Slađa was a lawyer, and Srđan, who had earned his PhD in Canada, had worked at the Vinča Institute for Nuclear Sciences in Belgrade. Their path to Athens was different: in the mid-1980s they moved to Norway, then to Australia where their son was born, and finally settled in Athens.

Srđan became the director of the university's Institute for Corrosion and Multiphase Technology, possibly the largest corrosion research lab in the country. Soon, he started producing results and earning awards for his work. Today, he is considered one of the leading experts on corrosion in the United States.

We met by chance at a local video club, agreed to get together, grew closer over time, and started seeing each other now and then for dinner and good wine.

One day, I asked Hajrudin why he had never mentioned that a man from Belgrade had joined the College of Engineering and Technology. Briefly he said he knew a Serb had come, and that was it. I mentioned Hajrudin to Srđan, who said they had met, but he realized that Hajrudin was not interested in much more than that.

The wounds of war were still fresh.

Athens, Ohio, 2005

Ana decided that it was silly for us to hide from them the fact that we socialized with the other and decided to make a dinner and invite them all, without telling them in advance.

This is how *La Grande Bouffe* happened. She put a lot of effort into it— set the table perfectly, prepared several exciting courses, good wine, a cake, and a serious selection of cheeses.

From that day on, we met up at least once a month. These were carefully prepared dinners which ended in long talks. Every table told its own story. Ana prepared fish and Mediterranean food; Nađa, magnificent pies, *burek*, and other traditional Bosnian specialties; while Slađa made *sarma* (stuffed cabbage) and unforgettable cakes.

When we were away, which happened often, they still met up and had dinner together. They still get together on the Adriatic where they have summer houses, one family in Herceg Novi, the other on the island of Korčula.

Our friendship lasted for ten years, until Nađa and Hajrudin retired and bought a house in California to be closer to their grandsons, daughter-in-law, and son, who became a big shot at Apple.

Whenever we are in Athens, Slađa and Srđan, Ana and I keep the *La Grande Bouffe* tradition alive by buying finer and finer wines, and making more sophisticated dinners. And, of course, during dinner, sometimes we give Nađa and Hajrudin a call.

Food Movies II

"A functional link between the brain region responsible for taste memory and the area responsible for encoding the time and place we experienced the taste had been found at University of Haifa. The findings expose the complexity and richness of the simple sensory experiences that are engraved in our brains and that in most cases we aren't even aware of" (Science Daily, September 22, 2014).

The experts claim that in the memory of a taste, in that compartment of our brain where we keep the secrets of our childhood, the taste that remains the longest and most vividly is the taste of the first saltwater fish we have ever eaten. The salinity of sea water supposedly has something to do with this.

I grew up eating fish. Fish from Brela: all the mackerel, tuna, dentex, and European conger are stored and preserved in my taste memory as its first denizens. When I first tasted fish in France, or, later, around the Mediterranean—in Italy, Spain, Greece, Israel, and Albania—I was always disappointed. Fish which look the same, go under the same name, and come from the same Mediterranean Sea, have a totally different taste and cannot hold a candle to the fish from the Adriatic. I've been told this is because the sea along the Croatian coast is considered the cleanest in Europe, that it has many islands, warm sea currents, and a slightly different salinity than the rest of the Mediterranean. I cannot say if all this is true, but we all know that when you believe something as I believe this, then accuracy is what matters least.

Los Angeles, New York, Athens, Ohio, 1991–2018

At home, no matter where our "home" is, we mostly eat fish. This is the reason why the place that took the longest to get adjusted to in the United States was the kitchen, its rhythm, culture, language, and rituals, or, to be more precise: it took us time to develop a taste for the fish that was available here. It took us years to accept that the oceans are not the Adriatic, and that there is no point in expecting fish that look the same to have the same—or even similar—taste.

In the end, cod was proclaimed our "at home" fish. Salted and dried, imported from Norway, it had been a typical dish for Christmas or New Year since our childhoods. We knew how to prepare it many different ways, each one better than the next. Fresh cod was a novelty for us until we discovered that it was closest to the fish stored in our taste memory, especially the Chilean and Icelandic varieties.

Athens, Ohio, 2018

I frequently talk over the phone with my brother-in-arms in the realm of scriptwriting, Ante Tomić, who lives in Split on the Adriatic coast. We shoot emails back and forth with ideas and hints for potential film stories even more often. When his mother-in-law, Vesna, a magnificent cook, went into the hospital, Ante embraced the role of family chef. He approached the new task in all earnestness. The recipes and the photos of the dishes he prepared slowly elbowed the movie script ideas out of the emails. Sometimes, I fired back in kind.

The other day I sent him a picture of fish soup I had made, inspired by what we had eaten at the Cull & Pistol Oyster Bar at Chelsea market, one of my favorite New York fish restaurants. He immediately asked for the recipe. I sent it to him, saying that I call it Athens/Venetian Fish Soup:

> Take a kilo or two of white fish, cleaned and cut in chunks. Here in Athens I use cod, but in Istria I take monkfish, which is, in my experience, by far the best fish for this. Also, you need half a kilo of shrimp, or, better yet, Adriatic scampi. If you can't find a monkfish head, which makes the fish soup of soups, boil the scampi and use that as the soup base.
> You also need:
> A can of peeled tomatoes
> three diced onions, shallots or, to make it milder, leeks
> 6 garlic cloves
> 2 bay leaves
> 1 bunch of parsley
> 1 twig of rosemary
> a bit of pepperoncino
> 2 carrots
> 1 stick of celery
> 3 salted anchovies olive oil peppercorns, salt
> 3–4 deciliters red wine
> Sauté the onion thoroughly. Add the finely diced garlic, then after a minute or two add the grated carrot, finely chopped celery, and half the

bunch of parsley, chopped. Sauté this for a good 15 minutes. Possibly longer.

Then, add the wine, bay leaves, rosemary, salted anchovies, salt, and pepper. Let this simmer for another 15 minutes, or until the wine evaporates.

After that, pour in the soup base made of the fish head or scampi. And then let it again boil and evaporate over high heat for another 10–15 minutes.

Then remove the bay leaves and rosemary, add the fish, and, finally, the cooked scampi. Cook for another 5–6 minutes, depending on how fatty the fish is. Before serving, add the rest of the parsley.

Fry a few slices of bread and put one in each soup bowl before you pour the soup over it.

The very same day, he replied to my email with the simplest lunch possible: fried red mullet and boiled chard. My recipe was obviously too ambitious for him. He is just a writer, after all.

P.S. Mrs. Mother-in-law recovered after half a year of treatments and resumed her command in the kitchen again. Ante lost his everyday task. We might actually write another script or two.

Gentleman

A man of pleasing appearance and courteous conduct. These were gentlemen in the movies: Clark Gable, Humphrey Bogart, James Stewart, Jean Gabin, Laurence Olivier, Vittorio De Sica, Tito Strozzi, Erland Josephson, Max von Sydow, Rade Marković, Vanja Drach, Relja Bašić . . .

In my life, my grandfather Aleksandar was a gentleman, a pharmacist in Zagreb's Upper Town, born in 1883 on St. Mark's Square on the second floor of Baroness Kušlan's old palace, today's Banski Dvori, the residence of the Croatian government. Until his second year at the Upper Town secondary school, he lived with his mother and brothers on Bregovita Street, now Tomićeva Street, in the home of his grandfather, Julius Hühn. At the age of seventeen he escaped to Paris where he spent two hungry years working as a guide at the Louvre and a night watchman in a girl's lycée. He returned, remorsefully, right before World War I and started studying to become a pharmacist. While still a student, he was called up, promoted to an officer of the medical corps in the Austro-Hungarian Army, and was sent to the Russian front. As an officer, he was entitled to twelve cigarettes or two cigars a day. From then until the day he died, for seventy-three years, he smoked two cigars a day: one after lunch, one after dinner. When he died, I inherited his cigar cabinet. It contained about two dozen boxes, a few cigars in each, and handwritten notes, such as "after fish," "after chicken" . . .

Zagreb, 1945

At the Croatian National Theater, actors were the ones who ran the legal trials of other actors. The judges (the actors who had returned from the Partisans) were on stage, while the defendants (the actors who had performed on that same stage during the war during the reign of the fascist Independent State of Croatia) sat in the audience seating. Actor Borivoj Šembera was sentenced to a three-year ban on performing at the National Theater. As the story goes, he shouted, on his way out, to his colleagues up on the stage: "You'll need gentlemen, and there won't be anyone to play them!"

Zagreb, 1980

For the closing scene of *You Love Only Once* (1981), I needed a gentleman for the role of show host. I asked Borivoj Šembera to play it. That's how the movie ends, with his lines after the main protagonist commits suicide: "Everything's fine, everything's fine ... Nothing happened. Our international program is about to begin!"

Gentleman Borivoj Šembera died several years later, while on stage in Graz, in the midst of a performance of *Countess Marica*.

My father didn't use the word "gentleman" very often, but when he did, it meant he held the person in high regard. This meant that he considered this person to be a man of integrity, a man whose conduct and actions commanded respect. When he used the same word with a different accent and a smile, though, it was with cynicism. He would do this to describe someone who was trying to be something he was not.

When I started making movies, I met very few gentlemen indeed. Still, I did manage to meet some among the directors: Oktavijan Miletić, Branko Marjanović, Branko Bauer ... Amazingly decent, cheerful people, both considering their profession and the surroundings in which they lived and worked.

Zvonimir Berković once wrote: "Rajko Grlić often says that Bauer was the last gentleman in the Zagreb world of film. The first time I heard that, I flinched, but then I remembered that that's what I thought, too, back in the day."

Zagreb, 1994

Berković, too, was a gentleman.

There was a hint of old-fashioned pathos in his conduct, which he skillfully balanced with an ironic grin. We did not know each other well. We met a few times in Prague when he, as a professor at the Zagreb Film Academy in its first years, visited to see how Prague Academy worked. We rarely bumped into each other in Zagreb.

This is why I was surprised when, in the summer of 1994, a few days after I had returned from the United States for a visit, he called and suggested we get together.

We met at in the *Gradska Kavana* café and talked about this and that. In the end, in a seemingly offhanded aside, he asked: "Rajko, are you Jewish?" "Yes, on my mother's side." A smile of relief lit up his face. "Oh, good, I was afraid it was that they'd sent you packing. But this is obviously in your genes, you're doomed to wander."

I went on looking at him and realized he was trying to justify maintaining his gentlemanly distance from the fact that a person could simply be jettisoned from the Croatian cinema. I wanted to say: "Sure, Berk, I'm the wandering Jew, the one the priests use to scare little children," but I said nothing, I just gave a polite chuckle.

Zagreb, 2004

Ten years later, I tried to even the score. I called to inform him that Motovun Film Festival would be giving him the *Fifty Years in Film* award. Without letting him get a word in edgewise, I told him the award was not based on artistic merit or for any special quality in one's movies, but simply for enduring for so long in Croatian cinema. I heard him laugh, amused by the cynicism. He later wrote about our conversation.

Motovun, 2004

I had difficulty persuading him to come to Motovun. He was afraid it would be something totally antithetical to his habitus. He did eventually come but made sure to let us know straight away that he was staying just for the day and that he and his wife would be leaving for Zagreb first thing the next morning. He stayed on until the end of the festival. He sat in the garden, on the grass, talking to young people all day long. His wife made several attempts to persuade him to go back to Zagreb. He wouldn't leave. He seemed to be a happy man who was truly enjoying himself.

A few months later, he wrote an article about Motovun for *Jutarnji list*, probably the best thing anyone has ever written about what we were doing on that hilltop.

Zagreb, 2008

The last time I saw him, it was in front of *Charlie*, a popular café. He was already visibly ill. He had just been given yet another lifetime achievement award, so I said, congratulating him, "Berk, you've received more awards than you've made movies." He winced and laughed, "Don't rub it in. If only I'd made five movies ... It sounds so much more impressive than four."

Great Movie Quotes

Movie lines which have found their way into everyday parlance, such as: "Frankly, my dear, I don't give a damn." "You talkin' to me?" "Play it, Sam. Play As Time Goes By." "Well, nobody's perfect." "I'm ready for my close up now, Mr. DeMille" . . .

Here are several lines which belong in that category, taken from the life of my grandfather who, toward the end of his life, reminded me of Victor Sjöström, a director considered the father of Swedish film, who played the lead in Bergman's *Wild Strawberries*.

Zagreb, 1918

After three years on the front, my grandfather returned to Zagreb, and knocked at the door of his family home on Tomićeva Street. His mother opened the door and said, alarmed: "Alzo, my dear Nano, but where are you going to sleep?"

Gračanica, 1992

My grandfather bought the pharmacy in the Zagreb Upper Town, but according to the contract, the previous owner could stay on for a few more years. This is why my grandparents went to Gračanica, a small town in Bosnia, where he ran a different pharmacy in the meantime, hence the reason why Gračanica was where my father was born.

One day, while Grandfather was away on business, a man bitten by a viper walked into the pharmacy. My grandmother, who was a painter and knew nothing about medicine, gave him a bottle of pure alcohol to use for rinsing the snakebite. The man left, drank it, was in a coma for two days, and survived. From that moment till the end of their stay in Gračanica, no one wanted to take the medicine my grandfather gave them. Whoever walked into the pharmacy and saw him at the counter would say: "I'd like a word with the lady pharmacist!"

Zagreb, 1944

The bestsellers at the Upper Town pharmacy were aspirin, "dog fat ointment," and condoms. The best customers were the priests. During the war, my grandfather sent supplies from the pharmacy to the Partisans. One morning, his brother Štef walked in wearing a full-dress general's uniform. He had come to boast about being promoted from colonel in the regular Croatian Domobran army to an Ustasha general. My grandfather told him, in front of the customers: "Štefek, you cannot go parading around all gussied up like that. Get out!"

Štef turned around and left. That was the last time they saw each other. A year later, Štef died at Bleiburg, a place in Austria where the remaining members of the Ustasha forces, Serbian Chetniks, and other stragglers from the Quisling armies of ex-Yugoslavia, who, having escaped the Partisans, continued fighting even after World War II was officially over.

Every year, on All Saints' Day, my grandfather would light a candle at the cross at Mirogoj cemetery where candles are lit for those whose burial places are unknown. He never told me for whom. His serious expression made it clear that he would rather not talk about it. The first time I heard this story about his brother was during our last walk through Mirogoj cemetery, a few months before he died.

Guarantee

A guarantee, usually in the form of a written contract, that vouches for the payment of an agreed sum after a job has been done, or after a film has been completed.

London, 1986

After three months of postproduction, we finish *That Summer of White Roses* at Twickenham Studio. English producer MacCorkindale hands me the check with my fee.

Zagreb, 1986

At Zagrebačka Banka, at the foreign-currency counter, I deposit the check. The teller, who has known me for years, does not wait for the mandatory validity check which takes a few weeks, but enters the sum—as procedure demanded at the time—in my savings account booklet right away.

Two weeks later, she phones me, in a panic. She asks if I have spent the money. No, I haven't. The check has bounced due to insufficient funds. I go to the bank. The teller erases the sum from my savings booklet. She is eternally grateful that I haven't spent anything. If I had, she would have had to reimburse the bank out of pocket for the amount.

I try to reach MacCorkindale by phone. He is out of the country; he will call. "Don't worry, it must be a misunderstanding." Long story short, he never calls.

I phone my friends in London. I ask them to check on what it would cost to retain a lawyer. A few days later, all of them tell me the same: too much. It's not worth it because this might take years and come to more than my fee.

London, 1987

That Summer of White Roses has its royal premiere at the cinema at Leicester Square. Our invitation provides detailed instructions for royal protocol. We decide not to go. I do not want to sit there with the man who robbed me. Old London friends of ours, Vera Machiedo and Petar Janković, both very elegant, attend instead of Ana and me, a source of consternation for protocol.

Denver, 1993

Seymour Cassel, Cassavetes's actor from the cult movies *Shadows* and *Faces* and I are given the same award at an event in Denver. The two of us are introduced to each other at the bar where we have our first drinks. We keep meeting up and talking at the same bar over the next few days.

New York, 1993

The movie *In the Soup*, with Seymour in one of the two leading roles, premieres at Lincoln Center. I wait for him afterward to go for a drink. A long line of people is waiting there to come up, one by one, congratulate him, ask questions, comment, leave their business cards.

I stand to the side, waiting. Next to me stands a well-dressed man. He asks if I am also waiting for Seymour. Unfortunately, he has to leave. He hands me his business card. He is a lawyer. I should give him a call, he says, and then off he goes.

I doubt I will ever call him. I have been in New York less than six months and my Filofax is already full of lawyers' business cards. He calls me, however, after a few days. He says he has talked to Seymour and he would like to invite me to lunch.

We meet at a fancy Italian restaurant on 56th Street. At some point, he asks jokingly, probably out of courtesy, if he could be of some assistance. Somewhat surprised, I answer: "No, no, thank you. I don't need anything." And then I remember. "Actually, yes, I do have something for you. I just don't know if it is within your remit." I tell him the story of the checks. He tells me to fax him the contract. Uncertain of what to do, I offer 10 percent of anything he manages to get. He laughs.

Seven days later, a FedEx envelope from London arrives at our Bleecker Street address. In it is MacCorkindale's check. I call the lawyer. I thank him. I ask him what he did. He asks if the sum is right. It's a thousand and two hundred less than it should have been, but that doesn't matter, I say. "Oh, no," says he. "It certainly does matter. How much lower is the sum? Don't cash it. Wait."

Five days later, a new envelope arrives with a new check. This time, the sum is as it should be. I call the lawyer and ask when I can give him his 10 percent.

The next day I come to a building on 56th Street, close to where we had lunch. I stare at the marble entrance and only then do I realize that the name on the business card and the name on the plaque at the building entrance are the same. He of one of the four partners in the law firm whose offices are in the building.

I approach the doorman and, and as if he is expecting me, he escorts me to the lift with a smile and over-the-top courtesy. On the thirty-fifth floor, a smiling secretary is waiting. As we walk down the long corridor, she tells some of the people as we pass: "This is him!" People are grinning, an older woman even applauds. I do not get it.

Eventually we reach the lawyer's office. I give him the check. He explains what happened.

They do not usually deal with such small matters. They work in international trade and insurance. They have a building like this in London, with as many lawyers there as they have here. They took a look at the contract, saw it as a chance for a little fun at the office, and went for it.

First, they asked MacCorkindale to pay. He was evasive and then declined. It took them two days to puzzle out a way to shut down MacCorkindale's production through the bank. Then they gave him twenty-four hours. He objected but finally sent the check. The second one, with the correct amount, accompanied by a huge apology, was sent a few hours later. The lawyers on both sides of the Atlantic found this enormously amusing. They even placed bets on the day and hour he would send the check. "So that's why everyone knows about the case, that's why they were greeting you along the way. It's like using a destroyer to attack a small fishing boat. It isn't fair but sometimes it helps."

That is the only unpaid fee I have ever been able to recover.

Head & Final Shot

The first and final shot of a scene, sequence, or movie.

Zagreb, 1950

Of my mother's entire family, thirty-two people in all, only Mother, my sister Vesna, and Uncle Moritz survived the war. My grandfather Osias was killed by the Ustashas in 1941 while he was trying to escape from the Kerestinec concentration camp, and my grandmother Katarina, whom Mom brought with her into the Partisans, disappeared in 1942 after the Chetniks burned the village where she was going to spend the winter. Whatever property was left in Zagreb was expropriated by the Ustashas.

My mother found out that some of their belongings—a piano, carpets, paintings—had been taken by a family on Martićeva Street, in the neighborhood referred to as the "Vatican." She went there and rang the bell. A burly man, who turned out to be a high-level member of UDBA, the Yugoslav secret police, opened the door. As soon as he heard why she had come, he slammed the door shut. Infuriated, Mom yelled after him: "You're worse than the Ustashas!" Soon, that sentence proved to be fateful.

My father hadn't been at home for over six months.

As editor-in-chief of the *Narodni list* daily, predecessor of *Večernji list*, he was taken to Goli Otok, an island prison camp on the Adriatic. There, with all the other editors-in-chief of the other Croatian papers, he was put through "training." After this, he was assigned to "voluntary work"; first to building the Brotherhood and Unity highway, and then on to the Černomerec brickworks, which at the time were in a remote Zagreb suburb.

Then one morning there was a knock at the door. Vesna was at school.

My mother opened the door. Two men in long leather coats walked in. Mother stood by my crib and took me by the hand. The men in leather coats searched the room.

I was not yet three, but I remember the scene by the smell of their leather coats and the huge pile of papers they cleared out of my father's desk.

I remember nothing else. I do not remember how they took Mom away, or what happened afterward. Years later, I learned that these were the UDBA officers and Mom was taken first to a prison on Savska Street and then to the Goli Otok prison camp, where she spent the next three years.

That is the first image in my mind, my first memory.

Zagreb, 2008

After five years of galloping Alzheimer's, my mother had almost completely lost touch with reality in the last few weeks of her life. She stopped eating and mostly slept. Day after day she withdrew, shrank, grew more fragile.

I sat at her bedside at the *Lavoslav Schwarz* nursing home, holding her hand. She woke, turned to look at me, and I saw her eyes fill with an infinite kindness and peace. She reached over with the other hand and took my palm between hers. Her eyes smiled. That smile was her farewell, it was everything a mother should tell her son as she departs. This was the last time I saw her awake.

Tel Aviv, 2011

At the Tel Aviv Cinematheque, I was at a Q&A after the screening of *Just Between Us*. An elderly woman stood up to ask: "How are you related to Eva Grlić?" "She is my mother," I said. And she, with the two other elderly women sitting next to her, clapped vigorously. Afterward they came over to explain that, for them, my mother's book *Memory (Sjećanje)* was precious.

Hollywood Blacklist

The Hollywood blacklist was drawn up in 1947 when the House Un-American Activities Committee called in for questioning ten scriptwriters and directors who were suspected of being sympathizers of the Communist Party USA. They did not appear for the questioning. Soon, a blacklist *and a* gray list *of suspects were drawn up. These included some five hundred writers, directors, actors, and musicians who, over the next two decades, could not find work for Hollywood studios if using their real names.*

New York, 1984

My mother phones me from Zagreb to let me know that the Executive Committee of the Communist Party of Croatia has issued a *White Book*, in which several pages are dedicated to me as one of the people who use culture and art to spread "politically unsuitable messages."

Zagreb, 2005

Twenty years later, the *White Book* was printed and publicly exposed as a sample of the sort of criminal act that was typical of the previous regime.

White Book, published by the Central Committee of the Communist Party of Croatia.

Translation:
>Price: 49 kunas
>WHITE BOOK By Stipe Šuvar
>About: "Stipe Šuvar's WHITE BOOK" was the popular name used to refer to a document issued on March 21, 1984 by the Executive Committee of the Communist Party Center for Information and Propaganda, led by Stipe Šuvar.
>
>Its original title was *On Ideological and Political Tendencies in Art, Literature, Theater, and Film Criticism, and the Public Actions of a Number of Cultural Workers Conveying Politically Unacceptable Messages.*
>
>Šuvar said it was dubbed the "White Book" because of its white cover.
>
>The book is a document that proves the degree of repression in the former communist state. It was aimed at mobilizing people against ideological opponents.
>
>The document was a witch-hunt led by the Communist Party against certain intellectuals, artists, writers, and other political opponents whose work and ideas opposed the party's ideological frame as set by Šuvar and his Party colleagues. Among the people tagged as unsuitable at the time were: Igor Mandić, Predrag Matvejević, Stanko Lasić, Dimitrije Rupel, Vuk Drašković, Dobrica Ćosić, Ljubomir Tadić, Stjepan Čuić, Drago Štambuk, Edvard Kocbek, Antonije Isaković, Lojze Kovačič, Rajko Grlić. The list shows that in Serbia and in Slovenia, it was the local nationalists or pseudo-nationalists who were deemed ideological opponents, while among the names in Croatia are also artists with a leftist orientation (Matvejević, Grlić).

Rumor has it that the new regime has their own white books but, having learned from the past, they have not published their list. On the regime's behalf, everyone's suitability is tested by various right-wing led veteran-widow-Catholic-neo-Ustasha-movement websites that publish their own "blacklists."

Screenshot of a "blacklist" published by a right-wing Croatian website.

Translation:
THE MOVEMENT FOR THE RENEWAL OF THE FAILED FABRICATION OF COMMUNIST YUGOSLAVIA!!

1) ANTE TOMIĆ, author and journalist
2) DEJAN JOVIĆ, political scientist
3) SAŠA PERKOVIĆ, former national security advisor to the President of the Republic
4) BUDIMIR LONČAR, the last Minister of Foreign Affairs of Socialist Yugoslavia
5) RAJKO GRLIĆ, film director
6) EUGEN JAKOVČIĆ, peace activist
7) GORAN RADMAN, former director of the Croatian National Television
8) HRVOJE KLASIĆ, professor of history
9) TVRTKO JAKOVINA, professor of history
10) DRAGAN MARKOVINA, journalist and politician
11) IGOR MIRKOVIĆ, director of Motovun Film Festival
12) ZORAN PUSIĆ, mathematician and peace activist
13) VESNA TERŠELIC, peace activist
14) VESNA PUSIĆ, former Minister of Foreign Affairs of the Republic of Croatia
15) TOMISLAV JAKIĆ, journalist and a former advisor to the President of Croatia
16) MATE KAPOVIĆ, professor
17) MILORAD PUPOVAC, leader of the Croatian Serbs and professor
18) ZRINKA VRABEC, journalist and former adviser to the President of Croatia
19) ANTE NOBILO, lawyer
20) STIPE MESIĆ, former President of Croatia
21) DAVOR BUTKOVIC, journalist
22) KREŠIMIR MACAN, marketing agent and the former adviser to the Prime Minister
23) JELENA LOVRIĆ, journalist
24) SAVO ŠTRBAC, Croatian Serb politician
25) ZRINKA BADRIĆ, strategic communication director
26) DRAGO PILSEL, journalist and theologian
27) HRVOJE ZOVKO, the president of the Croatian Journalist Association
28) BORIS DEŽULOVIĆ, author and journalist
29) MILJENKO JERGOVIĆ, author and journalist
30) INGRID ANTIČEVIĆ, politician
31) JADRANKA KOSOR, former President of Croatia
32) IVAN FUMIĆ, chairman of the Croatian Anti-Fascist League
33) BRANIMIR PROFUK, journalist
34) IVANKA TOMA, journalist
35) GORAN GEROVAC, journalist
36) IVO JOSIPOVIĆ, former President of Croatia
37) ZORAN MILANOVIĆ, former Prime Minister of Croatia
38) BRANIMIR ČAČIĆ, politician and manager

LISTEN UP, CROATIAN PEOPLE—THESE PEOPLE ARE DESTROYING CROATIA

Or, as the Croatian rock band *Prljavo Kazalište* would say, with apologies for my rewording:

> My name is Rajko Grlić
> And all around me is a
> Black-and-white world . . .

Horror Movies

Horror movies disturb viewers and sow panic. They awaken our repressed fears, in hopes that this will free moviegoers and allow them to reach a catharsis.

Zagreb, 1945

As a court-martial judge, film director Vojdrag Berčić (1918–2004) sent almost half of the former Croatian Ustasha government to their deaths, from Mile Budak, the number-two person in that hierarchy, and on down.

As a former Jesuit student, he spent the rest of his life meticulously investigating Ustasha crimes. He gave thought to the daunting dilemma: had he convicted innocent people?

Prague, 1993

When a communist army general, Franjo Tuđman, and a Canadian pizza maker, Gojko Šušak, came to power, this meant a semi-official rehabilitation of the spirit and iconography of the Ustasha movement; so at this point Vojdrag left Zagreb and spent the rest of his life in Prague.

He lived in poverty. He ate seldom and little. He lived on the outskirts, repeatedly humiliated by his landlady.

"They were crueler and bloodier and committed crimes more gruesome than I'd thought when I took the bench in 1945," said Vojo as we sat in a Prague brewery. "And almost ninety per cent of the worst criminals among them came from Serbian families, or were Orthodox Serbs who had converted to Catholicism."

I don't know if that's true and I doubt I'll ever find out, but our conversation in the brewery could serve as the opening scene of a horror movie about one of the main sources of the Croatian calamity today—the new regime's flirtation with the Ustasha movement.

How to Film in Front of a Mirror

A technique involving the filming of a shot and the reverse shot of a mirror from the same spot, and then blending the two shots, in postproduction, into one to avoid the reflection of the camera.

Los Angeles, 1950

My favorite movie about movies, Billy Wilder's *Sunset Boulevard*, was scorned by Hollywood, and the director was told not to bite the hand that fed him.

Galway, 1952

John Ford told a story about how *The Quiet Man*, one of the finest movies ever made in and about Ireland, irked the Irish. They claimed it gives a distorted image of their character.

Prague, 1967

Miloš Forman's *The Firemen's Ball* (*Hoří, má panenko*), a merciless portrayal of the Czechs, was sincerely despised by my Czech colleagues in Prague. They called it a flawed and malicious image.

It feels good to remember this from time to time. Encouraging.

How to Make Your Movie

Whoever embarks on a filmmaking adventure—from an amateur with an iPhone in his hands to a director surrounded by hundreds of professionals—everyone asks themselves this same question.

Paris, 1981

I am visiting my sister Vesna. She and her husband Malcolm Scott Hardy, director of the British Council for France, and their children, Daniel and Tanja, live in a beautiful apartment on Île Saint-Louis, an island in the Seine.

It's Sunday. I cross the bridge between the island and Le Marais.

It has been snowing for several hours and the city is blanketed in white. On the bridge there is a painter, a skinny Japanese man in a long coat. He is standing in front of an easel, and on it, a sheet of white paper. The Japanese man is painting a watercolor while dipping his brush in the snow. The strength of his pressure on the snow produces the range in the shades of black.

I watch him and find myself thinking that making movies is like this. The entire skill of filmmaking lies, in fact, in this ability, in the feel for how deeply and where to dip the camera in order to achieve the desired shade of reality.

Imaginary Line

The imaginary line is a fictional boundary drawn between two actors. To help the viewer understand who is to the left and who to the right side of the screen, the scene is filmed from one side or the other of the imaginary line.

Setúbal, 2007

Setúbal is Lisbon's fishing port. Not long ago, it had over two hundred fish-canning factories. Not a single one is left, but the smell of sardines is still there. They fry them in front of every restaurant and sprinkle them with coarse sea salt. Želimir Brala, the Croatian Ambassador to Portugal and his wife Nina, take Ana and me out to dinner. Toward the end, over Setúbal Moscatel wine and soft Azeitao cheese, Želimir talks about the connections between Portugal and Brazil.

To bring order to his new colonies, Pope Alexander VI, the notorious Rodrigo Borgia, declared the *Tratado de Tordesilhas* in 1494. The treaty established an imaginary line that would divide the New World lands ruled by Spain and Portugal. This is how Brazil and a part of Africa became Portuguese territories. Although these countries have been independent for many years now, their languages and cultures still bear vivid traces of the Pope's imaginary line.

Leningrad, 1978

The imperial train takes us from Moscow to Leningrad. A gilded compartment upholstered in brocade, furnished with armchairs and a desk, a bathroom and shower, and a huge samovar stoked from the corridor. We drink шампанское (champagne).

The railroad follows an imaginary line that Peter the Great drew across the map of Russia, connecting Saint Petersburg and Moscow. As he ran his finger over the map to explain to the architects the route he envisioned, he paused for a moment with his finger resting on a point mid-route. They immediately started drawing the line, but none dared ask Peter the Great to lift his finger. Hence the railroad between the two cities runs along a straight line but there is a large bend at only one spot. This is the bend around Peter the Great's index finger.

London, 1986

Ana and Boris Zenić have us over for dinner. Darko Bekić talks about a note from Churchill he held in his hand a few days earlier at the British Museum.

Yalta, 1943

During the meeting between Roosevelt, Churchill, and Stalin, while they were talking about the postwar division of their spheres of interest, Churchill sent a note to Stalin with a sketch of several countries, each divided into halves. On the halves, Churchill had penciled in his suggestion for how the countries might be split: Romania 90 percent to you, 10 percent to us; Greece 90 percent to us, 10 percent to you; Yugoslavia 50 percent, 50 percent. Stalin looked at the paper, laughed, and signed. Over the following fifty years, those lines determined the lives of millions of people. Including mine.

Moscow, 1988

We are sightseeing in Moscow. The guides stop in front of an enormous neoclassical building. There are seven like it in Moscow. The most famous is Lomonosov Moscow State University.

Six of the seven buildings are identical. Stalin signed the architectural plan for each. We stand in front of the seventh. For this one, the architects summoned the courage and offered him two plans. The only difference between them was the size of the windows. They thought to cheer him up by offering him a choice. Stalin was too busy that day, however, and signed them both. The architects were confounded. Afraid of making a mistake and possibly losing their lives, they made the building and drew an imaginary line through its middle—on one side they put the windows from the first draft, and on the other, the windows from the second.

Near Vinkovci, 1993

Actor Ivo Gregurević, who plays the infamous robber Čaruga in the movie *Charuga*, tells us a story about two opposing units during the war—Croats and Serbs—stationed somewhere near the town of Vinkovci, both using the name "Čaruga." They proudly bore the name of the outlaw who was a Serb, but who was born, worked, and died in Croatia. The only thing that separated the two "Čaruga" units was an imaginary line called the border or, more aptly, back then: the front.

London, 1996

I am at dinner with producer Pepa Ponce. A few tables away sits the British politician, Paddy Ashdown, known in Croatia as the person who was witness to "Tuđman's cocktail napkin."

During the war in ex-Yugoslavia, to celebrate the signing of a truce, Tuđman took a napkin and drew a map of Bosnia and Hercegovina for British diplomat Paddy Ashdown, and then he drew a line down the map splitting it into two parts—the Croatian half and the Serbian half.

Over the following years, a great deal of lives and property would be destroyed just to prove the validity of the idea represented by that imaginary line. Word has it that the napkin has been saved.

Rocky Mountains, 1993

I am on one of the peaks in the Rocky Mountains, right above the spot where the line of the continental divide is carved into a stone cube. All the waters of North America to the left of the imaginary line drain into the Atlantic, while those to the right drain into the Pacific.

Grožnjan, 1995

We open the Imaginary Academy. It runs for seven years and involves two hundred students from some thirty countries.

An imaginary line divides it into workshops for fiction film and workshops for documentary. This is how, directly and indirectly, it spawns the Motovun Film Festival, a fiction film festival, and ZagrebDox, a documentary film festival.

Memphis, 2001

In their attempt to solve the problem of land registry in the early eighteenth century, surveyors Charles Mason and Jeremiah Dixon drew a line between Pennsylvania and Maryland. That line, named the Mason–Dixon Line after the two of them, became known during the Civil War as the imaginary line that divided the abolitionist North from the slaveholding South.

And this is still visible. It can readily be discerned during elections, and in the laws of the states that lie to the south or the north of it. But there is yet another thing that makes it visible: at all the airports south of that line, smoking is permitted. North of it, smoking is an unpardonable sin.

Independent Production

Production companies that are not owned by or under contract with any of the Hollywood studios. The term applies not only to the US cinema but to other countries as well, where it refers to the production houses that have not been built into vast media or state systems.

Zagreb, 1989–91

Maestro Film was a production company through which we tried to produce Ivana Brlić Mažuranić's famous children's story *Lapitch the Little Shoemaker* (*Čudnovate zgode šegrta Hlapića*).

I persuaded Ivan Kušan, a writer, translator, and playwright, to write the script. We spent months searching for the key to the story and finally found it—it should be told from the point of view of the boots. This would preserve the unique charm of the book, which mostly stems from the author's descriptions, plus it would allow the movie to step away from the book.

Director Branko Bauer, a long-forgotten master of filmmaking at the time, was making a living by directing magazine shows for television. He joyfully accepted the offer. We believed that the Mažuranić-Kušan-Bauer trio would be a winning combo for a great children's movie.

Ivo produced several versions of the script, we developed the project and applied for state funding.

Right about that time, Ivo Škrabalo became Tuđman's man in charge of film at the Ministry of Culture.

Several months after the call for submissions for funding requests closed, we received Škrabalo's letter in which he informed us that the project would not be funded. Those several sentences were so insulting that I never showed them to Branko Bauer. I was embarrassed by the new government's arrogance.

Prague, 1997

April 1st. April Fools' Day. Alex Koenigsmark, one of the rare if not only friend with whom Kundera spends time when he comes, very rarely, to Prague, says: "Today is Kundera's birthday."

Exactly fifteen years earlier, while he was walking through Zagreb, Kundera stopped by the bookstore on Preradovićeva Street where T-Com sells cell phones today and spotted *Lapitch the Little Shoemaker* in the store window.

"My mother used to read this book to me. It's the first book I remember!" We went into the bookstore and bought *Lapitch the Little Shoemaker*.

In Memoriam

Movies are often dedicated to people who have died. When this is the case, the words "In Memoriam," or "In Loving Memory" appear at the beginning or end of the movie.

Plzeň, 1969

The first time I heard about relationships between US soldiers and Czech women was in Plzeň, from Alex Koenigsmark, who was born and raised there. He told me about abandoned girls who were not allowed to go to the United States, about family separation, children who never knew their fathers, little Black children in white Plzeň.

Zagreb, 1982

Next time I heard of this, it was from writer and scriptwriter Branko Šömen. He had just returned from Prague and was totally thrilled with a script by a Slovakian writer, based on one of those American-Czech destinies. It was in that version that I heard for the first time of Mexico as the meeting point of these couples. If I remember correctly, Mexico is also where the plot was mainly set.

Athens, Ohio, 1995

The third time I came across this, what I heard was from a witness, my Athens neighbor Bill. He served in the US Army during World War II, first in the 88th Glider Infantry Regiment, and then in the 97th infantry, one of the divisions that liberated parts of West Germany and Czechoslovakia, including Plzeň.

While Alex's and Branko's stories were told from the point of view of the women left behind, Bill's was from the point of view of the soldiers who left. He remembered an infatuated African American man who was as stubborn as a mule and who did manage to get to Mexico, but whether he made it all the way to Plzeň, Bill couldn't tell.

Athens, Ohio, 2012

In memory of my neighbor, William Diles, 1924–2012

Plzeň, 1945

John Butler, a burly Black man with a deep Southern accent and a wide smile, enters Plzeň as a twenty-four-year-old soldier on a 5th United States Army tank.

At a dance that the *Prazdroj* brewery organizes in the honor of the liberators, John falls in love with Jarmila Soukopova, a nineteen-year-old blonde. Gallons of beer are drunk that night and the brass band plays on and on. John and Jarmila dance the night away.

They spent their first days together on long walks, gesturing instead of talking, because they do not speak the same language. A few days later they kiss for the first time, and two weeks later, Jarmila decides to introduce him to her parents.

The introduction, however, does not go well. Her mother faints when she opens the door to the huge Black man with the big smile. They don't let him in. They are appalled at the idea of having a Black grandchild one day.

But, Jarmila is so in love that she won't let herself be dissuaded by their rage. She leaves her family home in tears and goes to a cheap hotel.

The next day, Captain Winters officiates for John and Jarmila's wedding ceremony at the 97th division headquarters. After a modest reception, John is granted a one-week leave. Three months later, Jarmila is already pregnant.

The deployment is ordered out of the blue. Most soldiers are sent to the south of Germany. A few of them, mostly mechanics, are sent to Tahiti, to maintain vehicles at a military base.

John's attempts to bring Jarmila along to Tahiti fail. As a foreign citizen, she is not allowed to travel with or live with American troops.

John swears he will leave the army, sort out her documents, and bring her to the United States before the birth of the child.

So off he goes to Tahiti and she stays in Plzeň.

Plzeň, 1946

Jarmila has the baby. The dark-skinned baby girl, Sue, is named after John's mother. Jarmila's parents die a few years later without ever having seen their granddaughter. Apart from John's letters, Sue is Jarmila's only joy.

Port-au-Prince, 1946

In his letters, John draws rather than writes. He does what he can to explain what he is doing and how much he loves the two of them. He ends every letter with a promise that the documents for his demobilization will be ready in a few days. Those "few days" turned into almost two years.

As soon as he steps out of his uniform, he goes to Washington.

Washington, 1948

The Czechoslovak Embassy is clear: Jarmila cannot leave the country nor can he, as an American citizen, move there. Gotwald and the Communist Party have won the elections. Soon afterward the passports of Czechoslovak citizens are annulled.

Being an auto mechanic, he finds a job at a Georgetown workshop. He is in charge of the maintenance of government vehicles.

As soon as he finds a place to stay, he gets a library card. He reads everything that is linked in any way to the term "communism." The more he reads, the more he likes the idea of social equality. In the end, he is glad the communists have taken over Jarmila's country. He wants to join them. But he can't understand why he, an ardent supporter, keeps being refused a visa.

It is more than two years since he has stopped receiving Jarmila's letters. During this time, John keeps writing, or drawing, almost twice a week.

In the spring of 1950, he becomes a member of the Communist Party of the United States. The same day, he goes to the Czechoslovak Embassy and shows his membership card. Again he is denied a visa.

He writes a long letter to the Ambassador. He never receives an answer. Then he writes a long letter to the president of Czechoslovakia. That too goes unanswered.

Plzeň, 1951

Those letters mean that Jarmila is brought in four times for questioning. The police kept telling her that her marriage to John is a cunning plan cooked up by the CIA, that they are using her and her daughter as an excuse to have him brought to Czechoslovakia to undermine the state. Soon after these interrogations, Jarmila loses her job and has to leave the hotel where she is staying with five-year-old Sue.

Washington, 1951

Senator McCarthy issues an announcement: "I have here in my hand a list of 205 names that are known to the Secretary of State as being card-carrying members of the Communist Party and who nevertheless are still working and shaping the policy of the State Department."

Auto mechanic John Butler is on the list and is fired immediately with no explanation. Over the next three months, the same thing happens to him in another four mechanics workshops in Washington.

Charleston, Jackson, Austin, 1951–53

Searching for a job, he sets off for the South. He finds jobs easily but loses them even more easily. And always the same way: after an anonymous phone call, his boss pays him out and asks him to go.

In early 1953, he can no longer find work.

Juarez, 1953–60

He goes to Mexico. He finds a job as an auto mechanic not far from the border in a small town on the Sabinas River.

A few days after his arrival, he hears that Stalin had died. He puts on a black suit, goes to the baroque church on the main square and lights a candle.

Over the following months, he visits all the motels along the border. He tips the doormen and ask them to let him know if anyone from Czechoslovakia comes through. And sometimes they do. These are mostly people waiting for American visas. When they meet this Black man who speaks Czech, they think it must be a police trap and refuse to speak with him.

Sometimes, he comes upon someone willing to hear his story, look at his pictures or to take a parcel. None of these parcels ever reach Jarmila and Sue.

Trnova, 1960

Police keep summoning Jarmila for questioning once a month.

The two of them live a secluded life in a village half an hour away from Plzeň. Jarmila's grandmother, an elderly deaf woman full of compassion, takes them in.

That winter, a man in a leather coat knocks at the door and gives them a bag of John's letters. Jarmila and Sue don't understand why this happens, but they never ask. It takes them a month to read them all. They laugh, cry, and hug each other for joy. In the end, they write John a long letter.

The police examine it and decide to let it go through. So finally, John, Jarmila and Sue are in touch. They go on to exchange countless letters and pictures. John sees how big his daughter has grown, and Jarmila sees that John is going grey.

Fearing the police, Jarmila writes only about pleasant things, and carefully checks Sue's letters.

Juarez, 1965

John is happy to hear that his loved ones have such a pleasant life and that what is written in the American newspapers is nothing but capitalist propaganda.

Prague, 1968

That spring, Dubček becomes First Secretary of the Communist Party of Czechoslovakia. For the first time in twenty years, the borders open.

Juarez, 1968

Finally, John is granted a visa. He quits his job and sells his car. He uses all his savings for his plane ticket and expensive gifts.

Prague, 1968

It takes him three days to travel from Juarez to Prague.

Forty-two-year-old Jarmila and her twenty-two-year-old dark-skinned beauty, Sue, wait for him at Ruzyně Airport with bated breath.

On the bus to Plzeň, Sue tells him how they have really lived all those years. Her English is perfect, and John occasionally interrupts in Czech, a language he has mastered over the last twenty-two years.

That night, John is devastated to see his daughter's loathing of everything socialist and the gleam in her eyes at any mention of capitalism. Their conversation turns into a heated argument.

The dust has settled and John and Jarmila fall asleep, when Sue rushes into their bedroom in tears, and turns on the radio that is playing *Má vlast* by Bedřich Smetana. The announcer keeps repeating that Czechoslovakia has been occupied by Russian troops with the help of five fraternal nations.

Two hours later, a long line of tanks passes by their house on their way to Plzeň. The soldiers wave. They are moving along the same route that John traversed twenty-three years before.

It takes Sue two days to persuade Jarmila and John that they must go to Vienna and then to the United States.

Pecos, 1983

Jarmila and John live in Texas. After fifteen years of working as a mechanic, he retires.

Sue earned her degree and works in Washington as a marketing advisor at Republican Party headquarters.

Whenever Sue comes to visit, once a year for Thanksgiving, Jarmila implores John to refrain from political disputes. And John does. Not only does he not talk about politics with his daughter, but while she is there, he does not even go to Mexico for the meetings of his small but very active branch of the Communist Party of Mexico.

In Memoriam II

In memory of Predrag Lucić (1964–2018)

The first cabaret—an inn, a small witty theater—opened in Paris in 1898. It had the pompous name *Chat Noir, Cabaret Artistique*.

Between the wars, Zagreb had seven cabarets.

Jazavac (*Badger*), which opened in Medulićeva Street in 1964, was the first cabaret I had ever been to. Its biggest stars were Mladen Crnobrnja (called Gumbek) and Drago Bahun.

Prague boasts a long tradition of cabaret entertainers. They were mostly duets: before World War II—Jiří Voskovec and Jan Werich, and in the 1960s—Jiří Suchý and Jiří Šliter, whom I watched at *Semafor*.

Zagreb, 1960–83

My parents had a cherished family cabaret tradition. Every New Year, they would write a *vrabac* (a sparrow). These were rhymed songs, and each married couple—the Kangrgas, the Supeks, the Petrovićes, the Majdaks, the Pejovićes, their friends, who always spent New Year's Eve together—had four stanzas dedicated to them, two for the husband and two for the wife, which cheerfully described what had happened to them that year.

Several days before New Year's Eve, our home percolated with tension. Deep into the night, my mother and father paced up and down, sharing ideas, experimenting with how to express them through song, discarding or jotting them down. Once written, the song would go through many edits and, eventually, a few hours before the party, Mom would write the final version down on a fresh page. At the party, before midnight, Mom and Dad would stand, take a bow and sing the entire *vrabac* to their friends.

They kept the *vrabaces* they had written for over twenty years, and Mom managed to save almost all of them. I see them today as chronicles of an immensely joyous circle, a document of their times.

Zagreb, Japetić, Oštrc, Rude, Smerovišće . . . , 1964–83

Circus Praxis was the second cabaret I saw. It was started by my father and Milan Kangrga, one of the leading philosophers and thinkers in Yugoslavia and Croatia who, with Dad, was one of the founders of the magazine *Praxis* and the Korčula Summer School. The two of them also performed at the *Circus*. If we think of the *vrabac* songs as prepared and dedicated to private life, then *Circus Praxis*, as a complete improvisation, was intended for the public sphere, for politics, for politicians, and for the one thing politics has never lacked—utter stupidity.

With all the meetings about *Praxis* and the Korčula Summer School—the biggest annual gathering of philosophers from the East and West at that time—they met at least once a week at dinners, parties, and regular hikes in the Samobor Hills, despite all the pressures and threats they faced. These were places of leisure, where *Circus Praxis* took place.

I remember the two of them, often stripping off their shirts for their performances, proud of their bodies, sweaty, holding their glasses, cheerfully singing political quotes, imitating speeches, poking fun at those who were out to destroy them. They danced, sang, recited. Sometimes, Dad also played the accordion. The performances were short for a small, intimate circle who enjoyed them tremendously.

Motovun, 2009

The first time I saw Predrag Lucić and Boro Dežulović, writers and journalists, perform *Melodies of Flash and Storm* (*Melodije Bljeska i Oluje*), which were Croatian military operations in the 1990s war, I thought back to Dad and Kangrga. They had a similar energy, joy, and the same blasphemy.

Unlike Dad and Kangrga, though, who were always amateurs, Predrag and Boro honed their cabaret to perfection. And their perfection, the professional approach that made it so easy for them to seduce the audience, did not detract a jot away from the penetrating acerbity they used to get under the skin of everyday issues.

I have seen many cabarets, but I doubt I have ever seen a better duo. They had the power, the wisdom, and the courage; nothing was sacred to them, and they thoroughly enjoyed the shenanigans. There's nothing higher and finer than that.

Over a few years, I saw them at various places, using various titles, and they were always filled with fresh energy, inspired by fresh idiocies, wittier, naughtier, braver. One could learn more about Croatia from them in that hour and a half, than from the newspapers and television in months.

I thought this was something truly worth preserving no matter what. I offered the recordings to various television channels—Croatian national television, RTL, to Nova TV . . . I offered to do them as a pilot, with no fee for any of us. We were flatly rejected. Nova TV toyed with the idea for a while but ultimately got cold feet.

Split, 2018

Good, wise Predrag died. Boro was on his own.

In Memoriam III

In memory of Nebojša Glogovac (1969–2018)

Čenej, Salaš 137, 2015

Once I'd begun preparing for The Constitution, I asked Nebojša to come to Zagreb and work through the script with a speech and accent coach. In short, to start the language training that would turn a man from Herzegovina into a man from Zagreb.

Zagreb, 2015

Mrs. Đurđa Škavić is the most famous speech and accent coach in Zagreb. She has spent her entire life teaching actors how to pronounce words properly. I have worked with her on several movies. Unlike many of her colleagues, she does not suffer from language purism, she loves it when language is alive. I phoned her, told her I was working on something new, that I had an actor with whom I would like her to work, and asked if I might send her the script. She said: "Mr. Grlić, please don't. I'm old and I'm not doing that anymore. I haven't even been going out much lately." It took me more than fifteen minutes to persuade her to have a look at the script, then to come by to hear him, and tell us where to start. "Half an hour, no more!" Mrs. Škavić was firm.

She was on time and as soon as she walked in, she glared at us and threw the script onto the desk. "Mr. Grlić, I do not understand why you would do something like this. I love your movies, you're a talented young man, but this . . . please, why would you make a movie about Croats and Serbs? I mean, please! This is beneath you," she said and sat down. Nebojša and I exchanged glances. I introduced them and did what I could to reassure her: "Mrs. Škavić, this is not going to be a movie about Croats and Serbs, but about a lonely man, about the misery of loneliness and what it leads to." She shook her head, dismissed this with a wave, opened the script and said: "Like I said, you have thirty minutes, not a minute longer."

We started reading. At first, she corrected him mechanically. Within ten minutes, though, she was listening with close attention, and as we neared the end of the text, she was explaining specific nuances with real zest. I watched Nebojša win her over with his skill and composure, bit by bit, slowly, no rush. And I observed how she, a seasoned speech coach, regardless of her age, was enjoying the back-and-forth more and more.

The reading lasted more than three hours. Finally she stood, shook Nebojša's hand, and said: "Sir, you don't need me. You're wonderful. I can't remember ever meeting someone who has such a good ear right from the start." I tried to persuade her to go through the text once more before we started filming, but she refused and, on her way out, said: "Mr. Grlić, you were right. Now that I've heard this gentleman, I know this won't be a movie about Croats and Serbs, it will be about human loneliness. A poignant story, indeed!"

Almost everyone on the crew went through the same transformation Mrs. Škavić experienced. Slowly and subtly, with his smiling eyes, Nebojša won them over.

The filming lasted for two and a half months. We spent them in peace. The crew cherished and pampered Nebojša. He was equally caring in return. No one ever raised their voice, lost patience, or said something mean. As a director, I cannot remember ever having felt such peace emanate from an actor as I did from Nebojša, such curiosity, such a readiness to play.

He was calm, wise, very simple, but at the same time a highly complicated man. That is what made him such a fine actor. Both his life and his acting stemmed from his humanity, from his inner sensibility and external stamina, and this is the very contradiction that spurs actors. I consider myself incredibly lucky to have had the chance to work with him and to enjoy our mutual play.

Belgrade, 2018

Nebojša died. I'll miss him terribly.

Intermission

A break, a pause, disruption, breather... during a play, movie, or concert. In Zagreb, we call it a čik pauza, or cig break.

Trieste, 1973

My first time in an Italian cinema. I am startled by the ten-minute-break in the middle of the screening.

Athens, Ohio, 2017

I remember the obsolete Italian ritual and think that here, halfway through this lexicon of untold tales, might be the right place to take such a break.

I check to see if the custom endures.

Ten minutes later, I am sent the answer.

Rome, 2017
From: Inoslav Besker
To: Grlic, Rajko

My dear Rajac,

I'm glad to hear from you. If only this happened more often.

The custom of intermission started back in the days when cinemas had only one projector, and there were two reasons for it: first, to take the first roll off and put the second one on; second, to let the folks in need go out and take a piss or have a smoke. Longer movies, the ones on three rolls, had two intermissions (one per change). It is preserved even now when there are two projectors, and even when the projection is electronic. For the second of the two reasons.

The break is called "intervallo," just like in soccer, and, again like in soccer, the first and the second part of the screening are called: "Primo tempo" (1° tempo), and "secondo tempo" (2° tempo). We use different terms: in soccer, these are "first halftime" and "second halftime" (not sure, but I think that's what they still call them in Croatia), but in cinema we called them "first act" and "second act," with the terminology of theater, not sports.

Take care, Ino

Internal Dialogue

A conversation the protagonists have with themselves or with voices only they can hear. The audience, unlike the other protagonists, can hear the dialogue.

New York, 1993

"Is it better to be a foreigner in your own country or abroad?"
 "Abroad."
 "Everything is new?"
 "It hurts less."
 "Do you know what it is that you miss from your previous life?"

"No."
"People? Things? Space? Taste? Smell?"
"No, I don't know."

V.R.: I'm too young to stay and too old to leave.

D.U.: It would take a few million dollars for me to solve the question of "Homeland." I'd move a dozen friends over here and a few precious things, and everything would be like it used to be.

R.M.: This morning's *New York Times* says: "Hate is local."

S.B.: José Saramago says: "Inside us there is something that has no name. That something is what we are."

D.T.: Death chimes the hours on Prague's Astronomical Clock.

Invisible Editing

A splice between two shots, which viewers do not notice. Hitchcock's Rope is one of the most famous examples.

Sarajevo, August 15, 1992

The vast majority of Jews leave Sarajevo under siege on a single bus exactly five hundred years after they settled there, when they had been banished from Spain, and arrived via Istanbul and the Sandžak or Venice and Dubrovnik.

Zagreb, September 1, 1992

Mother asks: "Did they bring with them the Haggadah?"

A few days later, she gives me her reprint edition to take to New York. "It's safer with you!"

Italian Neorealism

A film movement which came about as a response to the hypocrisy of the film industry and also as a protest against the poverty which, thanks to Fascism, had stricken Italian society.

Zagreb, 1950

After a falling out with my grandfather, his sons left their family home on Glogovac, an elite part of Zagreb. Of the three brothers, only my father already had a family.

This is how we started living on Kulušićeva Street. The two-bedroom apartment housed four families; two families were in the two "big rooms," one in a small maid's room, and one in a glassed-in space created by splitting the bathroom in two with a wall. Twelve people in slightly less than eighty square meters.

The kitchen table had a lead cover, and the nicest cake was my mother's halva made of flour, lard, and sugar.

Zagreb, 1954

Almost every Sunday, around noon, right before lunch, the singer would appear.

Tall, skinny, in an old but tidy suit and a tie. He would stand in the middle of the inner courtyard the size of an entire city block, set down his bag, and spend a long time adjusting his voice by massaging his vocal cords. Then he would take a piece of paper from of his pocket and start reading aloud from his medical report. He would finish by reading the sentence: "I am certified insane. Comrade Bakarić issued the certificate!" At the time, Bakarić was the leader of the Communist party of Croatia and Tito's close associate.

After this introduction, he would sing a few songs, usually old hits, and then take a deep bow to each of the four buildings overlooking the courtyard. This was the end of the performance. And then, coins wrapped in twists of newspaper would fly to him from all the kitchen windows. And there was a feeling of haste in it, as if everyone wanted to get rid of him as quickly as possible.

Only then would Sunday dinner begin: soup, fried chicken, mashed potatoes, and a green salad. Halfway through dinner, my dad would take me to our room and say: "Now start bugging me to take you to the soccer game, and I'll try to get out of it by saying I have to write. Okay?"

So I would do it, I would play my part and the two of us would spend the afternoon at Maksimir stadium, in west-side seats, enjoying the mastery of Čonč, Lipošinović, Čajkovski, and Horvat.

Jewish Film Festival

A festival mostly showing movies about Jewish life and history. The oldest is the San Francisco Jewish Film Festival.

Los Angeles, 1991

The first car I bought in the United States was a six-year-old Buick Skylark. It was white, with light-blue leather seats. Beautiful but, sadly, not perfect.

Every now and then, and somehow this would usually happen on a Friday, it would refuse to start. The engine would rumble, let out a cloud of black smoke, shudder briefly, and die. Any further attempts would be futile. In the end, I would have it towed to a Russian auto mechanic at the corner of St. Monica and St. Vincento Streets. He would take the keys and, without a glance at me or the car, say: "Come zavtra" ("Come tomorrow").

Late Saturday afternoon, the Buick would usually be at the exact same spot where I had left it. Taking the keys, I would ask the Russian what the problem was, but he would just shrug, wave it off, and tell me how much. I would pay and drive the Buick away.

The following Friday, the same thing would happen again.

It took me a while to understand that the Buick's Shabbat had to have something mysterious to do with the fact that its first owner was Jewish.

Jump Cut

An editing cut that disrupts the continuity of time and space, creating an effect of acceleration.

Ogulin, 1947

It is wintertime. Twice a year, the chief of Croatian police, accompanied by his secretary and closest associates, visits all the police departments to ensure their work is up to standard. The town of Ogulin is their final stop.

At dinner, surrounded by sweaty waiters bringing out trays of young lamb, the chief of Croatian police notices that the Ogulin police chief, despite his wife's presence, cannot take his eyes off the chief of Croatian police's secretary.

Zagreb, 1947

A few days later, the secretary enters her boss's office and laughs while showing him a letter she has received from Ogulin.

In it, the Ogulin police chief declares his love for her. He says he cannot live without her and he is willing to leave his job, his wife, his kids—in a word, everything.

The same day, the chief of Croatian police issues an order to have all the mail his secretary receives, both private and business, delivered directly to him.

The very same evening, in her name and without her knowledge, the chief of Croatian police writes a love letter to his subordinate in Ogulin.

The reply arrives immediately.

Thus begins a passionate correspondence.

The chief of Croatian police starts by preparing his subordinate meticulously, in the name of his secretary all along, for their escape over the border. He guides him to a new, exciting, and utterly uncertain life in an unknown world.

Three months and twenty-one letters later, everything has been planned: the day and place they will meet, when and where they will cross the border, who will carry what and where to.

In the last letter he sends to Ogulin, in which he tells of his distress at leaving "her" homeland behind, the chief of Croatian police implores the beloved to go to the village where her parents live, to take a stone from a particular pile and bring it along. This will be her only link to her birthplace.

At eleven o'clock sharp, in front of the Singer sewing machine store on Zagreb's Republic Square, the Ogulin police chief sets down his suitcase. He turns, anxiously checks the big clock in the Square, compares it to his watch, and pulls down his black hat.

Upstairs at the City Café, sitting by the oval window and sipping his coffee with cognac, the chief of Croatian police watches the Ogulin police chief. He lets him stand there waiting and fidgeting, checking the large clock against his wristwatch for the umpteenth time. He watches the man suffer in fear for over an hour. Meanwhile, he drinks four cognacs and six coffees and smokes almost half a pack of Drina cigarettes.

It is past noon when the chief of Croatian police finally leaves the City Café and goes over to the Singer store. To his own surprise, he, too, is suddenly excited. He slows his pace. He calms himself so he can relish his sweet victory.

The moment he sees the chief of Croatian police, the Ogulin police chief goes numb. For a few seconds, it seems as if he is about to say something or finally move, but the words will not come, his lips can't move. They keep changing hue until they go dark, nearly black. The only sound coming from them is a high-pitch hissing like the squeak of an iron door.

The unbearable sound, the dark trembling lips, and the petrified look in his victim's eyes suddenly sour the triumph.

Furious, the chief of Croatian police kicks the suitcase and snarls: "You piece of shit! Dump the rocks, go home, and I never want to see you again! Is that cleeeaaar?"

Not waiting for an answer he strides briskly down Jurišićeva Street.

Lady

A dignified high-society woman marked by composure and good upbringing. In the movies, these were Greta Garbo, Katharine Hepburn, Maureen O'Hara, Ingrid Bergman, Liv Ullmann, Jeanne Moreau, Ana Karić ... In my life: my great-grandmother Guga.

Zagreb, 1962

Guga had one of the first electronic hearing aids. The mic was in a metal box that was placed on the table, connected by wire to the Bakelite piece inserted in her ear. From time to time, she stealthily switched it off, and continued "listening" with equal interest.

Zagreb, 1870

She was baptized at Saint Mark's Church in the Upper Town and registered as Isabella Aloysia Stephania Schwartz.

Samobor, 1875

She lived for a few years in Samobor, with her mother Adelaida Mihić, and her father Franz Schwartz, whose ancestors, bell smelters, came to Zagreb about three hundred years ago. Her father owned the pharmacy on the main square, and the family lived in the quarters above it.

That apartment is where I filmed the opening scene of *You Love Only Once*.

Zagreb, 1880

They moved to the Zagreb Upper Town a few months before the earthquake which left not a single building untouched. Guga used to tell the story of how, a few minutes before everything started shaking, the cat raced frantically around the kitchen table.

Zagreb, 1891

She married Čedomil Cekić, son of Đuro and Ana Cekić from Karlovac, who were Orthodox Croats, as was said back then. Over the following seven years, she gave birth to three daughters and a son. They lived on Zrinjevac Square and up on Pantovčak they had an estate surrounded by vineyards.

Čedomil was a high-ranking official. For a while, he was deputy governor of Lika-Krbava County, and then a member of the Royal Seat of Seven—the supreme court during the Triune Kingdom of Croatia, Slavonia, and Dalmatia—presided over by the Ban.

I remember two of Guga's stories from those days.

The first is how she caused a major public scandal. In protest against the politics of Ban Khuen-Héderváry, she failed to curtsy properly in front of his wife at a reception. The following day, Zagreb newspapers covered the incident in a very serious tone.

The second is about force-fed geese. The back door to their Zrinjevac Square apartment, which led straight to the kitchen, was often approached by women from the Dolac outdoor market who would bring a gift of foodstuffs to the door from someone hoping to bribe her husband with them. Guga kept a close watch on the door. She feared one of the servants might take the "gift" instead and then it would look as if Čedomil had accepted the bribe. She admitted she was sad to see the women take back all the tasty treats.

Zagreb, 1902

"The clash between Croats and Serbs culminated on August 10, 1902 ... Raging crowds set fire to Serbian flags, destroyed Serbian institutions, shops ... ," claims the Croatian Wikipedia in an Ustasha-like tone. Their holiday home on Pantovčak was destroyed in the rampage. She used to say how they smashed all the windows, and all the plates and bottles too, and smeared jam everywhere.

Zagreb, 1947

Čedomil died at the age of fifty-seven.

Zagreb, 1930–50

Her three daughters died before she did, and she buried them: Ljubica, married name Kostinčer, in 1940; Belka married name Moačanin, in 1947; and Olga, married name Grlić, in 1948. Her son Čedo, a well-mannered, elegant gentleman, the only one of her children I have met, long-standing president of the Cynology Association of Croatia, married Čona Brigljević, from a noble family of swineherds from Turopolje. The family had been granted nobility in the thirteenth century by Béla IV, King of Hungary and Croatia, out of gratitude for hiding him from the Mongols in their pigsties. Among other things, the Brigljević family owned a large apartment block in Zagreb called *Wellerovo*, between Petrinjska and Palmotićeva Streets.

During the 1930s, Guga sold the five-room apartment on Zrinjevac Square and gave the money to my grandparents to build their family home. In the same villa at Glogovac 4, where she lived during World War II, she lived long enough to see Zagreb liberated from Nazi occupation and celebrate the wedding of one of her grandsons—when my parents, Danko and Eva, married.

Zagreb, 1950

Cica, my grandfather's second wife, drove Guga out of the house on Glogovac.

So that is how Guga came to Kulušićeva, our two-bedroom apartment, which was housing twelve people. Over the next three years, while my mother was held at the Goli Otok prison camp where Tito, after he parted ways with Stalin, locked up his political opponents—Guga shared a room with me and Dad. She was not only my great-grandmother but also my grandmother and mother. In those years, Dad earned his living by loading coal at a railway station at the west end of town, and my sister Vesna was staying in a dormitory for school children on Tuškanac.

Zagreb, 1954

When Mother returned, Guga moved to the house she and her husband had built on Pantovčak to live with her son. I remember the house. They were allowed to stay on in one of the apartments after the war. There, in the *altdeutsch speiszimmer* (the dining room furnished in nineteenth-century style), Guga taught me how to eat properly. I had to hold a notebook tucked under my arm while I ate. At the time, in Zagreb, this was called *Kinderstube* (good manners).

Zagreb, 1956

Under an unwritten agreement, the house on Glogovac went to the father, and the summer house in Brela on the Adriatic Coast, to the sons. Going to that house was something we dreamed about all year long.

Come early spring, my father would go the central railway station and find a railroad worker who—for a small sum of course—would disclose the whereabouts of the train that would be leaving for Split that night. My father would find it, enter a third-class compartment and take three seats on the wooden benches.

Guga, Vesna, and I came to the station in the evening, two to three hours before the train was to leave. We would sit on our suitcases and wait. As soon as the train pulled into the platform, we would search for Dad in the crowd until we saw him waving from a compartment.

I can still clearly remember Guga peering out into the darkness, leaning on a window. She was frail, her white hair carefully combed back; Guga was always elegant, always in a black dress with a subtle white pattern, and a delicate brooch on her bosom. There was a mildness in her eyes and her demeanor. And she maintained some unusual and utterly tranquil joy, at least on the outside, throughout her life. She was a lady at any time and in any place. A true one, invisible and unobtrusive. Even in that smoky, smelly, and overcrowded train that clattered slowly toward the sea.

Zagreb, 1965

She died at the age of ninety-six.

P.S. The current occupant of the Brigljević apartment, where Guga died, is Ivo Josipović, former president of Croatia.

La Paloma Blanca

A Mexican folk song that can often be heard in Spanish-speaking movies.

Prague, 1970–New York, 1993

Elmar Klos spent his entire life searching for strange examples of connections between the south and the north of Europe. One of these was a legend according to which a Czech and a Dalmatian wrote the Mexican song *La Paloma Blanca*. This tidbit, which sounded intriguing but could not be corroborated, was, unfortunately, all he had. The last time I visited him in Prague, in the summer of 1993, was also the first time he didn't talk about *La Paloma Blanca*. He was ill and we both knew this would be the last time we would see each other.

Two months later, he died. That same day, in his honor, I wrote this story.

Puerto Ángel, 1952

What follows are the words of Lopez de Silva Zanetti, the great-grandson of Kruno and Violeta Zanetti. The document is dated June 2, 1952 and was delivered to the court in Puerto Ángel, Oaxaca province, with the intention of filing a motion requesting an evidentiary hearing with regard to establishing the copyright for the song *La Paloma Blanca*:

In the fall 1845, a lighthouse is built in the south of Europe on Palagruža Island, a solitary craggy outcropping on the Adriatic Sea. The same year, right before Christmas, the first child is born on the island—my great-grandfather, Kruno Zanetti.

The childbirth is grueling, and his mother Lucia dies that same night.

The father, Antonio, is left alone with his little Kruno. He raises him with love and care. He is a hard-working, reserved man, who relaxes only during storms. When that happens, the falkuše, the fishing boats from Komiža, find shelter on their shores, and fishermen sing mournful songs very softly all through the night.

Growing up next to his taciturn father, Kruno finds companionship with birds. He learns everything about their comings and goings, their habits, language, and birdsong that drowns out the roar of the waves.

In 1858, imperial protocol announces an extraordinary guest: Princess Sophie of Bavaria, who is cruising in the southern Adriatic and wishes to see Palagruža.

Antonio, the lighthouse keeper, and the fishermen from Komiža who are fishing around the island are asked to prepare a small program in her honor. The night before the event, one of the singers falls ill. Kruno, thirteen years old at the time, is the only one who can replace him.

Sophie's visit is brief. The fishermen sing only one song—*I Loved You, My Dove* (*Jubi sam te, golubice moja*). Sophie is enchanted by the song, but most of all by little Kruno's voice.

Less than two months later, an imperial dispatch is sent from the Viennese court. The Princess Sophie of Bavaria is inviting Kruno Zanetti to Vienna to join the famous *Wiener Hofmusikkapelle*—the Viennese Imperial Court Music Ensemble.

The lighthouse keeper is the proudest father in the world. Kruno, however, does not share his enthusiasm. He does all he can to stay on the island. He cries, begs, implores. To no avail. Eventually, in utter despair, he spends an entire day stark naked outside during a raging storm, hoping he will lose his voice for good. But his father is adamant.

Vienna is dusted with the first snow when Kruno Zanetti enters the *Wiener Hofmusikkapelle* in 1859.

Three months later, he performs with the Vienna Boys' Choir. At the time, this is the most famous choir in the world, made up of one hundred and fifty boys from across the Austro-Hungarian Empire. In the Viennese cathedral, they sing *The Shepherd on the Rock* (*Der Hirt auf dem Felsen*) by Franz Schubert, who himself had been a member of the choir.

For Kruno, life in Vienna is difficult. Performances are frequent, the rehearsals long and exhausting, the discipline strict, the punishments harsh, the food poor, and the room in the boarding school, always cold. On top of all this, he has to spend three hours every night practicing the cello.

He becomes tight-lipped and withdrawn. More and more like his father. One night, after Mass in the boarding-school chapel, Kruno decides to go home. He hides for two days on the streets of Vienna and tries to slip onto one of the coaches going south. He is found and taken back, frozen to the bone. He is punished with isolation and a six-month performance ban.

Over that solitary summer, Kruno starts enjoying the cello, talking to it, playing it with more enthusiasm. There are even moments of deep grief, when he recreates the sounds of the Palagruža birds with amazing veracity.

The next time he performs with the Vienna Boys' Choir, it is Christmas, 1859. They sing *Stille Nacht, Heilige Nacht* in the great hall of Schönbrunn Palace. In the audience are His Royal Highness Franz Joseph, his mother, Sophie of Bavaria, and her younger son, Franz's brother, the tall and elegant crown prince, Ferdinand Maximilian. All of them are visibly moved by the beauty of the children's sweet voices, and then the Princess spots Kruno and waves to him.

In the early spring of 1860, Kruno's voice starts changing. This means an end to his membership in the choir. While other boys are saddened by this when it happens, Kruno is elated. But his hope of going home is short-lived.

At the recommendation of Director Kraus, and with his father's written consent, Kruno becomes a member of the Gift Quartet, a string quartet sent by His Royal Highness Franz Joseph as a birthday present to the Emperor's brother Maximilian who lives in his castle, Miramare, a Habsburg summer residence in Trieste, Italy.

Maximilian is thrilled. His wife, princess Charlotte of Belgium, however, sees this as yet another slap in the face from his powerful older brother. It is well-known that Maximilian enjoys music and abandons himself completely to it during frequent bouts of melancholy. The entire Miramare Castle is steeped in sorrow—the sorrow of a crown prince who will never come to the throne, and the even deeper sorrow of a princess who will never be queen.

Music is often performed in the garden behind the castle where Maximilian whiles away the days by planting oranges, and, only sometimes, on the deck of the *St. Marco* yacht, while it cruises the Adriatic Coast. During these cruises, Maximilian sits for hours on deck, dressed in his admiral uniform, watching the sailing boat tack across the seascape. His string quartet, also in white uniforms, softly plays Mozart.

On his way back from one of these melancholic cruises, the *St. Marco* nears Palagruža. The night is moonless, and the lighthouse shines its beacon in a steady rhythm. Alone at the stern, Kruno softly sings *Jubi sam te, golubice moja*. He suddenly stops, brushes away the tears, leaps into the sea, and strikes out toward the lighthouse.

They raise the alarm. Maximilian orders the ship stopped and sends a rescue boat after him.

Kruno swims vigorously toward the island. Once the boat catches up with him, he does what he can to evade them. The sailors catch him and pull him on board. Kruno jumps overboard again. The boat catches up with him again, the sailors grab him and do not let him out of their sight.

Kruno spends the next few weeks in bed, running a fever. In his attic room, he hears strange sounds. Something important is happening at Miramare Castle. As if everyone is happier, louder. He even hears laughter.

From the perch at his window, Kruno sees delegations from other countries visiting Miramare. With joy, Maximilian and Charlotte welcome and see off ministers and envoys from the courts of Europe: Napoleon III, King Leopold, even the Pope himself.

Kruno begins feeling better the same day that Gutierrez d'Estade, leading the Mexican delegation, officially offers the crown of Mexico to Maximilian.

The flag of Mexico is hoisted over the ramparts. Festivities go on into the night. Seven days later, the royal Novara frigate anchors in the waters off Miramare.

An ornately decorated craft ferries Maximilian and Charlotte to the Novara. They are escorted by seven boats. Three of them are loaded with personal belongings, three with furniture, cutlery, and other sundries. On board the seventh, there are twenty-two members of the entourage who have been personally selected by Charlotte and Maximilian: the secretaries and notaries of the future king and queen, the councilors, courtiers, chamber maids and cooks, and the string quartet.

Kruno Zanetti clasps his cello, wrapped in an oil cloth, and stares into the distance. Again he is setting sail, and again this is against his will.

On May 22, 1864, the cannon at the San Juan de Ulúa castle announces the arrival of the Novara in the port of Vera Cruz.

Austrian Crown Prince Ferdinand Maximilian, the new emperor of Mexico, and his wife, Princess Charlotte of Belgium, the new empress of Mexico, step off the ship onto Mexican soil. The noise of the cannonade does not conceal the silence of the city that greets them with empty streets and closed windows.

Maximilian is deeply hurt. He decides he will impress Mexico. He has two royal castles, Chapultepec and Cuernavaca, completely renovated and readied for luxurious balls. Between the balls, Maximilian travels through Mexico in his gilded coach, pulled by a dozen snow-white mules.

Mexico remains silent. Maximilian gets the message.

He begins riding, dressed in a close-fitting black suit with gold embroidery and a matching sombrero. He attends folk festivities and church feasts. He starts eating unbelievably spicy food, listening to music he has never heard before, his Spanish rapidly improves, and he does his level best to become Mexican.

All of this leaves little room for Kruno, the string players, and their music. They are renamed the *Royal Trumpeters* and dressed in military uniforms. Their task is to provide flourishes for Maximilian's departures and arrivals, his speeches, toasts, and decorating ceremonies, which become frequent.

Kruno spends his nights burning the midnight oil. He toils to calculate the time and money he will need to secure a berth on one of the ships that sets sail, from time to time, for Europe.

One of the nights, just before the dawn, as he is going yet again over the numbers, he hears a voice from the cellar of Chapultepeca Castle. He follows it and, in the semidarkness, sees my great-grandmother, Violeta de Caravaho, for the first time. She is peeling potatoes and singing *Gracias a la Vida*. She is seventeen and surely the most beautiful girl Kruno has ever seen.

Over the following months, Kruno visits the cellar more often. Withdrawn and shy like his father, he sits quietly next to Violeta, peeling potatoes with her, enjoying her voice.

On one occasion, making sure no one sees him, he brings along his cello. He unwraps it, tunes it, and begins to play. The instrument makes bird-like sounds. Violeta recognizes almost all of them. She gestures, singing over the cello, sketching the shapes of the birds in the air. That is how my grandparents begin to talk. Like birds. With sounds and gestures, not words. This is all that the differences between their languages allow. But, day by day, they understand each other better, and Kruno soon learns that Violeta was also born by the sea, and that she, too, knows all about birds and loves to sing.

Meanwhile, Maximilian and Charlotte's spirits are flagging. Their hopes of being embraced by Mexico slowly fade. And Europe, who sent them to Mexico, obviously does not need them anymore. Disenchanted, Charlotte spends days, even weeks, alone in her room with the curtains drawn. Maximilian, on the other hand, turns to music, as he always has in his moments of melancholy.

The *Royal Trumpeters* again becomes a string quartet. The costumes from Europe are brought out of storage, the wigs combed.

In the most secluded chamber of Chapultepeca Castle, Maximilian sequesters himself with the musicians and spends hours listening to them. While they play, he sits by the window in an armchair given to him by Napoleon III and gazes out at the park where Aztec king Montezuma II hunted. They play only Mozart, whose *Laudate Dominum* is the first piece played at every session.

Benito Juarez, Maximilian's sworn enemy, returns to Mexico, and marches with a large army on Ciudad de México. Charlotte sails for Europe, hoping to find help.

Kruno and Violeta devise an escape plan. She makes a sketch for where and when to meet, how to leave the city, and which route to take to reach Puerto Ángela, a small port in the Oaxaca province where her parents live.

A few hours before the planned escape, soldiers come for Kruno. They put him in a coach with Maximilian's secretary, with their musical instruments, and the other three musicians. Maximilian has chosen the five of them as his only escort in the battle to come against Juarez. The two coaches and about one hundred horsemen slip furtively out of Chapultepe.

Maximilian and his small army set up camp at a place known as Querétaro. A week later, Juarez's army surrounds them. Kruno gives up all hope that he will ever escape.

Once again, the string quartet switches to serving as an ensemble of field musicians. Almost every day, always at different times, the four of them climb the hill above the village carrying their trumpets and drums. Once there, with all their strength they imitate the sounds of a false attack by a nonexistent army. Meanwhile, Maximilian watches the opposing forces through his telescope, enjoying their confusion.

But this isn't the only change Maximilian undergoes. Facing death, he grows more relaxed and amicable. The few Mexicans who have stayed by his side finally like him. He doesn't care about the title; he entertains them all and receives young women from the village in his tent.

At the beginning of the summer of 1867, Juarez's troops enter Querétaro. They capture Maximilian and some thirty soldiers and members of his escort. On June 19th, Maximilian and his last two loyal generals—Miramón and Mejía—face a firing squad.

On a hilltop, three high wooden posts are mounted. The two generals are bound to the outer posts, and Maximilian to the one in the middle. The eight-man firing squad faces them. The commander and the priest to their right, the string quartet to their left.

The quartet is Maximilian's last wish. In their Austrian costumes, wearing their wigs, they play the fourth movement of Mozart's B-flat major Divertimento, *Zweite Lodronische Nachtmusik*.

After its finale, Maximillian calls out: "Viva Mexico!" His words are followed by the command: "Fire!"

Kruno spends the next two weeks in prison. He waits for his turn to be executed.

But my grandmother Violeta has reached Querétaro prison. She bribes the guards, Kruno is released, and they set off for Puerto Ángelo.

The journey is long and arduous. Bounties are offered for Kruno and Maximilian's whole entourage. They have been sentenced to death, and anyone who kills one of them is promised a generous reward.

Violeta dresses him inconspicuously. Afraid he might be recognized by his pronunciation, she won't let him speak to others. He uses sign language to talk with her, as if he were a deaf-mute. When they are alone, Violeta tutors him in Spanish. She sings songs and explains the lyrics with mime.

During the journey, Violeta sings to earn a little money. She usually performs in villages, at fêtes and weddings. This is how she earns the money for Kruno's first guitar. From then on, to the end of their lives, as soon as she starts to sing, he accompanies her on the guitar.

They reach Huajuapan de León. It is the Day of the White Dove. A white dove is chosen, red ribbons tied to its feet, and then released. It flies up to the church steeple and circles around it.

Meanwhile, down on the square, pigeon breeders gather, each holding an ornate cage with a white pigeon.

The master of ceremonies opens one of the cages. The pigeon flies up and circles with the dove. If their beaks touch, it will fly back to its cage. Then the next cage is opened, and so on, cage by cage, until the right one appears—the one that flies a full circle with the dove without touching. After making several triumphant circles, the pigeon, followed by the dove, flies back to its cage. The master of ceremonies closes the cage, drapes it with a cloth, and pronounces the festivities open.

That night, my grandfather, Kruno Zanetti, proposes to my grandmother, Violeta de Caravaho. She says "Yes," and Grandpa composes the melody for *La Paloma Blanca* that night. A few days later, Grandma Violeta writes the lyrics, and the song is still sung today.

When they arrive in Puerto Ángelo, Kruno asks Violeta's father for her hand in marriage. Her father, Juan Carlos, gives his blessing three months later, when the new government amnesties all of Maximilian's subjects.

At their wedding, Violeta and Kruno perform *La Paloma Blanca* for the first time in public, in front of their four hundred guests. The date, engraved on the guitar we still have, is celebrated by the Zanetti family and all the fans of the song in Mexico and around the world, as the day the song is born.

My late mother, Blanka Zanetti, who married Lopez De Silva, is named after the song. My grandparents have eleven more children. They live in a small house on the outskirts of Puerto Ángelo by the sea, quietly, happily, peacefully. The children grow up, a few move to the city, others stay by the coast.

The only thing to disturb the harmony, is old Kruno's habit of disappearing from time to time. He sneaks out of the house at dawn, slips into the sea, and disappears, swimming off toward the horizon.

Only Grandma Violeta knows he is spending the day on a nearby peninsula dominated by the great Maria-Magdalena lighthouse. Kruno sits in its shade and spends hours talking with the birds.

Kruno Zanetti dies on September 1, 1941 at the age of ninety-six. Over one hundred Mariachi bands from all over Mexico come to the funeral. They sing *La Paloma Blanca*. Grandma Violeta dies that same night.

Signed: Lopez de Silva Zanetti
Notarized: July 1st, Puerto Ángel, province Oaxaca, Mexico
Notary: Claudio Estrada

Ciudad de México, 2002

I told this story to Ademir Kenović, Bosnian film director and producer, during our visit to Chapultapec Castle, which hosted an exhibition dedicated to Maximilian. A few years later, he tried to start a production based on the story, was granted project-development financing from the Vienna fund and the Media fund, but he got no further than that.

Larger Than Life

Someone or something magnificent, more interesting and better than usual.

Zagreb, 1992

Right before the elections, Croatian National Television broadcasts Mladen Kušec's documentary about Franjo Tuđman, President of the Republic. A ten-year-old boy is his guest. At the end of the broadcast, the president asks him: "And who are we to thank for our happiness and prosperity?" and the boy quips: "You, Mr. President!"

Zagreb, 1996

Tuđman invites a dozen prominent Croatian painters to the Brijuni Islands to paint his portrait from their "artistic perspectives."

Zagreb, 2010

I surprise the painter Zlatko Kauzlarić Atač when I show him that I have his triptych *Tito*. It had been commissioned by the Dubrovnik theater where it hung in the foyer until 1990. For the next few years it was stowed away in a basement, and then in 2006 it found its place on my kitchen wall.

It was given to me by Klica, my friend Tomislav Klička, a collector of modern Croatian art, who invested the funds needed to create *Lauba—House for People and Art (Kuća za ljude i umjetnost)*, one of the key cultural institutions in Zagreb. He gave me Atač's *Tito* as a present in celebration of the premiere of *The Border Post*. He called me and asked: "Are you home?" "Yes." "Good, I'm sending the boys over. If Serbs were able to furnish you with Tito's Blue Train, why would we be any worse. We have something for you, too!"

The Blue Train is a luxury train once used by Josip Broz Tito to travel through Yugoslavia. The distributors of *The Border Post* obtain it to promote the film: in the train, which was used for the first time after Tito's death to run between Belgrade and Novi Sad and back, they organize a press conference for our opening night in Belgrade.

So the boys from *Lauba* bring over the enormous triptych. Later I hear Klica had bought it from the architect, Nikola Filipović, who had been doing work for the Dubrovnik theater. They did not have the wherewithal to pay him, so they gave him Atač's *Tito* as compensation.

While I show the triptych to Atač, I ask if he knows that toward the end of the 1990s, painters also painted portraits of Tuđman. "Do you know who organized them?" Atač laughs and says: "I did!"

The Last Picture Show

The Last Picture Show (1971), *a black-and-white movie by Peter Bogdanovich, one of the cult films of the American New Wave.*

Zagreb, 1994

I am watching old people wander about the Dolac outdoor market. Quickly, to get there before the street sweepers do, or, even more so—not to be seen by an acquaintance—they are gathering what the sellers have discarded under the stalls: rotten bananas, blackened vegetables, overripe tomatoes...

While I watch them, I think of my grandfather. Of our last walk through Mirogoj cemetery on All Saints' Day in 1983.

Zagreb, Mirogoj, 1983

He was in great shape. We walked from grave to grave. He lit dozens of candles and talked about the people by whose graves we were passing: "This one... See Franc over there? He was with Marieta, over on the other side... See? Yes, that's the one. He had a fling with her in 1927, and her husband..." He talked about them as if they were still alive.

A few months later, Grandpa died. Dad died less than a month after him. "Good thing they didn't live to see this war," said my mother.

Certain that I am finished with moviemaking, I compose the story for my last movie, my farewell, in case it does happen. The title is *Old Folks*. Later, I turn it into a synopsis, some fifteen pages long and call it *The Last Bite* (*Stidak*), named after the last bite left on a plate, which everyone is ashamed to take.

"Quit pretending and eat it," as my great-grandmother Guga would say, passing it to me.

Zagreb, 1992

The story is about elderly but still spry pharmacist Edo who lives in a large downtown apartment. His wife died several years earlier, the children left the country and started their own lives long time ago, and he leads a solitary life, trying to stretch his pension which seems to be buying less and less each day.

His friends deal with similar troubles. Five of them—all university professors, engineers, lawyers—people his age, hiking buddies for the last fifty years, are facing the same hardships. They also used to live better, they are also frightened by the war that is roaring from their television screens and holds no promise for a better tomorrow.

In spite of everything, they still go for a hike every Sunday, to Sljeme or Japetić, mountains near Zagreb, they tell each other the same old stories over and over and complain about their health, they despise politicians, they complain about the money.

In the basement of Edo's building lives Matilda, a stout old woman. She has spent her life cleaning other people's apartments, washing other people's dishes, watching other people's children. For years she worked at Edo's, as the main cleaner in the Central Pharmacy lab on Republic Square. She never married and never revealed who the father of her son is. She raised the boy with care, led a modest life, and worked all day long. Ten years ago, her son emigrated to Germany. He married there, now he comes less often, but he sends his mother one hundred deutsche marks every month.

Amid the calamities that the war has brought, the money is a tiny source of happiness for Matilda. It has turned her, in comparison to the rest of them who live off their pensions, into a rich woman. And, like anyone of the nouveau riche, she wants it to be known.

Matilda and Edo have never been close. She is a "basement sweeper," and he, the "gentleman from the third floor." They respect each other. This relationship, their social distance, has never been disturbed.

And another important point: Matilda has Axi, an old poodle. One of the ilk described in the books as the most intelligent representative of the dog species, loyal to its master, sensitive to the elderly. In his dotage, at the age of eleven—his dog years being that times seven—Axi is just a tad older than Matilda and, as such, her ideal partner.

The mountaineering squad regularly meets at Edo's. There, in his kitchen, they trade helpful information: where groceries are on sale, where to hock the family silverware, antique furniture, or an old painting by a famous artist. They know exactly who goes to buy cheap bread, and when, and who has been promised onions at the market, which would, otherwise, be thrown away. Around noon, after a round of their favorite card game, preference, they make lunch together—vegetable stews and potato dishes. Meat is a rare addition.

The only thing that mars the idyllic atmosphere in the cozy kitchen is what goes on in the yard, and they have to see it whether they want to or not.

Almost every day around noon, Matilda comes out into the backyard, Axi after her. Softly whispering, she sets down a tin plate for him in the corner and on it a bone with a chunk of meat, or a few slices of salami.

At first, the old folks do their best to ignore the scene. They joke that the dog lives better than they do, laugh at themselves, and shrug it off. But this happens so often that it starts getting to them—the dog, the barking, the food, and the cleaning lady who seems to be doing this just to needle them.

And so, one day, while they watch the happy dog devour a chunk of ham, they reach the conclusion—without ever exchanging a word or a glance—that the only thing to put an end to their suffering is its death.

As if hypnotized, they roll up their sleeves. The approach is more than scientific. They bring in books, translate the relevant pages, consult friends and acquaintances.

But in spite of their energy and enthusiasm and the aphrodisiac grip of the group fixation on them, playing with death is harder than any of them cares to admit. Not a single one of them can kill a dog just like that.

They have trouble sleeping, they pace their unheated apartments for hours, they toss and turn in their beds, in the morning they promise they will not do it and yet, later that day they dive again into their murderous plans with undiluted zeal.

A week later, in the evening, three boys find Axi, poisoned, and they rush him to Matilda.

For two days and two nights, the backyard echoes with her sobs. No one objects to the noise, no one protests, no one shouts or bangs on her basement door.

On the third day, Matilda, in deep mourning, comes out to the backyard. With dignity, she carries a cardboard box with Axi in it.

On the third floor, in Edo's kitchen, standing by the same window where they made the decision to kill Axi, the same window out of which they threw the poison, the old folks watch the funeral. Their ashen faces display a shame they can barely face.

Matilda starts digging a hole next to her basement window.

Edo goes down and offers help. He doesn't have the courage to tell her the truth, but he wants her to know that he sympathizes and understands.

Matilda neither accepts nor refuses his help. Her eyes red from crying, she gazes at the cardboard box as Edo covers it with dirt and then shapes it into a mound.

Edo can't sleep that night. The next day, he goes to Matilda's and invites her up for dinner.

A bit after seven, Matilda rings his doorbell. The door is ajar, so Matilda comes into the front hall. Light and soft music come from the dining room.

The old folks are in suits, white shirts, with ties. Edo stands in the middle, holding a groomed poodle with a red bow around its neck.

When he hands it to Matilda, she bursts into tears. She hugs the poodle and, stroking it, walks out of the dining room like a moonwalker, leaves the apartment and, laughing and crying, goes to her basement apartment.

They dine without Matilda. They know they have done the easy part of the task, and that the confession—and they have agreed to confess everything—will be much more painful. But no one wants to talk about this at the time. They have done something good and this is more than enough for a start. If anything, it is a good excuse for them to have a few *gemischts*, which they had been denied by their doctors and poverty.

That evening, while they talk about Matilda and the white poodle they found out on the street and groomed, they come upon an idea which by the next morning seems absolutely plausible, and which is supposed to solve the poverty which has begun taking its toll on their dignity. Innumerable purebred dogs are wandering the streets of Zagreb, abandoned by their impoverished owners.

The old folks spend more than a week carefully observing the dogs. They take notes, memorize things, come to agreements. Once again, they consult the literature, dictionaries, and encyclopedias. They come and go. They phone each other enthusiastically to share what they have found or learned. All the information points to the fact that they should focus on poodles.

Gathering them takes more than two weeks. The most difficult part is to separate the ones they want from the ones they do not. Everything else is easier. Hungry poodles will let themselves be lured by a few pieces of dry bread.

And so it is that seven select poodles are brought to Edo's apartment. The dogs are dirty, smelly, neglected. They try to wash them, but the dogs, starving and already feral, will not let themselves be ruled so easily. The old folks run out of steam. Realizing that they may have bitten off more than they can chew, they agree that the dogs should be put back out onto the streets. The old folks silently disperse to their homes.

Edo is left alone. The poodles scamper around, jump, pull, tear and knock things over. He watches them, helpless. He is not strong enough to stop them or to chase them away. Exhausted, he falls asleep in his armchair.

After the dogs wake him at the crack of dawn, Edo rings Matilda's doorbell. She answers the door in high spirits, rejuvenated, her new pet in her arms. Edo asks for her help. Worried by his demeanor, she agrees.

Never leaving Axi II out of sight, she quickly brings the dogs to order. She washes them, powders them, feeds them, yells at them, and pets them. And they—seven feral dogs—obey her. The old folks, who are making lunch in the kitchen, watch her in amazement, and stop saying they will leave the dogs on the streets.

From that day forth, Matilda comes to Edo more often. She does not go back to her basement apartment till night. The old folks try offering her money for her work, but she refuses, insulted.

They stop mentioning it. Slowly, they come to love her and treat her as an equal, which she enjoys. With a modest lunch and a trip to Medvedgrad, Matilda officially becomes their partner in their promising business.

She never buys the idea that the "business" is really promising; she avoids thinking about it but enjoys her new situation. Edo's attitude to her has changed too, and this is what has always mattered most to her. He is more caring, has patience for her long stories, does not show off, is not sarcastic.

While Matilda takes care of the dogs, Edo and his friends write exhilarating ads about the noble backgrounds of the dogs they are selling, post them up on gates and lampposts, put them into mailboxes, call people who they think might buy a dog.

Two weeks later, after they have spent almost all their savings, not a single person has expressed an interest in buying a dog. Matilda consoles them. They are not the only ones afflicted by poverty, although they find getting used to it so painful.

Finally, without ado, they agreed to take the dogs out into the street to release them. They have neither the money nor the stamina to care for them. Besides, they cannot watch Matilda waste her savings on them. While the rest of them talk, Matilda watches Edo. The look in her eyes is clear: if he lets the dogs back out into the street, she will leave.

The old folks go home.

Only Edo, Matilda, Axi II, and the seven priceless poodles are left in Edo's apartment. When, after long deliberation, Edo nods and saves the dogs' lives, Matilda kisses him on both cheeks.

That night, Edo asks Matilda to spend the night in his apartment. He prepares the guest room, warms it up, puts clean sheets on the bed. It makes no sense for the old woman to go back to her basement apartment only to come back in the morning. "Unnecessary walking!" says Edo, worried about her health. Matilda agrees.

The next day, in Edo's kitchen, Matilda makes a modest dinner for the two of them and the dogs. After dinner, Matilda goes to the guest room. Edo washes up.

An hour later, Edo knocks at the guest room door. Matilda is not sleeping. She is sitting in the armchair, Axi II in her arms, expecting Edo.

Edo enters and stands next to her. It is more than obvious that he is about to say something important and is summoning the courage.

Zagreb, 2005
Koraljka Meštrović writes two versions of the script based on the story, but I have obviously never managed to summon the courage to film my truly last movie.

New York, 2015
From: Olga Grlic
To: Rajko Grlic

i've read old folks again and if you don't make that movie i'll be sorely insulted and the history of telling stories about Zagreb in movies will never forgive you. just saying.

Zagreb, 2016
Some elements of this story are incorporated in the script of *The Constitution*.

The Last Picture Show II

Zagreb, 2006
I'm at Filip Trade, waiting for Klica—Tomislav Kličko—to finish a meeting at his company so we can go. Meanwhile, I'm talking to his doorman, a man from Hrtkovci in Vojvodina (Serbia). A quiet, kind, and somewhat anxious man brought to Zagreb by the war.

Klica comes, we go to the car. The doorman waves as we go.

In the car, Klica talks about the doormen he employed during the 1990s. All of them had been officers in the Yugoslav People's Army, unmoored, impoverished, and ready to take any job to feed their families.

Zagreb, 1993
One of them was particularly vigilant. He would record anyone who came, even the ones who only stopped by outside the company's offices. People

and cars. He conducted routine patrols of the property every fifteen minutes and wrote detailed reports. One day, he was diagnosed with cancer and committed suicide a few weeks later. He had concluded that the treatment would have been too costly and probably pointless, and would have been financially too great a burden for the family. He decided to spare both himself and them the trouble.

Legal Movies

Movies about laws, lawyers, and trials. Some of the most famous are: 12 Angry Men *(1957),* Anatomy of a Murder *(1959),* Judgment in Nurnberg *(1961),* To Kill a Mockingbird *(1962),* A Man for All Seasons *(1966),* Philadelphia *(1993),* Erin Brockovich *(2000),* The People vs. Fritz Bauer *(Der Staat gegen Fritz Bauer, 2015), and one of my favorites,* The Verdict *(1982), directed by Sidney Lumet, starring Paul Newman.*

Zagreb, 1991

Čedo Prodanović, by nationality a Serb, was fired, or, rather thrown out of the prosecutor's office for having the wrong sort of blood. To make a living, he opened a law office. While he was not allowed to in Zagreb, he was in Sisak, still someone planted a bomb under his car.

We walk along Bogovićeva Street. Zagreb is a small town. The two of us know most of the people we pass. Some of them have not been greeting us for the last few months. One of these is Vladimir Šeks, who has been playing a very important role in the party in power, the Croatian Democratic Union. He and Čedo know each other. As soon as he sees Čedo, Šeks turns toward a store window and stares fixedly at one spot. It is so obvious that we start laughing. Čedo laughs: "Just you wait, all of them will be asking me to represent them one of these days."

Zagreb, 2001

Less than ten years later, literally everyone, from the generals accused of war crimes in The Hague to the Croatian bankers and prime ministers accused of theft, all of them call and beg him to represent them in their major trials.

Zagreb, 2005

"To do what he does, one has to have balls. Big balls," says lawyer Vladimir Rubčić of Čedo. Like Čedo he was a Zagreb city kid. He is also a great music lover—moreover he was the front man of the famous *Bijele strijele* band.

Both of them are the best Zagreb exemplars, yet completely different people.

"In times like these, it's best to be anonymous!" says Vladimir.

Lifetime Achievement Award

An award given for one's overall contribution to a science or artistic field.

Denver, 1993

The Denver International Film Festival and the city of Denver gave me an award "In Recognition of Outstanding Achievement in the Art of Film."

Witold-K Kaczanowski, a Polish painter who lived in Denver, took me to the Rocky Mountains. We spent all day driving through red rock outcroppings, visiting abandoned mines, and taking refreshments in elegant hotels. Along the way, Witold-K regaled me with stories about how he smuggled dissident texts by Polish and Russian writers to the West, about his wanderings across the United States, about his friendship with Picasso, for whom he worked for a few years and who painted his portrait.

Finally, on our way back into Denver, he talked about his father, a Polish surgeon, who hid Jews in his hospital during World War II. He spoke volubly and in detail about most things. But about his father he spoke only briefly, in a low voice.

That same evening, fearing I would forget, I noted down a few lines.

Warsaw, 1943

On a hill above the Vistula River, about twenty kilometers from Warsaw, is a castle that belonged to the Kociolek family. In the early twentieth century, the castle was given to the Faculty of Medicine in Warsaw, renovated, and made into the *Marianist Brothers Sanatorium*, the most famous psychiatric hospital in Poland.

The war rages. Russian and German troops traverse Poland several times.

The manager of the hospital is Dr. Witold Zdena, a forty-two-year-old widower. With his son Andrzej he lives in a villa next to the castle.

The hospital suffers from a shortage of food and medicine. Dr. Zdena often spends sixteen hours a day at work to keep the hospital going. Only a few doctors and nurses come to work regularly. There are fewer patients, too. Only the most difficult cases, about a hundred of them, have been retained.

Once a week, a German military inspection team comes to the hospital. They examine the rooms, the doctors, the nurses, and each of the patients with meticulous care. They are on the lookout for fugitive Jews from the Warsaw ghetto and members of the resistance.

The head nurse, Jadviga Kutorowski, makes sure they are prepared. She even organizes an information network right outside the castle. Several local women inform her of the German troops passing by, and she pays for the information with food and money. This is how the hospital knows when the Germans are coming, five to seven minutes before they arrive.

Once they know of an imminent arrival, they bring a patient to the operating theater, followed by nurses and assistant doctors. The operation begins after just a few minutes. Each patient is chosen carefully in advance, only among those with incurable conditions. While Dr. Zdena operates, the head nurse, Jadviga, takes the Germans through the hospital, showing them the documents and the people.

The sound signal marking the beginning of surgery is also a signal for complete silence beneath the operating theater. And there, in the basement, in just a few rooms, a dozen Jewish families have been living for almost two years.

All the entryways to the basement have been walled up and carefully camouflaged. The only possible entrance leads through the operating hall and is located directly under the operating table.

Dr. Zdena first brought the family of his late wife to the basement, and then the families of their friends.

The only people who know about the Jews apart from him are head nurse Jadviga and the eldest staff member, Czesław Kiszczak.

Czesław is the hospital undertaker, always in search of the deceased. He is the first one to enter the rooms in the morning. He checks the beds and wakes the patients. They shout at him, threaten, and curse. Ignoring them, Czesław wraps the deceased in sheets, places them onto his squeaking gurney and takes the bodies out into the hospital graveyard. And while the people upstairs call him the "angel of death," he is joyfully welcomed downstairs because he brings food, medicine, looks after them, and is their only link to the outside world.

That spring, two badly wounded German officers are brought to the hospital by members of the resistance, and they want Dr. Zdena to save the Germans' lives and hide them for the time being, so that later they can be traded for the resistance's brothers-in-arms. Once they are operated on, Czesław places them in the basement.

And this is where the story should start.

Warsaw, 1944–45

And it would be best told by Czesław, the hospital undertaker who visits the basement several times a day. From his perspective, from a slightly skewed point of view, we could follow a love story between Greti Klingerberg, a nineteen-year-old Jewish girl and Alexander Tong, a twenty-two-year-old German officer. A story which happens in the most improbable of all places, in times of fear and in the space of just one year—from the moment they first set eyes on each other to her pregnancy, her grandmother's attempt to kill the child while it is still in the womb, and the birth of the baby girl, Saphira.

With Czesław's help, we would find out what really happened, how the two people come to like each other in that cramped place filled with intolerance, even hatred, the bond that forms, the reactions of the others, of her people, of his people, of how they find a way to have privacy and make love.

And how eventually, at the end of 1944, Russians liberate them, and, the very same day, take Tong away. That is when the hospital undertaker Czesław might try to buy out Tong and save his relationship with Greti, and finally reveal his own identity and his real reasons for telling the story.

Location

The place where a movie is shot. The choice of location is very important because every location tells us a lot, directly or indirectly, about the person who we see in it, whether they live there or are just passing through.

Belgrade, 1971

For *All Eat Each Other*, my first short film after graduation, I won the Best Yugoslav Short Film Award in 1971. This was my first professional award and the first cash prize I had ever won. Absolutely certain, although I cannot remember why, that I would never win another prize unless I immediately spent the money, I booked one half of a famous club and invited some fifty people over for dinner: all my colleagues from Prague, the actor Branko Cvejić and his wife, Otašević the painter, writers Kovač, Kiš...

Later that night, when the dinner was almost over, I headed for the men's room. A young man came after me and, mixing Italian and Serbian, asked me if I am the one who reserved half of the club. We pissed and talked. His name was Paolo Magelli, he was an Italian, and had come from

Romania where he was directing a play. That night, he had his first opening night in Yugoslavia at the club of the Serbian National Theater. They had booked the other half of the club.

Zagreb, 1985

Someone is at the door. I open it and see a man who introduces himself as Duško Ljuština, the producer of the World University Games opening ceremony. He has come to tell me that I am the one who will direct the ceremony. I look at him in shock, and invite him in.

I explain that I do not do that sort of thing, but I have just the man for him. His name is Paolo Magelli, he is a communist from Tuscany, a Catholic. I have seen a dozen of his productions throughout Yugoslavia. He is a bit crazy but has a good hand. He is a great director.

Zagreb, 1986

Paolo arrives, directs the World University Games opening ceremony, and settles in Zagreb.

Ever since then, Zagreb has been the base he leaves to live his life in various European and South American countries, and the place he always comes back to. It is a place where, he claims, he feels best, although he is not sure why.

Zagreb, 2017

We are at lunch at Draško's club and think we might, at least temporarily, renew the tradition of cooking together that Ana began long time ago.

We go to the Dolac open market. We find Caesar's mushrooms and porcinis.

I make hors d'oeuvre, and he, since he is Italian after all, cooks the main course—Tuscan black pasta with mushrooms, pine nuts, and ricotta. Jadranka and Čedo, who join us for lunch, and Ana and I, unanimously agree that this is the best pasta we have ever had. He laughs. He is feeling good. He is a director. He likes to hear public declarations of love.

Yes, a fine director—but even a finer cook.

Lost in Translation

A Sofia Coppola movie (2003), with Bill Murray as the lead. It takes place in a Tokyo hotel where an American actor spends sleepless nights at the hotel bar.

Tokyo, 1987

Many years before the movie was made, I stayed in the same hotel and, due to the time difference, spent sleepless nights at the very same bar.

Athens, Ohio, 2003

The movie takes me back to that floating feeling of murky sleep deprivation. I do not know if I have ever felt such painful, almost physical compassion for the protagonist of a movie and his torment.

Zagreb, 1970

Editing the philosophy journal *Praxis*, my father and Gajo Petrović had phone conversations that went on all night long. In German. "Since they've tapped our phones, they should at least have to take on a translator," as Dad used to say.

Zagreb, 2012

At Draško's club, I'm at dinner with a big crowd. We talk about translations. I share the anecdote about the conversations in German. A woman at the table smiles and says: "We didn't have to take on part-time translators. Because of the two of them and others like them we had a staff of full-timers."

Lost Movies

Due to the brief lifespan of film emulsion, many movies have been lost forever.

The figures I find on the internet illustrate the extent of the tragedy: the *Martin Scorsese Film Foundation* claims that over 50 percent of the American movies made before 1950, and 90 percent made before 1929 have been lost forever. *Deutsche Kinemathek* estimates that 80–90 percent of the silent movies are gone. Their archive records the loss of 3,500 movies. A study by *the Library of Congress* in Washington DC, confirms that 75 percent of silent movies no longer exist.

The situation in Croatian cinema is no better. Most of what was made between 1945 and 1990 has, without any legal right, fallen into the hands of the mafia that got their hands on production houses Jadran Film and Croatia Film during the war. From time to time, masters of digital postproduction Robert Vidić and Tomislav Vujnović reconstruct and digitize a few films for the Croatian Film Archives, but for the most part, Croatian film production is simply disappearing.

And no one seems to care that this means the disappearance of an important segment of Croatian culture. That traces of existence are being erased, documents of times that could one day help reconstruct life in the region.

And once all the documents are gone, falsifying the past will be easier. That is why this recklessness, like any other, follows its own logic.

Zagreb, 1998

I saw the first roll of my movie *If It Kills Me* (1974). It is almost completely discolored, and the image is several times lighter than the original. I am afraid the negative is not in a much better state either.

Where have I been, what have I done?

But the imperfection of the emulsion is not the only reason movies disappear.

Belgrade, 2001

The organizers of my Belgrade retrospective tried to find *The Return*, my thirty-minute thesis movie with Božidar Boban in the lead. I made it in 1970 for FAMU, produced by Zora Korać and Television Belgrade. After a long search, they found two of the three rolls—the first and last. The middle part of the movie is lost.

Zagreb, 2005

Croatian Radio Television was coproducer of *Charuga*. Alongside the fiction film, we also made a sixty-minute documentary. The editing was almost done when Television interrupted the project.

Some ten years later, I start searching for the documentary. It is not in the Croatian National Television archives. The archivists "console" me with the story that in 2000, after the Croatian Democratic Union lost the elections, the television crew drove away a full load of documentaries in their truck. They believe my documentary was also on that truck.

The people who appeared in that movie died a long time ago. The village where Čaruga's family lived, like many of the other nearby villages, was ransacked in the war. The documentary would have been the proof of their existence, archaeological evidence of what was destroyed. Maybe that is exactly why it disappeared, maybe that insanity, too, follows its own logic.

Love Letters

The title of many movies. The most famous is one by William Dieterle, 1945, with Jennifer Jones and Joseph Cotten. In Croatia, Zvonimir Berković made a movie with a similar title: Love Letters with Intent *(1985).*

Požega, 1992

I am traveling with Ana in our Renault 4 from Zagreb to Požega, and the drive takes us seven hours. Before the war, this used to take us an hour and twenty minutes. The final stretch of the detour runs through villages which have been destroyed. In the only village still standing, there are huge Croatian flags waving.

Night falls on Jozefina's terrace. Explosions echo from downtown. Ana's brother Danko checks his watch. He notices they are a bit early tonight. Serbian houses are being blown up in Požega. By strangers that the locals do not know. The Croats from Požega have protested. Their houses are being damaged too. But the protests do not help. Nobody knows who the people are or who is sending them, but everyone knows how much it costs. To have someone's house blown up costs two to three hundred deutsche marks, depending on the size.

Slavonia, 1991

The war in the former Yugoslavia has turned a part of northern Croatia into a landscape of death. Many villages have been burned to the ground. At the same time, on the slopes of Papuk Mountain the village of Kula with some twenty houses, with a school, a church, and shops is intact.

Kula, Hrtkovci, 1986–90

This is a story about that village, and about Hrtkovci, a similar village on the other side of the front. In these two villages, two fourteen-year-olds—Vera in Kula in Croatia, and Tomislav in Hrtkovci in Serbia. The two villages are less than a two-hour bus ride apart.

They meet a few years earlier at a school competition of video amateurs. Since then, they visit each other frequently. Exchanging films, showing each other their work. Then the war breaks out and interrupts any contact. The phones stop working, there is a barrier across the road. The front runs between their two villages.

Some of the inhabitants of Vera's village are Serbs. Her family are Serbs as well. They have been living in Croatia since forever.

Some of the inhabitants of Tomislav's village in Serbia are Croats. They have also been living there for centuries.

At the beginning of the war, a scene takes place in both villages that is almost identical.

Kula, Hrtkovci, 1991

One night, a house is torched in Tomislav's village. The followers of Vojislav Šešelj (a far right- wing Serbian politician) go from house to house and, wearing Chetnik uniforms, smash windows and threaten the Croatian inhabitants that they will slit their throats unless they move away.

At the same time, the first house is blown up in Vera's village. Anonymous perpetrators, under the protection of the Minster of Defense Gojko Šušak, walk from house to house, telling all the Serbs to move out immediately.

Both villages are gripped by fear. People stop going out into the fields, they stop working. Everyone stays home and keeps silent. They know they have to leave but they do not know where to go. They watch television for days, staring at the scenes of slaughter and destruction, images which display more or less the same scenes on both sides of the front lines but with different texts, calling for hatred and revenge.

Watching her frightened parents, Vera decides to do something.

She takes her camera and has her father walk around the house and describe it in detail, room by room. They repeat the same thing in the stable. Her father shows the tractor, the three cows, the pigs, then he opens the barn, the smokehouse, and finally walks over the rich, fertile land. She films everything.

That same night, Vera leaves the house.

Harkány, 1991

She hitchhikes in a truck full of refugees and with them crosses the Hungarian border. With very little money and no knowledge of Hungarian, she makes her way to the Serbian border. There, she uses what money she has left to have a taxi driver put her in the trunk of his old Ford and drive her across. Two days and two nights later, she reaches Tomislav's village.

Hrtkovci, 1991

Vera's video started moving from house to house. The villagers watch it without a word. Tomislav has his father do the same thing. He also walks around his property describing everything. It is hard for him, but he is beginning to realize he has no choice.

In those few days, Vera and Tomislav grow closer. And too serious for their age.

Kula, 1991

Vera goes home along the same route, experiences the same troubles. Her parents are in a panic. She starts taking Tomislav's footage from house to house to show people. Folks in her village are equally distrustful, watching an unknown man show his property. Soon, another man asks Vera to make a movie of his house.

Kula, Hrtkovci, 1991

The footage started traveling across Hungary. With each footage of a house and estate, Vera and Tomislav send their messages. Bit by bit, the video-friendship starts turning into teenage video- love.

Having seen hours of the video material, one man spots a house much like his own. He sends a video message that he is ready for an exchange.

The surrounding villages are being torn down, people banished. War drums pound louder and louder. Less than a week later, all the houses have found adequate replacements.

The final video that sets off across Hungary also carries a suggestion about the exchange. The basic rule will be to leave everything as-is in the houses. Nothing should be brought along. Only documents and photos albums.

The departure is wrenching on both sides.

Harkány, 1992

They met up at dawn at the train station of a Hungarian town. For a while, the people eye each other. Suspicious and frightened, holding only small bags, they finally come closer. All of them have seen their footage many times and know exactly which face they are looking for. Hardly saying a word, one by one they exchange keys and set off with their families into the unknown.

The only people left at the train station are Tomislav and Vera. With their bags full of footage. Looking at each other, holding hands, they do not know where they can go.

Athens, Ohio, New York, London, 1994–95

Several scriptwriters and producers consider turning the story into a script. I am not too happy with any of the versions because right from the start I think the story should be a "mocumentary," a fake documentary.

The movie will be made only of the video material the two of them shot. Sadly, no one is interested.

Lunatic Asylum Movies

Movies which take place, in part or entirely, in a mental institution. The most famous are The Three Faces of Eve *(1957),* One Flew over the Cuckoo's Nest *(1976),* Frances *(1982),* 12 Monkeys *(1995),* Shutter Island *(2010) . . .*

The Ridges, officially the Athens Lunatic Asylum, was a mental hospital which operated in Athens, Ohio from 1874 until 1993. During its operation the hospital provided services to a variety of patients including Civil War veterans, children, and the criminally insane. It is perhaps best known as a site of the infamous lobotomy procedure, as well as various supposed paranormal sightings—says the English-language Wikipedia.

Athens, Ohio, 1996

In the abandoned hospital, one of only four or five such hospitals in the United States, we took about three thousand photographs that were used for staging the virtual interior of a film school in the multimedia project *How to Make Your Movie—An Interactive Film School*.

Athens, Ohio, 2002

While I was making a feature-length omnibus about the institution with my students, I heard hundreds of stories about patients and doctors who left their lives in the massive Victorian red brick buildings.
The story of Billy Milligan was the most interesting one.

Columbus, 1977

At the age of twenty-three, Billy abducts and rapes three students on the Ohio State University campus. He is captured and, during the trial, in the courtroom, he "turns" into a woman. Suddenly, he starts speaking in a high-pitched voice, with a pronounced Southern accent, he starts walking like a woman, and claims that he, as a woman, would never rape a woman. The judge is sure he is faking it and orders a psychiatric assessment.
The psychiatrists reach the conclusion that Billy suffers from dissociative identity disorder and he is acquitted. This was the first such case in the history of the American judiciary.
"Dissociative identity disorder (DID) is a rare condition in which two or more distinct identities, or personality states, are present in—and

alternately take control of—an individual" (Psychology Today website, https://www.psychologytoday.com/us/conditions/dissociative-identity-disorder-multiple-personality-disorder#:~:text=Definition,as%20an%20experience%20of%20possession).

Athens, Ohio, 1978

Instead of being sent to prison, Billy is referred to Athens Lunatic Asylum for treatment, where he spends more than ten years. First, he is held for five years in an isolated and closely monitored space, and the remaining time in an open section which he can leave during the day.

After several years of close inspection, doctors find that Billy has twenty-four distinct personalities. Out of these, four are women, six are migrants. When Billy, who has never left Ohio and never met a foreigner, enters one of the immigrant characters, he immediately starts speaking English with a strong German, Russian, or Polish accent.

Over the ten years Billy is in Athens, he paints as an amateur. Finally, he produces a painting in which he portrays all twenty-four of his personalities, face by face.

Athens, Ohio, 2001

I saw the painting, and I saw an amateur video made by a local man. It shows Billy who, while standing by the town swimming pool in his swimming trunks, "turns into" a woman in a matter of seconds. His breasts grow slightly, his movements and gestures all of a sudden have nothing to do with the person who was standing there just a few seconds earlier. I have read a book about him written by a local professor and heard that Hollywood has been planning to turn this into a film for decades.

What I have always found the most interesting, though, is one issue the book never tackles, something we are told by his doctor's wife—exactly how one of the personalities takes the place of a previous one, how he jumps from one to the next. It happens when one personality cannot tolerate the pressure anymore and uses another personality as an escape route. While he is in any of those twenty-four personalities, he behaves according to the personality's ethical standards. While he is inside a personality, he represents no hazard to his surroundings. He is dangerous when he is in-between, in transition. No one knows—this has never been established—how long the "black hole" lasts: two seconds or a few minutes. While it lasts, he does not respect rules or social norms, there are no scruples, and he feels absolutely free to do anything, even commit murder.

A film about Billy should be about that space in-between, the "black hole" in time, and the uncertainty it holds.

Columbus, 2014

The *Columbus Dispatch* reports that at the age of fifty-nine, patient Billy Milligan has died at an almshouse.

Los Angeles, 2015

The Hollywood Reporter publishes an article titled "Leonardo DiCaprio and New Regency Moving Ahead with *The Crowded Room*."

  "Leonardo DiCaprio is getting closer to playing a role he's eyed for nearly 20 years—that of Billy Milligan, who was the first person to successfully use multiple personality disorder as a defense in a court of law . . ."

Magic Hour

The time of day just after sunrise or before sunset, when there is a special warmth to the light. In movies, this is called the magic hour although in reality it lasts for only a few minutes.

Prague, 1970

On weekends, Prague would literally fill with East German tourists armed with *Zenit* and *Praktika* still cameras. This unpleasant phenomenon gave rise to a game called "hop-to-picture," invented by FAMU students.

The point was to photobomb all the pictures of an East German tourist who was on a three-day trip to Prague with his family. So, once the tourist went home and developed the film in a basement lab on the outskirts of Leipzig, he would realize that all the family photos he had taken included a complete stranger.

But, we doubted right from the start that such a sublime aim was truly attainable; yet since we still wanted a winner, we agreed on a precise score list for photobombing. The only thing I remember is that the highest score was given for appearing in a photograph of a child in a stroller. This virtually impossible but technically doable accomplishment was worth fifty points.

The game was based on the honor system. And it was played mostly on Sundays, when tourists roamed Malá Strana and Hradčany. On Monday, the players reported on the pictures they had bombed, which would then be calculated in points, so we could know who was ahead.

Two students of dramaturgy finessed the game to perfection. They watched a French film crew preparing a scene that, if you are really lucky, may only be possible to film once a year, for no more than ten minutes.

On that day, the sun shines at a particular moment between two baroque palaces at the top of Neruda Street. This was a fiction film, a nineteenth-century romance. Once the "magic hour" set in, the director called out "action!" The FAMU duo let the actors begin, they waited for the sun to move into exactly the right position, then calmly walked into the frame, turned to the camera, and waved.

This barbaric act won them victory and the "hop-to-picture" game played by the FAMU students ended once and for all. The East German tourists could finally breathe easy.

Master Class

Merriam-Webster Dictionary states: "a seminar for advanced music students conducted by a master musician." A Croatian dictionary defines the word "master" as: a skilled craft worker; a renowned artist.

Prague, 1966

I enroll in Fiction Film Directing at FAMU, in the class of professor Elmar Klos.

Seven of us from Yugoslavia are at FAMU at that point: five in the department of Directing Fiction, one in Directing the Documentary, and one cameraman. Every single one of us is an ambitious kid hungry for life; in love with film and confused about the sexual freedoms and political non-freedoms that mark these new surroundings. Prague in the 1960s. The culture of everyday life runs deeper and is more firmly rooted than is the one where we come from, while socialism is more grim and rigid than it is where we have grown up.

After a few weeks, I come to understand that the similarity between the Croatian and Czech language is just an illusion. I listen to a lecture by Milan Kundera and can barely understand a word.

I write my scripts for student exercises in Croatian and have them translated by Jessica Horváthova. Klos never comments on them. He talks about all the other scripts but mine. Are they bad? Is it the translation? Eventually, I summon the courage and ask him why he keeps skipping me. "Because you placed as a second-year student and this isn't your assignment," says Klos.

This is how I find out that I scored so high on the entrance exam, which I took with the help of a translator, that I am a second-year student. Someone may have tried to explain this to me earlier, but I had not understood.

On Jenstenska Street there is a film studio in the Roxa building; it used to be a Jewish movie house and now is the FAMU cinema as well as a studio for making films. I am given three days there to shoot a short fiction film, my first second-year exercise. This is going to be my first time of working with a big camera, with 35 mm film, my first time with sound sync, actors, a real studio, and a professional crew.

I arrive an hour before anyone else. I have no idea what to tell the crew. How am I going to manage such a shoot? Everything I have ever filmed, I had done with two friends, possibly three. Klos tells me he will come half an hour earlier to explain the technical details.

I am sitting in the production room, smoking cigarette after cigarette. Klos arrives. He is angry to see me smoking. He does not take off his hat or set his bag aside. He is worried about how I will direct in a studio where, like in any other studio, smoking is banned. I will be forced to interrupt the shooting and leave every now and then. Actors will lose their continuity, the shooting will suffer. He asks me to stop smoking and walks out. Not a word about what I am hoping he will show me, the things he will teach me. I am absolutely panic-stricken.

New York, 1993

I teach a Directors Master Class at New York University in a film studio close to Washington Square. It is a good studio, well-equipped. The only problem is that, like in any other studio, smoking is not allowed.

At a faculty meeting, I ask for permission to smoke. The very idea of making such a request is tantamount to blasphemy at NYU. But, it passes, with a large majority. The next day there is a large ashtray waiting for me at the studio. The students are ecstatic. Now they, too, can smoke. I look at the ashtray, somewhat embarrassed. I think of Klos.

A few weeks later, on New Year's Day, I quit smoking.

Mexico City, 2002

I hold out for almost seven years. Until the director's workshop which I run at the Mexican Film Academy. There, after roasted duck with red cabbage, in an excellent Polish restaurant, Ademir Kenović persuades me to try a fresh Cohiba, one of those *magicos a petit robusto* that just arrived from Cuba through private channels, to which one simply cannot say no.

Prague, 1971

Klos's first "lecture" is about smoking and his last is about women. Between these two concerns, these two points in time, imperceptibly led by his help, clarity and wisdom, "I finally became a man"—as Bubuleja, Bane Bumbar's father would say in *The Reckless Years*, the popular television series.

When Lordan and I graduate, we invite Klos out to a farewell lunch at *Valdštejnská zahrada*.

Toward the end of lunch, his voice shifts. We know that what is to come will be the professor's final words to his students. First, he says we are about to leave to live our own lives and make our own movies, and these lives and these movies will be completely beyond his control. And this, in his opinion, this is good for us. He has just one small request which has nothing to do with our future lives and future movies. He begs us not to fall in love with our actresses, not to sleep with them. These relationships can be extremely complicated and might destroy the movie. This is all he wants to tell us now that we are leaving.

In order to understand how hard saying this must have been for him, one would have to have known Klos. He was more prim and proper than anyone I have ever met. Venomous tongues claim he never even saw his own wife naked. Once, when Goran Marković and I showed him an unfinished version of our "porno movie" *L. V. Kuleshov*, which later won us the *Grand Phallus of Dušan Vukotić* award at the GEFF festival, Klos was more than nervous during the screening. We had learned by then, that when he didn't like what he was watching, he would tap his finger on the chair in front of him. And during that entire screening, he never stopped tapping. At the end, he walked out—a pained smile on his face and not a word uttered.

And yet another thing which may or may not have something to do with the two "lectures" by Klos: in Prague, on Kampa Island, on a wall across from the house where Alex Koenigsmark was living, there was sprawled a graffiti: "Woman is woman, but a cigarette, now that's smoking!"

Prague, 1968

The last movie Klos and Kadár make is the first American movie they make in MGM production: *Adrift*, based on the Lajos Zilahy novel *Something Is in the Water*, with Milena Dravić and Rade Marković as the leads.

I read the script while it is still in the making, I am even present at one of their scriptwriting sessions. I strongly believe that, alongside Carrière's script, *The Tin Drum*, based on Grass's eponymous novel, this is the best script I have ever read. Klos and Kadár work together, but the script is Klos's domain. He is the grand master of story structure. Kadár directs and Klos edits. This how they had been collaborating for seventeen years: Klos, a wise, elegant gentleman, and Kadár, his total opposite: a smoker, a drunkard, a colorful character.

They film it in a Slovakian village at dawn. The camera is atop the church steeple, and someone is supposed to cycle down along the street that led directly to the church. The directing assistants call for camera and sound.

Into his walkie-talkie Kadár says "Action," but then, from where the cyclist was supposed to come, a tank appears instead. First one, then another, then another. The assistants on the tower yell at the assistant who was to let the cyclist pass through: "You idiot, what are you doing? Move the tanks!" And he responds calmly: "I can't. Those are Russian tanks." It was August 21, 1968.

Several months later, they resume shooting. After that, Kadár emigrates to the States, and Klos finishes the editing. Just like any other film that was at some point touched by misfortune, this one never recovers.

Like my *Josephine*.

Prague, 1977

Sulejman Kapić asks me to go to Prague and find interesting unpublished stories and novels.

Ana and I land at Prague-Ruzyně. We take a cab. I talk to the driver and find out that eleven years earlier, when I came to Prague to study, he was the general secretary of the Czech Movie Workers Association, an important and powerful institution at the time. On the way to the hotel, he tells me that over the course of a few months at the beginning of the 1970s they were all "disposed" of. That's when Klos was kicked out of FAMU.

We visit Klos. Not a single word of complaint does he utter. He has withdrawn into the silence of his home with dignity. He earns a living in other ways. We talk about my *Bravo Maestro* script. He has prepared some notes.

Cannes, 1978

Bravo Maestro is in the competition. We are at Montfleury Hotel. I bump into Kadár. He is there to promote a movie he is about to film in the States that fall, with Muhammad Ali, in the leading role. He invites us over for breakfast the next day.

So, Ana and I have breakfast with Kadár and Ali, closely watched by Ali's bodyguards. The most vivid memory from the breakfast is that great Ali, whom I had always admired, was thoroughly entertained by Kadár's stories and kept laughing out loud, slapping him on the shoulder. And short, skinny Kadár, a cigarette forever in his mouth, sank deeper into the chair with every slap. At some point he would pull himself up, but then it would happen again.

Prague, 1979

With Goran Marković, I am at a dinner at Klos's. After dinner, we ask if we can go out onto the terrace for a little fresh air. Klos laughs. How can we still be smoking? We shrug, out we go, we light up. Less than ten minutes later, we come back in.

Klos is sitting there, his eyes full of tears. He's staring silently at a sheet of paper.

The mailman has just brought a telegram from Los Angeles, Kadár has died. A chain smoker, he died of lung cancer.

Prague, 1984

The Czechoslovakian Movie Workers Association organizes a "Prague Yugo-student's" retrospective. At the opening, we have a press conference at the Association, on Národna třídi, above *Laterna Magika*. The audience is packed. Klos sits in the last row. He was kicked out of Czechoslovakian cinema years before. Journalists pretend not to see him.

But we honor him. We openly state that they have ruined their cinematography, they have lost their reputation in the world, banished their finest directors or prevented them from working. We tell them all sorts things, and watch Klos savoring it all.

The journalists listen, take notes, the cameras roll. But both we and they know full well that not a single word of this will be published.

The next day, they organize a reception at the back of the then still great and powerful Barrandov Studios. They seem compelled to persuade us that they would like us to return to Prague and make our films there.

The Yugoslav Ambassador organizes an official reception that same day for us at his residence. He urges us to invite our friends. We explain that most of them are dissidents, but we meet with them every night so there is no need for him to get into any trouble because of them. But he insists that we invite not only Klos but our other friends as well.

We arrive with Klos. The Ambassador greets him. He thanks him for looking after us all those years. In the garden of the Ambassador's Residence, where lunch was served, the Czechoslovakian Minister of Culture, the president of the Association of Film Workers, and the director of Barrandov Studios are standing there, side by side. They extend their hands to shake Klos's but he doesn't even look at them. He walks by them in silence.

The friends we have invited are Alex Koenigsmark, Karel Steigerwald, Rudolph Ruzicka, Jessica Horváthova. At the very beginning, while the soup course is being served, Karel and Alex launch a series of political jokes. We cast furtive glances at the serious people across the table. They will not put up with this for long. Some ten minutes later, all three apologize and leave. "The protocol required that I invite them, but it's good that they've left. Now we can dine in peace," says the Ambassador.

Intervallo: I send an email to the last Ambassador of Yugoslavia to the United States.

From: Grlic, Rajko
To: Darko Silovic

Darko, would you happen to know, and you should, it's your bailiwick, what the first name was of Vlahović (I think he was Veljko Vlahović's brother) who was the SFRY Ambassador to Czechoslovakia, in Prague at the end of 1970s, beginning of 1980s?

Best, Rajko

From: Darko Silovic
To: Rajko Grlic

The man's name was Miso (read Misho), that's what we called him, but was it his full name? He was Veljko Vlahović's brother. I knew him well, I worked with him a lot. An insightful and even-tempered man. He wasn't at all indoctrinated. His wife, Vjera, was terrific, attractive, intelligent, educated. From a wealthy Montenegrin family, educated in France, England before the war. When Vladimir Velebit went to London during the war as Tito's envoy, Vjera was more than a secretary to him. Anything else?

Best, Darko

Prague, 1990

Klos phones me, begging me to come to Prague. He is organizing a review of his students' films. I'm editing *Charuga*. I try to bail. But judging by his voice, I understand I should say yes.

Almost all of us come. He is afraid he could die without saying goodbye. In short: he had a legitimate reason to summon us.

One of those days, we were in a tavern: Klos, Goran Marković, Aleksandar Petrović, and me. Petrović is a great director. I have huge respect for his movies, especially *Three* (*Tri*, 1965). My relationship with him is far better than his with my FAMU Belgrade colleagues. He praised me sometimes in the newspapers, and once even came to a premiere of mine in Paris. This is probably because I was far enough away, I was not trespassing on his territory. To my colleagues from Belgrade, he was inexplicably hostile.

He himself was a FAMU student. For two years. In 1948, after the Informbiro rift (when Yugoslavia broke with the Soviet Union), he interrupted his studies and returned to Yugoslavia. And he was not the only one. Cameraman Slavko Zalar (father to cameraman Živko Zalar), and cameraman Jure Ruljančić (father to cameraman Dragan Ruljančić) also had to interrupt their studies. Years later, though, their sons graduated with flying colors from the same school.

Goran and I comment on the two years of Petrović's studies and tell Klos: "Can you imagine the films he would be making had he studied, like us, for five years?" Klos laughs. Petrović does not laugh. He looks at us, unsure if we are pushing his buttons or if we mean it.

Prague, 1993

With Michael Miller, Associate Dean of the Tisch School of the Arts at NYU, I tour Eastern Europe. Tisch has decided to open film and theater departments in Warsaw, Krakow, Prague, and Budapest.

In Prague, I contact Klos. His wife tells me he is sleeping. He has not been well the past few days. He is not seeing anyone. She hopes he will feel better soon.

The same evening in the hotel, they give me a message from her. Klos would like to see me.

We talk for almost an hour. In the end, although weak and barely able to walk, he insists on seeing me to the gate. This is where we say goodbye.

New York, 1993

At dawn, I open the front door and pick up the *New York Times*. Under *Obituaries*, I read:

> Elmar Klos, 83, Czech Film Maker Who Won Oscar
> By ERIC PACE
> Published: August 2, 1993
>
> Elmar Klos, a Czech film director who shared an Academy Award for the 1965 film *The Shop on Main Street*, died on July 19 in Prague. He was 83.

Karlovy Vary, 2010

When accepting the Best Director Award, I dedicate it to my professor, Elmar Klos.

Maverick

Merriam-Webster Dictionary offers two definitions: "an unbranded young animal (especially a calf); an independent individual who does not go along with a group or party."

Branko Bauer was, above all else, a gentleman. He was mild-mannered, level-headed, dignified. He was the master of what is called the art of film directing, the art of storytelling. He had a gift which, like being a gentleman, is not common in our filmmaking world.

Another disadvantage was that very early he realized film is more than just a local toy. He despised petty nationalists and local geniuses. He worked with the best screenwriters, actors, and production crews in Yugoslavia. When they would not let him work in Zagreb, as happened more frequently and viciously than is generally thought, he would go somewhere else and there he would make his films.

With these three virtues that are little valued in Croatian film history, Branko Bauer has not even remotely received the place he deserves in the "national cinema."

If we are talking about Croatian directors, he is the one who has always been my weak spot. A kind and unassuming gentleman who made films with a particular feel for space, background action, and the drama of the face.

He was always a "maverick." And this word is used to describe only the great and solitary masters of film art. Loners who never belong to anyone or any place and who have paid a high price for this. In world cinema, the term describes Orson Welles, John Huston, Sam Peckinpah, Ken Russell, Ulrich Seidl ... In the former Yugoslavia, Žika Pavlović, Boštjan Hladnik, Dušan Makavejev ... In Croatian cinema, there were two: Vlado Kristl, a distant relative of mine, in animated film; and Branko Bauer in fiction film.

Motovun, 1973

I met Branko, though not by accident, in Motovun, on the empty town square. He was visiting his father who had a house there, while Điđa and I were writing the script for *If It Kills Me* at Hotel Kaštel.

Motovun, 1979

Caricaturist Davor Štambuk made a series of documentaries for TV Zagreb about masters of art—painters, sculptors, composers. Each of the episodes represented a meeting between an "old master" and an "up-and-coming" one. In the episode about film, Branko was the old master, and I was the spokesperson for the young generation. It was filmed, again, probably also no accident, in Motovun.

Zagreb, 1989–91

When the Ministry of Culture refused to provide financial support for *Lapitch the Little Shoemaker*, Branko gave up on making movies for good.

Zagreb, 1990

Krešo Golik, who had been teaching Film Directing to fourth-year students at Zagreb Academy, retired. They approached me to take his place. This was the second time I taught there. I heard from my students that they had never had the chance to meet and talk with people like Branko Bauer or Tomislav Pinter, a director of photography who had shot two Orson Welles movies. Despite the disapproval of the Academy, I invited them both, separately, to talk with the students.

Grožnjan, 1997

Branko sold his father's house in Motovun and bought an apartment in Poreč. He visited us in Grožnjan. He brought Ana a short movie he made about her in Oprtalj with his small video camera. I took him to the Imaginary Academy. In the classroom on the third floor, there was a lecture in progress. I cracked the door open and asked a little anxiously: "Do you know whom I've brought?" They all shouted: "Yes! Branko Bauer" and burst into applause.

Grožnjan, 1998

We opened a movie theater at the Imaginary Academy. I named it the *Branko Bauer*. Branko came to the opening with his wife Snježana. We organized a short interview before the screening of his movie *Three Girls Named Anna* (*Tri Ane*, 1959). Standing room only. He was thrilled. That was his first "public appearance" in years.

For many of the students at the Imaginary Academy—who are referred to today as "young Croatian cinema," "young Bosnian cinema," etc.—this was the night they watched Branko Bauer's directing for the first time. We screened *Three Girls Named Anna*, my favorite movie of his, from a poor-quality VHS, as this was the only copy Branko had. Several years later, Boris Matić managed to retrieve a 35 mm copy, not from the Croatian film archives but from the Macedonian *Kinoteka*, and we screened it in Motovun. Branko was there then, too.

Motovun, 1999

In order to rectify, at least to some extent, the carelessness with which Croatian cinema treats its own people, the Motovun Film festival inaugurated an award called *50 Years*. This was the first award Motovun had ever given. Branko Bauer and Tomislav Pinter were the first laureates. When they came up on stage in the packed town square, the audience greeted them with standing ovations. And the two masters, visibly moved, wept on stage. I, too, wept, standing between them and watching the audience give them back the dignity they so deserved.

Zagreb, 2002

We returned from hospitals at almost exactly the same time. Each from our own surgery. We spent a long time on the phone, talking about Motovun, Istria. I told him how shocked I was by the local intolerance, the nationalism by a different name, by the fact that Istria, in spite of my illusions, had not passed so innocently through the decade of hatred. He consoled me, saying: "Rajko, remember, you and I, we're the city kids. This is something we simply cannot understand."

Motovun, 2002

He died in spring. That summer, we dedicated the opening ceremony to Branko. His wife and I opened the *Bauer* movie theater. On the same square where we'd met almost thirty years earlier.

P.S. *I'm reading a book of conversations between the recently deceased Billy Wilder and director Cameron Crowe. Cameron asks: "Is Sunset Boulevard a black comedy?" "No, it's just a picture," says Wilder. Reading that answer, I remember Branko.*

Mediterranean Cinema

"The Mediterranean seems to have all of the characteristics of either a multicultural utopia, or an imminent global existential crisis," writes Elena Past in her essay with its wonderful title: Lives Aquatic: Mediterranean Cinema and an Ethics of Underwater Existence.

Lordan Zafranović and I come from different backgrounds, different families, we have different temperaments and interests, a different take on film, and often very divergent political views. In short, we come from different worlds. But despite this, or perhaps because of it, we have been through a great deal together.

Since the moment we met, regardless of our relationship, regardless of whether or not I like some of his films, I have always thought he was one of the greatest talents of Croatian cinema, a rare director with a "feel for movies," with what, in the world of music, is called "perfect pitch." Moreover, he is the only Croatian director whose films grew organically out of the iconography of the Mediterranean—out of the sun, salt, poverty, out of the baroque-sugary Catholic kitsch, and the bitter world of red-black ideologies.

Zagreb, 1965

We shared the first prize at the Festival of Croatian Amateur Film, which is where we met, on the stage of the Technical Museum in Zagreb. In the name of the Croatian Filmmakers Association, Zlatko Sudović gave us the award and offered us scholarships to FAMU in Prague, provided we passed the entrance exam.

Prague, 1966–71

We came to Prague together, took the entrance exam together, and were the first students in the history of FAMU who—he, owing to the short films he had already made, and I, owing to my entrance exam success—were able to skip our first year and were taken straight into the second year of Fiction Film Directing, the class of Elmar Klos. For the first two years we were roommates. After the first two years, the scholarships we had been granted were stripped from both of us by the Communist Party secretary of the Croatian Filmmakers Association, in an attempt to erase us from the national cinema we had not yet even entered. He claimed he had "reliable information" that we were spending our scholarships on whores and cab rides. The cameraman, Živko Zalar, whose scholarship was already taken away, replied, before a full hall: "I don't know about you, Comrade Vrdoljak, but I still fuck for free!"

Zagreb, 1971–91

We graduated in 1971 and returned to Zagreb together, to make movies at the FAS, the Film Author Studio led by Kruno Heidler. A few years later, we almost simultaneously moved to Jadran Film, to Sulejman Kapić, with whom over the next fifteen years we each made seven films.

And then, in 1985, came the *White Book*, the roster of enemies in culture, published by the Executive Committee of the Communist Party of Croatia. Lordan was a member of the Party Committee and one of the authors of the book. I was not a member of the Party, and the book listed me as one of the bad guys. We didn't speak for the next ten years. Possibly even longer. Meanwhile, both of us went into exile—he to Prague, I to New York.

Exile, 1991–?

From that moment on, we have been treated in Croatia as the worst outcasts. They have removed us from the encyclopedias, from the Artists

Association, we have been denied social coverage, length of service, and any other benefits. Not a single movie we made was screened in any of the Croatian movie theaters or on Croatian Television for over ten years.

Being in exile was tough on both of us. We were at the peak of our artistic powers so leaving and starting our lives over again was far from easy.

To paraphrase Michael Chabon: the pain of exile—a buried pain that lasts like a high-pitched, elusive sound, dwelling in the subconscious, that never stops reminding the consciousness that there is no oblivion.

I turned out to be luckier in exile. But, frankly, our homeland hated him far more boisterously than it did me. The pack of nationalistic Croatian filmmakers could never forgive him the scene of Ustashas committing atrocities in his movie *Occupation in 26 Pictures* (*Okupacija u 26 slika*, 1978). Anyone who had ambitions to be recognized as a Croatian film critic was required to spit on this movie of his at least once. I think, however, that what he found more hurtful than anything was the fact that he was publicly renounced by writer Mirko Kovač, a close friend of his, with whom he not only made that movie and three others, but also shared a great deal of his life.

Karlovy Vary, 1996

The festival organized a Prague School retrospective. This is where, after many years, I saw Lordan again. We bumped into each other in front of Hotel Pub. We stood there for a long time until finally I said: "Fuck it, kiddo?!" He laughed, flung wide his arms, shrugged, said: "Fuck it, kiddo!" and gave me a huge hug. "Kiddo" was what we had always called each other. We drank plenty of beer that night. We almost outdid our own record when, the night before graduation, at the Vinohrady theater, we each downed twenty-one beers.

Gorjani, 2013

We came back from Rovinj, from Mirko Kovač's funeral. He was badly shaken by Mirko's death. We talked after dinner over a glass of Malvasia. He and Mirko had made peace two years before, after twenty years of silence. When he heard Mirko had cancer, Lordan visited him at the hospital.

After the funeral, in the garden at Boba's, Mirko's wife, Lordan entertained some twenty people with witty anecdotes about his and Mirko's erotic misdeeds. I asked him where he found the stamina for this performance: "I owed him that," said Lordan. "Regardless of what he did to me, I owe it to him to see him off with joy."

Once again, he was witty and—despite all the calamities that had befallen him over the past twenty years—full of life. Deep into the night, he talked about a move he would like to make, although we both knew it was never going to happen. In turn, I told him about my idea for a movie which, like his, stands very little chance of being made. So it was that we came back to the point we had set off from into the world of filmmaking—our *Festival of Spoken Movies*. It was an idea we had entertained as students in Prague—a festival that would take place in a city which had no movie theater, where each director would have two hours to tell the story of a movie he would never been able to make.

It took us less than fifty years to put the idea to work.

The Melody Haunts My Reverie

A line from the Nat King Cole's song Stardust, *and the title under which the distributor screened my movie* You Love Only Once *in the United States.*

>...Sometimes I wonder, I spend
>the lonely nights dreaming of a song, the melody haunts my reverie...

From: Vesna Hardy <domanay@icloud.com>
London
Today, September 2, 2019, 2:54 a.m.

I think I'm the only one left who remembers the day you were born. It was a big event in my six-year-old life. A few months before you were born, we moved from the studio on Ribnjak into the big apartment with a garden on Torbarova Street. Then, despite Mom's advanced pregnancy, we went to the seaside and spent a few days at Grandma Olga's in Brela. I remember Dad's excitement when, a few days after we came back, his son was born. Family legend has it that he exclaimed, "A dragon!" I got a brother and started school on Kaptol, all at once. Across the street from school, I could drop in at Grandpa's pharmacy. He'd always give me sweet lozenges. I have a vivid memory of those few days of my childhood years when my little brother was the center of attention. Up to when Dad was arrested, then Mom, too, and then, less than two years later, when you and I were separated. Seventy-two years later, I'm happy to be able to wish you, once again, a happy birthday!
Vesna

Military Movies

A subgenre of war-movies, focusing on soldiers and their destinies.

Belgrade, 1974

The barracks of the Yugoslav People's Army. It is winter. For ten days I have been serving in the army. One of the hundreds of scared, confused, frozen novices, "lizards," as we were called. Assigned to the Convicts Battalion of the First Proletarian Brigade made up of "convicts and spies." The convicts are murderers and thieves who were released from prison to serve in the army, and back they will go once they are done. The "spies" are those of us who studied in art academies abroad, mostly musicians and painters. I represent the cinema.

"Why the hell would you study abroad unless you're a spy!" cheerfully declares a sergeant major.

The ones who do not belong to either category in the unit are few. I don't know why they are there, but I know for sure that Hrastić is neither a "murderer" nor a "spy," at least not at the start of this story.

Belgrade, 1974

We have been standing in line for dinner for two hours. It is dark and snowing. Our heavy coats are drenched. We stink, the coat is scratchy, and we are groggy.

Hrastić is in front of me, a little guy from Zagorje. From day one at the barracks, we are in the same lines, the same trenches, navigating the same obstacle courses, marching together. I carry a bazooka, while he, as my assistant, carries an imitation grenade. In the ten days we have spent together, we have not exchanged a word. Except for the question he comes with every two to three hours: "Got a cigarette?"

I nod, take out a pack, light one for him and one for myself, and we smoke in silence. That night, around six thirty, Hrastić turns to me, I take out the smokes and the ritual repeats. He inhales and, in a low voice, says: "So what do they think, that we're animals?"

After this first sentence I have ever heard from him, Hrastić turns with a wave and disappears into the dark.

It is the seventh night in a row that Hrastić's bed has been empty. They wake us before dawn. They yell, scream, drive us from the rooms. The officers line up the entire barracks, several thousand sleepy soldiers.

Around six o'clock, two military policemen, escorting the colonel in command, appear, leading young Hrastić in handcuffs.

On an elevated stage, the show begins. The MPs surround Hrastić who is standing, short and confused in his cut-off coat, staring at the ground. The colonel delivers a speech. "This soldier deserted, he willfully left our People's Army, abandoned the army born of the revolution, of blood and ashes, the army begun by our beloved Marshal Tito. Desertion means betrayal of Comrade Tito. And whoever commits such a crime must endure the punishment." The MPs take Hrastić away. Orders are issued in silence and the soldiers disperse. It is freezing cold.

A nocturnal exercise is underway. We lie in a water-filled trench. We wait for the "enemy." Hrastić is next to me. He did his two weeks of time in prison. After a few hours of silence, over a cigarette, he shares his story.

Varaždin Breg, Belgrade, Zagreb, Varaždin, 1974

He was born in the village of Varaždin Breg and, until the age of twenty-one, when he was called up for the army, he had left his village only once to go to Varaždin, the nearest town. When he was drafted, his father was on his deathbed. He tried to postpone his military service, but he did not succeed.

The first few days, he waited for a letter from his sister to let him know what was happening with their dad. He feared that while he was away, his sister might sign the house and the land, and everything their father had owned, over to herself, and only then let him know that their father had died. The days passed, her letter did not come, and they had no telephone. So that night, while we were waiting for dinner, he decided to go to Varaždin Breg to see what was going on.

His village was five hundred kilometers from Belgrade. From Belgrade to Zagreb, he stowed away in the bathroom on a train. From Zagreb to Varaždin Breg he did not dare do the same, but he could not afford a bus ticket. Walking along the road was also risky, because he was afraid the military police might pick him up as soon as they saw him wearing a uniform. So he set off on a sixty-kilometer trek along the railroad tracks.

When he reached his father's house the next day, he was so tired that he walked into the kitchen, dropped onto the couch, and fell fast asleep. The next thing he remembers is the military police taking him to the military prison in Varaždin. He did not see his sister and he did not find out whether his father was still alive. In prison he mostly slept, and then was transferred to Zagreb. He was brought from Zagreb to Belgrade, and then to military prison. Now he is here, afraid to ask anything, and unsure of what to do next.

Belgrade, 1975

I ask him almost every day if his sister's letter has arrived. He shakes his head, occasionally asking for a cigarette and smoking in silence.

A few months later, the weather warms, everything is green, again we are standing in line, waiting for something, when Hrastić turns to me and asks for a cigarette. When he takes it, he asks if he might have a few more. Knowing what this means, I nod. Hrastić, again, disappears, that night.

Varaždin Breg, 1975

Hrastić has been missing for over two months. They have organized a "hunt for the deserter." Our sergeant and a corporal go to Varaždin Breg.

Ten days later, when the search party comes back empty-handed, the corporal explains why they have failed. Apart from them, there are some fifteen other search parties from all over Yugoslavia scouring the Zagorje hills for deserters. The only thing they discover is that the fugitives are living in the woods in improvised treetop shelters. The villagers bring them food and water. More experienced search parties explain that there is no way they will catch any of them until autumn when the trees shed their leaves. In the past, deserters like these were dubbed the *Green Cadres*. The term dates back to Austro-Hungarian soldiers and fugitives who returned from the Russian front, under the sway of the October Revolution. In 1918, there were one hundred thousand of them in hiding in the woods of northern Croatia.

Belgrade, 1975

And sure enough, they bring Hrastić back in the fall. This time they make no show of it, he is simply taken to prison. He could be sentenced to ten years behind bars. A sensitive captain finds a way to have him sent to the military hospital, and finds someone willing to declare him unhinged, insane, not responsible for his behavior.

The last time I see him is when he is discharged. As he is leaving in civilian clothes, he tells me his father did die and his sister did sign everything over to herself. A neighbor has written to him to tell him this while he was in the hospital. After that, he again asks for a cigarette, inhales, nods, and off he goes to his Varaždin Breg.

Monologue

A long speech, confession or an address directly to the audience.

Castroville, 1998

Ruth Bradley talks about her friends from Texas, painters, who had twins, a boy and a girl, fifteen years ago. A few weeks after the birth, the little girl becomes very sick and the doctors prepare them for the worst: she might not live through the night.

When she hears this, the mother lies down next to her and starts whispering in the baby's ear. She keeps this up for a full twelve hours. The father goes in and out. He cannot bear watching the child die and his wife who cannot face it.

The girl lives through the night. But the mother keeps talking. She does not stop until the doctors assure her that the worst is over and that the baby is safe.

MOS

A film segment shot without sound. This is an abbreviation of the phrase mit-out sound, *used by German directors in the late 1930s when, escaping fascism, they came to Hollywood. Instead of saying: "We're filming this without sound," they would mix English and German, and say: "We're filming this mit-out sound."*

Athens, Ohio, 1974

There is a big house on the hill above the university campus. An elderly couple lives there, both of them professors.

One day, she catches him *in flagrante* with a student. A few nights later, she sneaks into his bedroom and pours a significant quantity of glue between his legs.

The surgical procedure for separating the professor's penis from his thigh takes more than four hours. Eventually, parts of his penis have to be reconstructed.

When he leaves the hospital, he goes straight home and sets the house on fire. She only narrowly escapes.

Over the scene of the house vanishing in flames and the two of them watching it wordlessly roll the opening credits.

The sound gradually comes on with the titles. The roar of the blaze grows louder.

Movie Star

A famous movie actor or actress, an actor or actress with high market value. And the value is precisely gauged and announced every year, as defined by box office results.

Zagreb, 1987

The movie *That Summer of White Roses* was based on Borislav Pekić's novella *The Apology and the Last Days* (*Odbrana i poslednji dani*, 1977). We had several scriptwriting sessions at his London apartment. And I enjoyed each of the sessions with this perfect gentleman.

And then we began preparations in Zagreb, thinking we would make it locally. We even managed to persuade Pavle Vujisić—an old Serbian actor who had gone into voluntary retirement, swearing never to film again—to come back. But all in vain. After more than a year of futile attempts, we could not pull together enough funds to begin production.

We were about to give up when Jadran Film received an offer from London. They would finance the movie if we made it in English. The offer implied production money, and—there is not an offer in the film world that does not have a "but"—the producer, a famous English actor, would have to play the lead. After seeing his movies, I said: "Thanks but no thanks." I remember thinking this was the most expensive phone call in my life.

Once again, we had kissed the movie goodbye when, less than a month later, another offer came from the same producer, this time without the condition that he play the lead. This time, the condition was to cast his wife, Susan George, famous for Sam Peckinpah's *Straw Dogs* (1971), where she had held her own with Dustin Hoffman reasonably well. Long story short, she had a few good films behind her, and in this movie she was going to play a far lesser role.

London, Karlovac, Zagreb, 1988

After long deliberation, and not overly thrilled about it, I started making my first movie in English. I knew what I was going to lose, but not what, if anything, I was going to gain.

I ran the casting in London. The US lawyers for Jadran Film insisted that I cast a US actor for one of the leads. I received videos. Nothing special. But the lawyers kept after me. On one occasion, just to tell them something, I suggested that, if this had to be a US actor, they should go for Rod Steiger. A few weeks later, a phone call from Los Angeles woke me up. I heard them yelling: "You have Steiger! He said yes!"

We filmed in Mrežnica, close to the town of Generalski Stol. We stayed in Karlovac, at Hotel Korana. This production was funded more richly than anything I had done till then.

Steiger arrived two weeks before his first day of shooting. They organized a dinner for just the two of us, so we could get to know each other. At some point, I was about to pour wine into his glass, but he quickly covered it with his hand. I looked at him in surprise and asked: "How long?" He readily answered: "Six years, three months, and eight days!" I said: "So, it was serious, then?" For the first time he laughed.

I looked at him, wondering if this had been a mistake. Had I given them the wrong name? (I have always been terrible with names.) Or had they maybe misunderstood? But this was definitely not the man I had asked for. What should I do with this major production that had begun filming a few weeks earlier? How was I going to get myself out of this shit?

Steiger was a wise man. My anxiety did not escape him. He slowly set his fork and knife aside, rested his hand on his head, and watched me intensely. Then, with an abrupt gesture, he whisked the wig off his head, and asked: "Happier?" I breathed a sigh of relief: "Oh, yes! Rod Steiger!" Yes, this was the man I had been expecting. One of the famous members of the Actors Studio. The actor who more than held his own with Brando in Kazan's *On the Waterfront*. He was wearing a wig because he had married a very young woman a few months earlier and felt it improper to be walking around bald.

On the first day of shooting we had a terrible fight. He did what almost all actors do. No matter how long you talk to them, no matter how thoroughly you prepare the movie, they always test the limits of how far they can go; they test your power, your skill, patience, and determination. Like a cat, they mark their territory. Some do it deliberately, with a grin, others subconsciously—but they all do it.

We were in my trailer going over a scene, waiting for the rain to stop. I explained what I needed. He was reading it in a completely different way. He had come with an idea for how to play the old fisherman and he would not budge. I kept interrupting, asking him to reread the lines. At some point he said: "Listen, no one directs me. Kazan didn't direct me. Leave me alone." I completely understood what he was saying, but what he was doing was so far from what I had in mind that I simply could not let him go through with it. We reached a point when I had to say: "If that's how it is, if we cannot reach an agreement, let's stop and call this quits before we start!" I was startled to hear my own words, but there was no way back. He gazed at me for a long time and then asked, with a smile: "So today's your birthday?" I did not understand the question since he knew it was my birthday. After all, he had already brought me champagne and a Sacher torte from Vienna that very morning. I nodded. He winked and said: "Fine. Today we do it your way. It's your birthday."

Never again did we lock horns. After all, when and if one passes this "actor test," once it becomes clear who's who, whose job is what, and how much wiggle room there is, a film shoot becomes a lot of fun. I enjoyed working with him although I never managed to strip him of his high-pitched Actors Studio pathos. He was good-natured, cheerful, curious above all else. Agreeable and unpretentious, like any real star.

We had a small ritual. Each time he came onto the set, he would walk past me, then stop, and ask, without looking at me: "Is she going to ruin our film?" In the same tone, I would respond: "So far so good." A cunning old fox, he realized right from the start that the lead actress, the one who came with the package, represented the greatest hazard to the movie. Tom Conti, who played lead, was more direct: "If half of the crew doesn't feel compelled to fuck the lead actress right there on the set, this generally means she's a bad choice for lead actress."

Toward the end of the shooting, I added a scene in which Steiger gets hit by a burst of gunfire and falls, dead, into the river. The scene was not in the script, i.e., in his 150-page-long contract. It was a scene that required fulminates and wires and was to be shot in a shallow part of the river which was full of sharp rocks. Such scenes are usually done by stunt doubles, not sixty-year-old movie stars. The producer and Steiger's wife advised me against even asking him. They told me I was just going to infuriate him. But I did. And he said, yes. But no retakes. In only one go.

I made sure I had enough cameras, I rehearsed the scene with stunt doubles and pyrotechnicians, and then we filmed. And it worked. Everything went as we had agreed. But I had the feeling we could do better. I went to Steiger and, while they were pulling him from the water and taking off the fulminates, I asked if we could do another take. Everyone started turning around, averting their eyes, certain he would fly into a rage. But he laughed. He said: "Okay! One more time! But let's make a bet that in the end you'll go for the first take." I said: "Deal, fifty bucks." We shook on it.

We had another take. The next day, as I was reviewing the footage, I told Steiger, one of the rare actors who never watches the material filmed the day before, that I was going to go for the second take. He trusted me. He gave me a fifty-dollar bill, I asked him to sign it and I taped it to the shooting script right in front of him. The fifty is still there.

Paris, Tokyo, London, 1989

The movie did well. It was in English, which opened doors all over the world. It ranked first on the annual box office results in Zimbabwe, in Paris it was screened at the two biggest cinemas on the Champs Élysées—with and without subtitles—it won the Grand Prix and Best Director awards in Tokyo, an "A" festival. It ran on television in the United States, and received excellent reviews everywhere except, naturally, in England, where the critics were irritated by the language, that is, the variety of English accents used in the movie. In short, it enjoyed a destiny any director could only dream of.

Still, it never felt completely mine. If I were forced today to renounce one of my movies, *That Summer of White Roses* would probably be on the shortlist.

I never tried to rationalize this strange and for me quite atypical sense of distance from my own movie. But simply put, I believe it stems from an uneasiness and feeling of guilt at choosing actors who, despite their great skill and fame, still were an unnatural element in the landscape. In terms of language, in terms of their mindset . . . in terms of everything. I tried to turn a local story into an international one, and that rarely succeeds.

A story is international only if it is truly local. Rooted in time and space. Only then can it become accessible to a wide audience. And in that game, the choice of actors is what basically makes it rooted, genuine, and true. The face, the gestures, and the language of Pavle Vujisić would have been integral part of that landscape. Rod Steiger simply could not be that. The only thing he could do was interpret.

This was a painful lesson learned working on the movie that brought me my greatest "international renown."

Los Angeles, 1991

"After such a movie, one goes straight to Hollywood," my new agent scolds me.

Movie Theater (Cinema)

Where movies are screened.

Zagreb, 1928

My father once told me that the first time he saw a motion picture it was in a packed movie theater, on a small screen with a barely visible image. A man with a long stick was standing right by the screen showing who was where and explaining out loud what was going on: "And now they are carrying him around, now the king, here, see, this one here, that's the king, yes, he is arriving in . . ."

Dojran, 1975

In Macedonia, at Lake Dojran, we film one of the six episodes of *Wild Stories* (*Žestoke priče*), a documentary series. Movies about Dojran made in the early 1950s are brought to us from Skopje. If we want to watch them, we will need to hire a movie theater.

We enter a large theater. In the middle of it, an iron barrel. Around it, two dozen chairs in various shapes and sizes. They explain that in winter, the audience members must not only bring a ticket but also a log. People watch movies sitting around the barrel with a fire going in it and every so often someone adds a log to keep it going.

Gorjani, 2017

I'm reading a wonderful book, *A Memory of Woods* (*Sjećanje šume*), by Damir Karakaš, in which he describes a movie theater from his childhood, and says that the man who was in charge, in an attempt to save on logs, lit a candle and put it in the wood stove to trick the audience into believing there was a fire burning.

Movie Violence

Any violence depicted in a movie.

My movies have always been somehow mysteriously linked to the reality around me as I film them. I have often wondered if this was because as I prepared my focus narrowed and I would start observing the world through the eyes of my protagonists, or whether there is a sort of conditional link between life and fiction, which cannot be rationalized.

To illustrate the phenomenon, here are two scenes I experienced while preparing *Charuga*, my only movie with scenes of violence.

Valencia, 1988

Actress Snežana Bogdanović, theater director Paolo Magelli, Ana, and I go out for dinner. It is ten o' clock in the evening. For Valencia, this is indecently early. Decent people do not sit down for dinner there before midnight, or even later.

We find a peaceful restaurant with a somewhat old-fashioned interior and promising aromas. There are only a few guests. We take a corner table at the back of the room.

The front door bursts open, and four young men run into the restaurant with nylon stockings pulled down over their faces. Each of them is gripping a Magnum. They shout and wave the guns. One of them tears into the kitchen, the second stands by the door, the third holds the bartender and two waiters at gunpoint, while the fourth starts going from table to table. He makes all the guests stand and hold up their hands. He wants everyone to take out all their money and put it on the table. Once he is done with the people at one table, he makes them squat and stare at the floor. Since the restaurant is half-empty, our turn comes soon.

Snežana and Paolo take out all the money they have. Ana lifts her wallet, opens it up and the money falls out (later, she shows us how she opened it and let the coins slip out but kept the large bills in). The nervous man with the stocking over his face asks me to hand him my jacket which is over the chair. I do as he says. He drapes it over his arm next to the hand with the Magnum and with his other hand he pats the jacket nervously. The Magnum swings only centimeters from my head. There is nothing in the jacket. He makes us squat. There are two more tables left, and everything is over very quickly. The restaurant is wrapped in silence. The waiters need a few minutes to catch their breath and call the police.

Plainclothes officers go from table to table. While taking our statements, an older officer tells us we were very lucky. These were obviously amateurs, and very young too. They were after money for drugs and they are usually more scared than their victims. So, they often use their guns. In this sort of situation, professionals do not kill but amateurs do.

The restaurant offers everyone dinner on the house. Several people leave, most of us stay. We finish our dinner in peace. We go over the story again. We laugh. As if nothing happened.

Afterward, we go to a nearby café to have a cognac. Only when we've been served the cognacs and raise our glasses do we notice that our hands are shaking. Seriously. It took an hour for the fear to kick in.

Zagreb, 1989

It is afternoon, and Mića Carić's Tiffany, a restaurant where we have been regulars for years, is empty.

I am near the doorway at a small table by the bar with my friends Dražen Vrdoljak, a music critic, Vlatko Stefanovski, a Macedonian guitar virtuoso, Vladimir Rubčić, a lawyer who used to be the front man for one of the first rock bands in the Balkans. We sip our drinks and talk.

Two big, brawny men walk in, come down the stairs, pass by us and go on into the restaurant. Later we find out they are well-known thugs, brothers from the Zagreb outskirts. Right behind them come two men just as big, with crew cuts, and the language they're speaking identifies them as Albanians from Kosovo. The bartender goes over to them, takes their order, brings them their drinks, and slips, unnoticed, out the door.

From where we are sitting, we can't see what's happening, but the place is small, so we hear everything. They are talking about numbers. The volume cranks up. Soon, the first blow falls, and then a real brawl breaks out. Two of them start fighting in the middle of the restaurant, the other two come to the entranceway between our table, the bar, and the stairs leading out to the street. They go at it, kicking and punching. Their blood sprays us. There is not enough room for us to squeak by them and get out of there. We stand with our backs up against the wall.

This is the first time I had ever seen a fight up close. It is different from what you see in the movies, because only one in ten punches actually lands. But when it does, there is a thud and then more blood than I would have thought sprays. The wall behind us slowly turns red. They snarl while pounding each other and show no intention of stopping anytime soon. We withdraw into a small restroom. In silence, we listen to the fight as it goes on and on. I have no idea how long it lasted but I would say—long. We leave only when we are sure that they are gone.

Meanwhile, the waiter is back and starts rinsing the walls. He ignores us. As if nothing happened.

Movies with a Number in the Title

Numbers are often associated with magic powers, and this may be one of the reasons why they appear so often in film titles: 12 Angry Men (1957); 3:10 to Yuma (1957); Ocean's 11 (1960); 8 ½ (1963); Three (Tri, 1965); 1900 (1976); Occupation in 26 Pictures (Okupacija u 26 slika, 1978); 4 Weddings and a Funeral (1994); Se7en (1995); 101 Dalmatians (1996); 21 Grams (2003); 4 Months, 3 Weeks and 2 Days (4 luni, 3 saptamâni si 2 zile, 2007), District 9 (2009) . . .

Athens, Ohio, 2015

For fifteen years Ruth has been circulating a Friday email to remind a group of about ten of us to come to Jackie O's & Brewery at five p.m. and celebrate the end of the work week.

> From: Bradley, Ruth
> Sent: Friday, January 29, 2015 10:47 a.m.
> Subject: Friday
>
> Hello All,
> At our last Friday get-together, there was an initiative underway to promote world peace. Our Muslim and our Jew shook hands and vowed to break bread together this Friday.
> As the senior Protestant of the group, I agreed to organize this attempt at a peace accord, because, after all, we the Protestants started this mess and need to try and fix it, the whole world peace thing.
>
> See You Then, RB

If Ohio University had ever asked me, and they have not, undoubtedly for good reason, to make a movie about Ohio University, I would start it with this email. This message that gathers such different people: white and Black, Africans, Arabs, Europeans and Americans, Muslims and Jews, Christians and all the subgroups. A diverse crew, along with the inborn human need for laughter and drink, can be brought together only by a great American university.

So, if Ohio University had ever asked me to make a movie about Ohio University, it would be called *Jackie O's at Five*, and would have the following cast: Dr. Ruth Bradley, director of the Athens International Film and Video Festival; Dr. Jenny Nelson, Media Arts and Studies; John Butler, Peterson Sounds Studio; Dr. Alia Ziyati, Communications and Media Studies; Steve Ross, School of Film; Alexandra Kamody, Athena Cinema; Gary Kirksey, Photography; Dr. David Descutner, Dean of University College; Dr. DeLysa Burnier, Political Science; Cindy Trueman, Jack Wright, musicians; Dr. Arthur Cromwell, School of Communication . . .

That is the crew, sometimes bigger sometimes smaller, that convenes on Fridays at Jackie O's, and drinks—as one would expect from such a diverse group—very diverse drinks: Ruth, Bushmills; Steve, Dry Bombay gin martini; Jenny, Budweiser; Alexandra, Mystic Mama IPA; John, Grey Goose vodka martini; Ali, Firefly Amber Ale . . .

Strangers overhearing our Monty-Pythonesque conversations would be horrified that such serious professors are prepared to trample on all the rules of political correctness, one of the sacred cows of American universities. He would hear the Muslims rib the Jews, and the Jews retort, the Sephardis razz the Ashkenazis and vice versa, the Protestants zing the Presbyterians and back, and all other possible combinations that take part in the vociferous exchange filled with laughter, irony, and sometimes quite savage teasing at all levels: political, racist, religious. And, what is important: hardly anyone in the group practices any religion or belongs to a political party.

But back to the movie I was, luckily never asked to make. Just when the conversation was sizzling along with zest, I would have to cut it. To the client, who could probably see this coming and never offered, I would not be able to explain that *politically incorrect* laughter, the spiritual exercise, is crucial for maintaining mental hygiene, the most effective cure against any form of repression and hatred, against superficiality, in short—against stupidity.

Multimedia

"As the name implies, multimedia is the integration of multiple forms of media. This includes text, graphics, audio, video, etc." (The Tech Terms Computer Dictionary).

New York, 1993

At NYU, in the Tisch School of the Arts, Graduate Film Program, I taught the Master Class in Film Directing. I prepared my lectures seriously, I kept copious notes. I was working to set up a system in the scattered madness known as Directing.

A man came to one of my lectures and introduced himself as the editor at a publishing house. He had heard of me from his friend's son, and he was wondering if I had ever thought about publishing a book, a textbook based on my lectures and exercises. I told him I hadn't, but I would consider it. If I should decide to, he was interested, he said.

A few days later, I walked into a bookstore at Broadway and Astor Place. I flipped through the books on film directing; there were about twenty of them, ranging from "how to become a director in three days" to the ones that were somewhat more complex. All of them were more or less like cookbooks with precisely formulated recipes.

Athens, Ohio, 1994

At the Graduate Film School at Ohio University, I also taught the Master Class in Film Directing. My notes were beginning to pile up. I gave some thought to the idea of investing the funds available to me as "seed money" for a new project into something that would not be a book, and certainly would not be a movie, since I firmly believed at the time that I had abandoned filmmaking for good. For the first time in my life, I bought two CD-ROMs, the CDs that came before DVDs, hoping they might hold the answer.

The first of the two was educational: blocks of text narrated by a monotonous voice. The second was a simple game with a lot of shooting and killing. The experts assured me there is no third kind of CD-ROM.

I decided to come up with the third kind—an educational game. I plunged into it as a computer ignoramus, as someone who knew nothing about computers, programming, multimedia, or how it is all made. After all, had I known anything, had I had the faintest idea of how time-consuming creating multimedia is, I probably never would have embarked on the project in the first place.

The initial idea was simple: a point-and-click virtual film school. A school, housed in an old three-story building, full of rooms dedicated to film grammar, techniques, and short film production. A place where you could read and write scripts, recut movies, play in a studio with lights and camera, mix, watch a movie and, eventually—provided you did the work yourself—you could earn a real degree. In short: to create a school for those who would like to make movies but could not afford to attend one of the expensive film schools.

What I found the most difficult at first was the transition from the "linear" thinking of filmmaking to the "nonlinear" thinking of multimedia. I taped index cards up in various colors all over the walls, so I could explain all the possible combinations to myself. When I pulled it all together, some six months later, and fed it into the computer, the script was more than a thousand pages long.

The university bravely invested in the project. I found a coproducer: *Electronic Vision*, a local computer company. Tom Erlewine soon became the project art director, and Deric Christian became the main programmer.

And so, off we went, groping in the dark.

Ebeltoft, 1997

We were invited to present the project at the Danish European Film College, at an international congress of film schools. It took us time to decide whether we could present it at this point when, three years in, we were still only slightly more than halfway through.

I started the presentation in a Barnumesque manner—I warned the audience of about one hundred film school directors that what they were about to see was motivated by the general idea of shutting down the institutions they managed. They gave me strange looks. At the end of the presentation, though, Tom and I received a standing ovation. Walter Murch, a famous editor, exclaimed from the balcony: "This is the best multimedia ever!" The director of Ohio University School of Film, Dr. David Thomas, wandered around, saying in excitement: "Home run, home run..."

Athens, Ohio, 1998

It took us four years to complete it. Aside from the three of us, about ten professors worked on the project with thirty students, several programmers, and fifteen professionals from all over the world who were there as visiting lecturers at the school.

Just when we thought we had only a month or two left to work on it, we heard that Steven Spielberg's film school was about to be published. Our blood ran cold. We knew that if it was in any way decent, Spielberg's name would blow our efforts out of the water. We stopped and waited. We found out when and where it would come out first and sent an assistant to be there in front of the store before it opened.

Once we saw what was being sold as Spielberg's school, we all breathed a sigh of relief. It was a fairly weak game about money and film production. After a few weeks and bad reviews, it was pulled from the stores. Someone had simply used Spielberg's name.

Washington, DC, 1998

The project *How to Make Your Movie—Interactive Film School* had its first public launch at the New York Festival, whose multimedia finale that year took place in Washington, DC. In the Best International Multimedia category, we were given the Grand Award, the Award for Best Educational Media, and for Best Design.

San Francisco, 1998

Ours was the first multimedia project ever to be selected for the official program of a festival—one in San Francisco. Since then, we have taken part in about twenty festivals—from Telluride to Cannes, where Kodak, in the American pavilion, presented it as American Film Product of the Year. Everything went so smoothly that at one point we were number one on the Barnes & Noble Bestselling Multimedia list—for only two weeks, but still—with Lucas's *Star Wars* game right behind us at number two.

That may have been what prompted Lucas Art Entertainment game builder Hal Barwood to say: "Film School in a jewel box. No kidding. Deftly arranged as a point-and-click adventure game, this is the most intelligently realized, most informative multimedia production I have ever experienced."

Athens, Ohio, 1999

Ohio University earned back its investment and then some, and it became known as a place for developing new technologies. After all, that is why they brought me there in the first place. They were clearly thankful, and so am I to them for believing in me even when I was not completely sure what I was up to.

Awards followed one after the other as did invitations from various world universities; there were about a hundred articles and reviews published, television coverage, while two computer magazines, one in Europe, the other in the United States, pronounced us multimedia of the year.

These were rare magical times we were not ready for. Francis Ford Coppola was preparing a virtual studio and he wanted it to be a film school. In the layout, one of the buildings was already named the Rajko Grlić Film School. Sony undertook negotiations to link our school with the sales of new professional video-cameras; a Mexican computer magnate weighed the idea of a Spanish-language version; Alan Parker thought of joining the British Film Institute educational team; the NYU Graduate Film Program required its prospective students to first go through our multimedia program; we used it for teaching film in dozens of schools in China and Africa . . .

Many great things happened at the same time, and Ohio University and Electronic Vision did not have the people to keep track of it all, or the money which, we realized too late, should have been invested. The toy, as we dubbed our School, had simply outgrown us all.

Athens, Ohio, 2004

When Ohio University returned the copyrights to me, Tom, Deric and I drafted, in our own production, a 2.0 version, a new, extended edition.

However, computer programs were changing so quickly that, in order to remain competitive, we needed to undertake a new round of programming for each new edition, and this would have to happen every two years or so. And I had neither the stamina nor the time, since I had gone back to making movies.

That is how I left multimedia, such an exciting journey into the unknown.

Athens, Ohio, 2010

I have tried to describe these events without sounding too boastful. As I am reading it now, though, I would say that when it comes to this story, I was not much of a success. Probably because this was my first project since I had come to the United States and, like any newcomer, consciously or not, I was eager to prove myself. Or better yet, I was looking for a way to heal my wounds which came from walking away from my "natural habitat" and filmmaking. But also, perhaps, because I had entered a new world, totally unknown, through which I wandered, banged my head against the wall, and eventually, to my own and everyone else's surprise, came out of it alive. In Croatian, situations like this are described with two sayings: "More lucky than smart!" and one that is even more forgiving: "Even a blind chicken finds a kernel now and then!"

At the end of the whole journey, I was still as computer illiterate as I was to start with. Ed Talvera, a cameraman with whom I filmed more than a hundred and twenty minutes for *How to Make Your Movie—Interactive Film School*, offered the best explanation. Once I called him to help me with a frozen screen, and after he had solved the problem in a matter of seconds, he laughed: "You became an American computer guru, they invite you every day to present your miracle, yet you can't even turn your computer on properly."

The New Hollywood

A movement in the American film that lasted from the late 1960s to the early 1980s. From Penn's Bonnie and Clyde *to Cimino's* Heaven's Gate.

New York, 1992

At one of the first lectures I held at NYU, when talking about the opening shot, I mentioned Bob Rafelson's *Five Easy Pieces*, one of the most important movies in the second half of the twentieth century. Out of the forty students, only a few had seen it. I organized a screening.

Telluride, 1998

Telluride is one of the best conceived movie festivals in the world. The hip 1960s feel, simple, unpretentious, and well-funded. It takes place at the end of the summer in Colorado, in a small town in the Rocky Mountains. Every year they select about twenty movies, accompanied by around twenty directors and actors. The group of people dines together every evening.

One of those evenings, I sat next to Bob Rafelson and his young escort. He was getting older and was drinking quite a lot. He is witty. I told him about the lecture, that his movie was the first one I screened for my students. He was glad. He talked about *Five Easy Pieces*. But, since he had mixed his drinking with consumption of a powdery substance, the conversation quickly became impossible. The escort slowly led him away from the table and the same thing repeated every night.

The next day, I saw them on the other side of the only street in Telluride. We waved to each other. He shouted: "Is it true that that was the first movie you showed them?" I shouted back: "Yes, it was!" He laughed, lifted his fist in a sign of victory, grabbed his escort, and ducked into a bar.

Newsreel

Short documentary films with news stories of topical interest. They were screened before the feature film in cinemas before the advent of television.

New York, 1984

I am a visiting lecturer at the Columbia University School of Arts. We are living in a rented apartment on 59th Street, between First and Second Avenue.

We have been there for a month and this is the day we are finally staying in for an "at home" evening. We sip wine, read. At some point, we notice more than the usual ruckus of blaring police sirens, but since this is New York, where police sirens are the dominant sound, we do not pay much attention. At about ten p.m., Ana goes over to the window. And down below, police cars, parked in rows of three, have filled the entire space between First and Second Avenue. All their lights flashing, some with sirens blaring. We open the window and immediately are blinded by a powerful spotlight. A serious voice commands through a megaphone: "You, on the fifth floor, get out of the apartment now! Everyone's already out. Get down here! Now!"

We come down immediately. There are police officers at the entrance. They tell us to hug the wall and get away from the street. The rest of our neighbors are already there. No one knows what is going on.

The neighboring streets are lined with restaurants. The owners compete to treat the police officers. A dozen waiters inch, crouching, from police car to police car, carrying trays with cups of coffee, sandwiches, and cake.

The restaurant owners also invite us to come in for a free drink. Ana and I end up at a bar on the corner. We sit, drink, get to know our neighbors. From time to time, I go out to find out what is going on. At some point, I see a TV news reporter giving live coverage.

This is how I find out that in the building next to ours, on our same floor, the apartment adjacent to ours, a man suffering from depression has wrapped himself in dynamite, surrounded with revolvers. He is threatening to blow himself up if anyone comes near him. Why he is doing it, they still do not know. The police are afraid that an explosion that size, what with the gas mains, might detonate the entire neighborhood.

Only around dawn do they manage to move the man out and let us back in.

The next day workers come to turn the gas back on. We hear from them that dynamite man was released that morning and went home. They were planning to send him to a mental institution but as he had no medical insurance, not a single hospital would take him.

On their way out, the workers grin: "We may meet again!"

No & Yes Man

No is a Chilean drama directed by Pablo Larraín with Gael García Bernal in the leading role. It is a story about a plebiscite in 1988, which determined the destiny of dictator Augusto Pinochet. Yes Man is an American comedy directed by Peyton Reed, with Jim Carrey in the leading role. It is a story about a man with a negative take on the world, so his friends made him attend a Yes workshop.

My family calls me a "Yes Man" who can never say "No" to anyone who asks for anything.

Zagreb, 1976

They call me from Kosovo Film. They ask if I am in Zagreb that week. They would like to visit. They would like to offer me a movie to direct for which they have the funding. I hasten to explain that they should first send me the script. I explain that I will not be in Zagreb tomorrow anyway. I am going to the Pula Film Festival. No problem, they say, they will come to Pula and bring me the script.

Pula, 1976

A delegation of six men and a woman, the entire Kosovo Film Arts Council, comes to Pula and brings me the script. They beg me to read it overnight and meet them the following day on the terrace of Hotel Riviera. They are dead serious.

I read the script. It is a Partisan film. The dramatized biography of a national hero who is now a high-ranking politician. I stop in to see Sulejman Kapić, director of Jadran Film. I ask him, in case they check with him, to confirm my excuse: I cannot accept the offer because I am committed to a Jadran Film project which will begin production by the end of that year.

I do my best to explain this to the delegation from Kosovo. They do their best to persuade me. If I think the script needs improving, I am free to do it. To make things less awkward, I ask them how they came up with the idea of offering it to me. They tell me they spent a lot of time thinking about what kind of film they want and realize that it "should have a world-class look." And as something like that can be guaranteed only by the work of cameraman Tomislav Pinter, they have been to see him at the Plitvice Lakes National Park where he is filming *The Times of Haiduks* (*Hajdučka vremena*).

Pinter accepts, and they ask him to tell them who he thinks would be the best director. Pinter mentions a few names. They make a list. I am first on the list, so they come to me first. I ask them to tell me, if it is not too indiscreet, who the second one is. "Your friend Srđan Karanović." They ask me to give them his contact information. They will go to Belgrade to meet him that same day. I call Điđa from the front desk of the hotel. One of the men from the art committee is standing right next to me. I explain to Điđa that I have talked with people from Kosovo, they are preparing a movie and are willing to come to Belgrade to talk to him about potential cooperation.

Điđa catches my impersonal tone and asks if they are standing next to me. "Yes, Điđa," I say. "Is the script bullshit?" he asks, and I answer, "Yes." Then I hand the phone to them so they can arrange a meeting directly.

Điđa reads the script and politely refuses. Number three on the list is Žika Pavlović. Once the movie is made, I see his name among the credits, as directing supervisor. Next time I see him, I ask him why he said yes. He laughs, shrugs, and says: "In return for the handful of appearances at the film location, I built myself a weekend house in a mountain resort. That's how."

Athens, Ohio, 2015

On a website dedicated to the history of Kosovo cinema, I find this text:

> Feature-length war movie about Kosovo Partisans, *When Spring Is Late* (*Kur Perevera Vonohet*, 1979), is based on the eponymous war diary of Fadil Hodža, a national hero and high-ranking political official from Kosovo, written by brothers Azem and Imer Škrelji. It was to be directed by famous Serbian filmmaker Živojin Pavlović, but after official Belgrade intervened because of Pavlović's political unfitness, actor Bekim Fehmiu agreed to direct it, and after he withdrew, Ekrem Kryeziu took his place. Director of photography [was the] famous Serbian cameraman Milorad Jakšić-Fanđo, and Živojin Pavlović was credited as filming consultant.

No & Yes Man II

Zagreb, 1987

I am called by a colonel from Belgrade, the person in charge of political supervision of the Fourth Army Corps—if I have remembered his full title correctly. He sounds like someone of authority who knows what he wants. After a few introductory clichés, he explains that the Army has decided to make a movie about a young officer, and he would like me to direct it. He says he knows I am always plagued by financial woes, and wouldn't it be nice if for once I had no worries about funding, and was able to focus completely on my art. Long story short, he will send the script the same day and call me next week.

And he really does call in a week. I try to explain that this is not a movie for me. And the script is not something that should be made into a movie. Simply put, it is bad. He doesn't hear what I'm saying. He has decided to have it made and he has decided I should be the director. He says I can fix the script. And he offers a contract where I can enter whatever figure I feel I should be paid. He will leave a blank space. "You've had enough financial hardship, you should, for once, be paid what you deserve."

(This is a sentence not a single producer has ever said to me, before or since. The one who came closest was Ivan Maloča, the wonderful producer of *The Constitution* [2016]).

In the end, I thank him and repeat that this truly is not a film for me.

The next day, while I am not at home (what a coincidence), he phones again and speaks with Ana. She is the one he wants to talk to. He explains that I am missing out on a great opportunity, that he will give me complete freedom, and I would be crazy to say no. He asks her to talk with me.

Belgrade, 1988

The movie is made. The title: *The Best* (*Najbolji*). Director: Dejan Šorak.

No & Yes Man III

Athens, Ohio, 2017

Times change. Movie projects used to be offered by the side that won World War II, and now, spurred by the new Croatian reality, they are offered by the side that lost.

I receive an email from California. A man is coming to Athens and would like to meet me. He has a book he wants to give me, and he thinks it would make a great movie. Điđa's typical response would be: "When you secure the funding, I'll be happy to read your book." I am not that harsh. I try to get out of it by saying I am not making movies anymore, that I am old, but after three or four emails I give in.

We meet for coffee. A very decent man in his late fifties. He speaks no Croatian. He has an American whose wife is of Croatian descent. He says: "Her father was a war hero who was forced to leave Croatia in 1945 to escape the bloodthirsty communists." The hero wrote a book about this. Or, more accurately, a *samizdat*—a self-published book, about one hundred pages long, with a drawing of the church in Međugorje on its front cover and on its back, a photo of Jure Francetić, one of the most savage of the Ustashas in World War II. He has the book in both Croatian and English, but he recommends the Croatian version, because the translation is not very good.

I ask him how he found me. "On the internet. I spent a lot of time browsing through Croatian directors, and finally chose you. Especially when I saw you were in the United States, in Athens, where my daughter is studying . . ." I gently do what I can to explain that it is pointless to leave the book with me, but he persists. He is certain that the time has come when they will be able to secure funding in Croatia for a movie like this.

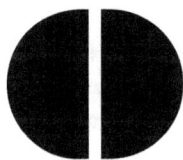

Opening Scene

The first scene, usually the key to the entire movie.

Pula, 1966

I was accepted at FAMU. At the end of the summer, I would be going to Prague. I had no idea what to expect—were the winters cold, should I bring food with me?

NIN, a Belgrade weekly that was very popular at the time and which, just like *VUS* in Zagreb, was published in broadsheet at the time, dedicated its entire back page to an interview with an aspiring young director, a student of Film Directing at the prestigious Prague Film Academy—Srđan Karanović.

I was in Pula, right next to the Triumphal arch, when I saw Karanović walk by with two girls. He was tall, skinny, with buoyant hair. I recognized him from the picture I had seen in *NIN*. He was loud, gesticulating with his long arms, the girls laughed, they gazed at him adoringly, hanging onto his every word. I waited for them to walk by, followed them hesitantly, and finally summoned up the courage to speak to him. I apologized, introduced myself, told him I, too, would be going to Prague, soon, that I would be studying at the same Academy, and that I'd like to ask him a few questions, such as what to bring, what I'd need. He listened, slapped me on the shoulder with a paternal air and said: "Busy now. Stay in touch," and left, awash in the girls' laughter.

Belgrade, 1945

His grandfather, Milan, was the curator at the Sarajevo Museum of Ethnology; painter Vladimir Becić was his great uncle; his mother, Višnja, born on Svačićev Square in the center of Zagreb, made the best cheese pastry I have ever tasted; while his father, Milenko, founded the Yugoslav Film Archive in Belgrade. So, this was the legacy Điđa carried with him into his life, fueled by his determination to become a great composer. No need to add that, like all the rest of us Yugoslav students in Prague, he was actually tone-deaf.

"The first director (who founded the Central Film Archive at the state-owned company Zvezda Film, which marked the beginning of what was later to become the Yugoslav Film Archive), was the first Yugoslav film archivist, famous professor Milenko Karanović (father of director Srđan Karanović)," reports Belgrade *Novosti* on an anniversary of the Yugoslav Film Archive.

What they do not say, however, is that he founded it in 1948 after coming upon a group of workers who were chopping up reels of film with axes in the center of Belgrade. With their help he discovered a storage room filled with films in a bunker underneath Kalemegdan fortress. After this, he began posting ads all over Yugoslavia, and in this way collected the first movies. This is how the Film Archive began.

Belgrade, 1969

Over one of Višnja's delicious cheese pastries, Milenko told us how he met my mother.

It was a few days after the liberation of Belgrade. As a man who could draw well, he was invited to Agitprop, to a meeting about the launch of a children's magazine. The meeting was chaired by writer Branko Ćopić and a young Partisan woman in uniform, my mother. As Milenko recalls, she sat down, took out her gun, placed it on the desk in front of her, and said:

"We're starting a children's magazine." We checked on the story about ten years later, in Zagreb, when Điđa's father visited my parents. It was true.

Milenko spent most of his life teaching film. He opened children's movie-making camps all over Yugoslavia. This was how Điđa, barely fifteen, at a camp on Koločep—an island near Dubrovnik—directed his first and only "spectacle" film, which eventually changed the destiny of the composer he was simply never meant to be.

Prague, 1966

With Goran Marković, he became the first Yugoslav student to attend FAMU after the 1948 break with Stalin.

He made amazing movies while still a student. We were roommates for two years. In the room we shared, we wrote our first script. Mira Trailović ordered the script for the opening of the first BITEF—the Belgrade theater festival. With Goran, we put together a blasphemous game that not even she dared to stage. We were too disrespectful regarding the Yugoslav national anthem. Later, the script was published in the Belgrade magazine, *Vidici*.

We also wrote our first "real" movie script with Goran. Each of us took one of the first three sentences from Ernst Bloch's *Tübingen Introduction to Philosophy* (*Tübinger Einleitung in die Philosophie*) and put together a story based on one of them.

Zagreb, Belgrade, Dubrovnik, Motovun, Trsteno, Bled, 1971–81

After FAMU, Điđa and I started writing together. Three of his movies, three of mine, the television series *The Reckless Years* ... Whoever was directing the film wrote the first and last draft, while the other played devil's advocate to poke holes in what the one who was directing had come up with.

But that story has already been told.

Long story short: he was talented, upbeat, and appealing. The movies and women liked him. He had his share of good and bad days. He traveled the world, cultivated his looks, and appeared, or at least did what he could to appear, a touch aristocratic.

And then, one day, he said *enough* and has stayed true to his decision: he hasn't written a word or filmed a single frame since. For years now I have been after him to write something about his dramatic interruption, and about everything he used to be. Nothing yet. Not a line.

Gorjani, 2013

It's hot. We're sipping chilled Dešković Malvasia.

"I have never envied anything about your life. Not your movies, your way of life, what you've had. The only thing I've ever envied is Ana," he says after a long silence.

He is tired and dispirited. He has difficulty walking. He is deeply hurt by how the producers of his last movie treated him. Over and over he says: "For me, filmmaking is something in the past perfect tense. A fond memory."

He was the first to give up, yet, possibly, the best among us.

Between the two scenes in Istria, in the fifty years that passed between that day in Pula and the evening in Gorjani, the two of us have been through a lot—from our dormitory room to serving as each other's best men, from the many wine bottles to the many hotels and cities where we wrote together, the festivals we attended, from friends to girlfriends, from the summers we spent together to our simultaneous moves to the States . . .

We have been and remain more than friends.

Athens, Ohio; Belgrade; Athens, Ohio, 2017

> From: Rajko Grlić
> Today, 8:14 a.m.
> To: Srđan Karanovic
>
> I dreamed of you last night.
>
> We're in a city, maybe Prague, but it could also be Paris. I ask you: "Why are you here?" You dodge, evading an answer. "Is this about a lady?" You say nothing. Finally, with a boyish, shy smile, you nod. I say: "Wow, has this been often lately?" You shrug and with pride you say, "Yes!"
>
> From: Srđan Karanovic
> Today, 4:54 p.m.
> To: Rajko Grlic
>
> Hahahaha! Like any other dream, this one has nothing to do with reality. That must be why they're so nice . . . I dream of you often too, about making movies or summer vacations but I forget it all when I wake up.
> Đ.

Oscar

The award given annually by the American Motion Picture Academy for artistic and technical merit in the film industry.

Zagreb, 1980

Erland Josephson tells a story about Bergman's thank you letter for his Oscar nomination. He mentions it as an example of a brief letter that says everything in just a few sentences.

Athens, Ohio, 2001

Ruth shows me a copy of the letter Erland is referring to—which Ingmar Bergman sent to the Academy when he declined the nomination for *Wild Strawberries* (1957):

Sweden
Solna 12/5 1960

ACADEMY of Motion Picture Arts and Sciences
9038 Melrose Avenue
H O L L Y W O O D /California

Dear Sirs,

As "SMULTRONSTÄLLET" ("WILD STRAWBERRIES") didn't compete for "OSCAR" I think it is wrong to nominate the picture and therefor I want to return the "CERTIFICATE OF NOMINATION".

I have found, that the "OSCAR"-nomination is one for motion picture art humiliating institution and ask you to be released from the attention of the jury for the future.

Sincerely

Oscar II

There are only two men in the history of the Oscars who have won Best Director two years in a row: John Ford (The Grapes of Wrath, 1940, and How Green Was My Valley, 1941), and Joseph L. Mankiewicz (A Letter to Three Wives, 1949, and All About Eve, 1950). Only one scriptwriter did the same: Joseph L. Mankiewicz (A Letter to Three Wives, 1949, and All About Eve, 1950).

San Sebastian, 1987

That Summer of White Roses is in the San Sebastian competition. One of the most famous Hollywood actresses of all time, Bette Davis, who played Margo in Mankiewicz's *All About Eve*, is staying in the apartment next to mine at Hotel Maria Cristina.

We bump into each other a few times. She smiles, a little muddled. A petite, almost transparent eighty-year-old woman, she walks with the help of an aide. Several hundred photojournalists are waiting for her out in front of the hotel. The aide has her lean on a palm tree and stands aside, staying close in case she is needed. Bette Davis waves absent-mindedly to the photographers.

New York, 1993

David is my TA at NYU. One night he takes me and Ana to Forum, a small art cinema in the Village. There, he introduces us to his grandfather, Joseph

Mankiewicz. The Library of Congress has restored the copy of *All About Eve*. Mankiewicz tells us that he is about to see it for the first time after nearly forty years.

After the screening, the vigorous old man tells us about his beginnings. His father, disappointed by his son's lack of ambition, essentially punishes him by sending him to Berlin to work. There, Mankiewicz finds a job at the UFA, translating German films into English. This is, however, in 1936 or 1937, and Berlin is not a pleasant place to live. He moves to Paris and then to Los Angeles. Once there, he starts subtitling sound movies. Movies were already using sound by then, but there were still movie theaters that only had projectors without sound. By adapting sound movies to silent ones, which meant condensing several pages of dialogue to a few lines, he learned the trade of screenwriting.

It is already late at night when we bid farewell to the wise man and his wife. On the way home, David talks about the tragedy that befell them.

After *Cleopatra* (1963), Mankiewicz decides to leave Hollywood and move back to upstate New York, to the farm where he grew up. They pack everything onto two large trucks. One is packed with their household furnishings and the other with everything related to his movies. From all his Oscar statuettes to the autobiography he had been writing for the past few years. The two trucks set off across the United States, but only one arrives at its destination. The one with their furnishings. The other crashed and burned.

Joseph Mankiewicz dies less than a month after the screening at the Forum.

Athens, Ohio, 1998

Harold Edwards, my neighbor, a sculptor, brings me a gift: two ceramic letters, an R and a G. He had bought them a few days earlier at an auction in San Francisco. One of the biggest American companies providing subtitling services has gone bankrupt. They started back in the days of the silent movies. These letters were used for the titles. I look at them and wonder: these letters might be the very ones Mankiewicz used for his work.

Paradox

A statement contrary to expectations and the ordinary; a conclusion that seems to fly in the face of logic.

Zagreb, 1983

It was Christmas Eve. First came "Cingula–Bingula." That's how Guga, my great-grandmother, swinging a bell, announced the unwrapping of the gifts under the Christmas tree that had been set up on the fridge. But before that, the three jolly brothers—my father Danko and his brothers, Ljubiša and Braco—solemnly sang *Silent Night, Holy Night* in German. After the gifts, my mother brought out a roast turkey with a pâté and roasted chestnut stuffing. With it, baked noodles, and sautéed red cabbage. The turkey, made following a recipe her mother had found in a woman's magazine in Budapest years before, was a "historic compromise" in our household. This is because Christmas Eve was the only proper annual gathering of the Grlić family. Around the table, enjoying the conversation and the good food, "baby Jesus" was celebrated by a crowd of atheists, descendants of three religions.

After dinner, over wine and cake, Petrograd cookies and vanilla crescents, we sat in my father's study surrounded by his book collection.

On one side, my grandfather, a pharmacist, aged ninety-three. In his youth, he spent a few years in France. In his old age, he read only in French. The last book he asked me to bring him was Goethe's *Faustus* in French.

Across from him, my father. He was sixty-one and full of energy. As a philosopher, he was deeply attached to German philosophy, he had translated several masterpieces, wrote books on some of the philosophers, on several occasions taught courses on the German philosophers at German universities.

With such backgrounds, the two of them talked about the two cultures. A Francophile and a Germanophile laid out their trump cards, theses, and antitheses, while all of us gathered around, listening. The conversation was both earnest and unassuming, ironic at times but also very affectionate.

Listening to them deep into the night, I thought for a moment that, if there were such a thing as absolute harmony and happiness, this was it.

Less than four months later, within a month of each other, both my grandfather and father had died.

Partisan Movies

As an amalgam of the American Western and the Russian war movie, the Partisan movie is a unique genre not only for former Yugoslavia but for all of Southeastern Europe. Often constrained by ideology and spiced with propaganda, but sometimes, in the exceptions that prove the rule, it can be very real and, at the same time, cruel to the politics and the times it addresses.

Zagreb, 1979

Kruno Quien worked as a dramaturge at Zagreb Film, and as one of the rare, if not only, professional scriptwriters in Zagreb at the time. One of his scripts was for an excellent film directed by Vatroslav Mimica's *Kaya, I'll Kill You* (*Kaja, ubit ću te!*, 1967).

We shared a fascination with the Zanović brothers from the Bay of Kotor, who were adventurers, writers, thieves, cellmates of Casanova's. The brothers were famous in eighteenth-century Europe as canny shysters. Among other things, they are said to have founded the first insurance company, which they used to insure nonexistent ships, then sink them in imaginary storms and seek real compensation. Dozens of European kingdoms and principalities issued warrants for their arrest.

Several times Kruno and I discussed the possibility of making this story into a script. They were enjoyable conversations that never went any further, because both of us knew full well that there would be no money for such an expensive story.

On one occasion, Kruno told me a story about an undertaker from Split whom he knew personally.

Split, 1939

Twenty-year-old Ante, an almost two-meter-tall albino with white hair and a pinkish complexion, has only one love: goldfinches. He catches them in the cypresses of the Sustipan graveyard. He chooses the best singers among them and releases the rest. Some of them he sells, and some he keeps.

Split, 1940

He finds a job at Sustipan as an undertaker. He spends his free time snaring goldfinches with a slender twig coated in resin. He tucks under a cypress branch, and, attracted by the smell, the goldfinch lands on the twig and cannot pull free.

He tries to mix up his own resin but without success. The one he buys, manufactured and sold by a store in Trieste, Italy, is very expensive. His spends almost his entire salary on resin. He orders a quantity of it and encloses, with the payment, a flattering letter to the owner of the store, begging him for the formula. He is a poorly paid undertaker, he explains, and can barely afford the expense. The parcel arrives always with the exact amount of resin he ordered, but Ante's plea is never granted.

Split, 1942

Italian solders bring more and more corpses to the Sustipan graveyard. This is too much for Ante and he joins the Partisans.

Trieste, 1945

As a member of the Dalmatian Brigade of the Yugoslav People's Army, he marches into Trieste. The same night, while the others are celebrating their victory, Ante finds the store he has written to so many times. He fires several rounds into the lock, breaks it open, rolls up the shutters, and enters the store. Frantically he searches for the resin formula. He overturns everything, opens every drawer, but it is nowhere to be found. At dawn, he takes all the resin he can fit into his backpack, rolls down the shutters, and leaves.

Split, 1951

Again he is the Sustipan undertaker. Goldfinches are still his only avocation. The resin he brought back from Trieste was used up long ago. All efforts to prepare the resin in his own kitchen remain futile. Finally, he gives up and sends a letter to the store in Trieste. He spends days composing a remorseful letter in which he writes about himself as a regular customer before the war, and about breaking into the store. He begs for the formula, again presenting himself as a poorly paid undertaker. He orders two boxes of resin and encloses payment.

After a month, the package from Trieste arrives. In it are the two boxes of resin. No formula, and no response.

Partisan Movies II

The Mid-Adriatic, 1943

An Italian cargo ship sails twice a month between Ancona and Split. It brings a number of ladies to Split and takes back to Ancona the ones who have finished their shift at one of two Italian brothels—one for officers, the other for soldiers. The ship also brings food for both of the "institutions."

By this time, the Partisan navy has already built several "warships" by mounting a machine gun or two on the two-masted *trabaccolo* sailing boats used for dredging sand and transporting it.

One of the *trabaccolos*, crewed by seven young Partisans, waylays an Italian cargo ship underway to Split. Their idea is to requisition the food the cargo ship has on board. In the below decks they do find the food, but they also find the ladies.

Negotiations don't take long. Seven ladies and the food are transferred ship-to-ship. After a few hours, the *trabaccolo* sails into a Kornati Islands cove where there is a freshwater spring.

The idyll lasted for fifteen days. This should be the backbone of the movie.

Meanwhile, the mainland Partisans mourn the crew which, they assume, have died in action, and hold a commemorative gathering in their honor.

Fifteen days later, just as they have promised the ladies, the Partisans intercept the same cargo ship, now underway from Split to Ancona, and return the ladies. Two of them refuse to leave and choose, instead, to stay with the Partisans.

Everyone is absolutely shocked when the ship with the seven murdered sailors and two unknown crew members sails into the Partisan harbor. They are court-martialed and sentenced to death. Every single one of them. But at that moment, the Italians attack, and the execution is postponed.

In the ensuing skirmish, the seven sailors show tremendous courage. The death penalty is commuted to a shorter sentence.

The two ladies stay with their sailors until the end of the war, and one of the two couples even marries.

Zagreb, 1983

I hear this story from producer Sulejman Kapić. I wonder why he doesn't find someone interested in turning this Partisan version of *Seven Brothers for Seven Sisters* into a script.

"Unfortunately," he says, "both the sailor and his lady are still alive and happily married. And, to make matters worse for the potential movie—he is an active rear admiral in the Yugoslav Navy."

Partisan Movies III

Athens, Ohio, 2015

Tomislav Jakić, journalist and former adviser to the President of the Republic, forwards his friend's email to me from Zagreb:

> Children are ashamed of their parents who were Partisans. Today we buried one of our members, a Partisan, who went through the Matić-field ordeal (he did not freeze to death), and his children wouldn't allow us to see him off with a few warm words. They fear the right-wing extremists, or so they say.

Performer

A person who performs for an audience, an actor.

I met actor Danilo Bata Stojković back in my student days, on Korčula Island. He used to come regularly and listen attentively to the lectures at the Korčula Summer School, the preeminent gathering, at the time, of philosophers from Europe and the United States.

Many years later, he played the role of Sreten, Bane's father, in *The Reckless Years* television series. That was when I had the opportunity to see how thoroughly and seriously this good-natured man—actor and entertainer—prepared his roles.

Belgrade, 1975

Halfway between the *Atelje 212* Theater and the *Politika* newspaper building, someone bellows "Soooldieeer!" Recognizing the voice, I know what is coming and pick up the pace. But an even louder "Sooooooooldieeeer!" rings out. I stop and look across the street. There is Bata, waving to me to come over.

In a split second, there is an audience. I cross the street and stand in front of him. He pulls his billfold from his pocket with theatrical flourish, pulls out a thousand-dinar bill, and tucks it into my army coat pocket. "Here you go, soldier! Might come in handy!" he says so everyone can hear, he winks and slaps me on the shoulder with fatherly care. "Yes, Bata, yes!" "Bravo, Bata!" "Show the kid how Serbs treat soldiers!" comment the passersby.

Bata bows ever so slightly, waves, and on he goes down the street.

Phobia

An irrational fear of certain situations or objects. Also, the most frequent word in horror movies titles, from the United States to Asia.

"Horror movies are frightful delights. But do you know what scares us more than a razor-fingered, chainsaw-wielding, summer camp attendee? Ourselves. It's because we're susceptible to phobias, conditions in which our minds run rampant with terror over an object or situation—a terror *that we know to be irrational*. If that sounds like you, you're not alone: There are 19.2 million Americans who suffer from phobias. And, as it happens, there's also a horror movie that brings almost every one of them to life," reads an internet website dedicated to phobias (https://www.syfy.com/syfywire/the-top-10-american-phobiasand-the-horror-movies-that-embody-them).

Zagreb, 1947

Dražen Juračić and I were born on Torbarova Street, in adjoining buildings. We held hands while taking our first steps. Both of us have older sisters. He still lives in the same building, he is a fine architect, and a great expert on the history of architecture.

Florence, 1977

We enter Duomo to climb up to the dome. It is the only place in all of Florence which he, who knows the city like the back of his hand, has not yet visited. The staircase has 436 steps, and it is very narrow and steep. It was built for the builders who worked on the dome, not for the tourists. That is why there is a warning at the entrance: "If you suffer from fear of heights or dark and narrow places, do not climb these stairs."

Dražen suffers from acrophobia, a fear of heights, I suffer from claustrophobia, a fear of narrow spaces. We are an ideal tandem for this enterprise.

We reach the top and come out onto a narrow balcony at the base of the dome. First, Dražen closes his eyes, and then tells me that Filippo Brunelleschi won the competition in 1418, and in 1515 Michelangelo stopped painting it. After that, he turns around, faces the wall and, while testing his knowledge, asks if I can see such-and-such to our right, and such-and-such above us. I carefully describe each detail he asks for.

We spend fifteen minutes doing that. Never once does he look to see the dome above or the depths below.

That is why the way back down the steep stairs is easy for him but challenging for me.

Photographer

The word "photography" comes from the Greek roots φωτός (phōtos), genitive of φῶς (phōs), which means light, and γραφή (graphé), which means drawing, writing. Therefore, photography means drawing with light; a photographer is a person who draws with light.

Zagreb, 1975

My grandfather gave the Zagreb City Museum his entire collection of Hühn's lithography and photos. The museum organized an exhibition.

> More than one hundred years ago, an educated lithographer, Julius Hühn, traveled by stagecoach from Chemnitz via Vienna to Zagreb, which back then was a small, barely visible dot on the map of the Austro-Hungarian Monarchy. He arrived in Zagreb which, only a few years later, in 1862, would be more closely connected to Europe by the first railroad, and where the Commercial exhibition (1864) would display not only pigs, wheat, and honey, but also the first *locomobile*. Hühn arrived at a moment when this small provincial town had aspirations, perhaps a little overblown, to become a serious city. (mgz.hr)

These are the opening words of Vanda Ladović's webpage at mgz.hr about one of the first Zagreb photographers, my great-great-grandfather Julius Hühn, a man who was, as she says, "the first photo-chronicler of Zagreb." That text, published on the occasion of the exhibition, ends in these words:

> The personality of Julius Hühn stands apart from the rest of those who represented this era of bourgeois prosperity. The dominant aim of his many activities was not his own economic prosperity. Less of a trader, more of an innovator, less of an artisan, more of an explorer with openly artistic ambitions, this naturalized citizen of Zagreb deserves a visible place on the still, regrettably, unwritten pages of our cultural history of the nineteenth century.

Zagreb, 1980

During a random conversation with one of the museum curators, he tells me that a portion of Hühn's collection has disappeared—it was stolen.

Zagreb, 2017

In Zrinka Paladino's book *Zagreb—an Anti-Guide* (*Zagreb—Antivodič*), a wonderful collection of material about a city that has neglected its own heritage, I find a text about Julius Hühn's villa: "Once the family Hühn had left Zagreb, the villa became the residence of fascist leader Ante Pavelić during World War II, and after the war it served as the residence for the President of Yugoslavia, Josip Broz Tito, until 1960."

This doesn't sound right to me. I check with Malcolm, my sister's husband, who has been exploring the family past with an almost professional passion. My suspicions turn out to be well-founded. The owner of that villa was not Julius Hühn, my great-grandfather, lithographer and photographer, proprietor of a house on Bregovita (now Tomićeva) Street, but his son, Dr. Kurt Hühn, founder of Croatian ophthalmology.

Photographer II

Oprtalj, 1970

I filmed my thesis movie, The Return, with Božidar Boban playing the lead, in Oprtalj. Back then, only a few people were living there: two elderly women, the tavern owner, the chaplain, the parish priest and his mother. They tell me that before 1945 the town numbered twelve thousand inhabitants. The monument to Mussolini in front of the Town Hall was the biggest in Istria. After that, many houses collapsed, worn down by time. Some of them still bore traces of slogans such as, "Noi siamo Croati—Vogliamo Tito!"

Sunday mornings, the town came alive. Its former inhabitants and their descendants came from Trieste to attend mass. While they were there at church, the cellars of the dilapidated houses opened their doors and became butcher shops. During the week, the modern refrigerators stayed hidden behind wooden planks and massive doors and were now suddenly well-lit and full of meat.

A ghost town full of Sunday butcher shops. Nostalgia mixed with a pragmatic need for cheap meat.

On the last day of the shooting, while the grips and electricians were loading the equipment onto the trucks and the crew was off to the tavern for a well-earned drink, I go for a stroll, as is my custom, around the "field after the battle."

I run into the parish priest on an empty street. He is tall, pale, and clearly very upset. Staring at the ground and cracking his knuckles, he whispers that his mother has just died. And he has a request: could I take a picture of her on her deathbed? Shaken, I accept. Sure, I will find my cameraman and ask him to take some pictures of Mom.

Živko Zalar and I go into the man's house. We tiptoe in and knock softly on the door through which we can hear sobs. The parish priest opens the door. His mother is laid out on her bed. She has been dressed and tidied, her hair is combed, his arms crossed over her chest. By her side, an older woman is crying. Živko switches on his light meter and holds it near the mother's face. He gestures to me there isn't enough light in the room. I open the windows. Živko measures again. Nothing. Not even the small chandelier in the middle of the room helps. The parish priest notices something is wrong. We explain that there is not enough light. The pictures will be too dark. If necessary, he will wait, it is very important that the pictures turn out well.

We return after half an hour, and bring two small redheads, the simplest lighting instruments. Now there is enough light. If we are going to light the "scene," we should do it properly. The parish priest agrees.

We go out and bring back the electricians. They leave their drinks behind, grab the spotlights, carry them over. They work in silence. The spotlights are set up. The room is beginning to look like a real studio. Živko is pleased. The parish priest asks me to arrange the family around the bed. I start "directing." At the last moment, the priest fusses over his mother. He cannot decide whether she looks better with her head higher or lower on the pillow. Her cousin daubs a little more rouge on her cheeks. The children are getting fussy. Everyone is loud. I have trouble hushing them up. The long photo session begins.

Zagreb, 1970

The pictures are developed. I send them to the parish priest. Ten days later, I receive a poignant thank you letter.

Photographer III

Athens, Ohio, 1999

I answer the phone. "Pompeo Posar speaking. I'm calling from Chicago. I've been following your work for quite some time. I'd like to meet you." I quickly remember who he is, and we continue a pleasant conversation. "Next time you come to Chicago, do come to dinner."

Zagreb, 1940

My grandfather's pharmacy on Kaptol has on staff a young, beautiful pharmacist, Matilda. One morning a young man comes in and introduces himself: Pompeo Posar. He is from Trieste and lives in Zagreb. In the same sentence he informs my grandfather that he wishes to marry Matilda and the two of them will soon be moving to the United States.

Chicago, 1953

With one thousand dollars borrowed from his mother, Hugh Hefner starts *Playboy*. The very first photographer he persuades to work for him is Pompeo Posar.

Zagreb, 1970

Whenever a copy of *Playboy* appears at our house, or whenever my father and his brothers talk about it, sooner or later "our man at *Playboy*" comes up. And "our man" is Pompeo, the same man who "stole the beautiful pharmacist" from my grandfather.

Zagreb, 1981

On the Adriatic, Pompeo is making *The Girls of the Adriatic Coast*. This will be the first time our beauties appear in *Playboy*. Pilaš (Mladen Pleše) the editor-in-chief at *Start*, a magazine modeled after *Playboy*, talks about meeting him. Pilaš raised its circulation to 230,000, amazing at the time and, and now—impossible to imagine.

Zagreb, 1984

Ana's brother, Ivo, a Swedish photographer, tells me how he met Pompeo in the States. He mentioned my grandfather's pharmacy.

Chicago, 2000

We are at dinner at Matilda and Pompeo's, in their penthouse in a skyscraper by the lake. She is still beautiful; he exudes old-world charm.

After dinner, he shows us some unpublished photographs. Among them, a nude of Matilda. She really was beautiful. In the end, he shows us a series of pictures he did with Salvador Dalí.

During the evening he talks about Zagreb, my grandfather, his first years in America, how he met Hefner, who, with a little money, sent him to Europe for the first time.

Munich, 1971

For days Pompeo stands on Marienplatz, just watching. He does not know how to begin. After a few days he summons up the courage and starts approaching the beautiful women walking by, telling them why he is there. He does not embellish. To his surprise, a few of them say yes. I ask him for his theory, what he thinks made those young women agree to be photographed naked by a stranger who came up to them on the street.

He laughs. Yes, he was puzzled too. So he asked them. All of them said the same thing: "Because you didn't have hungry eyes."

Chicago, 2004

He died at eighty-three. The many obituaries read more or less the same: "He was one of the most respected and prolific photographers in *Playboy* history."

Photographer IV (& Painter)

Athens, Ohio, 2003

At the Dairy Barn Art Center, I was introduced to Lloyd Moore by my friend, Ron Kroutel, a painter and professor at the Ohio University School of Art.

The first photograph I saw of Lloyd's was of an older man, sitting in his bedroom, holding a can of beer and looking directly into the camera. In this picture I found a simple, strong story that had stayed with me since my arrival in America. The mother of all stories: the story of loneliness.

A week later I visited Lloyd. He is a quiet old gentleman with a gentle smile. Most of his working life was spent as a lawyer in Ironton, OH, a little town on the banks of the Ohio River. He took up photography for practical reasons to help gather legal evidence for his cases. He soon discovered more than mere legal evidence in the faces of his subjects.

On the wall of his kitchen he projected countless photographs for me. Most of them were portraits of poor people. All of them had faces showing no embarrassment, or fear that his camera would cheat them, or humiliate them in a sea of irony. All of them had confidence in their photographer, so much so that they permitted themselves the greatest of human luxuries; to be who they really were. No matter how bitter or tragic their recollections, their eyes told us stories with affection, directly and purely, without pretense.

Few photographers are awarded such a gift by the people they photograph. Even fewer know how to return this gift with the affection that Lloyd has achieved in his photographs.

As I listened to his stories and looked at his pictures, I suggested to Lloyd that I could organize an exhibition and, with the help of Art Director Tom Erlewine, a book of his photographs.

Athens, Ohio, 2004

The *Face to Face* book and show at the Kennedy Museum were a simple distillation of those long kitchen gatherings: a photographic record of one man's passion, honesty, and sense of community.

Athens, Ohio, 2018

Fifteen years later I embarked on a similar process with the work of Ron Kroutel, the man who introduced me to Lloyd.

Under the title *50 Year Journey* I organized a retrospective of Ron's work at the Kennedy Museum. Again, with the help of Tom Erlewine, we published a book in which we follow his path from black and white drawings of a brutally honest Ohio industrial landscape to his first use of color, then leading to his last body of work: big canvases of flying, almost completely liberated, people.

The circle was closed. My curatorial career in search of the "real Ohio" had come to an end.

Plagiarism

Merriam-Webster online dictionary offers these definitions:
  –To steal and pass off (the ideas or words of another) as one's own.
  –To use (another's product) without crediting the source.
  –To commit literary theft.
  –To present as new and original an idea or product derived from an existing source.
In other words, plagiarism is theft. And it means both a theft of someone's work, and the subsequent lies about it.

Zagreb, 2010

In one of my mother's books, I find this clipping from *Feral Tribune*, a satirical weekly that was practically the only opposition newspaper in Croatia during the 1990s.

> Translation:
> THE WAR AGAINST PLAGIARISM
> April 15, 2004
>
> I recently read a newspaper article about how someone has proposed raising a monument to Franjo Tuđman. I'm therefore sending you this note which may add or detract from the proposal. More than twenty years ago, Franjo Tuđman stopped by our house at 2 Vrbanićeva Street. At the time, he was teaching at the Faculty of Political Science in our neighborhood.
>
> Tuđman had come to suggest that my husband Danko Grlić might write a text for *War Against War* (*Rat protiv rata*), a book he was preparing for publication.

Danko Grlić did write an article on the topic, about twenty pages long, and gave it to Franjo when he came next.

Danko was paid for the text.

After a while, a rather thick tome appeared in print: *Franjo Tuđman—War Against War (Franjo Tuđman—Rat protiv rata)*.

Soon after this, Franjo brought a copy to his associate, Danko.

However, not one of the associates' articles was signed in the book, leaving readers with the impression that the entire book was actually written by Franjo.

To be fair, Franjo did, at the very end of the book, append a note listing all the associates and thanking them for their cooperation.

The book remained on one of the lower shelves of our rather large library, and then, after a time, miraculously disappeared.

My kindest regards to everyone at *Feral* which I read with a passion every week!

—Eva Grlić

Point of View—POV

Someone's view of something. This shot usually comes in the movie right after or before the shot of the person gazing.

Zagreb, 1954

My father and I walk down Masarykova Street. He points for me to look across the street. A tall man in a Hubertus, a green overcoat, with a hat, a briefcase, and, in his mouth a cigarette, is coming out of Blato, a famous tavern often frequented by poets and artists. "That's Tin Ujević," Dad says respectfully, pointing to one of the greatest poets in the history of Yugoslavia and Croatia. He waves to Tin, Tin waves back at us, and on we go. "He used to come to our rooms at the Journalists Club early in the morning, straight from the tavern, he'd pick up one of the Proust novels and, pacing up and down, start dictating the translation to your mother straight into the typewriter."

Cannes, 1973

Điđa and I enter the Le Grand Palais to see the morning screening of Truffaut's *Day for Night (La Nuit américaine)*. The lights have gone down. The screening is about to begin. We take our front row, balcony seats. Seconds later, Điđa nudges me: "Look who's right next to you!" I turn—it's Grace Kelly. With Ingrid Bergman.

Paris, 1985

I am walking along Boulevard Raspail with Milan Kundera. He stops me and points across the street. "The tall skinny guy over there, that's Samuel Beckett." Becket is about to go into Gallimard. Kundera grins and says, proudly: "We have the same publisher."

Porno Movies

Movies that explicitly show sexual intercourse.

Dr. Wilhelm Reich, the man about whom Dušan Makavejev made his movie *W.R.: Mysteries of the Organism* (*Misterija organizma*), claims than the average man can have about 20,000 orgasms in his lifetime.

Graz, 1980

Bruno Jager is a bank clerk, an erotomane who has been diligently noting down each orgasm he has had since childhood. At the age of fifty-seven, he has reached 19,995. He has only five left to go. After a long deliberation, Bruno leaves his job, his family, his hometown, takes the money he has been secretly shaving off of his clients' bank accounts over the past ten years, and sets off in search of the remaining five.

This could be the beginning of a road porno movie which, in the honor of Makavejev, might be called—*W.R.: The Magnificent Five*.

Pula, 1981

One night, I tell this story on the terrace of Hotel Riviera. The director of Vardar Film, who is there with us, stops me the next day and asks if I'd turn the idea into a script for them. He sees this as an excellent commercial success. It is a challenge to dissuade him.

Porno Movies II

Zagreb, 1967

People show me a middle-aged man in a tattered grey overcoat, walking down one of the streets in the center of town. They tell me to be patient and observe. He is not doing anything much—he strolls down the street and, when he notices a middle-aged woman standing in front of a store window, he straightens up, approaches her, and looking into the shop window, says something. The woman takes a few steps back, looks at him in shock, and hurries off.

It is just a simple sentence, a question, actually: "Would you happen to need a fuck?" He claims, allegedly, that ninety-five per cent of the women are shocked. Most of them swear at him, some even smack him with their purse. But at least five per cent of them ask, taken aback: "What do you mean?" or something along those lines. In short, at least one of the women who enters into conversation with him takes it a step further.

In 1969, while making a feature documentary about the weirdos on the Zagreb's streets, I look for him, but he has stopped his wandering.

Porno Movies III

I come upon an internet ad in Croatian for a healthcare workshop, containing an almost imperceptible typo: "Radionica za prevenciju rajka dojke i grlića maternice."

Glossary:
rak = cancer   Rajko = first name
Grlić = last name   grlić maternice = cervix

It should read: "Workshop on prevention of breast cancer and cervical cancer." It actually reads: "Workshop on prevention of breast Rajko and cancer of the Grlić."

Preproduction

The entire preparation process covering the period from the moment a script is approved, to the first day of shooting.

Osijek, 1989

Several days before I start filming *Charuga*, a movie about an infamous Croatian robber from the 1920s, I visit Čaruga's grave with Ivan Kušan. Legend has it that if you leave a lit cigarette on the grave, you will be successful in whatever you are up to.

While we are lighting the cigarette, a policeman stops by. He tells us that every year on the day before All Saints Day—November 1—flowers from most of the graves at the town cemetery are piled up on Čaruga's grave, until the grave looks like a flower pyramid. They have tried to ambush the perpetrator on several occasions and waited there all night long, but they still have not managed to discover who has been doing it.

Zagreb, 1986

Ivan and I spent a long time working on the script for *Charuga*. With some interruptions, it took us three years. And so, with lunch after lunch and dinner after dinner, we discovered that we both enjoy eating and cooking and drinking. Ivo was a passionate cook. In America, he mastered the secrets of Chinese cuisine. From each of my trips abroad, I was tasked with bringing him spices, sauces, and special woks that couldn't be found in Zagreb back then.

The only thing he loved more than Chinese cooking was French cheeses. The writer who dedicated the best pages of his *Beggar in Disguise* (*Prerušeni prosjak*) to Paris, could spend hours talking about French cheeses.

Paris, 1987

I was in Paris for only two days. Right before I left, I visited the Marché Alimentaire Saint-Germain and bought thirty different cheeses.

Zagreb, 1987

Ana and I arranged the cheeses so they covered our large kitchen table. I invited Ivan. He came over, stopped at the table, and slowly, like a true connoisseur, inhaled and closed his eyes with pleasure.

We stay at the table deep into the night. Nibbling, sipping, enjoying it all. Ivan talked about his gourmet trips through Provence, about restaurants, dishes, cooks.

It took us a few days and a few more sessions to finally clear the table and get back to *Charuga* again.

President Movies

Movies whose lead or main focus is a real or imaginary president.

Tito's Handmade Vodka *is produced in Austin, in the oldest Texas distillery, and is considered the finest American vodka. Their website explains the name Tito*: Tito is a Latin child's name. In Latin, it means "saved" . . .

My mother and father come from relatively affluent city families. Reading Miroslav Krleža's works, and after they had followed what was going on during the Spanish civil war, they joined the left-wing movement as high school students and became members of SKOJ—the League of Communist Youth of Yugoslavia. Despite all the wars, the prison time, and the other "historical adversities" they went through, they remained loyal to leftist social thought to the end of their lives.

Comrade Josip Broz Tito was rarely mentioned in our home, and when he was, he was mentioned with respect for what he had done during the war, and with rather frank irony for his subsequent lifestyle. So I did not have the chance to become someone who either loved or hated him. As a kid, I used to see him as someone larger than life, like a John Wayne, except he turned up on our black-and-white newsreels instead of in technicolor American Westerns.

Pula, 1974

If It Kills Me wins the Best First Motion Picture Award. I will accept it at the closing ceremony, after the screening of *Guns of War* (*Užička Republika*). Comrade Tito, one of the characters portrayed in the movie, is coming to watch the movie and see the closing ceremony.

I have been given several different passes and exhaustive instructions regarding the appropriate time and manner of entering the Pula Arena. I am wearing a light-blue denim suit I bought in Paris the year before, on my way back from my first Cannes.

At the special entry point, opened just for the occasion, I face a stern middle-aged man. He takes a long serious look at my passes and IDs. Finally, he scans me head to toe and clicks his tongue in disapproval. (I tried to recreate that clicking with Bata Živojinović in the movie *In the Jaws of Life*). "You can't go like that before the Marshal," he says anxiously and clicks his tongue. "What's wrong?" I ask. "You can't appear in jeans before the Marshal." I start explaining that the suit is the most elegant item of clothing I possess and it is fashionable in the world ... I keep talking until, eventually, he shrugs, clicks his tongue and, visibly disgusted, lets me through.

The screening in the arena is held in complete silence. The idyll is occasionally disturbed by the crunch of footsteps on the gravel. They come from a waiter who is taking a glass of whiskey from the small trailer in the corner to the presidential box where Tito is seated. When he approaches the box, the waiter bends forward so as not to block the view for the people inside and lifts the tray with the drink above his head. Once he is in front of Tito, he slows down so Tito can take the full glass and place his empty glass on the tray, and then the man turns around and trots back to the trailer. This happens every ten minutes or so. He is quick. He moves like a ball boy at a tennis game.

After the screening, the crew takes a bow: Marko Todorović, in the role of Tito; Boris Buzančić; Božidarka Frajt; and the grand master of directing, Žika Mitrović, although this was not one of his finest movies.

After that, the award ceremony. The audience greets all the laureates with rounds of applause. No one stands, no one whistles, no one moves.

Once the seven of us accept our awards, we are brought down to stand in front of the stage.

Out of the VIP box comes Tito in a white suit and his wife Jovanka in a dark dress. Behind them, Trpe Jakovlevski, the Minister of Culture, and his wife.

A brief digression in the manner of *The Good Soldier Schweik*.

When we were studying in Prague, Trpe Jakovlevski was the Yugoslav Ambassador to Czechoslovakia. During World War II he spent a few years in prison in Sofia, having assassinated an important Bulgarian fascist. Twenty-seven years later, in Prague, Russians tried to kill him in a perversely devised plot. He barely survived.

We used to visit his residence often when we were students. Mostly because of his daughter and the two girls from Macedonia who worked there as cooks. Years later, when asked about any one of us, he would say that our names always reminded him of the refrigerator. "They were always hungry," Trpe used to say.

Once, toward the end of his term as ambassador, we were playing cards at his residence, but he kept running upstairs where he had a radio link with Belgrade. In Yugoslavia, there was a session of government or the Central Committee of the Communist Party in progress; an important meeting where they were deciding on ministry assignments. He finally came back, utterly downcast, and said: "Well, of course. Had I been there, they wouldn't have screwed me over. I'd have gotten industry or something else serious. Not culture." And really, to his sincere dismay, he was made the Minister of Culture—the last Minister of Culture of Yugoslavia. But, back to the arena in Pula.

Tito and Jovanka come up to the laureates. Right behind them, the Jakovlevski couple.

Tito approaches the first person in the row—Žika Mitrović. He shakes his hand and says: "Congratulations." That's it. I'm right next to Žika. Tito comes to me. I am surprised to see how short he is. I extend my hand, but he does not move his. He keeps it at his side, so I lean forward and move toward his hand. By the time I clasp it, I am quite bent over. Later, I see he does this whenever he shakes anyone's hand, and this is how he deals with his height problem. Anyone he shakes hands with has to bow a little.

"Congratulations," he says. "Thank you," I say.

Then, comes Jovanka. A beautiful woman with a wide smile. A head taller than Tito. A small purse pressed against her chest. Rumor had it that she kept a small revolver in it; she was the last line of Tito's defense. She congratulates me in a high-pitched, slightly screechy voice, in stark contrast to her large body. "We watched your movie last night, and we loved it," she says. Tito nods. Just then, Trpe and his wife come over. He congratulates me, she blithely kisses me on both cheeks.

Žika Mitrović looks at me, baffled. He has made this spectacular film about Tito's greatest victories, while I made a small, cheap, almost underground movie about an idler from Zagreb.

Tito congratulates everyone and makes for the exit followed by his entourage. We do not move until given the sign. The arena is still shrouded in complete silence, nobody moves.

In front of the arena, there are a dozen Mercedes-Benzes, their engines revving. Next to each, a man in a black suit holds open the rear door. They show us who is to go where. One car for each group of seven. Tito's car is the first one. We see him get in. His car sets off but stops after several meters. Commotion. The car holds still for a few seconds, enough for someone to run up to it and take orders. We start getting into the cars that are to drive us to the seafront, several hundred meters away. There we will board a patrol boat that will run us to Vanga Island, where we are to join Tito for dinner.

Tito's car moves on. Someone yells: "Stop. Wait!" Soon, they tell us Tito is indisposed and the dinner is off. Later, we hear rumors that Tito actually had not liked the movie, so he canceled the dinner. Whatever the case, those two words are the only ones I ever exchanged with Comrade Tito.

They bring us back to arena, to the stage. We stand and watch the audience, who watch us in silence. It takes the administrators at least five minutes to find Ivan Hetrich, the official festival announcer, and have him explain to the audience that the ceremony is over, and they can leave.

Belgrade, 1975

I am serving in the army in Belgrade, at the barracks, following in the footsteps of the famous First Proletarian Brigade. As a member of the brigade, my mother marched into Belgrade in 1945. But in my day, to be assigned to it was seen as a form of punishment. Five months later, and with the help of Branka Čeperac, Điđa's editor, whose husband worked in Zastava Film, the army's film company, I am reassigned.

Zastava Film introduces me to Vule Milovanović, captain of a battleship, a stout balding man with a pleasant smile. He has been assigned to make a documentary about the Victory Day parade that will be held in Belgrade on May 9th to celebrate the 30th anniversary of victory over fascism. The only problem is that he has never made a movie.

It does not take long before we come to an agreement. I will move to Topčider, to a dorm with thirty "invisible" soldiers. These are men employed in various departments of military journals and radio, and allowed, unofficially of course, to sleep outside the barracks. I get a round-the-clock leave permit and rent a room at the apartment of Branko Cvejić's cousin, Dragan, in the center of Belgrade. The captain of the battleship picks me up there each morning, takes me to the Zastava Film Studios, and brings me back in the afternoon. In return, I will set the positions of the cameras and do the editing. On the condition that he does not set foot in the editing room.

At the parade, General Đoko Jovanić makes several attempts to deliver a report to Tito. Not once does he manage to utter properly the two simple sentences: "Comrade High Commander, the Yugoslav National Army units are ready. Let the parade begin." Finally, the Marshal interrupts the stammering and says with a smile: "Let it begin!"

This was the beginning of Tito's last parade. It ended on an even odder note. Namely, there was an additional stand built next to the VIP box, narrower and higher than the first. In it, with Tito, were all the war and peacetime generals of the Yugoslav People's Army. At the end of the parade, Tito came down first, and the rest of them followed. Only one man was left. He was not in uniform and proceeded down slowly, from the back row. Once he reached the position from which the Marshal had watched the parade, he stopped and stayed there for a few minutes. From my position, next to one of a dozen 35 mm cameras, I could not tell who he was.

Back in the editing room, I asked the assistant to pull up all the final shots. And then, as in Antonioni's *Blow Up*, I started assembling the puzzle. The mystery man was Koča Popović, one of the signees of the Third Manifesto of the Surrealists, the first commander of the First Proletarian Brigade who, when the brigade was formed in the town of Rudo, greeted Tito in a white safari coat.

Yet another Schweik-like digression, and I promise this will be the last.

I extracted all the material of Jovanić's stammering report. First, I edited the sound to produce a coherent sentence and then the picture to match the sound. After that, Đoko Jovanić appeared to be making his report without a stammer.

I still had four months of the army ahead of me, and I knew I could finish the documentary in a month or two. Afraid they might send me back to Voždovac once I had finished, I slowed down the entire process.

Moreover, the generals who were leading certain echelons in the parade—the infantry, navy, aviation—started visiting the editing room. They came to check on their piece, to bring a bottle of *vinjak* (brandy), and to plea for adding a few more shots where their men could be seen. A rare instance of generals bribing a common soldier.

A month before I was supposed to leave the army, Vule, all excited, rushed into the editing room, bearing news that General Đoko Jovanić would be coming the next day.

I went to the director of Zastava Film and told him I was going to ask the general for a month's leave. I had salvaged his report and that must be worth something. Out of the question, he said. A common soldier cannot address a general. I could speak only if spoken to. I tried to explain that this was an unusual situation, and the general might agree to hear me out once he saw himself giving the report without a stammer. Eventually, afraid I might do just that, the director of Zastava Film put a sheet of paper into his typewriter and wrote the order: "Soldier Rajko Grlić is granted a month's leave."

Đoko Jovanić was pleased. The report to the Supreme Commander was perfect. He praised Vule before all of Zastava Film.

The following day, I said goodbye to Vule who was eternally grateful, took my order of leave, went to the Voždovac barracks, returned my weapons and uniform, and went back to civilian life that same afternoon.

Los Angeles, 1992

I am watching the siege of Dubrovnik on CNN. I see units from Montenegro shelling the town. Next to a huge canon is a Yugoslav People's Army major who bears a striking resemblance to Vule Milovanović. I watch him in shock, wondering what led him to that place. At the same time, I am hoping I am wrong and that it is not him.

But, back to our main character—Tito.

Belgrade, 2014

The Museum of Yugoslavia organizes an exhibition called *The Great Illusion—Tito and Film* (*Velika iluzija—Tito i film*). I receive an email from them with a plea to "make a list of up to five movies (not necessarily made in Yugoslavia) which, to your knowledge, somehow influenced, i.e., impressed Tito or are, in your opinion, in some other way relevant to the topic *Tito and Film*."

They also say: "As you know, Tito loved movies (between March 1949 and January 1980, he watched some 9,000 of them) and he often said he 'eagerly awaits every Yugoslav movie,' that is, he had a soft spot for domestic films (for your information, and according to the archives, Tito watched your movie *If It Kills Me* on July 27, 1974, and *Bravo, Maestro* on June 22, 1978)."

I sent them the list of the movies they later screened at the exhibition, and I added a brief explanation:

> *The Great Gatsby* (1949)–Elliott Nugent
> *The Searchers* (1956)–John Ford
> *Spartacus* (1960)–Stanley Kubrick
> *Kozara* (1962)–Veljko Bulajić
> *The Ambush* (*Zaseda*, 1969)–Živojin Pavlović

I don't know if Tito ever watched any of them, if they are on the list of the nine thousand movies he watched during his presidency. I also do not know if any of these movies, had he watched them, would have influenced him in any way.

But that does not matter. I chose them because I would have enjoyed, had I had the opportunity, to sit next to Tito and watch him watch them. I would have enjoyed observing him take them in, I would have tried to discern where he might see himself, what amused him, and what he would find boring. Watching him watch the films would help me understand where it was that I was born and what kind of country I had been living in for forty-four years.

Zagreb, 2015

Croatia's Madam President makes her first presidential move by throwing Tito's bust out of the presidential residence.

Zagreb, 2017

The Neo-Ustasha movement enters the Zagreb City Assembly and changes the name of Marshal Tito Square, the city's last symbol of antifascism. This is their triumphant return to the city which they left as cowards in 1945, when they fled Tito's Partisans, the antifascists.

P.S. Ivo Andrić says: *"Whenever and wherever I have come upon people who display excessive concern for national pride and the general interest, or excessive sensitivity to their own honor and dignity, this always, almost without exception, goes hand in hand with a limited mind, undeveloped skills, a cold heart, and pure, shortsighted selfishness."*

Prison Movies

Movies that take place in prisons or are about prisons: 20,000 Years in Sing Sing *(1932),* The Grand Illusion *(1937),* Stalag 17 *(1953),* Dead Man Walking *(1995),* Midnight Express *(1978),* In the Name of the Father *(1993),* Green Mile *(1999),* Is It Clear, My Friend? (Je li jasno, prijatelju?, *2000),* Hunger *(2008) ...*

Chambord, 1991

To celebrate the fall of the Berlin Wall, the French Minister of Culture, Jack Lang, invites about one hundred artists from Western and Eastern Europe to Blois. This is officially called *Europe Continent Culture*. The invitees from

Yugoslavia are Dragoslav Mihajlović, author of the novels *When the Pumpkins Blossomed* (*Kad su cvetale tikve*) and *Petria's Wreath* (*Petrijin venac*), and me.

Mrs. Mitterrand, the president's wife, organizes a gala dinner at the most famous of the Loire Valley castles, Chambord. The dinner is attended by about a hundred European artists, and all the European ministers of culture. All but the Yugoslav minister. At that point, Yugoslavia had not had a minister of culture for over ten years.

In the castle, done up in style for the occasion, Dragoslav and I sit and wait for the dinner to begin. Over a glass of champagne, Dragoslav tells me, in but a few words, about his experiences at the Goli Otok prison camp. I tell him what little I know of my parents' stay there.

Hardly can the discrepancy be any greater between our sublime surroundings and the pain of our conversation.

I hear for the first time of a pretend Goli Otok and a French delegation that visited it. With about a hundred other prisoners, Dragoslav was brought from the real Goli Otok for a few days to be an extra in the background. This was more or less all he said about it.

Here is my version of the event.

Paris, Belgrade, 1949

The news that Yugoslavia, despite the rift between Tito and Stalin, has a camp for political prisoners, modeled after the infamous gulags, spreads across Europe.

French socialists send a vigorous protest to the Yugoslav Government. They ask to be allowed to visit the camp, so they can inform the world objectively. To their surprise, the visit is granted.

Zagreb, Rijeka, 1949

A delegation of French socialists arrives in Zagreb.

Three black Mercedes-Benzes take them to Rijeka where they spend the night, and then they continue, the next day, southward along the road that runs down the coast.

Bakarac, 1949

It is cold. A strong bora wind has been blowing for three days.
After less than an hour, they leave the paved road. This is the first time their documents are checked.

The second time it happens, they have come to a barrier where there is a guard and a barbed-wire fence. Through the wire they can see a village of some thirty stone houses, roofed in white limestone. Once again, their documents are checked, but this time the check takes a little longer.

In the village, they are greeted by the manager of the camp who delivers a speech. He explains that there are about six hundred prisoners, one hundred and eleven guards, and twenty-two members of staff.

The French spend the morning wandering about the village. They are taken to see the sheep, the olive groves, an oil mill, houses, the doctor's office. The guards and the translators never leave them, not for a second. Also, the prisoners stay out of the way.

The guests, however, insist on talking with them. They explain why they have come, that they want to help, that the international community will take care of them, that they have nothing to fear.

Only a few of the most courageous prisoners agree to talk. But even they speak in hushed tones. They are clearly frightened. They complain about the conditions: the poor nourishment, the strict regime, the hard labor.

At five, the delegation is given a little something to eat. They are served olives, cheese, warm bread, and full-bodied red wine. The manager starts his parting speech by telling them that everything they are eating has been made in the village by the prisoners for the prisoners.

Gabriel Passek, the youngest member of the delegation listens to him while thinking that the prisoners he has spoken with were probably carefully chosen and instructed in what to say.

Moreover, Gabriel Passek is the only member of the delegation who can speak with them directly. He is a teaching assistant in the Department of Slavic Languages at the Sorbonne.

The manager's speech drags on. Gabriel glances around and sets his glass on the table. He approaches the closest guard and asks, more in gestures than in words, where he might find a toilet. The guard smiles and takes him behind the house. He points him to a wooden latrine at the far end of the garden.

Through the round opening in the latrine door, Gabriel patiently watches the guard. Once a gust wind forces the guard back to the house, Gabriel slips out of the outhouse and starts running.

He is finally on his own.

Suddenly, a prisoner walks across an empty street. Gabriel rushes over to him and grabs him by the hand. He hurriedly explains why he would like to talk with him. The prisoner shakes his head without a word, pushes Gabriel away, and walks on. Once again, Gabriel runs over to him and stops him. He pleads. The prisoner is unsure. It seems suspicious that a Frenchman speaks the language so fluently. Gabriel explains.

After the initial quandary, the prisoner pulls him back to a covered alleyway between two of the houses and starts speaking with excitement. He blurts to Gabriel that this is terrible, the food is awful, they have no contact with the outside world, they receive no newspapers, all the books they are allowed are carefully vetted, there are four of them to a tiny room, they have no running water. Gabriel keeps interrupting him. He wants to know if they have suffered physical torture. Are there harsh punishments? Are the interrogations linked to any kind of torture? Are the political prisoners mixed with criminals? The prisoner gives brief answers: no, no, and no. They are not tortured. They are not tormented. But the isolation is worse than any physical torture. Suddenly, the prisoner stops. He gestures to Gabriel to keep quiet. He pricks his ears. The sound of faraway footsteps. The prisoner runs off without looking back.

Paris, 1949

When they return to Paris, the French delegation holds a press conference. The world is informed that the prison does exist. Fortunately, though, the conditions are not the same as those of Stalin's infamous gulags. Moreover, for a country undergoing a painful recovery from the consequences of World War II, the conditions are surprisingly decent and humane.

Paris, 1958

Gabriel Passek learns that the camp they were actually looking for was called Goli Otok, that it was some ten kilometers away from the village they had seen, and that at the same time when they were there, under the strictest regime and utterly inhumane conditions, some ten thousand political prisoners were incarcerated. Gabriel eventually faces his longheld suspicion that the Yugoslav government has tricked them.

Ashamed, Gabriel decides to evade these thoughts. The only thing that keeps puzzling him is who the prisoner was, the one he had the dramatic conversation with. Is the man still in prison? Is he still alive? What is he doing now?

Paris, 1978

In the spring of 1978, the Croatian National Theater from Zagreb performs in Paris. Playing the lead, famous actor Ivan Dobrić.

In 1950, the most talented actor of his generation, Dobrić was, without explanation, whisked by the police from Zagreb to the Adriatic Coast. He was placed in a village which was, after its inhabitants had been temporarily removed, made over to resemble a prison. He spent the weirdest three days of his life there. He was the only actor among several hundred men who had temporarily traded their police uniforms for prisoners' garb, and yet another hundred genuine prisoners who donned new uniforms and were forbidden to communicate with the guests. Ivan Dobrić never said a word to anyone about it.

That night in the spring, however, performing in front of the Paris audience, Ivan Dobrić was convinced that his Frenchman must be out there in the dark of the theater. He was certain his long-held secret was about to be exposed, that his Frenchman was about to hear the truth he had so passionately sought.

But Gabriel Passek was not there. He had died the year before of kidney failure.

Producer

The person who prepares, organizes, and oversees film production.

Los Angeles, 1992

In the course of my eight months at UCLA in Los Angeles, Branko and Mirjana Lustig were very considerate to Ana, Olga, and me.

Before we return, Branko, two-time Oscar winner, takes me to a farewell lunch.

At the end of the meal, he takes out his checkbook and writes a check for $50,000. He tells me I must stay. That, without a doubt, I'll be making a movie there within two to three years. That it would be ridiculous to go back to Zagreb. I return the check. No, thank you, I can't accept it because I don't know how, or if, I will be able to return the money. Plus, I can't see myself in Los Angeles. Branko pushes the check back. You needn't return it; I don't expect you to. I just don't want you to make the wrong decision. Again, I return it, thankful for his kind gesture, for which I remain forever grateful.

Product Placement

A marketing technique used by companies to push their products by working them into a film, a television program, or any other media.

Brela, 1957

A big part of my childhood took place in Brela, on Loznica cove, in a stone summer house by the Adriatic Sea, built by my grandparents in the 1930s. This is where I learned almost all I know about the sea, fish, and therefore, naturally, about wine.

As for the sea, I used to think that to the north, it only went as far as the foot of Marjan Mountain, that with fish, as with everything else, you can drink only wine, and that *the* wine would always, and without exception, be Plavac. As I grew older, people explained that this is not really how things were, and I nearly believed them. Luckily, not quite. Because, even today, if I really want to swim, I go south of Split, and I still drink red wine with fish. And as to the wine, I still believe, after all the wines I have enjoyed in my life, that the Plavac of my childhood in Brela, which my grandma used to serve me in drops, is the finest wine in the world.

And back in my childhood in Brela, one knew exactly what came from where and how. Cookies were brought by ferry from Split, fruit and vegetables came by a ship called Leut from the mouth of the Neretva River, fish arrived on Lukeša's green boat from Baška Voda, and wine on a trabaccolo from "over yonder," and over yonder meant the islands of Brač and Hvar.

Split, Metković, Baška Voda, 1980–90

Years later, I would visit these places with the awe one feels when approaching the archeology of childhood. In Split, I found the cake shop where my father, between the night train from Zagreb, his morning coffee with brioche at Belvi's, and the ship to Soline, used to buy the traditional Dalmatian cookies called *rafioli*. I discovered the Neretva River, where at dawn, in complete silence disturbed only by the sound of an old diesel-engine, I watched the Leut, piled high with vegetables, leave for the coast. In Baška Voda, I found the bench outside the barber shop where the late Lukeša taught me not only everything about fish but everything about the winds, and about the logic and protocol to which they so obstinately adhere.

Zagreb, 2004

And then, one Saturday on Kaptol in Zagreb, in Slavica and Vlado's famous Bornstein wine shop, during a regular inspection of Plavac wines, I spotted a bottle whose blue-white Dogan label displayed a picture of a few stone houses. The label said that the place was Murvice, on Brač Island. And so finally, after a range of wonderful Tomić's and Carić's Plavac wines from Hvar, after the love given to and felt in return from all the Stagnums and other Miloš Plavac wines from Pelješac, I finally saw the Plavac from Brač. And right after the first glass of Baković's wine, I realized that I drink both with tremendous pleasure and with overwhelming sentiment.

Brač, 2005

Zrinka, Ante, Ana, and I embarked on a quest for Baković. We found him in Murvice, at the end of a dusty road, in a house amid a vineyard, high on a cliff overlooking the sea. There, with him and his family, savoring a glass of his Plavac, I felt as if all the tastes of my childhood had finally come together.

Reality Check

thefreedictionary.com states:

1. *An assessment to determine if one's circumstances or expectations conform to reality;*
2. *An event that forces one to reassess one's expectations or one's understanding of one's situation.*

February 2, 2012

Erland Josephson has died. A quiet man from the north. A face that told many of Bergman's tales.

Cannes, 1978

Bravo, Maestro is in the competition. Erland has a movie in the Critics Week. We meet after our screening. He says: "If you ever need an old man like me, call me. I'll come!"

Zagreb, 1980

We are filming *You Love Only Once* on Tuškanac. Erland plays Vladica's father. In the morning, we finish his part of the scene. After lunch, we move from the first to the second floor.

A few hours later, waiting for a change of light, I go down to the first floor. There is the crew and Erland is with them. I call Vanja Pinter, first assistant director, and ask her why no one has told him he is done for the day. "They have," she says, "but he doesn't want to go. He says he's here in case you need him. It would be silly, he says, if you wanted to change something and he weren't here. So, he's waiting. He says he never leaves a set until the scene is finished, even if his part in it is done."

I'm not sure why I remember this. It is new to me, I guess.

Zagreb, 1983

Erland visits us for lunch in Zapruđe, a new neighborhood on the outskirts of Zagreb. He is at the window, watching a muddy field where a big, beefy man is taking apart an old car while listening to loud music. He turns and says: "I know why you live out here! You want to be closer to real people!"

I do not want to disappoint him by saying that we have been hopelessly trying to exchange the apartment for one downtown so that we can move to a place that will not be so closely tied to real people.

Zagreb, 1985

Dunja Klemenc, a producer from Ljubljana and Erland's friend, sends me a copy of a few pages from Erland's recently published autobiography. As one of three directors, I am given an entire small chapter. The text is in Swedish, I do not understand a word. Ana, who used to work in Sweden every summer while she was a student, tries her hand at translating it. The other two directors are, no less, Bergman and Tarkovsky.

Research

Collecting material directly or indirectly linked to the story or characters of a movie. The first stage of the process happens before work starts on the script, and the second stage, during preparations in the preproduction phase.

Zagreb, 1986

I am prepping *Three for Happiness*. Production organizes a meeting with a police inspector from the burglary and theft department. He suggests that instead of meeting up at his office we could go for a walk around Zagreb.

Our walk starts off with his monologue: "Everybody steals. Of course, they steal what they can—a secretary steals office supplies, a worker at a gravel factory steals gravel . . . Everybody knows this. We know it, their bosses know it, our bosses know it. This how this society works. If the tap were turned off, things might go sour . . ."

And then he gives several examples from everyday life. A lot of what I see goes into the movie. But not everything. Here are two cases that, unfortunately, do not fit in the script.

We are in front of a supermarket in Zapruđe.

He points to the cashier. "We know she steals on a daily basis. How does she do it? Here's an example. Every morning, when she comes to work, she props a new broom up next to the cash register. And then adds it to every larger receipt. Only one in ten people actually checks their receipt. And when they ask: "What's this?" she says: "The broom!" The customer says, "I didn't buy a broom!" She calmly deducts the amount and removes the broom, saying: "Sorry, someone must have left it here!" As soon as the customer leaves, the broom goes back to the cash register. And so, the broom finds its way onto twenty, thirty, sometimes even fifty receipts a day," explains the inspector.

"The bald guy pacing over there, he's the manager. He knows, of course, what she's doing. But she also knows that he steals much more, whenever merchandise arrives at the store or is sold, measured or counted. We can't arrest either him or her, since we can't prove anything until they push it too far. And when do they fumble? When they rush. When they need money quick. For a wedding, a christening, travel abroad ... Then they need more money quick, so they become more vulnerable because they have no time to cover their tracks. And then they blow it."

On Radnička Rd. we pull over in front of a factory.

He points at the flat roof with steep skylights. "See that roof? It's so low that you can barely stand in the attic beneath it. A roof a lot like this one caught fire in Borovo, at the shoe factory. The fire department came and put out the fire. And what had caught on fire? Shoes! The attic was piled with old shoes. Almost ten thousand worn-out, dirty, rotting shoes. How did they get there? For years, possibly decades, workers would come to work in old shoes they'd collected from relatives, god knows where the shoes all came from. They left the worn-out shoes in the factory attic and went home wearing new ones. Had there not been a fire, they'd still be doing it."

He showed me around for hours, telling stories. He could see theft in everything. He was obsessed with thieves. Probably for good reason.

Revenge Movies

Revenge movies are aggressive and often bloody. A character sets off on a journey of revenge and does not give up until he kills the person who has wronged him.

Belgrade, 1947

Soon after World War II, Hotel Moscow in Belgrade is nationalized. The owner's son stays on as an employee for the next seventeen years, more than twelve of these as the hotel accountant.

Melbourne, 1964

The Hotel Moscow accountant, also an amateur dancer, travels with the national dance ensemble to Australia. As soon as he arrives, he seeks political asylum. They grant it to him in no time.

Belgrade, 1965

Six months later, he writes a letter to the management of Hotel Moscow. He tells them he has spent the last twelve years diverting from the hotel accounts the precise sum of money the hotel was worth when it was nationalized. The enclosed check for $7,000 is surplus. He had taken that much more than what was owed him.

Road Movies

Fiction, documentary, and experimental movies are often referred to as forms, while horror, comedy, drama, etc., are described as genres. The genre in which the characters keep traveling is called a road movie.

Prague, 1966–Athens, Ohio, 2006

I was nineteen when I went to study in Prague. Like everyone who leaves, I also thought that this was temporary. Soon, however, I realized that once life is packed into a suitcase, it is never unpacked. The suitcase, therefore, made me an eternal foreigner, both in the places where I came and the place I came from. This might be the reason why I still cannot answer a simple question: is the suitcase my homeland or is my homeland wherever my suitcase is?

New York, 2007

Olga may have been asking herself the same question when she chose this drawing as the logo for her GO Studio.

Olga Grlic's GO Studio logo, used with permission.

Rock and Roll Documentaries

Music documentaries that follow a rock band's concert or its tour or reconstruct a rock event or the life of a famous rock personality through archival footage and interviews.

Zagreb, Lapidarium, 1991

Dražen Vrdoljak was the preeminent rock critic of my generation, and often, even more: he was father, sometimes even mother, to many rock bands.

That year, the year zero of the war, he turned forty.

Aware of the times we were living in, he organized a small concert in the Upper Town Lapidarium. He invited about fifty friends and as many rock stars. Everyone who was anyone on the Yugoslav rock scene showed up—from Vlatko Stefanovski coming from the southernmost part of the country, to *Lačni Franz*, a band from the north. They came to sing in Dražen's honor, obviously knowing full well that this was going to be the last time they would be able to gather. Yes, this was the farewell rock concert of a generation.

I have been told that before dawn, while I was sitting on the floor in front of the small stage where the Belgrade band, *Idoli*, was performing, apparently I asked to hear the song *Maljčiki* three times in a row, when I was, probably, pretty sloshed. And, sure enough, they played it for me three times.

I am thankful to them. I still hold it in my ears.

The cameras never stopped rolling that night. I hope the material has not been lost, I hope someone is still preserving it somewhere and will make a rock-and-roll documentary about Dražen and the end of a good rock story someday.

Romantic Comedy

A love movie with a simple plot, spiced with light humor. The greatest masters of that genre were Billy Wilder, Ernst Lubitsch, and Stanley Donen, while the most famous titles are: It Happened One Night *(1934)*, Ninotchka *(1939)*, Roman Holiday *(1953)*, The Forty-First *(Sorok pervyy, 1956)*, Some Like It Hot *(1959)*, The Apartment *(1960)*, Jules et Jim *(1962)*, Look at Me, Unfaithful *(Pogledaj me, nevernice, 1974)*, Annie Hall *(1977)*, When Harry Met Sally *(1989)*, Pretty Woman *(1990)*, Love Actually *(2003)* . . .

Zagreb, 1948

My grandma Olga died.

Zagreb, 1950

My grandfather fell in love with Miss Cica who ran a knitting shop on Petrinjska Street. His sons did not share their father's enthusiasm. They inquired and discovered that the lady had already been married several times, and always to elderly gentlemen. With an almost professional aplomb, and quite quickly, she had taken them for everything they had. The three brothers told their father what they had found. His response was to write a long letter, asking them to vacate the villa on Glogovac.

The father and sons did not speak for nearly fifteen years. Over that period, I was the go-between, the messenger who went up to Glogovac once a month, taking a message if there was any to take, and sitting for an hour with Cica and my grandfather, my reward being cake with my tea.

My grandfather was a tough cookie. It took Cica almost ten years to get him to deed the house to her: a villa with a spacious two-story apartment, a small swimming pool, a one-bedroom apartment on the ground floor, a large cellar, and an orchard.

And, just as the sons had predicted, a few weeks after he had signed the deed over to her, Cica kicked him out of the spacious apartment and moved him to the one-bedroom on the ground floor. Half a year later, she sold the house and disappeared. My grandfather stayed on in the small apartment with the approval of the new owner until his ninety-first birthday. Then he asked me to find him a place in a home.

On that same day, he gave me his memoirs, asked me to hold on to them and never publish them under any conditions.

Zagreb, 1965

My mother was the first one to break family silence and call my grandfather. From that moment on, until the end of his life, he came to visit once a week to Vrbanićeva Street for lunch. He spent Christmas Eve with his sons and took part in family gatherings in an attempt to make up for lost time.

Veliki Lošinj, 1976

My grandfather built yet another house in his old age. But he lost that one, too. He signed it over to his final companion, a certain Ms. Ange.

Romantic Comedy II

Prague, 1995

We are on our way down the stairs at the Rudolfinum. Seventy-year-old Vera K. talks without taking a breath:

" . . . the only thing I couldn't understand was why he ripped it off. The blouse, the dress . . . Everything. Why so rough? He knew I would've . . . Thirty-eight . . . nine . . . no . . . eight years ago. On the island of Hvar. Yes. Do you know him? Ivan Franičević? Tall. Handsome as Apollo. I wept when the war in your country started. Prayed nothing would happen to him. On Hvar . . . There wasn't war there, right?"

Rome

Federico Fellini's movie, made in 1972, in which the lead roles are played by the city of Rome and its residents.

In one sequence of the movie, the cameras, followed by spotlights, enter underground halls covered in frescoes. In contact with the light, the frescoes fade and disappear before our very eyes.

Going through my director's notebook which has given birth to this lexicon, I feel how my memories, like those frescoes, are fading as I tuck them in under these headings, lay them in one of the graves in this cemetery of my movies that have never been filmed.

Rules of the Game

The Rules of the Game (La Règle du Jeu, 1939) is a romantic comedy by Jean Renoir. A satirical movie that touches on French high society, it was banned by the Vichy government which forced Renoir to recut it. Today, there are several versions of the movie, which is considered one of the paramount films in French cinema.

Zagreb, 1982

My grandfather told me that when he was wounded in World War I, he felt he left his body and, floating above it, watched himself being operated on. At this point, he said, he felt he had a choice: to go back into the body or give up.

Zagreb, 1986

I toyed with using "leaving the body" in a film. I read a few books, I talked to people who had had the experience, but the story never took solid enough shape.

Zagreb, 1995

It was summertime. I was walking along streets I had been on many times. Suddenly I felt as if I were looking at them from above, as if I were floating. As if I had stepped away from myself and, like my grandfather, I had a choice, or at least felt I did: to come back or not.

That evening, I wrote this:

> The first ten minutes or so of a movie—known as the "first act" in ancient Greece and also in the Hollywood of today—are when the audience is given the vocabulary they'll need to follow the story. Within this block of time, the limits are set for the playground, the players are introduced, and their conflict explained. In short, the "rules of the game" are set to help the audience follow the fiction as if it were reality. The moviegoer decides whether to accept the rules as offered or walk out of the movie theater and abandon fiction for the real world.
>
> This game of fiction and reality is part of our real lives, too. In the darkness of the movie theater, the "rules of the game" are made explicit from the start, and the narrator mostly keeps to them all the way through. In real life, however, these rules often change. During a single lifetime, at a single place, the rules may change two or three, or even more times. And another small difference. We can refuse to comply with the "rule of the game" of a movie for the price of the ticket, while the price of refusing the "rules of the game" imposed by life is a little higher.
>
> If we walk out of a theater before the end of a movie, it is erased from our memory virtually forever. Leaving the parameters of our lives, unfortunately, doesn't guarantee such a clean cut. The body remembers a severed arm, the feet remember the street pulled out from under them.
>
> Life or cinema? I don't know. I tried making movies, and yet, life happened to me. I'm not sure whether things would've gone better had I taken the opposite road.

Russian Cinema

All the movies made since the days of the Russian Empire—from the ones made in the Union of Soviet Socialist Republics to those made in Russia today.

Prague, 1969

"The History of USSR Cinema" was by far the most challenging exam at FAMU. Students were examined by Dean A. M. Brousil and the exam sometimes lasted for a few hours.

Motovun, 2008

When the Russians decided to celebrate the centenary of their cinema at three places worldwide and chose the Motovun Film Festival as one of them, I was able to recite, off the top of my head, the historical chronology of their cinema in thirty movies. The festival sent my suggestions to the Russians and they approved the list. Brousil was a great dean, and probably deserves the most credit for Czech cinema being taken seriously in the 1960s and 1970s, but, apparently, he also taught us a little something.

Moscow, 1978

I received a phone call from Yugoslavia Film. The Russians had invited four young directors whose movies they had started screening: Srđan Karanović, Lordan Zafranović, Karpo Godina, and me.

We met up for a "farewell dinner" at Ivo's restaurant at the Belgrade Writer's Club.

On the airplane, with the kind help of stewardesses who loved our movies and to soften our fears, we drank a lot of whiskey.

In Moscow, we are greeted in style. They sweep us through the airport shouting: "Delegation, делегация, delegation." They usher us through passport and customs controls, seat us in long, black Chaika limos that drive along a special middle lane without having to stop at red lights, and deliver us to Rossiya Hotel on Red Square.

That evening, we attend an official dinner with the minister of culture of the USSR at the Film Workers' Club. In a grand hall, with only one table in the middle. All in black suits, there they are: the minister; the head of his Cinematography department; the director of *Mosfilm*, the central film studio; and the general editor of *Voprosy kinoiskusstva*, the official film journal. All in all, these are the decision-makers for the film industry of the Soviet Union.

Across the table from them sit the four of us, with only Lordan in a jacket and a tie.

The dinner kicks off with caviar, vodka, and banter. The editor of *Voprosy kinoiskusstva* casually asks me to explain to her, since I have studied in Prague, why it is that Czech movies are no longer as good as they used to be. I answer, equally casually, that this might be because they were occupied in 1968. She coolly skips over the answer and moves on to easier questions.

Everything goes smoothly until the moment when the minister rises to his feet and ceremoniously raises his glass. We follow suit. The minister holds a toast and several times he mentions Comrades Tito and Brezhnev and the great friendship between our fraternal nations. We drink our drinks and sit. At that point, the translators quickly explain that protocol requires the head of our delegation to respond with a toast. We protest that we are not a delegation and none of us is any sort of head. That we are four movie directors who represent no one but ourselves. Clearly this is not going to pass muster. We exchange glances and say: Lordan is the only one of us who is a member of the Communist Party, and we're in Soviet Russia, after all, so he is in charge. And so it is that Lordan gives a toast in which he mentions Comrades Tito and Brezhnev several times and the great friendship between our fraternal nations.

After this, the head of cinematography within the Ministry of Culture gives a toast and speaks of the fraternity of the fraternal cinemas of USSR and Yugoslavia. The translators explain that the deputy head of our delegation is now supposed to respond with a toast. We play a quick round of odds and evens. I lose, rise to my feet and propose a toast to Isaak Babel. I say I am glad to be visiting the country of this remarkable writer, the author of the story my thesis movie is based on. The third toast is Điđa's. He speaks of Pilnyak and his love for this author whose work has recently inspired a movie of his. We know full well that both Pilnyak and Babel are still blacklisted. Tensions rise.

All of this, however, is just a lead-up to the grand finale. After the general editor of *Voprosy kinoiskusstva* gives his toast, Karpo's turn has come. He stands up with effort and, as he raises his glass, being a large man and very drunk, he topples over right onto the table. The minister is seated directly across from him. Which means that whatever flies off the table ends up all over the minister and his lap.

An awkward silence. We jump to help Karpo up, an almost impossible task, while the Russians, and a few men who have been standing to the side, clearly the police, jump in to assist the minister.

Then a man appears. As we later understand, he is the Yugoslav cultural attaché who has been sitting at the back of the hall all along. He whispers that the dinner will end now, and he will be giving us a ride.

And indeed, after rather chilly farewells, the attaché piles us into his Volvo. Once we are on our way, he explains that today, or rather yesterday, as by then it is after midnight, was the Day of the Republic, and he is taking us to the Yugoslav Embassy. A reception for three thousand people is underway there. "The ambassador is expecting you" he says, to justify the endless drive through the empty Moscow streets.

When we arrive, he drops us off in front of the building and goes off to park the car. We decide not to wait for him but go straight in and climb the vast marble staircase, gradually realizing that everything in Russia is three times bigger than what we are used to.

At the top of the monumental staircase there is a monumental marble hall. The reception is clearly over. The guests have left. Numerous tables covered in leftovers are soaked in the pungent stench of cigarette butts. A tall man in a black suit is walking around the hall. He holds a small camera above his head, snapping pictures of the ceiling. With each click, he takes a playful little hop, mutters something, and reels drunkenly along.

Lordan goes over to him and says: "Hey, you, listen here. Why don't you take a picture of us? This is our first night in Moscow." The man looks at him steadily, points the camera at the ceiling, takes another little hop, mumbles a few words, and on he goes. Lordan catches up and nabs him by the collar. "Listen kiddo, don't fuck with me, take a picture of us."

"No, I will not take a picture of you. I am the ambassador here and I don't have to."

"You're a dick, not an ambassador," says Lordan and pushes him toward us, saying: "Hear me? Take the picture!"

At this point, a young man, apparently a plainclothes police officer, materializes next to the tall man, and says: "Comrade Ambassador, do you need help?"

Yes, this is, indeed, the Yugoslav Ambassador to Russia, Joža Smolej. He does snap a picture of us and soon afterward we end up at his home. Lordan instantly makes a move on his wife, while the three of us, slowly but surely, go about emptying the wine cellar.

In the morning, as the cultural attaché ferries us back to our hotel on Red Square, we fall sound asleep in the car.

We spend seven days in Moscow. We ask to see Tarkovsky and the movie he has just finished: *The Mirror* (*Zerkalo*, 1975). Over the seven days, they take us every morning to a small cinema for the screening of a different movie. Each day we stay for five minutes, then get up and leave. On the seventh day, they finally show us *The Mirror*. For the seven days, we are an official delegation, escorted around and shown amazing sites, while at night, after the official Chaikas drop us off at the hotel, we take a cab and embark on a totally different life. Our guide through nighttime Moscow is Larisa Shepitko, a student of Dovzhenko's. She won the Golden Bear award at the Berlin Film Festival the year before, but her movies are still being censored. While repeating the sentence: "Romanian officers do not charge for love," Larisa takes us, night after night, to an atelier or an apartment in the ugly new buildings. Inside, the apartments are furnished like the finest museums, and we meet writers, directors, painters, and many other strange characters there.

So, one night, on our way back to our hotel, just before dawn, we see Red Square covered with a dusting of snow. It has been falling for less than an hour and no one has walked through it yet. I can't remember whose idea it was, but soon we started taking little steps and dragging our feet across the vast Red Square and, imitating the original logo, write: "Coca-Cola." Then I hoist Karpo up onto my shoulders and he takes hundreds of pictures that are supposed to bring us—as he yells with excitement—untold riches. Ever since that night, Karpo has been promising to find the negatives, but it has been thirty years and he has not found them yet.

We take the Imperial Train from Moscow to Leningrad. We set off from a station they are just starting to demolish. The one from which Anna Karenina saw off Vronsky. So Larisa comes to see us off dressed like Anna Karenina. Besides—and good directors can arrange for that too—it is snowing. This was the last time we saw Larisa. A year later she died en route to the set of her new movie. Many claimed the traffic accident was staged.

Leningrad, 1978

A bluish northern dawn. We are in a car moving through the empty streets of Leningrad. Approaching the city center, we see people lying on the ground. Not actually dead, just dead drunk. Buses with Finnish plates move slowly along, stopping by each "dead guy." Two men get down off the bus, roll the man over and, if he is one of theirs, they drag him on board. If not, they leave him there on the ground. The translator explains this happens at the end of every weekend, when the guests from the Nordic countries are supposed to return home.

That afternoon, we are on the Aurora, the ship from which shots were fired, which marked the beginning of the October Revolution. Karpo takes pictures, we act the scenes we remember from Eisenstein's *Potemkin*. Needless to say, we have never seen any of those pictures either.

We are taken out for a dinner to the Grand Hotel Europe, if I remember correctly. We are in the grand hall, lined in dark wood and decorated with crystal chandeliers, and over champagne and red and black caviar served chilled in small crystal bowls over ice, we listen to the story of the hotel and the Leningrad siege.

At the end of World War II, Russians come across the detailed German protocol for a celebratory dinner to be held once Leningrad falls to them. Some thirty German generals and field marshals are supposed to be seated around the table. Everyone's place and the menu are clearly mapped out.

About fifteen of them are captured by the Russians. After they have been made to walk across Red Square alongside their soldiers and throw their squad flags at Stalin's feet, the generals are brought to Leningrad to the very hotel and the very hall, and they are seated around the table according to the German protocol, and served the dinner as planned.

Baku, 1978

We spend our last few days in the south, in Baku. A socialist version of the orient: no shops or bustle in the streets.

We pass the time mostly drinking with Azeri writers and directors. We drink copious amounts of their cognac. In order to survive it, we chew on chives, a sort of grass soaked in greasy oils. The oils, they claim, prevents alcohol from going from the stomach to the brain. There I finally understand why gypsy musicians, when performing at weddings that last for days, take a sip of oil every so often.

As we are leaving, Karpo—need I add that he was not completely sober?—lies down on the runway, flings open his arms and legs, and shouts: "I've lost my passport, I'm staying here forever." Azei air traffic shuts down for almost half an hour.

Motovun, 2012

Karpo arrives, with shouts of "I've found them! I've found them!"
 "What did you find?"
 "The pictures from Russia!"
 "Coca-Cola, too?" I ask.
 "Not yet, but soon. So far, I have this," says Karpo and hands me an envelope with four photographs in which he, Lordan, Điđa, and I are standing, in fur coats, in the heart of the medieval Russia, in snow-bound Zagorsk, in front of the Church of the Holy Trinity, adorned by icons painted by Andrei Rublev.

Script

The written text used for a movie, containing scenes with description of the action and dialogue.

Motovun, 2001

Igor Mirković introduces me to Ante Tomić.

Zagreb, 2002

After I read Ante's short story collection *I Forgot Where I Parked* (*Zaboravio sam gdje sam parkirao*), I told him that two stories from the book, one about the war and another about the prewar period, could be made into a script. But a proper triptych would need a third story, a postwar one with the same characters. Not only did he agree, but he was thrilled. He promised to send the story in no more than two weeks.

I did not hear from him for more than a year.

Athens, Ohio, 2003

And then, his email arrived amid my tranquil life in the States. It mentioned nothing about our agreement or his promise. What he did say is that he was attaching a few chapters from his next novel, a brief outline of what he was planning to write, and he asked me if I would be interested in making that into a movie.

The novel had as its working title, *The Border Post*. I read what he sent and answered that I was interested, I would like to start playing with it, turning the novel into a script, but if this were to become a reality someday, I would like for us to work on it together. His response was short and clear:

> From: Ante Tomic
> To: Rajko Grlic
> Subject: Re: Karaula
> Date: Wed, 26 Feb 2003
>
> Dear Rajko,
>
> Thank you for your comments, they're smart and will be very useful. The outline I've sent is still only in my head. I'd need a few free days to finish it. To hell with this, it has to be done by the beginning of March. And then you decide. To be honest, I don't feel like writing a script. That's something you can't make me do. As soon as I finish the story, I'll send it to you, and then it's yours to cut and change it any way you like, talk to the producers, but I'll already be doing something new. I'd like my work on this movie to be nothing more than one or two friendly visits to the set.
>
> Best, Ante

Zagreb, 1983

This was not the first time I had been rejected. When I suggested to Dubravka Ugrešić that we take her novel *Steffie Speck in the Jaws of Life* (*Štefica Cvek u raljama života*) and build another story around it to frame it, and then turn that into a script, she said more or less the same thing: "Take the book and do whatever you like with it. I prefer to stay out of it." Eventually, she did not stay out of it completely.

Athens, Ohio, 2003

I wrote the first draft of the script while Ante finished the novel.

Split, 2003

Three months later, in Meje, a neighborhood of Split, we wrote the second draft.

Zagreb, Athens, Ohio . . . 2003–5

We wrote the next drafts in an assortment of places: Zagreb, Athens, Ohio, Sumartin, Ohrid . . . And each of them took us a week or two to finish. We sequestered ourselves about nine every morning, wrote until lunch, had lunch, and then resumed writing until five or six in the afternoon. Billy Wilder used to say that scriptwriting is an uninspiring job, that there are no muses, that one comes to work as if you are working in a factory, that, unlike the shooting itself which can be joyful, scriptwriting is work, work, and work; blood, sweat, and tears.

The process is always similar. After each draft, we set aside the text to let it sit for a month or two. So, we can rest from it and it can rest from us. Then, in the tranquility of the US hills or Istrian dales, I set up a new structure, scene by scene, add new scenes, discard old ones, develop the ones that are already there. This always takes at least two months.

A discussion about changes kicks off each new session. This lasts for a day or two, and then Ante sits at his laptop, plays Lucinda Williams at full blast, and starts writing the scene we have discussed: meanwhile, I draft the outline for the next one. And, of course, I keep the coffee brewing, since Ante can drink it in enormous amounts. Finally, we read the scene together, tweak it if necessary, or, if it is beyond repair, he writes it all over again. A day of work ends in reading and an almost ritual abbreviation of dialogues. And his dialogues are not easily shortened; because of their internal rhythm, but maybe also because Ante feels sincere pain at every cut or change in his dialogue. The excuse I can offer for the pain I have been causing him for years is: I have never worked with anyone who writes better dialogues.

Also, I must admit that I have never laughed so much while writing a script. We respect Buñuel's motto that a day without laughter is a day wasted. We laugh a lot, talk a lot, and feel just as good about staying quiet. In short—we get to know to each other, realizing how different we are and how much personal space both of us need in this mutual game of ours.

Ohrid, Macedonia, 2005

While we were writing the first draft, we agreed that we would write the final one after we had had our final rehearsals with the actors. A month before the shooting was to begin, we brought to Ohrid the five actors who would play the main roles. I spent two weeks with them reading the script, talking, rehearsing, visiting buildings and sites, and setting up a few of the basic scenes. Ante was with us for the last seven days. In the beginning, he cringed at actors' suggestions to adjust a sentence or two, but he quickly rolled up his sleeves. He fought for every word and sometimes, lacking any other argument, he joined in to show the actors how to deliver the lines. He assumed the role of director for a while and clearly enjoyed it.

Then, we let the actors go so they could sort out their lives before they came to the set which they would not be leaving for the next ten weeks, and the two of us wrote the final, eleventh draft, over two days. We adapted the dialogue to each of the actors, their language and rhythm.

I did not introduce many changes during the shooting. Everything went relatively smoothly. I had an excellent crew. Every now and then something would crop up, I would add a short scene or shorten an existing one, I'd develop or shorten the dialogue, or I'd change a location and adapt the text to it. Only once, when I ran into a slightly bigger glitch, did I exchange a few emails with Ante, and move on.

Ante, true to his promise, joined the shooting and stayed for a few days. He loved sitting in the director's chair. At some point, watching me prepare for the scene at the open market, realizing that a single shot needs hours of patient orchestration of the actors, the crew of about a hundred people, and some two hundred extras, he worried: "How can you do this? It's an awful job!"

As he was leaving, he gave me a CD with a note:

Dear Rajko,

While I was packing last night, I realized I wanted to leave this album with you. I've had enough of it and you, I thought, while you're leaving for the set at the crack of dawn, might find something in these beautiful, wise rhymes of Kristofferson's, something we could use in our movie.

Ante

This messaging through music has continued throughout our collaboration. For each new project, Ante compiles a list of a dozen songs which, in his opinion, best express the spirit of the film in the making.

Athens, Ohio, Zagreb, 2008

We enjoyed our scriptwriting double scull so much, that we decided to do it again. This time we started from scratch, from what is called an "original script." This started, as is our ritual, with an email, but this time the nudge came from me. I sent him just a few sentences in which I tried to sketch out a possible connection between five characters: husbands, lovers, mistresses. We toyed with the Zagreb urban mythology of double lives. The name of the film was *Just Between Us*, and we wrote, as I recall, eight drafts of the script; Ante claims there were ten.

Athens, Ohio, Zagreb, Split, 2011

After that, we joyfully went to work on his novel *The Viper's Glen Miracle* (*Čudo u Poskokovoj Dragi*). Even before it was published. We wrote a script for a comedy, a love-adventure, for a spectacle which would be screened in huge tents, with beer in hand, and live gigs by the TBF band, inviting the audience to sing along.

We abbreviated it, developed it, we changed almost the entire second half of the novel. Ante objected only occasionally and when asked about it, he said: "We're ditching a lot and I know that after the movie opens, people will come over to me and say: 'What a pity he ditched such a great scene. That's the best scene in the book.'"

We spent two years on the script, in eight drafts or more, then we spent just as much time chasing the funding. We secured half the necessary budget but not all of it.

Split, Athens, Ohio, Zagreb, 2014

We decided to heal this bitter defeat, the open wound left by the unmade movie, with a new script. A film which, in case we could not find the money, I could make with three friends and an iPhone.

Once again, it was conceived over email. Ante sent me a late-night message from Split describing his neighbor, a professor who dresses up as a woman at night, and a woman who helps him do it. To his ten lines I responded with twenty, giving the professor a father and the woman a husband, and I moved them all into one building.

Two and a half years and six drafts later, we had a script built on our own experience with intolerance, intolerance that spurred several physical attacks on Ante, and sent me across the Atlantic. The movie was *The Constitution*.

Duško Ljuština, probably the best manager in culture in Croatia, persuaded Ante, with less effort than it took for him to convince me, that once the movie was out, the script should be adapted for the theater.

Novi Sad, 2016

After the opening in Zagreb, we went on a tour. We took a bow in Rijeka, Split, Ljubljana, Belgrade, and finally in Novi Sad.

We came out before the audience and received a standing ovation. A long one. At one point, Ante and I looked at each other and I said, "We're done now!"

He says: "Nothing's better than this!"

"It would be a pity to spoil it!" I add, he smiles and nods.

Athens, Ohio, Split, 2017

Emails with new ideas fly across the Atlantic. We send them timidly and bury them bravely. I am not sure I can make it through yet another movie, but the fear of stopping the game is even worse. He might fear the end, too. Over these fifteen years we have become friends.

P.S. As Billy Wilder says: "*a good writing collaboration is more difficult to achieve than a good marriage. And it's more intimate.*"

The Secret to Great Film Acting

Hundreds of books have been written on the secrets of acting in movies. Workshops worldwide reveal the secret every weekend for a modest sum. Numerous film and theater schools are sustained by the trust their students place in them, believing the school will open the door to this mystic paradise.

I spent a few years teaching the course—Acting for a Film. I wrote pages and pages to explain at least a part of the secret to myself. For a while, I entertained the idea of turning this into a book. But I gave up because I realized that an innocent soul might see my words as a "recipe," the truth on how to become and stay an actor.

After all the movies I have made and all the actors I have worked with, I still have not found the recipe; to be frank, I am certain now that there isn't one. I believe the decisive element is the actor's or actress's character, their inner world. If they are well-led, and if you, as a director, are lucky, what is inside them can, at least for a moment, be brought to the surface. If this human but also difficult and complex element is lacking, if they are empty, if they are not endlessly sensitive to a touch from outside themselves, there can be no acting. And no acting technique in the world will help.

Zagreb, 2015
While working on *The Constitution* with Ksenija Marinković and Dejan Aćimović, both fine actors for whom the roles were written, and with Nebojša Glogovac, a rare master, an actor whose self-possession and bearing I tremendously enjoyed, I wrote down these lines during one of our breaks:

> Acting in film is like a connect-the-dots game. This is what a good actor does. He gives the audience the dots, and then they have the task of connecting them and assigning to his face their understanding of his emotions, conditions, fears, and hopes. If the actor were to offer an already-finished drawing, if he were to connect the dots himself, the audience would feel superfluous. They would not have the right or privilege of being more than an equal player in the holy triangle of author, movie, and themselves in the darkness of the movie theater, as the one who deciphers the emotions and solves the puzzle.

Zagreb, 2015

Once the shooting was done, Nebojša sent me probably the most beautiful text message a director can get from an actor:

> I'm finding it difficult to find the words, and I've been trying since yesterday, for how inspiring, nice, important, pleasant—and everything else I'm still seeking the words for—it was at the shooting of our movie. Working with you was, beyond doubt, one of the best collaborations I've ever had with a director. The nuances you noticed and the ones which were lacking so we searched for them, inspired the feeling that we were exploring something new and yet something already known, which we'd invoke and find. I felt like a "real actor" ☺. Thank you so much for the opportunity, for accepting, understanding and developing my vision of Vjekoslav Kralj, and for this feeling of creative friendship you so easily and graciously established. This evening, I'm drinking with you.

Selfie

A photo or a recording we make of ourselves.

Split, 2014

She and He, both under thirty, enter a bedroom, kissing. We see them from the point of view of the small camera he is holding.

Bit by bit, we realize they have decided to make a homemade porno movie. They start stripping off their clothes, excited, hurried. But suddenly, she has a change of heart. She doesn't want to, she's scared. Some other time. She takes the camera from his hand and places it on a shelf by the window.

He refuses to give up. He tries to persuade her again, promises her face won't show. While trying to talk her into it, and making sure she doesn't notice, he slowly turns the camera toward the bed. But she does notice and pushes it away. She threatens to leave.

As of that moment, the camera is motionless. The planned love scene turns into an acoustic act.

Through the window which makes the outside sounds inaudible, the camera "sees" a not-so-busy street.

A man passes, a child runs along, a car drives by. In contrast to the peaceful image, the love play presented through sound grows more passionate.

On the street as we watch, two cars appear from opposite directions. One is bigger than the other. In passing they collide. The damage isn't bad:

scrapes on both cars and cracked rearview mirrors. Angry drivers jump from the cars. They yell at each other, waving their arms.

After a few moments, things quiet down. The drivers take out their cell phones. They make calls. Still on the phones, they get back into their cars. Nothing happens. Apparently, they are waiting for the police.

Suddenly, the driver of the smaller car gets out, goes over to the bigger vehicle, and kicks the driver's door. The driver of the bigger car comes out, shocked. He roars. Threatens. The driver of the smaller car returns calmly to his car. The driver of the bigger car goes back to his car and takes something from the glove compartment. He turns around, kicks the door closed, and then we see he is holding a gun. He marches to the smaller car. The driver of the smaller car rolls up his window in fear.

In terms of sound, the lovemaking is finished. Silence. Cigarettes lit. Someone gets up. It is him.

He approaches the camera, points it at himself, and winks smugly. A gunshot. His hand trembles and he turns off the camera.

The Seventh Seal

Ingmar Bergman's movie (1957) with its famous scene on the beach where a knight, hoping to prolong his life, plays chess with Death.

During World War II, Blažo Jovanović (1907–1976) was one of the most important leaders of the Yugoslav Communist Party of Montenegro and the first President of the People's Assembly of Montenegro.

The Grand Beach, near Ulcinj (Montenegro), is 13 km long and 60 m wide, and covered in fine sand. According to some estimates, it can hold up to 150,000 people.

Ulcinj, 1963

Five of us high school boys were the only, and possibly first, campers on the beach that year. No more than one hundred people came to the beach each day and took up the first one to two hundred meters. The remaining twelve kilometers were empty.

One morning, two muscular men in black suits came to the beach and gestured to the people to make room. The people obeyed submissively, then the men spread a blanket, set down a chess board, and arranged the pieces.

Half an hour later, a small speedboat arrived. A middle-aged man jumped out of it, and helped Blažo Jovanović, by far the most powerful Montenegrin at the time, climb out of the speedboat.

The man dragged the speedboat up onto the sand and the two of them, in swimming trunks, went over to the blanket, lay down and started playing chess. The game lasted for almost an hour. The bodyguards stood by their side, watching the people on the beach.

Once the game was over, the players stood up without a word, went to the speedboat, climbed in, and left.

The two men in black suits collected the pieces, placed them in a box, shook the sand off the blanket, and left without saying anything.

The people, also without comment, slowly went back to their places on the beach, as if nothing had happened.

Silent Movies

A movie in which dialogue appears in subtitles, and the sound is provided by live music that can be played by a solo pianist or a grand orchestra.

Leka Konstantinović, Tito's projectionist for years, told in a documentary made about him that out of all the Western films, Tito's favorite was one with Kirk Douglas. I am not certain which film, but I think it might have been *Lonely Are the Brave* (1962). He also said that during the movie—and Tito saw it a million times—at the exact moment when Kirk comes out of the saloon and faces the danger of being shot by a bad guy from a nearby roof, Tito would always shout: "Kirk, watch your back."

That sincere shout of a cinephile inspired this idea for a silent film.

Munich, 1921

Stipe goes to a movie theater, buys a ticket and shows it to the fat ticket-taker, who tears off half of Stipe's ticket. Stipe looks at him in shock, goes back to the box office and buys another. Once again, the fat ticket-taker tears his ticket in half. Stipe comes up with an idea, goes to the box office and buys two tickets. He shows one to the fat man and hides the other in his pocket.

The theater is half-empty. A Western is showing.

The lonesome cowboy is unaware of a group of villains creeping up on him from behind. Stipe is agitated and shouts a warning to the cowboy. The cowboy turns around and kills the gang. Fatso comes over to Stipe and presses his finger to his lips to gesture silence.

Stipe watches in silence. But the cowboy is in peril again. Stipe bites his tongue. He looks at Fatso and Fatso wags his finger at him, warning him to keep quiet. But the cowboy's life is now in danger. The bad guy shoots at him from the roof. Stipe cannot resist and shouts. The cowboy turns around and kills the bad guy in the nick of time. Fatso comes over to Stipe, waves his flashlight at him and warns him, angrily, that, if he does it again, he will throw him out.

Meanwhile, the cowboy pushes his way through woods. A new group of villains is lurking for him in ambush. Stipe grows more nervous. He turns, looks for Fatso, who gestures for silence with his flashlight. The cowboy nears the ambush. Stipe looks at the cowboy, then at Fatso. He doesn't know what to do. At that moment, the bad guys shoot and hit the cowboy. He is wounded but still alive.

Stipe leaps to his feet, jumps up onto the stage, barges into the screen and tells the cowboy that the fat ticket-taker is working with the bad guys. The cowboy from the movie kills Fatso in the audience.

Atlanta, 1921

Stipe comes out of the screen and finds himself in another movie theater on another continent. This is where his silent movie adventure begins.

Silver Screen

A reflective screen which, due to the actual silver or reflective aluminum embedded in it, becomes a highly reflective surface. This term was embraced by popular usage as a metonym for the cinema industry. So, the phrase "star of the silver screen" simply means: a movie actor.

New York, 2010

In his movie about Elia Kazan, Martin Scorsese describes the New York of his childhood, the streets he walked, and the people he met. He says that he saw it all over again in Kazan's movies that took place in the same setting, with almost the same faces. He says that, thanks to Kazan's movies, he began to understand the world he lived in.

While I am watching Scorsese's movie, I think how fortunate it must be to have the grounds for such comparisons, to be able to see on the screen something so close to your own life.

Zagreb, 1959

I grew up going to the movies and imbibed the moving pictures on the screen with equal eagerness. The difference is that these had almost nothing to do with my life, my street, and the people around me. Back then, Yugoslav cinema was either caught up in war without end or steeped in ponderous rural dramas . . . Hollywood was caught up either by Californian swimming pools, dusty prairies, or the distant past . . . Very little of what I saw on screen had anything to do with my life. For me, movies were something else, something larger or smaller than life, but certainly not the life around me.

Zagreb, 1974

I have never talked with Điđa about this, but I guess it was a shared feeling that gave birth to the idea for the series *The Reckless Years*. I suppose that while he was writing the script for the series, he must have, like me, had a vague need to bring image and life closer together, to make it possible for a filmmaker, someone coming after us, to recognize his own life through someone else's, to identify his own images through someone else's destiny, so near and yet so far.

Sound

The sound is recorded separately from the image and then they are synchronized. After the editing, the sound is processed separately and then, as an optical signal, it is transferred to a 35 mm sound negative. Through synchronization between the 35 mm negative of the image and tone negative of sound, we get a positive, a 35 mm film copy ready for cinematic screening. This is how things used to be while films were, as the term states, made on film. Digital technology has simplified all this.

Pula, 1974

In the Pula Arena (one of the world's largest open-air cinemas, located in a Roman amphitheater), a "technical rehearsal" of image and sound was typically organized one night before the official screening. In the dead of night, after the festival audience left the arena, the movies to be shown the next day had the chance to run one roll. While it was on, you went to different parts in the arena, and shouted to the people up in the projection booth: turn it up, turn it down, I can see it, I can't see it. And that's about it.

This was the first time I was showing a movie in the arena and went through the ritual for the first time. We synchronized the sound volume with the image and then went to Hotel Riviera for a drink.

If It Kills Me was the first movie shown that evening. The screening began. The image was fine, but the sound was virtually inaudible. For a minute or two, I thought they might have forgotten to play it, but then I realized it simply was not there and I would have to do something. But what? I was not the only debut author in the arena, everyone around me was also new to this and no one knew what to do. I realized I needed to get to the projection booth as soon as possible. But how? The night before, at the rehearsal, the arena had been empty, and that had been easy. But this evening it was packed, so what now?

I leaped to my feet and started running. I looked for a way through the increasingly rowdy audience. They started whistling in disapproval.

The movie was in its seventh or eighth minute by the time I reached the booth. The arena was ringing with whistles.

I opened the door and saw the two projectionists sipping drinks and playing cards. I shouted: "The sound!" One of them stood up calmly and said: "Oops, sorry," he turned it up and went back to his cards. I was gasping, unsure of what to say. Outside, the whistling subsided. The movie's sound, now at normal volume, filled the arena.

That night, someone who had had many screenings asked: "Did you take a bottle of whisky to the projectionist before the screening?"

"No, I had no idea!" I moaned.

"Well, now you know!" he said, winking at me.

Zagreb, 1989

Đorđe Milojević, known as Đoka Hrt, was the director of Centar Film from Belgrade which, with my Maestro Film, coproduced Điđa's movie *Virgina*.

When talking about the sound and the French partner who was supposed to provide the sound technicians and the equipment, Đoka casually mentioned as an aside: "We must make sure Điđa isn't screwed over like you were back then at the arena." I had no idea what he was talking about.

"That time, you know, when you had trouble with the sound?" he said and burst out laughing.

It slowly started to sink in, and so I asked: "That was you?"

He nodded and laughed even louder: "Well, that was your directorial debut, and we, too, had a few debuts in the competition. And back then, the Serbian Ministry of Culture gave a hefty bonus for each Pula award."

"So, what did you do?"

"Nothing. We gave the guys a little cash for a drink and to forget the sound for a while."

"But I won the award for directorial debut in the end!"

"Well, I know, fuck it, we tried!" said Đoka and went on about the French sound technicians.

Pula, 2010

Just Between Us had a screening in Pula. This was my eleventh movie in the arena. The lesson I learned with my first has stayed with me. Half an hour before the screening, just as I have done every time since then, I take a bottle of whisky up to the booth.

Pula, 2017

For the first time, I wasn't going to be present at the test screening. I asked Maja Vukić, the executive producer, who more than diligently worked on *The Constitution*, to take a bottle of whisky to the booth in my name. She said they told her: "Nice to know the old customs haven't been altogether forgotten."

Soundstage Isolation

The sound studio is a well-isolated space which offers optimum conditions for the recording of a sound movie.

Milan, 2000

With Pavel Schnabel as producer and a cameraman, I'm making a documentary for ZDF (German public television) about two Italian guest workers in Germany: the theater directors, Roberto Ciulli and Paolo Magelli.

At the bar of Grand Hotel et de Milan, on Via Manzoni, a few hundred meters from the La Scala, I sit with Roberto who is telling me that Giuseppe Verdi used that very hotel as his own Milan residence for over thirty years, and he composed his *Othello* and *Falstaff* right there. This is where he had a heart attack, and where he fought to survive for a full week, supervised by a crowd of doctors.

Roberto says the city government ordered that the busy Via Manzoni be covered with sand so the rattling of coaches would not disturb Verdi's recovery. He says Verdi commanded such respect that people lowered their voices or even stopped talking altogether while passing the hotel. The internet claims that the street was covered in straw, but Roberto's version sounds better.

In that hotel in an almost absolute silence, Giuseppe Verdi died on January 21, 1901.

Belgrade, 1997

Bernardo Bertolucci begins his movie *1900* (*Novecento*) with a scene of a peasant running through the fields, shouting: "Verdi e morte!" His death, thus, marks the beginning of a new century. I saw the original version of the movie, 317 minutes long, when Bertolucci brought it to Belgrade, to the FEST Film Festival, and had it screened in a small cinema, behind closed doors.

He was haggling at the time with the producer about the running time and had not been given permission for a public screening.

Athens, Ohio, 2013

I am reading Greg Grandin's *Fordlandia*, about a utopian project started by Henry Ford, the richest man in America at the time, in the Amazon jungle. The book mentions Teatro Amazonas, where the first opera was performed several years before Verdi's death, in 1897. Built in Belle Époque style, the magnificent building of the Opera still stands in Manaus, in the heart of the Amazon jungle.

The opera was built with money donated by the rich owners of plantations who were extracting latex to use in the production of rubber.

In order to ensure silence and create the ideal conditions for the visiting singers, the entire square where the opera stands was coated in rubber, as well as the nearby streets.

Werner Herzog's *Fitzcarraldo* begins with a scene in that opera.

Zagreb, 1895–2014

Two years after my grandfather was born, the Croatian National Theater was built. That is where I saw my first opera. My father took me in 1956 to see Mozart's *Così fan tutte*. Twenty-one years later, I filmed the closing sequence of *Bravo, Maestro* in that building.

Today, the building is surrounded by beaten-up stone steps and a battered sidewalk full of holes, where skaters go on rollicking sprees.

As far as that building is concerned, nobody cares about sound there anymore.

Special Screenings

Before it enters wide distribution, every movie goes through a number of screenings. Each has a name:

> Test screening–a screening of an unfinished movie to a group that reflects the profile of future audience
> Market screening–a screening for potential distributors
> Private screening–a screening for investors or those in the marketing business
> Preview screening–a screening of a finished movie where the audience is surveyed with questionnaires
> Critic screening–a screening for film critics
> Festival screening–a screening at festivals

Prague, 1968

Czechoslovakia was occupied. Russian tanks were all over the streets of Prague. The schools of Prague University were on strike. FAMU was in charge of filming anything that could be filmed. Eight crews constantly cruised the city, day and night. About a hundred of us camped out at the academy for days, in the Neo-Renaissance Palác Lažanských, on the bank of the Vltava.

It was snowing. The Russians had become very active that evening. They kept relocating their tanks and armored vehicles. They seemed to be preparing to oust us.

This did not prevent us from organizing our daily "special double-feature screening."

The first movie was *Love in the Afternoon*, one of the most romantic comedies ever made, directed by Billy Wilder, with Audrey Hepburn and Gary Cooper.

The lecture hall on the second floor was packed. People were even sitting on the floor. The excitement was intense, right from the start. We roared with laughter, wept without shame, and cheered noisily.

Screenings are not differentiated only by what their organizers are after—they differ, possibly even more, by the audience. By how emotionally they accept or reject the movie. And, of course, by the moment when they take place. In that heated cauldron of people who had barely had a wink of sleep, in that time of occupation, movies became more than just movies: they turned into a collective escape into something else, larger and nobler than our reality was.

Rudolph Ruzicka came into this emotionally charged room every twenty minutes, a skinny student of Directing who later became President Havel's first councilor and, even later, one of the chiefs of the Czech secret police. He would switch off the projector, flick on the lights, and address us anxiously: "We must reinforce the guard at the entrance. I need four men"; "Now there are three tanks in front of the building, and two on the side, on Narodna Street, between us and the theater"; "The waiters from the *Slavija* have brought us 524 bowls of soup as a donation. I need two people to bring them."

The volunteers stood and left in silence, Rudolph switched the projector back on, turned off the lights, and left. The smoky room was once again filled with the gypsy orchestra and its relentless sounds:

> It was fascination
> I know
> And it might have ended
> Right then, at the start
> Just a passing glance

> Just a brief romance
> And I might have gone
> On my way
> Empty-hearted...

Early the next morning, a Russian patrol, three soldiers and an officer, entered the Palác Lažanských. As soon as they started climbing the wide staircase to the first floor, they were stopped by Dean Brousil's resonant voice.

Elegant, dressed completely in black, with a wide red scarf, carefully articulating every word in Russian with pathos yet completely calm, without allowing the officer to interrupt, Brousil held a short lecture. He told them they had entered a temple of Soviet film, that this was a subject of study at the Academy, and he was kindly asking them to vacate the premises because everything was under control. His words echoed and obviously made a strong impression on the Russian officers. After a long silence, he gave them a military salute, ordered an about-face, and he left the building escorted by the soldiers.

FAMU thus remained the only official institution in Prague which was never occupied by the Russians.

Prague, 1989

A few months after the Velvet Revolution, FAMU invited us as their guests. At the front of the Palác Lažanských there was a sign that reads: "Djekujeme Vam Jugoslavci!" (Thank you, Yugoslavs!)

In the same lecture hall where we had screened the movies during the 1968 strike, the students were shown our student works. We felt a little embarrassed, but we endured bravely.

Sports Movies

Movies in which a sport, a sportsperson or a sporting event serves as the lead or the focal topic. Among the most famous are Blue 9 *(1951),* The Hustler *(1961),* The Loneliness of the Long-Distance Runner *(1962),* National Class *(Nacionalna klasa, 1979),* Raging Bull *(1980),* Chariots of Fire *(1981) ... and, among documentaries,* Hoop Dreams *(1994),* When We Were Kings *(1996),* The King *(2011) ...*

Zagreb, 1954

At the New Year lottery, my father won a pair of children's *Lušinke* skis named after the craftsman in the Zagreb neighborhood of Trešnjevka, who manufactured them.

Several weeks later, Dad, Vesna, and I climbed Sljeme, a hill above Zagreb. The snow kept falling. It was so deep I could barely walk. The road was totally snowed in. My dad trod a path through the snow, carrying me, my skis, as well as my sister's skis, and his skis. From Šestine, which we reached by bus, across the *Kraljičin zdenac* trail, to the Grafičar mountain lodge where, after the two-hour climb we entered the room with a huge warm furnace.

As soon as we entered, he stripped to the waist, shook the icicles from his whiskers, and laughed heartily, wringing out his sweat-drenched shirt. His entire body steamed like a train engine.

He was in his prime.

Sports Movies II

Zagreb, 1983

"Ever been ice-skating?"
"No."
"Never?"
"Never!"
"Excellent."
?
"And you were born south or north of Ilica?"
"North."
"Excellent. You'll play for the North."
"And what are we playing?"
"Hockey!"
?

The Sports Center in Zagreb organized a charity hockey game between the people of Zagreb who were born north of Zagreb's longest street, Ilica, and those born south of Ilica. Long story short: those who had never been on ice skates—the basic requirement—against those who had never been on ice skates. The proceeds would support renovations of the children's hospital.

Players from the Medveščak hockey club helped us dress for over an hour. And then, under all the clothes and equipment, we were supposed to go out onto the ice. Once we finally arrived, greeted by a round of thunderous applause, we were grateful to see a large number of plastic cups filled with *gemischt*—half wine–half mineral water—arranged neatly along the entire wall of the ice rink.

Zlatko Sviben, a Zagreb citizen by profession, was referee and host. He presented us, and the game began.

We, the Northerners, attacked first. Not very successfully. The Southerners, after a lot of pushing and falling, which made the audience tremendously happy, gained control of the puck. They launched a counterattack. I was left all alone, facing the opposing team's goal. I struggled to turn and join the rest of the team. Amid my anguish, someone hit the puck out of our half, and it stopped right in front of me. And so there we were, some three meters between us, eye to eye, the goal tender, the puck, and I. I looked at the goal tender, then at the puck, trying to figure out how to hit it without falling. While I was working on a tactic, the others arrived. But, as they did not know how to stop, they swept both me and, more importantly, the puck straight into the goal.

Sviben ceremoniously announced that I had scored the first goal at the game. Olga, who was in the audience with Ana, was very proud of her father, the goal-getter.

Spy Movies "Based-on-a-True-Story"

Among the best-known are North by Northwest *(1959),* The Day of the Jackal *(1973),* Spy Game *(2001),* Munich *(2005),* Charlie Wilson's War *(2007),* Fair Game *(2010).*

Columbus, 2005

We are having dinner at our friends' house. Our host Zdenka (thirty-five) has prepared a delicious meal using a recipe "from home." Her husband's story is even better, though, than the dinner. Not really a spy story, as the title promises, but out of respect for his profession, I categorized it as such.

San Francisco, 1989

John (fifty) is a low-ranking FBI agent in San Francisco. As a member of counterintelligence, he runs Russian agents in the Bay Area. His wife Sybil (twenty-seven), with whom he has a three-year-old son, is four months pregnant.

Sybil has been trying to enroll in medical school for two years. She travels from place to place, goes to interviews, but to no avail. As she is about to give up, a professor from a medical school in Philadelphia informs her she has been accepted.

John and Sybil come up with a plan: she will leave for her studies and he will stay in San Francisco and raise their son.

Philadelphia, 1991

Sybil comes home less and less. After a few months, she lets him know she's not planning to come back. She has fallen in love with Dušan (sixty-one), her professor and a renowned Philadelphia physician, originally from Novi Sad.

In long phone calls, John pleads with Sybil to return. All in vain. They go through an amicable divorce. Meanwhile, Sybil has another son. The court grants Sybil custody of the child. John can see his son only for two weeks, twice a year.

Sybil and her newborn son move in with Dušan.

Where Dušan is from, the war is raging. Dušan helps people from both sides of the conflict get out of the hell. He brings them to Philadelphia, sending them medical school guarantees, and gives them jobs bound to his home and his private doctor's office. To them, he is both a benefactor and a slave driver. He pays them meager wages and keeps their passports.

Zdenka (twenty-two) comes to Dušan's house from the suburbs of Zagreb as a future nanny for the unborn son. Without any knowledge of English, money or the proper papers, she quickly comes to the conclusion that she had be better going home. In phone calls, her parents beg her not to, she should at least wait until the war is over.

Zdenka is given the task of taking the six-month-old boy to San Francisco, handing him off to his father, returning to Philadelphia, and then, two weeks later, going back to San Francisco to fetch the baby.

San Francisco, 1993

John waits for them at the airport. He meets Zdenka who arrives with his son. He is stunned by her beauty.

The next day, he persuades Zdenka not to return to Philadelphia. He asks her to help him with the baby and stay at his place for the two weeks.

Six months later, Zdenka becomes John's wife.

Columbus, 1996

A few years before they retire, FBI agents get to choose the town where they would like to spend the rest of their working life. John's mother is in Columbus and she needs help. John and Zdenka move to Columbus. Over the next two years, Zdenka gives birth to two boys.

John retires. Zdenka works. They live happily with their children on the outskirts of town, in a big house on the edge of a golf course.

Stage Fright

Anxiety, fear of public performance. It is usually linked to the actors' jitters at being faced with an audience, but it refers to any fear we might feel before the beginning of something we believe is extremely important.

Zagreb, 1973

Angel Miladinov was an uncommonly smart and good-natured television editor at Zagreb Television. A mild, somewhat ironic smile played on his lips, he puffed his pipe and drank Mastika with a roasted coffee bean. He was the man I made my first documentaries for.

A week before the shooting of *If It Kills Me* was to begin, I bumped into him in the center of town. He looked at me and asked, dryly: "So, you're not scared?" Without giving it a second thought, I replied cheerfully: "No! Why?" He didn't answer but I could guess by the look in his eyes that fear had prevented him from stepping away from directing television programs, which, by the way, he was brilliant at, to venture into something bigger, something that would be his own.

I had been making movies since I was fourteen, I was trained not to be scared, and yet, whenever I was about to start a new one, whenever I was preparing to take the plunge off the high cliff into the abyss, unsure of whether I might expect deep sea or shallow rocky ground, I would remember the encounter with Angel. And, naturally, I thought of fear. I wondered if it is inside me or if I am just good at suppressing it, hiding it from myself. I don't know the answer, but I do know that at the start of every production I had to make a range of crucial decisions very quickly. Probably afraid the fear might catch up with me.

State Award

The highest award given by the state. For the purpose of honoring artists, in Croatia it is the Vladimir Nazor Award, and it is the National Medal of Arts in America.

Zagreb, 1974

At the Zalars's home, I am waiting for Živko Zalar. Živko's father Slavko— who had been the cinematographer on Tanhofer's movie *H-8* (1958)— and I watch the news. They announce the recipients of the Nazor Award. The Life Achievement Award in Film is given to cinematographer Branko Blažina. Aside from all the movies he worked on, including Bauer's *Three Girls Named Anna*, the crowning jewel of his career and possibly the key reason for this decision is historical footage he took of Partisan Vladimir Nazor entering Zagreb after liberation. His eyes on the screen, Slavko says: "Do you know how he did that?"

Zagreb, 1945

Slavko is a photographer, a Partisan. Among the first to enter liberated Zagreb.

On a motorcycle with a sidecar, he comes to the former Cinema Zagreb on Preradovićev Square. This is where the State Institute for Motion Pictures is situated, as well as all the film equipment of the fascist Independent State of Croatia.

Armed and in uniform, Slavko and his friends go into the Croatian Institute, the Ustasha propaganda center. Without introductions or explanations, he orders all the cinematographers to line up. He watches them for a time, and then asks each of them what they have filmed so far. Finally, he picks one and tells him to come along.

They put a camera, the necessary equipment and the terrified cameraman into the sidecar and off they go to the Sava River. Once they reach Red Bridge, Slavko helps the cameraman set up the tripod, the camera, and arranges the shot.

Two hours later, Vladimir Nazor, president of ZAVNOH (the State Antifascist Council for the National Liberation of Croatia), marches across Red Bridge and enters Zagreb.

The cameraman who filmed that historic moment was Branko Blažina. Years later, he confessed to Slavko that, up until the moment they came to the bridge, he had thought he was going to be shot.

Slavko Zalar never won the Nazor Award.

Subtitles

The printed line(s) of translated dialogue text optically or mechanically superimposed on a copy of the film. Apart from Asia, where they are displayed vertically, subtitles are displayed along the bottom of the screen, in one or two lines.

Zagreb, 1982

A Russian distributor bought *You Love Only Once*. They paid $36,000 for a movie which was made with no more than $150,000. They bought a double negative, neutral backgrounds, IT ribbons, and everything else in such quantity that Jadran Film thought it would come out in at least two or two and a half thousand copies in the USSR.

They paid for everything on time, but the movie did not appear in the cinemas. Years went by. And then one of our distributors came back from a film fair in Moscow with this story.

Moscow, 1985

The Russians made only one copy of *You Love Only Once*. They screened it at a small cinema in the building of the Moscow Central Committee. They screened it three or four times a week to delegations from small towns. And they, with due ideological disgust, they enjoyed it as pornography.

The woman who told the story to our distributor had made a living for years by simultaneously interpreting *You Love Only Once*. She knew all the dialogue by heart.

Moscow, 1987

At the peak of *Glasnost*, Gorbachev approved a list of about twenty foreign movies that had been banned for years. One of the movies on the list was *You Love Only Once* which then began its Russian life in major Moscow cinemas with one of the highest box office scores that year.

That same year in Moscow, film critic Mironenko published a book about the movie *You Love Only Once*.

Zagreb, 1997

An employee at Jadran Film told me that Russians had, again, bought the distribution rights for the movie. Jadran Film never officially confirmed this because, in that case, they would have to pay me royalties and they have not been doing that since they privatized. But that's another story, the story of the criminals who, with the encouragement of the state, have turned the Croatian cinema into private property which is literally being destroyed.

Superstar

A term used to describe only the biggest and most profitable stars among actors.

Los Angeles, 1929

Judy Garland, often called by Americans "the world's greatest entertainer," told the story that they took her to see Santa Claus when she was seven, and that he, when he saw her, asked for her autograph.

Pula, 1965

I was seventeen and had made my second amateur movie. Apart from the prize, I was also awarded seven days in Pula. That is how I attended the festival for the first time. I stayed in a student's dorm above the arena with about twenty film amateurs from all over Yugoslavia.

Almost every evening, before the arena, I would go over to Hotel Riviera. I had been told that all the important people in the industry sat on that terrace. And yet, despite my burning desire to see them, I could not summon the courage that summer to go up to the mythical terrace.

One evening, I saw about two or three thousand people out in front of the hotel. They were waiting for Milena Dravić. When she appeared, she was greeted with a round of applause and then escorted, as if they were her honor guard, to the arena.

Never, at any festival, have I seen such reverence for an actress.

That year, Milena Dravić won the Golden Arena for her role in Obrad Gluščević's movie *Turbulent Summer* (*A Lito vilovito*).

The Golden Arena for Best Actor went to Bata Živojinović, for his role in one of the most important Yugoslav movies—*Three* by Saša Petrović.

Zagreb, 1984

We were preparing *In the Jaws of Life*. I called Bata Živojinović, by far the most famous Yugoslav actor at the time, who, in terms of his popularity and charisma, could be called a Yugoslav John Wayne, begging him to take the role of Trokrilni. I launched into my explanations that we don't have enough money, that we're filming it on 16 mm, that we haven't received any state funding, that the role requires him to take his clothes off . . . He interrupted me and said: "I'm coming!"

We rehearsed and set his scene in great detail. We started filming. We did several takes. Each time, Bata skipped the line: "That's us, Serbs!" After the fourth or fifth take, I approached Bata and quietly asked him: "Is this line a problem? Does it bother you?"

Bata flashed me a grin and asked: "Does it matter to you?"

"It does," I said.

"Okay," said he, and we easily did several takes with the line.

Suspense

A state of uncertainty giving rise to uneasiness in anticipation of an important outcome.

Zagreb, 1989

The official committee of the RSIZ of Culture of Croatia, the state institution making decisions on government grants for film production, puts forward several projects. Among them is *Virgina*, by director and screenwriter Srđan Karanović, my colleague Điđa, in the production of Maestro Film, my company. At the meeting with RSIZ, directors Antun Vrdoljak and Dejan Šorak call for the decision to be rescinded, saying that a Serbian director is unwelcome in Croatian cinema. I take the floor several times to defend the project and the director. Vrdoljak and Šorak, taking advantage of the rising tide of nationalism, refuse to budge. Strong words are uttered, there is talk of betrayal, and homeland, all the watchwords that will soon become routine grounds for a death sentence.

Eventually, the project is approved by one vote. We are lucky. A few months later, even that one would have been against us.

Zagreb, Spring, 1990

What we are looking for is a barren, rocky, almost lunar landscape, and a stone house that would appear to be small, nearly imperceptible on the outside, while on the inside it would be big enough for filming. The director and the set designer go location-scouting and, in the end, they come back with two suggestions: one location near Imotski, where mostly Croats live, and the other near Knin, were mostly Serbs live. Mladen Koceić and I, as the owners of Maestro Film, the executive producer of *Virgina*, opt for the location close to Knin, in order to facilitate easier communication with Zagreb.

Polače, Summer, 1990

It takes them almost two months to build the house, which proves to be quite complicated. What they do first is hollow out a wide hole in the rocky terrain, and then build the house over it. Its walls can be moved as needed.

Polače, Summer, 1990

With Mladen, I come to the first day of shooting. I have barely stepped out of the car when I notice a man with a long beard standing to the side, staring at us. He is dressed in a black Chetnik uniform from World War II, a skull on his cap, traditional peasant shoes, a bandolier across his chest, and a rifle in his hand.

Virgina takes place toward the end of the nineteenth century, it is about a girl raised as a boy, so I cannot for the life of me imagine what this Chetnik costume is doing here. I find Maja Galasso, a wonderful woman and fine costume designer with whom I have often worked, and ask her to explain the joke, to tell me which of her assistants has dressed the man to look like this. With a sad look, Maja explains that the man has not been dressed by her assistants. She says this is a man from a mountain village, someone comes almost every day, wanders about, inspects them, only to disappear as unexpectedly as they have appeared.

I take another look at him and realize that my forebodings of war now have taken concrete form.

Knin, Summer, 1990

The Serbs in Knin decide to hold a referendum to assert the autonomy and sovereignty of Serbian people in Croatia. The Croatian government proclaims the referendum illegal. This is, at least officially speaking, the beginning of what came to be known as the Log Revolution. All the roads to and from the town are blocked and placed under strict control. The crew members are regularly stopped and threatened. They cannot reach the filming location nor are they allowed to go to Zagreb.

Zagreb, Summer, 1990

Two days later, we realize that this is more than just the temporary whim of some unhinged politician. We should pull the people and equipment out as soon as possible. In Zagreb, Mladen and I get into the car. The road across the Plitvice Lakes is closed. You can reach Knin only through Bosnia, via the town of Bosansko Grahovo.

Bosansko Grahovo, Summer, 1990

We are almost through Grahovo when we are pulled over by a police patrol. When we say where we are going, they regard us with suspicion. They suggest we turn on all our lights, blinkers too, and drive at a crawl. At some point, a car will appear behind us and it will turn on its fog lights. We should not stop but continue on at the same speed until we reach the first barricades. "Good luck," say the policemen, worried.

Golubići, Summer, 1990

Everything happens just as they said it would. Slowly, escorted by the car which suddenly appears behind us, we reach the first barricade. The term "Log Revolution" is not just a figure of speech. An actual pile of logs is blocking the road. It is getting dark. Two bonfires are burning. A dozen men around them, all of them armed. They look like a group of frozen pensioners.

A kid no older than sixteen, possibly seventeen, approaches the car on passenger side where I am sitting. An older man is right behind him. The kid holds a gun and gestures for me to open the window. When I do, he shoves the gun in my face and says: "IDs!" While we search for our IDs, he stares at us, defiantly. As if waiting for us to tell him to fuck off. He smells of cheap alcohol. His eyes are glassy. He is very proud that he is doing this. I hand him the IDs. He inspects them for some time and goes off with them into the dark. The old man remains next to the car, a rifle in his unsteady hand. He is not saying anything. He seems embarrassed, as if he would rather apologize.

Ten minutes later, the kid comes back and, brandishing the rifle, returns the IDs and gestures to us to pass slowly between the logs.

Knin, 1990

As soon as we arrive, we organize a meeting with the crew. The people are nervous. I try to calm them down. I explain that we must find a way to get out of the encirclement as soon as possible, all of us. I speak while certain that there is someone in the crew, among the hired local workers, who will pass on what I am saying, word for word.

Less than an hour later, a skinny man approaches me and takes me aside. He has a message: I should come, alone, one hour after midnight, to a designated tavern which is six kilometers outside of town. There I will meet someone I can talk to. No more, no less. He repeats once again that I am kindly asked to come alone.

We discuss what to do. Mladen is adamant that I must not go on my own. Ilija Prgomet, my driver on five or six movies, now Điđa's driver, insists on coming with me. He will drop me off at a certain distance and stay there in case I need him.

Kninsko Polje, 1990

Ilija drives me, headlights off. We arrive at the restaurant on a desolate spot.

The restaurant smells of lard. There are only two drunk men at the bar. I order a drink and wait. Fifteen minutes later, no one has come.

Suddenly, one of the two drunkards, the one who has been staring at me all along, throws himself at me, grabs me by the shirt and yells: "Mesić, you son of a bitch! You ruined Yugoslavia! Mesić, you motherf . . ." Stjepan Mesić was the last President of the Presidency of Yugoslavia. Due to a physical resemblance between us, the drunk man has obviously mistaken me for him. The other drunk man peels him off and drags him back to the bar. After a few minutes of complete silence, the same guy throws himself at me again, but more vigorously and more loudly. "Hey, Mesić, I am so going to fuck you over for everything . . ." I try to push him away, but I can't. He grabs and shakes me, gets in my face, shouting so loud that I'm covered with his spit.

At that point, another man comes in and shouts: "Leave him alone!" The drunkard instantly lets go of me. The man who has come in looks well put together and altogether decent. He approaches me, apologizes, and takes me to the farthest table. I do not remember his name. I just remember that he is a physician, deputy mayor to Milan Babić, who, many years later in The Hague, "pleaded guilty to crimes against humanity against Croatian civilians," and, soon afterward, hanged himself in his prison cell.

He explains that what is happening is beyond their control. The barricades are mostly held and controlled by people from Serbia. It would be wise for us to leave as soon as possible. No one can tell what will happen next. He will help as much as he can, he has a pass for us for the first barricade. He cannot vouch for anything beyond that, but he believes everything will be fine.

Knin, Summer, 1990

The next morning, we line up the vehicles. The crew, the equipment, the ARRI trucks. Mladen and I walk to the first barricade in front of the vehicles. We pass. They let us through the second one and the third one, too.

Zagreb, Fall 1990

Mladen and I request a meeting with Ivo Škrabalo, assistant to the Minister of Culture, who is in charge of film. He does receive us but refuses to help.

Polače, Fall, 1990

The filming of *Virgina* resumes after almost two months. The crew stays in Drniš. They go to the set escorted by the Croatian police. A few hundred meters before the set is the first Serbian barricade. This is where the soldiers of Serbian Krajina meet them and escort them to the set. In the evening, on their way back to Drniš, the same procedure.

Zagreb, Fall, 1990

Slobodni tjednik, an extreme right-wing newspaper controlled by the government secret services devotes two pages to an article claiming that behind the so-called filming of *Virgina* stands Slobodan Milošević, who is channeling funds into the uprising in Knin through me. The article provides extensive quotes from Antun Vrdoljak, the vice president of Croatia.

Smack dab in the middle of the article, they publish a picture of me with the caption: "This man is happiest when he's among Chetniks." At the time, this was like being put on the "ten most-wanted criminals" list. The hunt was on.

Los Angeles, November 1991

At the American Film Market, one of the biggest film markets in the world, a French distributor I have never heard of screens the movie. Early in the morning, in a Santa Monica cinema, with no one but me in the audience. This is when I saw *Virgina* for the first time.

Sync Sound

The image and the sound are recorded separately in film. The recorded sound that corresponds to the recorded image is called the sync sound.

Zagreb, 1959

I was twelve when I went to see the German western *Freddy Under Foreign Stars* (*Freddy unter fremden Sternen*), with Austrian singer Freddy Quinn, at the Mosor movie theater in our neighborhood, on Socijalističke revolucije Street.

On my way home, I realized I lost my wallet. I ran back, searched through the place very thoroughly, but could not find it.

For the next few days, I kept coming back to the theater hoping someone would return it. As a consolation, they let me in without a ticket.

I never found the wallet, but I did see the movie *Freddy Under Foreign Stars* at least ten times.

There is one scene from that movie that I still remember: a cowboy is sitting by a lake, strumming his guitar and singing a sad song in German. The lake behind him is crystal clear, the sky is blue, and the mountain peaks are covered in snow. I remember feeling that the mournful sound and happy image were not in sync.

New York, 1993

We are at dinner at Ljubica's and Žarko's, connoisseurs and collectors of all things movie-related. And, bit by bit, we find our way to the movie, *Freddy Under Foreign Stars*.

Our host stands, goes off to the next room and comes back with a single. Freddy and his sad cowboy song in German fill the room. It is snowing outside. Manhattan, aglow in all its winter luxury, is right there before us. Once again, I feel the discrepancy between the image and the sound.

Munich, 2000

I am mixing *Josephine*. I am on my way back to the hotel. It is late. Raining. Hungry, I look for a place to eat. I pick the first restaurant that seems at all decent. It is full of aging men who exude a German sort of sadness. Some of them are solo, some with company. They look over at me and grin. The waiter comes over. He, too, grins. He pats me on the shoulder, leaving his hand there just a little too long. This is a restaurant for aging and not very well-off gay men.

There is a song playing. Yes, it is cowboy Freddy and his sad song. At last the sound is in sync with its image.

Television

A system for transmitting images and sound.

Zagreb, 1960

A Philips television set arrived in our home. It was the first one in the building, perhaps on all of Vrbanićeva Street. Unpacking and installing it took two days. The procedure, in complete silence and in the presence of our neighbors, was handled by my father. By himself. No one else was allowed near the TV.

The only channel broadcast in Zagreb back then was Italian RAI. Therefore, the first program we watched was Studio Uno, a Mike Bongiorno music-dance show with Adriano Celentano, Domenico Modugno, Milva.

And yet, the real reason for the arrival of the television was not the Italian singers, but the Olympic games in Rome. Almost a month before the games, we set up benches in front of the set and spent days discussing whom to invite.

One of the evenings, Dad turned it on, but the screen remained black. Panic seized us all.

The next day, a repairman came, an engineer from the radio station, a short man with a big head. The reason I can still remember him so vividly is that for the few hours he spent checking the TV set in complete silence, all of us stood there and watched him. Eventually, he removed a lamp-like tube which was as big as a hand and said: "This burned out. You'll need a new one."

Back then in Zagreb, there was no such thing as a store or a service where you could buy spare parts, or anything television-related, for that matter.

My dad sat down and wrote a letter which started with "Lieber Philips." He described the disaster we had suffered, mentioned the neighbors, the Olympics, and promised to pay whatever it cost, just to get the part before the opening of the Games.

And so, we waited. We counted the days. You could easily say that all of Vrbanićeva Street was in the clutches of despair while we all waited for the reply from Philips.

And finally, just as we had lost all hope, two days before the Olympics, a parcel arrived from Germany. In it, two of the lamp tubes and a letter in which Philips expressed their hope that all the members of the household and the neighbors would enjoy the Games, and the tubes were a gift from the company.

Not a single seat was left empty. Standing room only. Dad ceremoniously switched on the television. The moment the image appeared on the screen was even more festive for all of us than the opening ceremony itself.

Yugoslavia took home a gold medal from that Olympics, for soccer, no less. After the semi-finals, when the Yugoslavia-Italy game ended in a tie, a slip of paper with the name of our country on it was drawn from a hat belonging to Dr. Andrijević, our team's doctor. By chance, he happened to be the only person on either team who was wearing a hat just when the team to be chosen to go forward to the finals match with Denmark would be decided by drawing lots.

Third Act

The third act: everything before, nothing after, as Aristotle says.

Belgrade, 2005

The papers published a news item that in the center of Belgrade, a married couple, she seventy-six, he seventy-eight, jumped from the sixth floor, holding hands.

Time

"*Time, an endless succession of changes, in which the moments or their transformations can be conceived as an endless series of shapes, one erasing another, forming a flow of various configurations and speeds, contained in the possibility of the new and the unpredictable*"
(*The Croatian Encyclopedia published by The Miroslav Krleža Institute of Lexicography*).

Zagreb, 1969

Miroslav Krleža sent me, by way of my father, his movie script for *Journey to Paradise* (*Put u raj*). I was twenty-something and at my studies of Directing in Prague, and had come home to Zagreb for a few days. I was overwhelmed to hear he would like to talk to me about this. I read the script and could not summon the courage to go to see him. How to explain to someone as famous as Krleža that "wind blowing the pages off a wall calendar" might not be the best way to describe the flow of time in a movie.

Zagreb, 1979

Ten years later, I had the honor of meeting Miroslav Krleža, who is regarded as one of the greatest literary figures and a major influence on the left-wing movement of twentieth-century Yugoslavia and Croatia. With actors Ljuba Tadić and Mladen Budiščak, I went to his office at the Institute for Lexicography to talk about a potential film adaptation of his novel *On the Edge of Reason* (*Na rubu pameti*).

As soon as we came through the door, he took off his wristwatch, placed it onto his desk, and said: "Gentlemen, you have exactly forty-five minutes. A full classroom hour."

It didn't take long for him to give us his permission for the adaptation, and then, in almost real time, he retold a play he had never written. Set at the Petrovaradin fortress, near Novi Sad, the drama plays out at a dinner of Austro-Hungarian officers, one night before the fall of the Austro-Hungarian Empire.

Meanwhile, he sat in a large leather armchair and slowly slid down. Every fifteen minutes he would straighten up, and then again he would begin to slide to an almost horizontal position.

He was an amazing storyteller.

His classroom hour lasted more than three hours.

Zagreb, 2005

My grandfather Aleksandar—who went to the Upper Town high school and was in the same class as Krleža—had three table clocks: a Biedermeier, a Rococo, and an *altdeutsch*. All three worked, beating time, and chimed every fifteen minutes. Ana once asked him how he could sleep with all that noise. He answered that the three clocks were his three sons for him, and he could sleep well only with them there. When he died, each of the sons inherited one of the clocks. The sons, too, have died. Now the grandsons have the clocks. I have the *altdeutsch*.

Athens, Ohio, 2008

On my way home from my studio at Ohio University, I pass a barbershop on Court Street. An old-fashioned barbershop with three big chairs. The eldest, best, most experienced barber works at the first chair by the window. He is the most heavily booked. Sometimes, his schedule is full a week in advance. The customers who do not make it onto his list go to the second chair, to a younger barber, and the ones left with no choice, or who are in a hurry, end up on the third chair, in the hands of the youngest.

Over these fifteen years, I have watched the transfer of barber number three to the second chair, and then to the first. One day, he, too, was gone. "Where'd he go?" I asked. "Retired!" they said.

I have been here too long.

Zagreb, 2011

On a corner in the center of town, next to the café where we often went for coffee, there was a small store that eluded ready categories. At first it was a workshop where you could have your clothes altered, hemmed, or mended, but it gradually morphed into a store that sold men's and women's intimate apparel.

It was run by a woman well into her forties. Some time ago, the man she had been living with died. For months she wore black and stood in the doorway, smoking cigarette after cigarette, gazing into the distance.

I was traveling a lot, and each time I came back, I could see her changing. First, she stopped wearing black, then she began frequenting the café, as she had before he died. The merchandise offered at the store also changed. First, it was only the most innocent underwear, pajamas, slippers ... Several months later, she was carrying only women's lingerie. The styles—anything but innocent. More erotic bras and panties. The look in the woman's eyes also began to change, as did her body language. She was eager, again, to live.

Timing

Position or occurrence in time. In movies, the term usually refers to finding the best moment to begin something, to sync the movements of the camera with the actor's movements, or for gauging time ratios when editing a chase ...

Venice, 1902

Painter Vilko Gecan walked all the way from Zagreb to Venice, about 250 miles. As soon as he arrived, he went straight to the Piazza San Marco, took out his easel, and looked for the best vantage point.

Once he had chosen where he would work, he sat on his chair, set a canvas on the easel, and took a good long look at the campanile tower. He decided to start the painting with it, as it was the only vertical element at the square. As he drew the first line, the tower collapsed and enveloped the square in a cloud of dust. Gecan quickly gathered up his things and left.

Venice, 2011

"And never again did he return to Venice," says my school friend Marta (Dalibor Martinis) as he finished the story.

Marta made one of my favorite video installations, or maybe I could call it a video concept: *Dalibor Martinis (1978) talks to Dalibor Martinis (2010)*. At the age of thirty-one he recorded himself posing questions about life and art. Thirty-one years later, he sat down again in front of the screen, facing his own young and arrogant self, and offered answers to all the questions.

Piazza San Marco is empty in November. We go up to the campanile, encased in scaffolding. The foundations are being reinforced. On the scaffolding wall, among the exhibited pictures which tell its history, there is one from 1902—the piazza with no campanile, veiled in a cloud of dust.

Zagreb, 2018

Ranko Mastilović says: "I find it hard to believe that Gecan, who was born in 1894, would have walked all the way from Zagreb to Venice as an eight-year-old, carrying his easel and paints." I defend Marta with the famous Italian proverb: "Se non è vero, è ben trovato!" (Even if this is not true, it makes a fine story.)

Travel Movies

Documentaries about a region or town, told by a traveler or explorer.

New York, 1993

Kevin Scott, a writer and a professor, our oldest New York friend, tells a story about his grandfather, a New Jersey Jew, who requested in his will to have his ashes put in twenty containers, each of them to be taken to a different part of the world by family members.

And so, for years, wherever they go, family members take with them one of the containers with his ashes.

Twist Ending

A sudden twist at the end of a movie which, when you analyze the story in retrospect, is not so surprising after all.

Athens, Ohio, 1994

"You may find yourself living in a beautiful town, and you may find yourself teaching at one of the finest American universities, and you may find yourself in a beautiful house, with your young, intelligent, and beautiful wife. That is how I imagine hell."

This is from a fax sent to me by one of my Prague classmates, film director Goran Marković, in the middle of the war. He sent it from Belgrade, a city terrorized by rampant criminal gangs, the city from which Milošević waged the war, the city where Aleksandar Berček—an actor Goran had worked with who had gone on to become a politician—called for Goran Marković to be charged with treason against Serbia on a live televised broadcast from parliament. In short: he had sent the fax from the heart of darkness, from hell itself.

Motovun, 2002

That hell gave birth to the movie *Serbia, Year Zero* (*Srbija, godine nulte*, 2001), a documentary-fiction essay, one of my favorites of the movies Goran has made. A movie which, more than any other, resembles him with his restful exterior and restless interior. Watching it in Motovun, on the square filled with people, I thought that each of us who plays with film should make such a record of our own life and the time of dishonor in which we have lived. So we leave no bills unpaid, never a shadow of a doubt about how we have lived.

Walt Disney

An American animator who, with Ub Iwerks, started making short cartoons in Kansas City in 1919. Their popularity helped them start their own studio. Several years later, Disney moved it to Hollywood. That studio gave rise to the modern empire of happiness.

Athens, Ohio, 2016

Charlie, a big ginger and white cat, a true member of our family, died at the ripe old age of twenty-three, silently, in his sleep.

Like so many others, Charlie led a double life.

Outside, he was a hunter, a beast. He brought in trophies from the woods behind the house: snakes, small rabbits, field mice. He would stand proudly next to his victim by the kitchen door, waiting to be praised for his atrocity. Only squirrels remained a pipe dream. He would lurk for hours, but they were faster. Even when he did grab one, the ensuing struggle typically ended with a visit to the vet. He outlived two of his vets.

At home, however, he was an infinitely cuddly kitten. He spent hours sleeping by my head or watching movies. He enjoyed being stroked, lying on the lap, "talking" to us with purrs of pleasure. But, like an old maid, Charlie generally adhered closely to his daily routine. At eleven p.m., he went down to the basement, where he slept. At seven a.m. sharp, he scratched at the door and, after breakfast he was ready for action.

Athens, Ohio, 1994

Our first Christmas Eve in the new house. In keeping with the Grlić tradition, Ana roasts a turkey with goose liver pâté and roasted chestnut stuffing. Olga and I decorate the Christmas tree. We share gifts, enjoy the dinner. After the cake, Olga goes out with her friends, and Ana and I go for a walk.

The empty town is buried under a blanket of untrodden snow. The students have gone home, the professors have scattered around the world.

On our way back, on a slope, we hear a soft *meow*. We turn, trying to gauge where it is coming from, and finally we see a kitten who has sunk deep into the snow and is struggling. We lift it up, warm it a bit, and leave it at the doorstep of the nearby house where it probably belongs.

After a few steps, we hear the whimper again. The kitten follows us, hopping from one footprint to the next. Ana suggests we take it. I am adamant that we mustn't. We are forever traveling, we are gone for months at a time, sometimes longer. Who will look after it? I am fishing for rational reasons, trying to convince us both.

And so, we reach the house. I stay out with the kitten. Ana brings it some food and milk. I sweep off the doormat so it can reach the bowls. It is hungry. It has probably been abandoned by a student on the move.

We sit inside and say nothing. Olga comes home after midnight. As soon as she opens the door, the kitten scampers in. Ana and Olga stroke it to dry it out. I am still the unbending villain. They finally cave. I return the kitten to the doormat.

Christmas morning. It's still early. The windows are framed in snow. The decorated tree is alight in the corner. I come down in colorful pajamas.

The silence is broken by a barely audible *meow*. I open the front door and through the storm door I see the kitten. Its fur is wet, it is frozen, it can barely make a sound. I open the door and say: "Okay, in you come. You've earned . . . !" And the kitten, afraid I might change my mind, streaks in even before I have finished.

Several hours later, Olga has named him Charlie. I watch them play and I think, with a secret smile, that Disney would be more than happy with this scene.

Western

Cowboy movies, *as we used to call them, are one of the oldest and most enduring American genres. They typically show a battle between good and evil taking place at the border between civilization and the wilderness, between law and lawlessness. Westerns are, easily, the purest descendants of ancient tragedy.*

I believe every film director should make a western at least once in their life. It is the bar mitzvah of our trade. My Western was *Charuga*.

Gijon, 1987

We are guests at the film festival. Every evening, the hosts take a group of about ten guests to one of the hip Basque restaurants. Jack Palance, one of the greatest Western villains of all times, is also among us. In Pennsylvania he was born Volodymyr Palahniuk, son of Ukrainian immigrants. His father was a miner. He changed his name and surname, or rather his agents did, but he always spoke proudly of his Ukrainian origins. This is why he, with genuine emotion, his eyes filling with tears, sings a few Ukrainian songs each night.

There is weird, almost sad disillusion in this scene. One of the most beloved cowboys of my childhood, a giant of the Wild West, a man of infinitely craggy features, singing sappy Slavic folk songs.

Wipe

A type of transition in a film where a shot replaces the one before by moving from one side of the frame to the other.

Zagreb, 1964

When you are sixteen, you write love poems steeped in pain. And you hope that the girl you're in love with, by some weird chance, finds this poem of yours, reads it with tears in her eyes, and finally understands everything.

At that tender age I was given a Bell & Howell 8 mm camera as a Christmas gift from my uncle, and started making movies driven, more or less, by that same motivation.

Soon, the game became my life. I made movies while trying to leave a trail behind me, enjoying the Eros of creation, the energy that births them.

Athens, Ohio, 2017

More and more often, I leave movies to my dreams.

I lay on the pillow, close my eyes, and let the screening of the movie in which I spent my day come to an end. Short clips of reality roll by like closing credits, repeat, and slowly fade. And then, sometimes sooner, sometimes later, another projectionist comes along and plays a "surprise movie," a movie ignoring logic or reality.

This one has neither beginning nor end, no acts or structure, no linear or nonlinear narration. No production, no money. The movies last for a few hours or a few seconds, they sometimes are but one tiny frame, while sometimes they are the most lavish of spectacles.

Here is one of those dreams with the fragrance of a finale.

New York, 2016

A policeman stands at the entrance to an accordion-like passage linking the airport to the plane. Passengers approach, one by one.

The policeman asks each passenger for their destination. The passenger whispers the answer in his ear. The policemen nods that he is pleased with the answer and the passenger may proceed to the plane.

It is my turn. I come up to the policeman.

> Policeman
> Where to?

> me (whisper)
> Zagreb!

> Policeman
> Where?

> me (louder)
> Zagreb!

The policeman cups his ear. He can't hear me. I come closer.

> me
> Zaaaaagrreeeeeeb!

The policeman shakes his head.

> Policeman
> No, I can't hear you. Sorry.

Wrap

A phrase used by a director to signal the end of filming.

Athens, Ohio, 1998

It is fall. Late afternoon.

With Hajrudin Pašić, Ohio University professor, I am hiking in the hills above town.

Skinny, tall and nervous, he stops by a dead bird, and chuckles: "Everything has its end!" and, after a long pause, in a more serious voice, he adds: "Except a sausage: it has two!"

Wrap Party

A party the production throws for the cast and crew to celebrate the completion of filming of a motion picture.

Zagreb, 2017

The sun is setting. The streetlights come on. I walk up the hill toward Mirogoj cemetery.

From a distance, I can hear my father telling his favorite story, imitating two country bumpkins.

>
> Jambrek: (o.s.) (absent-minded)
> Jožek!
>
> Jožek: (o.s.)
> Wha..?
>
> Jambrek: (o.s.)
> What do you say, does life go from inside out, or from the outside in?
>
> Jožek: (o.s.) (softly)
> Well...
>
> Jambrek: (o.s.)
> Hmm?
>
> Jožek: (o.s.)
> Well...
>
> Jambrek: (o.s.)
> (after a long silence)
> So?
>
> Jožek: (o.s.)
> I...
>
> Jambrek: (o.s.)
> (after a long silence)
> Well?
>
> Jožek: (o.s.)
> Well... I'd say no!

The camera descends.

The contours of Mirogoj cemetery appear against the red backdrop of the setting sun. Above the graves in section II G, where Dad and Mom lie, my uncles, my grandfather, grandmother, my great-grandmother and great-grandfather, the voices become more and more audible. These are my folks, telling their stories.

I listen to them, awaiting my turn. Crows caw.

It's dark.

Against the black background, white letters:
THE END

Over the end credits, while ordering late-night drinks at PJ Clark's New York bar, Sinatra sings in a smoky voice:

"... Make it one for my baby
And one more for the road..."

WORKS BY RAJKO GRLIĆ

Rajko Grlić was born in 1947 in Zagreb, Croatia (Yugoslavia). He graduated in feature film directing in 1971 from the FAMU in Prague, Czech Republic (Czechoslovakia). His films have been shown in movie theaters across five continents; they have been included in competition programs of leading world festivals, including Cannes; and they have received numerous international awards. Website: www.rajkogrlic.com.

Theatrical Features Films

Director and Screenwriter

2016	The Constitution
2010	Just between Us
2006	Border Post
2002	Josephine
2001	Who Wants to Be a President (co-director, documentary)
1991	Charuga
1989	That Summer of White Roses
1986	Three for Happiness
1984	In the Jaws of Life
1981	You Love Only Once
1978	Bravo Maestro
1974	If It Kills Me

Producer

2019	Departure
2007	How Ohio Pulled It Off (documentary)
2003	Happy Kid (documentary)
2001	Who Wants to Be a President (documentary)
1992	Virdzina
1991	Charuga

Co-screenwriter

1984	Early Snow in Munich
1981	Erogenous Zone
1980	Petria's Wreath
1979	Budimir Trajkovic
1978	The Fragrance of Wild Flowers
1972	Party Game

Short Films

Director and Screenwriter

2010	John "the Bear" Butler
2002	Boulder
1999	Drinkable Water and Freedom III
1997	Pasta Paolo
1991	Parizi, Istra
1987	Fairy-Tale about Zagreb
1986	Drinkable Water and Freedom II
1978	Zagreb
1974	Drinkable Water and Freedom I
1974	Tell Me a Story
1971	Preface
1970	All Eat Each Other
1969	Hamlet
1968	Misunderstanding
1967	Djurja
1967	Tell Me Something Nice
1966	Pass

Producer

1991	Award
1991	Parizi, Istra
1990	Consecration

Television

Documentary Feature Films—Director and Screenwriter

2017	Every Good Story Is a Love Story
2004	Roberto & Paolo
1968	All Men Are Good Men in Bad Society

Documentary Serials and Film—Director and Screenwriter

1976   *Wild Stories* (6 x 50 min) (documentary miniseries)
1975   *The Reckless Years* (10 x 55 min) (miniseries)
1971   *Praises* (6 x 30 min) (documentary miniseries)
1968   *We from Prague* (30 min) (fiction serial—co-screenwriter)

Multimedia

Director, Screenwriter, and Producer

2004   *How to Make Your Movie: an Interactive Film School* 2.0
1998   *How to Make Your Movie: an Interactive Film School* (set of three CD-ROMs)

Books

2018   *50 Year Journey* (editor)
2018   *The Untold Tales*
2016   *The Constitution* (co-writer)
2006   *Border Post* (co-writer)
2004   *Face to Face* (editor)
2003   *Motovun: The Book of Genesis* (co-writer)

INDEX

Academy of Dramatic Art in Zagreb, xvi, 53, 93, 103, 113
Aćim, Joca, 91
Aćimović, Dejan, 270
American Motion Picture Academy, 222
Ali, Muhammad, 187
Andrić, Ivo, 246
anti-climax, 7
Antičević, Ingrid, 131
Antonioni, Michelangelo, xi, 244
Apology and the Last Days, The (*Odbrana i poslednji dan*), 200
Arau, Alfonso, 116
Aristotle, 10, 295
Art Film Festival, Trenčianske Teplice, 77
Atač, Zlatko Kauzlarić, 163–64
Atelje 212 Theater, 229
Ashdown, Paddy, 136
Athens International Film and Video Festival, 208
Avala Film, 28
Axel, Gabriel, 116

Babel, Isaak, xii, 261
Babić, Milan, 291
Badrić, Zrinka, 131
Bahun, Drago, 143
Bakarić, Vladimir, 149
Barrandov Studios, 13, 115, 188
Barwood, Hal, 211
Bašić, Relja, 121
Bauer, Branko, 31, 93, 96–97, 122, 137, 191–93, 284

Becić, Vladimir, xxv, 219
Beckett, Samuel, 238
Beggar in Disguise (*Prerušeni prosjak*), 240
Bekić, Darko, 135
Béla IV, King of Hungary and Croatia, 155
Belgrade International Theater Festival, the (BITEF), 54, 221
Berček, Aleksandar, 299
Berčić, Vojdrag, 132
Bergman, Ingmar, xv, 124, 222, 252–53, 272
Bergman, Ingrid, 153, 237
Berković, Zvonimir, 96, 122, 177
Bernal, Gael García, 215
Bernhardt, Sarah, 88
Bertolucci, Bernardo, 277
Bešker, Inoslav, 147
Bijele strijele, 170
biopic, 12, 23
Biro, Yvette, 93
Biškupić, Božo, 110
Black Wave, 14
Blažina, Branko, 284–85
Bloch, Ernst, 221
Boban, Božidar, 232, 176
Bodine, Susan H., 6
Bogart, Humphrey, 121
Bogdanović, Snežana, 205
Bogdanovich, Peter, 96–97, 164
Bongiorno, Mike, 294
Boorman, John, 42–43
Borošić, Slavica and Vlado, 21
Brala, Nina, 134

Brala, Želimir, 134
Brigljević, Čona, 155–56
British Film Institute, 211
Brook, Peter, 29–30
Brousil, A. M., 259–60, 280
Brown, James, 111
Broz, Jovanka, 242
Broz, Josip, 163, 232, 241. *See also* Tito, Josip Broz
Bruce, Lisa, 91, 94
Brunclík, Bohumír, 115
Brunelleschi, Filippo, 230
Budak, Mile, 132
Budisavljević, Dana, xvii, 95
Budiščak, Mladen, 53, 296
Buffalo Bill, 42
Bukovac, Vlaho, 68
Bulajić, Veljko, 245
Buñuel, Luis, 81, 267
Burić, Željko, 94
Burnier, DeLysa, 208
Bush, George, 42
Butkovic, Davor, 131
Butler, John, 208
Bradley, Ruth, xxvi, 199, 207–208
Brando, Marlon, 83, 202
Brezhnev, Leonid, 261
Burcar, Nenad, 87
Buzančić, Boris, 241

Čačić, Branimir, 131
cameo, 19
camera angle, 20
Campbell, John, 59
Caesar, Julius, 4
Cannes Film Festival, xii–xiii, 41, 45, 59, 76, 90, 187, 211, 237, 252
Carić, Mića, 206
Carrey, Jim, 215
Carrière, Jean-Claude, 186
Cassavetes, John, 70, 126
Cassel, Seymour, 126
Cekić, Ana, 154
Cekić, Čedomil, 154
Cekić, Đuro, 154
Cekić, Olga, 18
Celentano, Adriano, 294
Čermák, Jaroslav, 12

Centar Film, 28, 276
Čeperac, Branka, 243
Chabon, Michael, 195
Chaplin, Charles, 6
character arc, 21
Charlotte of Belgium, Princess, 158–60
Christian, Deric, 210
Churchill, Winston, 29, 135
Cimino, Michael, 213
Ciulli, Roberto, 277
close-up, 31
Coburn, James, 100
Cole, Nat King, 196
Columbia Pictures Industries, 6
Columbia University School of Arts, xvi, 214
Communist Party of Croatia, 129–30
completion guarantee, 32
Conti, Tom, 203
continuity, 34, 58, 150, 185
Cooper, Gary, 279
Ćopić, Branko, 33, 220
Coppola, Francis Ford, 211
Coppola, Sofia, 174
Ćosić, Dobrica, 130
Crnobrnja, Mladen, 143
Croatia Film, 28, 91, 175
Croatian Democratic Union, 32, 68, 170, 176
Croatian Film Archives, 176
Croatian Filmmakers Association, 194
Croatian National Theater, 29, 86, 114, 121, 249, 278
Croatian Radio Television, 41, 56
  archives, 176
Cromwell, Arthur, 208
Cross, Pippa, 6
Crowe, Cameron, 193
Crystal, Billy, 69
Čuić, Stjepan, 130
Cunningham, Shawn, 109
Cvejić, Branko, 43, 92, 173, 243
Cvejić, Vesna, 92
Czech Movie Workers Association, 187

Dairy Barn Art Center, 235
Dalí, Salvador, 234
Danish European Film College, 210

Davis, Bette, 223
De Sica, Vittorio, 121
Degrassi, Moreno, 21
Denver International Film Festival, The, 171
Descutner, David, 208
Desmond, Norma, 87
Deutsche Kinemathek, 175
Dežulović, Boris (Boro), 131, 144
DiCaprio, Leonardo, 182
Dieterle, William, 177
Đilas, Milovan, 28
Đilas, Mitra, 27
Diles, William, 139
director's cut, 44, 45
Disney, Walt, 300–301
Dixon, Jeremiah, 136
Dolinar, Žarko, 22
Donen, Stanley, 256
Dörr, Miljenko, 115
Douglas, Kirk, 273
Dovzhenko, Alexander, xii
Downey, Mike, 58–59, 74, 94
Drach, Vanja, 121
Drašković, Vuk, 130
Dravić, Milena, 186, 287
Dubček, Alexander, 142

Edwards, Harold, 224
Eisenstein, Sergei Mikhailovich, 80, 263
Electronic Vision, 210–11
Erlewine, Tom, 210, 235–36
Esquivel, Laura, 116
establishing shot, 68
European Film Academy, 60

Face to Face, 235, 308
Faculty of Political Science (Zagreb), 236
Faculty of Humanities and Social Sciences (Zagreb), 3, 22
Faustus, 225
Fehmiu, Bekim, 216
Fellini, Federico, xi, 258
Feral Tribune, 236–237
Ferreri, Marco, 116
FEST film festival, 277
Festival of Croatian Amateur Film, 194
50 Year Journey, 236, 308

Film Academy of Performing Arts (FAMU), xi–xii, 19, 52, 70, 80, 99, 176, 183–84, 187, 189, 194, 219–21, 259, 279–80, 306
Film Author Studio, the, 194
Filmex, 42
Filipović, Nikola, 164
flash cutting, 114
flashback, 113
Flego, Fiore, 93
Foley, Jack Donovan, 115
Ford, Henry, 278
Ford, John, 71, 133, 223, 245
Fordlandia, 278
Forenbacher, Ivanka, 58
Forman, Miloš, 25–27, 133
Foster, Clare, 31
Frajt, Božidarka, 241
Francetić, Jure, 218
Francis I, 4
Franco, Francisco, xv, 79
Fumić, Ivan, 131

Gabin, Jean, 121
Gable, Clark, 121
Galasso, Maja, 289
Garbo, Greta, 153
Garces, Vincent, 81
Garland, Judy, 286
Gecan, Vilko, 298
GEFF festival, xii, 186
George, Susan, 201
German, Damir, 57
Gerovac, Goran, 131
Gillis, Joe, 87
Glasnost, 286
Glogovac, Nebojša, xx, 145, 148, 270
Gluščević, Obrad, 96, 287
Godina, Karpo, 260
Goethe, Johann Wolfgang von, 225
Gojanović, Toni, 55
Goli Otok prison, xi, 63
Golik, Krešo, 96, 103, 192
Good Machine, 6
Good Soldier Schweik, The, 53, 64, 92, 242
Gorbachev, Mikhail, 286
Görlich, xxiii, 18, 33

Graduate Film School at Ohio University, 209
Grandin, Greg, 278
Grass, Günter, 186
Grau, Josep Pons, 81–82
Green Cadres, the, 199
Gregurević, Ivo, 136
Grič literary group, xxv
Griffith, D. W., 31
Grlić, Aleksander, 18
Grlić, Ana, 14, 24, 26, 44–45, 54, 60, 74–76, 83, 90, 103–104, 107, 109, 111, 116–18, 126, 134–35, 174, 177, 187, 192, 205, 214, 217, 221, 223, 240, 250–51, 253, 282, 296, 300–301
Grlić, Danko, xi, 236
Grlić, Eva, 129, 237
Grlić, Olga (grandmother), xxv, 34, 155, 196, 256
Grlić, Olga (daughter), 3–4, 6, 24, 44–45, 47, 52, 54, 83, 90, 103–105, 107, 109, 111–12, 169, 250, 255, 282, 300–301
Grlić, Stjepan, 18
Grubac, Jordanka, 55
Guevara, Ernesto Che, 80–81

Habsburg, Ferdinand Maximilian, 158–59
Habsburg, Franz Joseph, 158
Hannewijk, Leo, 110
Hardy, Malcolm Scott, 133
Hardy, Vesna, 196
Hašek, Jaroslav, 64
Havel, Václav, 74, 279
Hefner, Hugh, 234
Heidler, Kruno, 194
Hepburn, Audrey, 279
Hepburn, Katharine, 153
Herzog, Werner, 278
Hetrich, Ivan, 243
Hladnik, Boštjan, 191
Hledík, Peter, 77
Hodža, Fadil, 216
Hoffman, Dustin, 201
Holland, Agnieszka, 52
Holloway, Ron, 90
Hollywood Reporter, The, 59, 90, 182
Hope, Ted, 6
Horváthova, Jessica, 184, 188

Hrustanović, Kemal, 16
Hühn, Julius, 121, 231–32
Hühn, Kurt, 232
Hühn, Maria, 18
Hunter, Lew, 93, 103
Huston, John, 20, 191

I Forgot Where I Parked (Zaboravio sam gdje sam parkirao), 265
Idoli, 256
Imaginary Academy, the, xvii, 60, 93–95, 136, 192
Indigo Filmproduktion GmbH, 75
Informbiro, the, 63, 189
Isaković, Antonije, 130
Ivanda, Branko, 94, 109
Iwerks, Ub, 300
Izrael, Osias J. Daniel, 17

Jadran Film, 7, 28, 40–41, 57, 175, 194, 201, 215, 285–86
Jakić, Tomislav, 131, 229
Jakovčić, Eugen, 131
Jakovčić, Ivan, 94
Jakovina, Tvrtko, 131
Jakovlevski, Trpe, 242
Jakšić-Fanđo, Milorad, 216
Janković, Petar, 126
Jasný, Vojtěch, 109
Jergović, Miljenko, 131
Jones, Jennifer, 177
Josephson, Erland, xv, 121, 222, 252
Josipović, Ivo, 131, 156
Jovanić, Đoko, 244–45
Jovanović, Blažo, 272
Jovanović, Dušan, 104
Jović, Dejan, 131
jump cut, 150
Juračić, Dražen, 108, 230
Jurkić, Vesna Girardi, 114
Jurković, Ruža, xiii, 86–87
Jutarnji list, 68, 123

Kaczanowski, Witold-K, 171
Kadár, Ján, 3, 115, 186–88
Kafka, Franz, 52
Kalajdžić, 8–9
Kalin, Boris, 22

Kaloper, Jagoda, 92
Kamińska, Ida, 3
Kamody, Alexandra, 208
Kangrga, Milan, 22, 144
Kapić, Sulejman, 7, 8, 28, 40, 187, 194, 215, 228
Kapović, Mate, 131
Karakaš, Damir, 205
Karaklajić, Dejan, 66, 91
Karanović, Milan, 219
Karanović, Milenko, 220
Karanović, Srđan (Điđa), xi, xvi, 27, 52, 57–58, 74, 87, 103, 216, 219, 220, 222, 260, 288
Karanović, Višnja, 219
Karić, Ana, 153
Kazan, Elia, 202, 274
Kelly, Grace, 237
Kennedy Museum, the, 235
Kenović, Ademir, 77, 163, 185
Kerestinec concentration camp, 128
Khrushchev, Nikita Sergeyevich, 63
King Nikola I, 12–14
Kirksey, Gary, 208
Kiš, Danilo, 173
Klasić, Hrvoje, 131
Klemenc, Dunja, 253
Kličko, Tomislav, 163, 169
Klingerberg, Katarina, 18
Klos, Elmar, xi, 3, 11–13, 115, 156, 184–90
Knifer, Julije, 14
Kocbek, Edvard, 130
Koceić, Mladen, 288
Koenigsmark, Alex, 64, 74, 87, 137–38, 186, 188
Konstantinović, Leka, 273
Korać, Zora, 176
Korčula Summer School, 144, 229
Kosor, Jadranka, 131
Kosovo Film, 215
Kostinčer, Ljubica, 155
Košuta, Josip, 28
Kovačić, Lojze, 130
Kovač, Mirko, 173, 195
Kožarić, Ivan, 14
Kozlović, Gianfranco, 21
Krleža, Miroslav, 68, 240, 296
Kristl, Vlado, 191

Kroutel, Ron, 235–36
Krupskaya, Nadezhda, 42
Kryeziu, Ekrem, 216
Kubrick, Stanley, 245
Kundera, Milan, xv, 137–38, 184, 238
Kušan, Ivan, 137, 239
Kušec, Mladen, 163
Kusturica, Emir, xi, 84
Kvesić, Pero, 87

Lačni Franz, 256
Ladović, Vanda, 231
Lang, Jack, 246
Larraín, Pablo, 215
Lasić, Stanko, 130
League of Communist Youth of Yugoslavia, the (SKOJ), 240
Lee, Ang, 116
Lee, Spike, xvi, 106
Leigh, Vivien, 29–30
Lenin, Vladimir Ilyich Ulyanov, 19, 25, 42
Leone, Sergio, xv, 44–45
Letica, Slaven, 41
Library of Congress, 175, 224
Linta, Branko, 101
Ljuština, Duško, 174, 269
Lončar, Budimir, 131
Lovrić, Jelena, 25, 131
Lubitsch, Ernst, 15, 256
Lucas, George, 211
Lucić, Predrag, 143, 144
Lumet, Sidney, 102, 170
Lustig, Branko, 113, 250
Lustig, Mirjana, 250

Macan, Krešimir, 131
MacCorkindale, Simon, 125–27
Macedonian *Kinoteka*, 192
Machiedo, Vera, 92, 126
Maestro Film, 137, 276, 288
Magelli, Paolo, 65, 173–74, 205, 277
Makavejev, Dušan, xii, 14–16, 40, 90, 191, 238
Maloča, Ivan, 217
Mandić, Igor, 130
Mankiewicz, Joseph L., 223–24
Manojlović, Miki, 53, 81
Marijan, Bojana, 16

Index

Marinković, Ksenija, xx, 270
Marinković, Ranko, 114
Marjanović, Branko, 96, 122
Marković, Goran, xi, 20, 84, 186, 187, 189, 220, 299
Marković, Rade, 121, 186
Marković, Vesna, 92
Markovina, Dragan, 131
Martin Scorsese *Film Foundation*, 175. See also Scorsese, Martin
Martinis, Dalibor, 298
Mason, Charles, 136
Mastilović, Ranko, 298
Matić, Boris, 93, 100, 192
Matošević, Ivica, 21
Matvejević, Predrag, 130
Mažuranić, Ivana Brlić, 137
Mejía, Tomás, 161
A Memory of Woods (Sjećanje šume), 205
Mesić, Stjepan (Stipe), 131, 290–91
Meštrović, Koraljka, 169
Mexican Film Academy, 185
Michelangelo (di Lodovico Buonarroti Simoni), 230
Midžić, Enes, 113
Mihajlović, Dragoslav, 247
Mihić, Adelaida, 153
Miladinov, Angel, 39, 284
Milanović, Zoran, 131
Miletić, Oktavijan, 96, 122
Miller, Michael (Mike), 105, 109, 190
Milligan, Billy, 180, 182
Milojević, Đorđe, 276
Milošević, Slobodan, xviii, 53, 103, 291, 299
Milovanović, Vule, 243, 245
Mimica, Vatroslav, 226
Miramón, Miguel, 161
Mirković, Igor, xvii–xviii, 95, 100, 131, 265
Mironenko, S. V., 286
mit-out sound (MOS), 200
Mitrović, Žika, 241
Moačanin, Belka, 155
Močibob, Pero, 20
Modugno, Domenico, 294
Montand, Yves, 83
Moore, Lloyd, 235

Moreau, Jeanne, 153
Mosfilm, xii, 260
Moskowitz, Gene, 90
Motovun Film Festival, xvi–xvii, 60, 95, 123, 131, 136, 192, 260
Mozart, Wolfgang Amadeus, 83, 158, 160–61, 278
Murch, Walter, 210
Murtić, Edo, 68
Murray, Bill, 174
Mussolini, Benito, 95, 232
Museum of Yugoslavia, the, 245

National Film School of Denmark, 98
National Medal of Arts, the, 284
Nazor, Vladimir, 285
   Vladimir Nazor Award, the, 284–285
Nelson, Jenny, 208
Neoplanta Film, 27
Nešić, Marko, 117
Nešić, Slađa, 117
Nešić, Srđan, 117
Newman, Paul, 170
New York Festival, 210
New York Times, the, 210
New York University, 93, 105, 106, 185
   Tisch School of the Arts, the, xvi, 105, 106, 190, 208
newsreel, 214
Nickson, Robert, 94
Nixon, Bob, 91
Njegoš, Nikola Petrović, 13
Nobilo, Ante, 131
Nugent, Elliott, 245
Nunn, Lucien, 88–89

Obradović, Dejan, 27–28
October Revolution, 11, 25, 42, 199, 263
O'Hara, Maureen, 153
Ohio University, xvi–xvii, xxiii, 93, 106, 107, 116, 207–212, 235, 297, 303
   School of Art, 235
Olivier, Laurence, 29, 121
On the Edge of Reason (Na rubu pameti), 296
Ostojić, Arsen, 105
Otašević, Dušan, 173

Pace, Eric, 190
Pakula, Alan J., 76
Palance, Jack, 302
Papić, Krsto, 88
Parker, Alan, 211
Pašić, Faruk, 116
Pašić, Hajrudin, 116, 303
Pašić, Mirza, 116
Pašić, Nađa, 116
Passer, Ivan, 26
Past, Elena, 193
Pavelić, Ante, 25, 232
Pavić, Nino, 68
Pavlović, Živojin (Žika), 14–15, 90, 191, 216, 245
Peckinpah, Sam, 100, 191, 201
Pekić, Borislav, 200
Penn, Arthur, xvi, 106, 213
Perković, Dušan, 28
Perković, Saša, 131
Pesaro Film Festival, 14
Petria's Wreath (*Petrijin venac*), 247, 307
Petrović, Aleksandar (Saša), 14–15, 189, 190, 287
Petrović, Gajo, 175
Picasso, Pablo, 171
Pilnyak, Boris, xii, 261
Pilsel, Drago, 131
Pinochet, Augusto, 215
Pinter, Nada, 58
Pinter, Tomislav, xiv, 14, 96, 115, 192, 216
Pinter, Vanja, 252
Playboy, 234
Pleše, Mladen (Pilaš), 234
point of view (POV), 237
Polanski, Roman, 20
Politika, 90, 229
Ponce, Pepa, 136
Pope Alexander VI /Rodrigo Borgia, 134
Popović, Koča, 244
Popović, M., 9
Posar, Pompeo, 233–34
Prague Spring, 10–11
Praxis, xi, 144, 175
preproduction, 253, 239
Prgomet, Ilija, 290
Prljavo Kazalište, 132

Prodanović, Čedo, 68, 105, 170
producer, 6, 16, 26, 28, 32, 44, 81, 94, 110, 113, 125, 136, 163, 174, 201, 203, 217, 228, 250, 253, 277, 278, 288, 306, 307
product placement, 250
Profuk, Branimir, 131
Projections, 43
Puhovski, Nenad, xvii, 93
Pula Film Festival, 8, 41, 215
Pupovac, Milorad, 131
Pusić, Vesna, 131
Pusić, Zoran, 32, 131

Quien, Kruno, 226
Quinn, Freddy, 292

Račan, Ivica, 68
Radio Sarajevo, 116
Radman, Goran, 131
Rafelson, Bob, 213
Rancaño, Honorio, xv, 78–85
Rankov, Mara, 54–55
Ređep, Draško, 27
Reed, Peyton, 215
Reich, Wilhelm, 238
Renoir, Jean, 258
Roosevelt, Franklin D., 135
Ross, Dick, 105
Ross, Steve, 208
Royal Shakespeare Company, 29
Rubčić, Vladimir, 170, 206
Rublev, Andrei, 264
Ruljančić, Dragan, 190
Ruljančić, Jure, 190
Rupel, Dimitrije, 130
Russell, Ken, 191
Ruzicka, Rudolph, 188, 279

Sami, Bilal, 16
San Francisco Jewish Film Festival, 150
Saramago, José, 148
Schamus, James, 6
Schell, Maximilian, 100
Schnabel, Pavel, 277
Schubert, Franz, 158
Schwartz, Franz, 153
Schwartz, Isabella Aloysia Stephania, 153

Scorsese, Martin, 45, 274. *See also* Martin Scorsese Film Foundation, the
Scott, Campbell, 116
Scott, Kevin, 298
Screen International, 58–59
Seidl, Ulrich, 191
Šeks, Vladimir, 170
Šembera, Borivoj, 122
Senečić, Željko, 6
Šerbedžija, Rade, 69, 76
Serbian National Theater, 174
Šešelj, Vojislav, 178
Shepitko, Larisa, xii, 262
Šibenik Folk Music (*Šibenska narodna glazba*), 55
Sikorski, Joseph, 88
Silovic, Darko, 189
Sjöström, Victor, 124
Škavić, Đurđa, 145–46
Škrabalo, Ivo, 137, 291
Škrelji, Azem, 216
Škrelji, Imer, 216
Škubonja, Fedor, 96
Šliter, Jiří, 143
Slobodna Dalmacija, 55
Slobodni tjednik, 291
Smetana, Bedřich, 142
Smolej, Joža, 262
Šnajder Slobodan, 41
Soldatić, Vergilio, 93, 95
Šömen, Branka, 113
Šömen, Branko, 87, 138
Something Is in the Water, 186
Sophie of Bavaria, Princess, 157–58
Šorak, Dejan, 217, 288
Spanish civil war, 240
Spielberg, Steven, 210
  film school, 210
Stalin, Joseph Vissarionovich, 15, 19, 63, 135, 141, 155, 220, 247, 249
Štambuk, Davor, 191
Štambuk, Drago, 130
Stanković, Nenad, 88
Start, 234
Stefanovski, Vlatko, 206, 256
Steffie Speck in the Jaws of Life (*Štefica Cvek u raljama života*), 266

Steiger, Rod, 100, 201–204
Steigerwald, Karel, 188
Stewart, James, 121
Stojković, Danilo Bata, 229
Štrbac, Savo, 131
Strozzi, Tito, 121
Suay, Ricardo Muñoz, 81
Suchý, Jiří, 143
Sudović, Zlatko, 194
Sullivan, Jeanette, 59
Šušak, Gojko, 132, 178
Šuvar, Stipe, 130
Sviben, Zlatko, 281–82

Tadić, Ljubomir, 130, 296
Talvera, Ed, 212
Tanhofer, Nikola, 284
Tarkovsky, Andrei, xii, 253, 262
Taylor, Sam, 60
Tel Aviv Cinematheque, 113, 129
Television Belgrade, 176
Telluride Film Festival, 211, 213
Terešak, Vladimir, 28, 91
Teršelic, Vesna, 131
Tesla, Nikola, 88–89. See also *Secret of Nikola Tesla, The* (*Tajna Nikole Tesle*)
Théâtre des Bouffes du Nord, 29
Third Manifesto of the Surrealists, the, 244
Thomas, David, 93, 107, 210
Tin Drum, The, 186
Tito, Josip Broz, xiii, xviii, xix, 15, 23–24, 29, 32–33, 41, 63, 121, 149, 155, 163–64, 189, 197–98, 232, 240–47, 260–61, 273
Todorović, Marko, 241
Tokyo Film Festival, 83
Tolstoy, Lev Nikolayevich, xxvi
Toma, Ivanka, 131
Tomić, Ante, xviii, 119, 131, 265–66
Tong, Alexander, 173
Toplak, Živka, 56
Trailović, Mira, 54, 221
Trninić, Slobodan, 74
Trueman, Cindy, 208
Truffaut, François, 237
Tübingen Introduction to Philosophy, 221
Tucci, Stanley, 116

Tuđman, Franjo, 32–33, 41, 53, 113–14, 132, 136–37, 163–64, 236–37
Tvorčni skupina, 13

Ugrešić, Dubravka, xiv, 266
Ujević, Augustin (Tin), 237
Ullmann, Liv, 76, 153
Universum Film-Aktien Gesellschaft (UFA), 224

Valencia Film Festival / Mostra, xv, 78–79, 81–83, 85
Vardar Film, 238
Variety, 59–60, 90
Večernji list, 57, 128
Velebit, Vladimir, 189
Velvet Revolution, 26, 280
Verdi, Giuseppe, 116, 277–78
Viba Film, 28, 100
Vidić, Robert, 175
Vidici, 221
Vištica, Olinka, 95
Vitez, Zlatko, 113
Vitti, Monica, 8
Vlahović, Veljko, 189
von Sydow, Max, 121
Voprosy kinoiskusstva, 260–61
Voskovec, Jiří, 143
Vrabec, Zrinka, 131
Vrdoljak, Antun, 57, 108, 194, 288, 291
Vrdoljak, Dražen, 206, 256
Vujisić, Pavle, 201, 204
Vujnović, Tomislav, 175
Vukić, Maja, 277
Vuković, Vladimir, 99

Waits, Tom, 43
War Against War (Rat protiv rata), 236–37
Wayne, John, 241, 287
Weber, Eugen, 86
Welles, Orson, xiv, 115, 191–92
Werich, Jan, 143
When the Pumpkins Blossomed (Kad su cvetale tikve), 247
White Book, 15, 129–30, 194
Wilder, Billy, 87, 133, 193, 256, 267, 270, 279

Wright, Jack, 208

Yugoslav Film Archive, 220
Yugoslav Navy, 228
Yugoslav People's Army, 32, 62–63, 169, 197, 227, 244–45
Yugoslav secret police / UDBA, 128–29
Yugoslav Short Film Award, 173
Yugoslavia Film, 27–28, 260

Zafranović, Andrija, 56, 75
Zafranović, Lordan, xi, 19, 91, 114, 193, 260
Zagreb—an Anti-Guide (Zagreb—Antivodič), 231
Zagreb City Museum, 231
Zagreb Film, 122, 226
Zagreb School of Animation, 115
ZagrebDox, 136
Zalar, Slavko, 92, 190, 285
Zalar, Živko, 92, 190, 194, 232, 284
Zastava Film, 243–45
Zenić, Ana, 135
Zenić, Boris, 135
Zilahy, Lajos, 186
Žilnik, Želimir, 14–15
Ziyati, Alia, 208
Živojinović, Bata, 241, 287
Zovko, Hrvoje, 131
Zubčević, Darko, 41
Žufić, Stevo, 94
Zupančič, Milena, 104
Zuppa, Vjeran, 68, 93
Zvezda Film, 220

Index of Films

Films by Rajko Grlić

All Eat Each Other (Sve jedno drugo pojede), 115, 173, 307
All Men Are Good Men in Bad Society (Svaki je čovjek dobar čovjek u rđavom svijetu), 39, 56, 307

Border Post, The (Karaula), xviii, xix, xxii, 16, 55, 59, 84, 102, 163, 265, 306, 308

Bravo Maestro, xii, xv, 42, 69, 71, 76, 90, 187, 245, 252, 278, 306

Charuga (*Čaruga*), xv, xvi, xix, 99, 102–103, 105, 136, 176, 189, 205, 239, 240, 301, 306

Constitution, The (*Ustav Republike Hrvatske*), xx, 59, 101, 145, 169, 217, 269, 270, 277, 306, 308

Croatia 2000—Who Wants To Be a President (*Novo novo vrijeme*), xvii, 100

Drinkable Water and Freedom (*Pitka Voda i Sloboda*), 40, 307

Fragrance of Wildflowers, The (*Miris poljskog cveća*), co-writer, 90, 307

How to Make Your Movie—An Interactive Film School, xvii, 43, 46, 113, 133, 180, 210, 212, 308

If It Kills Me (*Kud puklo da puklo*), xii, 7, 8, 92, 113, 176, 191, 241, 245, 275, 284, 306

In the Jaws of Life (*U raljama života*), xiv, 82, 110, 241, 266, 287, 306

Josephine, 25, 59, 73, 75, 112, 187, 293, 306

Just Between Us (*Neka ostane među nama*), xix, 85, 129, 268, 276, 306

L. V. Kuleshov, 186

Melody Haunts My Reverie, The (aka *You Only Love Once*), xiii, 196

Party Game (*Društvena igra*), 28, 90, 307
Praises (*Pohvale*), 39, 308

Reckless Years, The (*Grlom u jagode*), co-writer, 93, 185, 221, 229, 275, 308
Return, The (*Povratak*), 92, 176, 232

That Summer of White Roses, 82–83, 99, 125–26, 200, 203, 223, 306

Three for Happiness (*Za sreću je potrebno troje*), xv, 44, 82, 253, 306

Viper's Glen Miracle, The (*Čudo u Poskokovoj Dragi*, not made), 101, 268

Wild Stories (*Žestoke priče*), 204, 308

You Love Only Once (*Samo jednom se ljubi*; aka *The Melody Haunts My Reverie*), xiii, xv, xix, 8, 40–41, 78, 81, 87, 90, 102, 110, 122, 153, 196, 252, 285–86, 306

Films by Other Directors

Adrift (*Touha zvana Anada*), 115, 186
All About Eve, 223–24
Ambush, The (*Zaseda*), 245
Anatomy of a Murder, 170
Annie Hall, 256
Apartment, The, 256

Babe, 3
Babette's Feast (*Babettes gæstebud*), 116
Battleship Potemkin (*Bronenosets Potyomkin*), 263
Best, The (*Najbolji*), 217
Big Feast, The (*La Grande Bouffe*), 116
Big Night, 116
Black Peter, 25
Blow Up, 244
Blue 9, 280
Bonnie and Clyde, 213

Chariots of Fire, 280
Charlie Wilson's War, 282
Cleopatra, 224
Cross of Iron, 100
Crowded Room, The, 182

Day for Night (*La Nuit américaine*), 237
Day of the Jackal, The, 282
Dead Man Walking, 246
Deliverance, 42–43
Devil's Advocate, The, 34

District 9, 207
Down by Law, 65

Eat Drink Man Woman, 116
8 ½, 207
Erin Brockovich, 170

Faces, 70
Fair Game, 282
Firemen's Ball, The (Hoří, má panenko), 133
Fitzcarraldo, 278
Five Easy Pieces, 213
Forty-First, The (Sorok pervyy), 256
4 Weddings and a Funeral, 207
4 Months, 3 Weeks and 2 Days (4 luni, 3 saptamâni si 2 zile), 207
Frances, 180
Freddy Under Foreign Stars (Freddy unter fremden Sternen), 292

Gone with the Wind, 72
Grand Illusion, The, 246
Grapes of Wrath, The, 223
Great Gatsby, The, 245
Green Mile, 246
Guns of War (Užička Republika), 241

H-8, 284
Heaven's Gate, 213
Hill, The, 65
Hoop Dreams, 280
How Green Was My Valley, 223
Hunger, 246
Hustler, The, 280

In the Name of the Father, 246
In the Soup, 126
Intimate Lighting (Intimní osvetlení), 27
Is It Clear, My Friend? (Je li jasno, prijatelju?), 246
It Happened One Night, 256

Jaws, 3
Jazz Singer, The, 115
Jiro Dreams of Sushi, 116
Judge, The, 34
Judge Steps Out, The, 34

Judgment in Nurnberg, 170
Jules et Jim, 256

Kaya, I'll Kill You (Kaja, ubit ću te!), 226
King, The, 280
King Kong, 3
Kozara, 245

Lapitch the Little Shoemaker, 137–38, 191
Lassie Come Home, 3
Last Picture Show, The, 164
Letter to Three Wives, A, 223
Life and Times of Judge Roy Bean, The, 34
Like Water for Chocolate (Como agua para chocolate), 116
Lincoln Lawyer, The, 34
Lone Wolf, 3
Loneliness of the Long-Distance Runner, The, 65, 280
Lonely Are the Brave, 273
Look at Me, Unfaithful (Pogledaj me, nevernice), 256
Lost in Translation, 174
Love Actually, 256
Love in the Afternoon, 279
Love Letters with Intent, 177
Loves of a Blonde (Lásky jedné plavovlásky), 26

Mahabharata, 29
Man for All Seasons, A, 170
Midnight Express, 65, 246
Mirror, The (Zerkalo), 262
Miss Gay America, 53
Moscow Laughs (Vesyolye rebyata), 53
Munich, 282

National Class (Nacionalna klasa), 280
1900 (Novecento), 207, 277
Ninotchka, 15, 256
No, 215
North by Northwest, 282

O Brother, Where Art Thou?, 65
Occupation in 26 Pictures (Okupacija u 26 slika), 195, 207
Ocean's 11, 207

On the Waterfront, 202
Once Upon a Time in America, xv, 44–45
One Flew over the Cuckoo's Nest, 180
101 Dalmatians, 3, 207

Papillon, 65
Party Game (Društvena igra), 28, 90, 307
Paths of Glory, 34
People vs. Fritz Bauer, The (Der Staat gegen Fritz Bauer), 170
Philadelphia, 170
Pretty Woman, 256

Quiet Man, The, 71, 133

Raging Bull, 280
Ratatouille, 116
Reckless Years, The (Grlom u jagode), 93, 185, 221, 229, 275, 308
Roman Holiday, 256
Rome, 258
Rules of the Game, The (La Règle du Jeu), 258

Schindler's List, 113
Searchers, The, 245
Secret of Nikola Tesla, The (Tajna Nikole Tesle), 88
Serbia, Year Zero (Srbija, godine nulte), 299
Se7en, 207
Seven Brothers for Seven Sisters, 228
Seventh Seal, The, 272
Shadows, 126
Shawshank Redemption, The, 65
Shop on Main Street, The (Obchod na korze), xi, 3, 190
Shutter Island, 180
Some Like It Hot, 256

Spartacus, 245
Spy Game, 282
Stalag 17, 246
Star Wars, 211
Straw Dogs, 201
Success, 55
Sunday (Nedjelja), 20
Sunset Boulevard, 87, 133, 193

Tell It to the Judge, 34
Three (Tri), 189
Three Faces of Eve, The, 180
Three Girls Named Anna (Tri Ane), 192, 284
3:10 to Yuma, 207
Times of Haiduks, The (Hajdučka vremena), 216
To Kill a Mockingbird, 170
Tower to the People, 88
Turbulent Summer (A Lito vilovito), 287
12 Angry Men, 170, 207
12 Monkeys, 180
21 Grams, 207
20,000 Years in Sing Sing, 246

Verdict, The, 170
Virgina, 57, 103, 276, 288, 291–92
Viridiana, 81
Viva Mexico, 80

W.R.: Mysteries of the Organism (Misterija organizma), 238
When Harry Met Sally, 256
When Spring Is Late (Kur Perevera Vonohet), 216
When We Were Kings, 280
Wild Strawberries, 124, 222–23

Yes Man, 215

www.ingramcontent.com/pod-product-compliance
Lightning Source LLC
Chambersburg PA
CBHW072143100526
44589CB00015B/2066